THE ROUGH GUIDE TO

L

Restaurants

2005 EDITION

Written and edited by
Charles Campion

Additional research and reviews
**Jan Leary, George Theo, Tim Cooper,
Michelle Bhatia and Peter Buckley**

Welcome to the seventh edition of the Rough Guide to London Restaurants. If you used the earlier books, you will have spotted a few major changes: the book has changed shape, there is a new colour section at the front, and the reviews have been organised differently. The guide is still laid out area by area but the areas are now listed alphabetically, making them a good deal easier to find. There are also two maps on the inside cover flaps showing the overall view with the neighbourhoods covered in the book labelled in red; we start with "Aldwych & The Strand" and go through to "Wimbledon & Southfields". In the revision process the guide has also grown considerably and now there are full reviews of over 350 restaurants plus helpful "further choice" sections which list the address and phone numbers of other eateries in areas that are particularly promising. Perhaps the biggest change is the addition of a colour "Ideas" sections at the front. As the name implies each of these is a shortlist, so if you fancy a night out at a gastropub but need some inspiration the "Ideas" section will provide half a dozen alternatives.

Another important thing to note about the restaurants reviewed in this book is that they are all recommended – none has been included simply to make up the numbers. There are some very cheap places and there are some potentially pretty expensive places, but they all represent good value. The only rule we have made for inclusion is that it must be possible to eat a meal for £50 a head or less. In some of the haute cuisine establishments, that will mean keeping to the set lunch, while in some of the bargain eateries £50 might cover a blow-out for four. This guide reviews restaurants for every possible occasion from a quick lunch to a celebration dinner. It also covers many different kinds of food – some fifty cuisines in all. In reality, we cover even more, as, for simplicity we have used "Indian" and "Chinese" as catch-all terms.

PRICES, CREDIT CARDS AND SO FORTH

Every review in this book has at the top a spread of prices (e.g. £12 –£40). The first figure relates to what you could get away with – this is the minimum amount per person you are likely to spend on a meal here (assuming you are not a non-tipping, non-drinking skinflint). The second relates to what it would cost if you don't hold back. Wild diners with a taste for fine wines will leave our top estimates far behind, but the figures are there as a guide. For most people, the cost of a meal will lie somewhere within the spread.

For a more detailed picture, each review sets out the prices of various dishes. At some time in the guide's life these specific prices (and indeed the overall price spreads) will become out of date, but they were all accurate when the book left for the printer. And even in the giddy world of restaurants, when prices rise or prices fall, everyone tends to move together. If this book shows one restaurant as being twice as expensive as another, that situation is likely to remain.

The reviews also keep faith with original menu spellings of dishes, so you'll find satays, satehs and satés – all of which will probably taste much the same. Opening hours and days are given with every full review, as are the credit cards accepted. Where reviews specify that restaurants accept "all major credit cards", that means at least AmEx, Diners, MasterCard and Visa. Acceptance of Visa and MasterCard usually means Switch and Delta, too; we've specified the odd exception, but if you're relying on one card it's always best to check when you book.

You will also see that some restaurants have the tag "Disabled Facilities". As provision for the disabled varies so wildly this must be something of a catch-all, so when a restaurant is credited with "disabled facilities" it means that the establishment has some facilities specifically for disabled diners – that may be a lift, or ramps, or converted loos. It is always best to check exactly what's what before setting out – all restaurants should be keen to help.

It just remains to wish you "happy eating" and enjoy the Guide.

About the Author

Charles Campion is an award-winning food writer and restaurant reviewer. He writes a restaurant column for the London Evening Standard, and is a past winner of the Glenfiddich "Restaurant Writer of the Year" award, and contributes to radio and TV food programmes, as well as a variety of magazines including Bon Appetit in the USA. His most recent book publication was The Real Greek at Home, which he wrote with chef Theodore Kyriakou.

Before becoming a food writer, Charles worked in a succession of London ad agencies and had a spell as chef-proprietor of a hotel and restaurant in darkest Derbyshire.

Help Us Update

We've tried to ensure that this the seventh edition of The Rough Guide to London Restaurants is as up-to-date and accurate as possible. However, London's restaurant scene is in constant flux: chefs change jobs; restaurants are bought and sold; menus change. There will probably be a few references in this guide that are out of date even as this book is printed – and standards, of course, go up and down. If you feel there are places we've underrated or overpraised, or others we've unjustly omitted, please let us know: comments or corrections are much appreciated, and we'll send a copy of the next edition (or any other Rough Guide if you prefer) for the best letters. Please address letters to Charles Campion at:

Rough Guides, 80 Strand, London WC2R 0RL or
Rough Guides, 4th Floor, 375 Hudson St, New York, NY 10014.
Or send email to: mail@roughguides.co.uk

Ideas

Newcomers

Since the last edition of this guide, the restaurant scene has been on its usual roller-coaster ride; there have been closures, restaurants have moved, chefs have moved, and new restaurants have opened. Already some of the new kids on the block look like they will be here to stay. Here are some of the star turns among the newcomers.

Le Cercle

A new restaurant from the Gascon specialists, Club Gascon in Smithfield. High style, and all day eating with tapas-style dishes.

▸ P.231 ▸ KNIGHTSBRIDGE & BELGRAVIA ▲

Rasoi Vineet Bhatia

Amazing and inspiring Indian food, from a family team in a small, stylish Chelsea restaurant.

▸ P.72 ▸ CHELSEA ▲

The Burlington

A small neighbourhood restaurant with charm, atmosphere, and good French-inspired cooking. Good value.

▸ P.84 ▸ CHISWICK

Inn the Park

An amazing step forward in Park catering, this beautiful restaurant serves good, straightforward food and relies on British suppliers.

P.270 ▸ PICCADILLY & ST JAMES'S ▲

Yauatcha

Best ever dim sum, (unusually on a day-long basis) from this sibling to Hakkasan. Elegant and designery.

 P.322 ▸ SOHO ▼

The Wolseley

Very stylish, beautiful room, celebrity guest list and a menu inspired by the great Central European cafés.

 P.274 ▸ PICCADILLY & ST JAMES'S ▼

French

2003 and 2004 were good years for French food. Trends seemed to be leading chefs back towards simple dishes, and that meant a resurgence of interest in classic French cooking. Here are some of London's best French restaurants, some upscale and cluttered with awards and some more straightforward, but all of them good.

The Square

A very grown up restaurant indeed. Inspired dishes, elegant presentation and original combinations of ingredients. Serious stuff.

▶ P.252 ▶ MAYFAIR & BOND STREET ▲

Racine

Englishman Henry Harris cooks very genuine French dishes. Comfortable restaurant with Gallic service and a gently priced set lunch.

▶ P.329 ▶ SOUTH KENSINGTON ▲

South

Light and airy French restaurant in Hoxton that deserves more plaudits than it gets. Genuine food, friendly service and agreeable pricing.

▸ P.204 ▸ HOXTON   ▾

Gordon Ramsay

Very smart, top drawer cooking in a sleek Chelsea setting. Dishes are unusually sophisticated.

▸ P.70 ▸ CHELSEA   ▾

The Capital

Chef Eric de Crouillère-Chavot runs the kitchens at this elite restaurant, which underwent a much needed redesign during Summer 2004.

▸ P.230 ▸ KNIGHTSBRIDGE & BELGRAVIA▴

Chez Bruce

Very high standard of French cooking. Very interesting wine list and a splendid cheese-board. Bargain weekday lunch. A real favourite.

▸ P.97 ▸ CLAPHAM & WANDSWORTH ▴

Gastropubs

The past three or four years have seen an explosion in the numbers of gastropubs. Go back into the mists of time – to the end of the last Century – and we were all very grateful when a gastropub opened. Any improvement in pub food (which was generally very poor) was welcomed with open arms. Now the competition has stepped up, and to be great a gastropub has to serve restaurant quality food at reasonable prices.

The Rocket

A rather good Italian restaurant within a pub in Acton! Very friendly place with an ever changing, chef-led menu.

▶ P.137 ▶ EALING & ACTON   ▼

The Barnsbury

Practical (rather than fancy) gastropub that does a great job serving a large local following with sound food.

▶ P.208 ▶ ISLINGTON & HIGHBURY   ▼

The Anglesea Arms

Long established, local hero, gastropub. Daily changing menu runs in sync with the seasons.

▶ P.184 ▶ HAMMERSMITH ▼

The Eagle

This pub can claim to have been the first ever gastropub. It is still a good place to eat – loosely Iberian grub with the occasional Mozambican influence!

▶ P.106 ▶ CLERKENWELL & SMITHFIELD ▼

The White Swan

If the White Swan were a restaurant it would be a very good one. As a pub it is exceptional – very good cooking, intense flavours.

▶ P.111 ▶ CLERKENWELL & SMITHFIELD ▼

The Anchor and Hope

Cheerfully anarchic sort of place, no advance bookings taking, British ingredients get star billing. Cooking is occasionally inspired.

▶ P.361 ▶ WATERLOO & SOUTH BANK ▼

Indian

London can now boast more top-class Indian restaurants than any other city in the world. What's more, these elite restaurants are being pressed hard by a wave of up-and-coming middleweights, and there are still over 3,000 neighbourhood Indian restaurants, each central to its community. From the 70 or so Indian restaurants listed in this book the ones on this page are truly exceptional.

Painted Heron

Another award winning restaurant. Intense flavours and sophisticated presentation. At home in its Chelsea surroundings.

▸ P.71 ▸ CHELSEA ▲

Chutney Mary

Very Chelsea, very successful upscale Indian restaurant with a menu that runs from authentic homely dishes to food fit for a Maharajah.

▸ P.66 ▸ CHELSEA ▲

Cinnamon Club

Judge Cinnamon Club as a restaurant rather than as an Indian restaurant. Sophisticated food. Cocktail bar. Slick club downstairs. Good cooking.

▸ P.371 ▸ WESTMINSTER ▲

Rasoi Vineet Bhatia

Newcomer, and straight to the top of the pile. One of the first Indian chefs to win a Michelin star opens his own small restaurant.

▸ P.72 ▸ CHELSEA ▼

Sarkhel's

Udit Sarkhel is a very good cook and his restaurant is a labour of love. Good dishes, confident service, reasonable prices.

▸ P.378 ▸ WIMBLEDON & SOUTHFIELDS ▲

Madhu's

Stunning and sophisticated restaurant in far off Southall. Deserved winner of several awards. Gutsy cooking, friendly service.

▸ P.333 ▸ SOUTHALL ◀

Real Cheapies

Sometimes you just want to eat cheap. But the old saying that no truly awful meal can ever be cheap enough does hold good. What we need is a cheap restaurant where the food is sound at the very least, and preferably very good. The restaurants here offer a lifeline to anyone looking for that rare combo of cheap and good.

Jaffna House

You will not believe how cheap this small, scruffy Sri Lankan restaurant can be. A friendly, no-frills place.

▸ P.345 ▸ TOOTING ▾

Zen Satori

This place is the training restaurant of the Asian and Oriental School of Catering. Good, cheap Indian, Chinese and Thai food.

▸ P.205 ▸ HOXTON

Masala Zone

A modern take on Indian street food. Light and bright place with a good crowd of people keen on low prices and slick service.

▸ P.314 ▸ SOHO ▾

Centrale

For decades a reliable source of big bowls of pasta. Loved by students and others who have little money to spend and want value.

▶ P.311 ▶ SOHO

Chowki

A large and bustling Indian restaurant offering very authentic dishes at very reasonable prices.

▶ P.312 ▶ SOHO

Abu Zaad

Very jolly, very cheap Damascene restaurant. Perhaps the best value Middle Eastern meze in London.

▶ P.300 ▶ SHEPHERD'S BUSH & OLYMPIA

Chinese

Chinese food has always been a popular option, although the Chinese restaurant trade seems to lack the cohesion of its Indian brethren. But you can choose from a range of styles – from dim sum, through chic, to neighbourhood – and there are star turns to be found in each of them.

Yi Ban

A real surprise. Isolated in Docklands, a busy and bustling Chinese restaurant – dim sum good at lunch.

› P.131 › DOCKLANDS

Fung Shing

Old established Chinese restaurant, good for "specials" and authentic Cantonese dishes including fish.

› P.77 › CHINATOWN

Royal China

A very competitive dim sum house that has recently moved a few numbers down Baker Street. The roast pork puffs are best ever.

▷ P.244 ▷ MARYLEBONE

Hakkasan

Ultra modern style palace with food that lives up to the hype. Not cheap but with a good cocktail bar and a lively crowd.

▷ P.154 ▷ FITZROVIA

Yauatcha

Yauatcha is a new and stylish establishment, selling dim dum. Not expensive, a comfortable tea room on the ground floor.

▷ P.322 ▷ SOHO

Ecapital

A restaurant with a mission to popularise the lesser known dishes that come from Shanghai. Also has a decent wine list.

▷ P.76 ▷ CHINATOWN

Star Chefs

There are good restaurants that do not have star chefs, and there are also familiar faces who run restaurants that rely more on their chef's fame than on their abilities. Here are a few chefs who deserve our respect for their cooking skills.

Fergus Henderson – St John

Fergus Henderson has done more than any other chef for British food – his love of offal and unfashionable cuts is legendary.

▶ P.108 ▶ CLERKENWELL & SMITHFIELD

Vineet Bhatia – Rasoi Vineet Bhatia

Vineet Bhatia was one of the first Indian chefs to win a Michelin star and is an exceptionally gifted cook.

▶ P.72 ▶ CHELSEA

Richard Corrigan –
Richard Corrigan at the
Lindsay House

Richard Corrigan is a large, blustering, Irish chef and his dishes deliver strong flavours in original combinations.

▶ P.317 ▶ SOHO ▼

Gordon Ramsay –
Gordon Ramsay

Despite his rough-and-ready television image, Gordon Ramsay is a very talented chef.

▶ P.70 ▶ CHELSEA ▶

Phillip Howard – The Square
Phillip Howard is a retiring sort of chef who lets his cuisine speak for him – sophisticated dishes, cooking at the highest level.

▶ P.252 ▶ MAYFAIR & BOND STREET ▲

Giorgio Locatelli –
Locanda Locatelli

Giorgio Locatelli is a charismatic chef running a glossy and fashionable, (and Michelin spangled) Italian restaurant.

▶ P.240 ▶ MARYLEBONE ◀

Veggie

It remains the bald truth that you can eat much better vegetarian food in Indian restaurants than anywhere else. This dire state of affairs is changing however, particularly in French establishments, where more chefs are producing lighter Gallic dishes. Elsewhere veggie menus are appearing under a variety of cuisines and in more upmarket restaurants.

Morgan M's

Smart Islington French restaurant with an accomplished Garden menu on offer.

▸ P.489 ▸ ISLINGTON & HIGHBURY   ▲

Ram's

This may be London's finest (or only) Surti restaurant. Good Indian vegetarian dishes.

▸ P.193 ▸ HARROW

The Gate

Inspired veggie cooking. Just the place to take a non-believer.

▶ P.185 ▶ HAMMERSMITH ▲

Kastoori

Jolly, family-run Indian restaurant. Kenyan Asian dishes – strong flavours.

▶ P.346 ▶ TOOTING ▲

Roussillon

A much lauded French restaurant, with an able chef and an impressive Garden menu.

▶ P.359 ▶ VICTORIA ▼

Wild Cherry

Extremely reliable and homely cafe/restaurant, part of the neighbouring London Buddhist Centre – good karma, good food.

▶ P.54 ▶ BRICK LANE, SPITALFIELDS
& BETHNAL GREEN ▼

Italian

We have a very good spread of Italian restaurants in London, from regional specialists with often obscure dishes on offer, to those offering sophisticated cooking that calls itself Modern Italian. One thing is for sure, the days of red meaty sauces slopped out onto over-cooked spaghetti are long gone.

Zafferano

Despite (or perhaps because of) having an English head chef, Zafferano serves splendid Italian food. Regional specialities, decent wine list.

▶ P.232 ▶ KNIGHTSBRIDGE & BELGRAVIA ▼

Locanda Locatelli

Giorgio Locatelli's celebrity filled, slick and fashionable restaurant. The food is good and honest if sometimes elaborate.

▶ P.240 ▶ MARYLEBONE ▼

Sardo

Sardo has done more than anywhere else for the reputation of Sardinian food. Expect regional specialities and friendly service.

▶ P.159 ▶ FITZROVIA ▲

Enoteca Turi

Friendly no-nonsense, family-run Italian resto with a very good, very comprehensive wine list. Plenty by the glass.

▶ P.282 ▶ PUTNEY ▲

Riva

Run by Andrea Riva, the food is well cooked and authentic. The specials (often fish) are particularly good.

▶ P.33 ▶ BARNES & SHEEN ▼

Assaggi

Small, hard-to-get-a-booking-at, seriously expensive Italian restaurant serving exquisite and simple dishes.

▶ P.255 ▶ NOTTING HILL & KENSAL GREEN ◀

Restaurants

Aldwych & The Strand

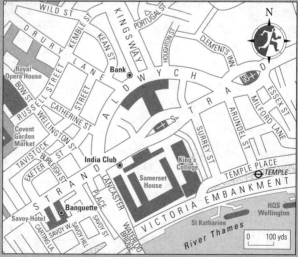

Bank

Modern British £17–£65

1 Kingsway (corner of Aldwych) WC2 & ☎020 7379 9797
Station Holborn **Open** Mon–Fri 7–11am, noon–3pm & 5.30–11pm,
Sat 11.30am–3.30pm & 5.30–11pm, Sun 11.30am–3pm & 5.30–9.30pm
Accepts All major credit cards ☏www.bankrestaurants.com

This restaurant may well be the closest London gets to re-creating the all-day buzz and unfussy cuisine of the big Parisian Brasseries. Bank opens for breakfast, lays on brunch at the weekend, does a good-value pre- and post-theatre (5.30–7pm and 10–11pm) and lunch prix fixe (both are £12.50 for two courses, £15 for three), and has a bustling bar. And then there's the other matter of lunch and dinner for several hundred. Whatever the time of day, the food is impressive, especially considering the large numbers of people fed, and if you like things lively you will have a great time. In the spring of 2004 Bank got a refurb and smart new colour scheme.

The menu is constantly changing, so dishes come and go. Start with something simple –

simple to get wrong, that is – a Caesar salad (£6.95), say, or push the boat out with a well-made foie gras parfait with apple and pear chutney (£8.50). Or go for shellfish. A key role in Bank's history was played by one of London's leading catering fishmongers, so crustacea such as dressed crab with ginger and wasabi dressing (£12.50) should be reliable. The fish dishes are equally good, from roast cod with boulangère potatoes and mussels (£14.95), to a traditional halibut fish and chips (£18.95), featuring mushy peas and tartare sauce. Meat dishes are well-prepared brasserie fare such as braised beef with parsley mash (£15.50) or confit of duck with amaretti and butternut squash purée (£15.95); Puds include an assiette au chocolat (£7.50), and brioche bread and butter pudding (£5).

✳ If you want a taxi after 10pm, go for the cabs arranged by the doorman – black cabs are an endangered species in Theatreland.

Banquette

Modern British £15–£60

The Savoy, Strand, WC2 & ☎020 7420 2392
Station Charing Cross **Open** Mon–Sat noon–11.45pm, Sun noon–10.30pm
Accepts All major credit cards except Diners ☏www.gordonramsay.com

When you are eating at the Savoy, Banquette represents the "informal" face of Capitalist excess. The restaurant is narrow, with the eponymous banquettes on one side and small window tables on the other. You can look out over what is allegedly the only piece of road in Britain where you drive on the right – set up for the

convenience of taxis. This would be a great eyrie for paparazzi if it weren't for the prices, which can seem fierce. Console yourself with the thought that diners in the Grill downstairs pay lots more for the services of the same head chef – Marcus Wareing heads up both these outposts of Gordon Ramsay's empire.

The food could be described as a sort of "faux common" take on old favourites. There are pickled sardines on toasted sourdough (£6); a beef burger with onion rings, gherkins and salad (£8.50); there's a classic Caesar salad (£8) with crisp enough Little Gem but maybe too gentle a dressing; there are soups; and you can order eggs Benedict (£8). From the main course list you could opt for fishcakes with tartar sauce (£12); spaghetti with lobster (£15); or shepherd's pie (£8) – a rich, comforting dish very much on a par with the kind you would find in a decent pub. This place is something of an enigma, and you can only surmise that it works because it offers a dab of reality to hardened Savoy hands. It's a pretty room, the service is sound and the wine list goes all the way from plain to pricey.

*"Barbara Barry's design evokes the interior of a 1950's Corvette Stingray."

India Club

Indian £6–£20

143 Strand, WC2 ☎ 020 7836 0650

Station Holborn **Open** Mon–Fri & Sun noon–3pm & 6–10.30pm, Sat 6–10.30pm
Accepts Cash or cheque only

When the India Club opened in 1950, the linoleum flooring was probably quite chic. Situated up two flights of stairs, sandwiched between floors of the grandly named Strand Continental Hotel, the Club is an institution, generally full and mostly with regulars, as you can tell by the stares of appraisal given to newcomers. The regulars are in love with the strangely old-fashioned combination of runny curry and low, low prices, and don't mind traipsing downstairs to the hotel reception to buy a bottle of Cobra beer. They can be split into two categories: suave Indians from the nearby High Commission, and a miscellany of folk from the BBC World Service down the road in Bush House.

The food at the India Club predates any London consciousness of the different spicing of Bengal, Kerala, Rajasthan or Goa. It is Anglo-Indian, essentially, and well cooked of its kind, although to palates accustomed to more modern Indian dishes it is something of a symphony to runny sauce. Mughlay chicken (£5.20) is a wing and a drumstick in a rich, brown, oniony gravy, garnished with two half hard-boiled eggs; while scampi curry (£7) is runny and brown, with fearless prawns swimming through it. Masala dosa (£3.60) is a well-made crispy pancake with a pleasantly sharp-tasting potato filling. Dhal (£3.30) is yellow and … runny. There are good dishes of bhindi or brinjal (both £3.50). The mango chutney (40p) is a revelation: thick parings of mango, which are chewy and delicious. Breads – paratha (£1.60), puris (two for £1.80) – are good, while the rice is white and comes in clumps (£2).

*Heed the kindly chilli warning of your waiter. Chilli bhajis (£2.60) are extra-hot green chillies deep-fried until crisp.

Barnes, Sheen & Kew

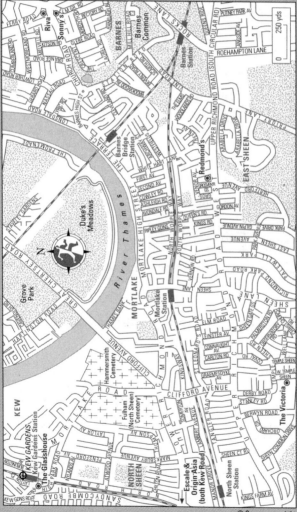

© Crown copyright

Escale

Turkish £15–£35

94 Kew Rd, Richmond, Surrey ☎020 8940 0033
Station Richmond **Open** Daily noon–11pm
Accepts All major credit cards except AmEx ⊕www.escale-richmond.co.uk

Among the ever increasing number of restaurants crowding into this area, Escale adds a Turkish option to your choice of dining. It has fast become a popular "local" – good unpretentious food with amiable efficient service and wallet-friendly prices certainly attracts the regulars. Booking is essential most nights but you will never be hurried on your way should you linger longer than planned. Weather permitting, there are pavement tables at the front.

Small samplers of meze with very moreish bread are served on arrival: a ploy that usually results in the mixed cold meze starter (£6.45 or £9.95 for two) being the first entry on the waiter's pad. Hot starters include patates kôftesi (£4.25), which are Turkish potato croquettes; particularly delicious felafel (£4.20); or perhaps kiymali

börek (£4.75), little filo parcels filled with minced lamb and herbs. Main course dishes are substantial, the mixed grill (£10.95) – consisting of lamb, chicken, lamb shish, kofte and lamb's liver, served with bulgar wheat and salad – will satisfy the healthiest of appetites, while the chicken shish (£9.25) is plentiful and perfectly chargrilled. The deep-fried sardines (£9.45) are served in a sharp lemon marinade and there is grilled seabass on a bed of spinach (£13.95). A small selection of vegetarian dishes is also available (from £8.55 to £8.75) and includes veggie moussaka; mushroom Stroganoff; or mücver (courgette and feta cheese fritters). Puddings include all the usual suspects including rice pudding (£3.50), ice cream (£3.75) and cheesecake (£3.95).

✳ Baklava, sweet enough for the sweetest toothed.

The Glasshouse

Modern British £18–£60

14 Station Parade, Kew Gardens, Surrey ☎020 8940 6777
Station Kew Gardens **Open** Mon–Sat noon–2.30pm & 7–10.30pm,
Sun 12.30–3pm & 7.30–10pm **Accepts** All major credit cards except Diners

The Glasshouse has settled into its dual role as local hero and Michelin-starred destination restaurant. Chef Anthony Boyd honed his craft at the much decorated Square (see p.252) and Chez Bruce (see p.97). At The Glasshouse he has made a good job of combining the rich flavours of Chez Bruce with the sophistication of The Square. What's more, the restaurant is on the doorstep of Kew Gardens' underground station, which makes it easily accessible. The interior has a clean-cut, modern feel to it and the comfortable chairs are worthy of a special mention. The food is good. Very good.

The menu changes daily offering eight selections for each course. Three courses cost £32.50, but there is a limited set lunch menu (two choices each course), which costs just £12.50 for two courses and £17.50 for three. All of these options are snatch-their-hand-off bargains. For the full Michelin experience there's a multi course tasting menu for £45. The imaginative and straightforward cooking owes much to French cuisine. Starters range from a warm salad of wood pigeon with deep-fried truffled egg, to mackerel and smoked salmon tartare with ravigote dressing. Main courses vary from a Navarin of venison with roast root vegetables; to an assiette of pork with apple sage and grain mustard; or roast halibut with wild mushrooms, braised celery and pommes cocottes. Puddings have a deft touch and include old favourites like hot chocolate fruit and nut fondant or rhubarb and custard. The wine list is short and thoughtfully drawn up, with one or two unusual selections.

✳ Heed the warning – "Please order taxis at least 25 minutes before they are required" – you are in the wilds of Kew.

Origin Asia

Indian £15–£30

100 Kew Rd, Richmond, Surrey ☎ 020 8948 0509

Station Richmond **Open** Mon–Sat noon–2.30pm & 5.30–11pm, Sun noon–2.30pm & 5.30–10.30pm **Accepts** Mastercard & Visa ⊛ www.originasia.co.uk

In the spring of 2004 Origin Asia went through a bit of a shake up when a new chef took over. Chef Ranga trained at the Taj Group and he has taken the menu up-market, which rather suits this aggressively modern, markedly stylish, somewhat over-the-top Indian restaurant. The eatery is divided into four sections, the most attractive of which is the one at the back with a grand view of the open kitchen. In the front section the "goldfish-bowl" feeling is just about mitigated by a rather splendid Indian glass chandelier; the middle sections are agreeable, but the back is the place to be.

Dishes like lobster pepper fry (£19.50) hide on the starter page of the menu under the heading "exotic" which it certainly is; or how about tandoori quails (£5.95); masala pomfret (£12.95); or lehsooni whitebait (£4.95)? There are enough old favourites to suit the more conservatively minded and the main courses include the simple things like gosht saagwala (£8.50), a combo of lamb and spinach. Lamb also stars in the lamb shank xacuti (£9.50), a slow-cooked take on the Goan classic. There's also a rogan josh (£8.50) and more adventurous dishes like kori gassi (£7.95) – chicken is so much better cooked on the bone; in this instance it's cooked with coconut, garlic and roast chillies, then the sauce tempered with sharp tamarind paste. The vegetable side dishes are imaginative, and there is a sound list of breads, including a roomali roti (£2.95). Heading the menu it says "Origin Asia, blissfully Indian" – the food here may not be complete bliss but it is certainly very good.

✳ Sunday lunch bargain buffet – each week different regions of India, (£10.95 adults, £5.95 children)

Redmond's
Modern British £18–£50

170 Upper Richmond Rd West SW14 ☎ 020 8878 1922
Station BR Mortlake **Open** Mon–Sat 6.30–10.30pm, Sun noon–2.30pm
Accepts Delta, Mastercard, Switch & Visa

When Redmond and Pippa Hayward opened this small neighbourhood restaurant it was head and shoulders above anything else the locale had to offer. A few years down the line and "Barnes, Sheen & Kew" may not quite be a match for Soho, but there are an increasing number of decent places to eat. Redmond's is one of the best, propelled by a telling combo of very good cooking and reasonable prices. They tweak the menu on a daily basis, so it reflects the best of what the season and the markets have to offer. The dinner menu is not particularly short – about six or seven starters and mains – and proves astonishing value at £29.50 for three courses. There is also a competitive "early" menu running until 7.45pm: £12.50 for two courses and £15 for three. What's even more agreeable is an absence of supplements. And the food here really is very good indeed: well seasoned, precisely cooked, presented elegantly.

If the terrine of ham hock, foie gras and baby capers is available when you visit, pounce. Redmond's charcuterie is accomplished: it will be multi-layered, multi-textured and yummy. There may also be a salad of crisp fried mackerel with orange and chorizo oil; or perhaps an open ravioli of Jerusalem artichoke and wild mushrooms. Main courses combine dominant flavours with elegant presentation – roast cod with a herb crust; crisp belly pork served with mash and rhubarb; fillets of red mullet with a fennel puree. The puddings are wonderful, too: Calvados and sultana parfait; crème brulée; a passion fruit panna cotta.

✳ A wine list littered with interesting bottles at accessible prices – some particularly good halves.

Riva

Italian £25–£50

160 Church Rd, SW13 ☎ 020 8748 0434

Station BR Barnes Bridge **Open** Mon–Fri noon–2.30pm & 7–11pm, Sat 7–11.30pm, Sun noon–2.30pm & 7–9.30pm **Accepts** All major credit cards except Diners

Andrea Riva has always been something of a darling of the media, and his sophisticated little restaurant exerts a powerful pull, strong enough to convince even fashionable folk to make the dangerous journey to the south bank of the Thames. When they get there they find a rather conservative-looking restaurant, with a narrow dining room decorated in dull greens and faded parchment, and chairs which have clearly seen service in church. As far as the cuisine goes, Riva provides the genuine article, so most customers are either delighted or disappointed, depending on how well they know their Italian food. The menu changes regularly with the seasons.

Starters are good but not cheap. The frittelle (£9.50) is a tempura-like dish of deep-fried Mediterranean prawn, salt cod cakes, calamari, sage and basil, with a balsamic dip. Serious Italian food fans, however, will find it hard to resist the sapori Mediterranei (£21 for two), which gets you grilled scallop and langoustines; baccalà mantecato and polenta; eel and lentils; mussels in tomato pesto; and grilled oysters. Among the main courses, rombo al rucola (£18.50) is a splendid combination of tastes and textures – a fillet of brill with a rocket sauce and boiled potatoes. Fegato and polenta unta (£15) – calf's liver served with garlic polenta and wild mushrooms – delivers a finely balanced blend of flavours. The house wines are all priced at a very accessible £12.50. Of the whites, the pale-coloured Tocai is crisp, light and refreshing.

✳ Brodetto "Mare Nostrum": chunky, saffron-flavoured fish soup (£7), subtler than its French cousins.

Sonny's

Modern British £18–£40

94 Church Rd SW13 ☎ 020 8748 0393

Station BR Barnes Bridge **Open** Mon–Sat 12.30–2.30pm & 7.30–11pm, Sun 12.30–3pm **Accepts** All major credit cards

Perceptive Barnes-ites have been supporting Sonny's since Modern British cuisine was just a twinkle in a telly chef's eye. The interior of the resto is modern but gratifyingly unthreatening and there is a busy, casual feel about the place. Sonny's shop next door sells a good many of those little delicacies that you would otherwise have to journey to the West End to secure. But do not be deceived into thinking that the cooking here is suburban, the kitchen is headed by Helena Puolakka – formerly head chef of the much acclaimed and sorely missed La Tante Claire.

The menu changes on a regular basis to reflect the seasons, so you might find starters like velouté of sweet potatoes with goats cheese mousse (£5.50); or a pressé of rabbit and baby vegetables with pistachio duxelles (£8); a salad of Bayonne ham and black pudding with potatoes and confit shallots (£6.50); or pan-fried scallops with oyster beurre blanc (£9.50). Main courses may team John Dory with choucroute, carrots and pancetta (£15); or pan-fried calves' liver with creamy polenta (£15). There is even room for a retro classic like Tournedos Rossini (£17) and something simple but good like shoulder of "Middle White" pork served with Brussels sprouts and wild mushrooms (£14). The service is welcoming and the wine list provides some sound bottles at sound prices. Puddings are

comfortable: sorbets, jellies, raspberry brûlée, served with biscotti (£5.25). There's also a set dinner: two courses for £16, three for £19.50 Monday to Thursday.

Bargain set lunch – two courses £13 and three courses for £16.

The Victoria   Modern British/Gastropub £15–£32

10 West Temple Sheen, SW14 ☎020 8876 4238
Station BR Mortlake **Open** Mon–Fri noon–2.30pm & 7–10pm, Sat noon–3pm & 7–10pm, Sun noon–3pm & 7–9pm **Accepts** All major credit cards ☻www.thevictoria.net

It would be nice to live in West Temple Sheen. The name has a good ring to it. The houses are palatial and pricey, both Sheen Common and Richmond Park are close at hand, and then there's The Victoria, a fine gastropub. The Victoria made the transition to gastropub in late 2000. Since then it has flaunted the obligatory conservatory, squashy sofas and painted floorboards. But what you're paying for is restaurant cooking in an informal setting, plus a restaurant wine list and restaurant service, and although

prices have been creeping up, what you pay seems pretty reasonable.

The menu changes daily – or even more frequently than that, should dishes run out – and features half a dozen starters and the same number of mains and puds. Starters may offer a sophisticated soup of white almond gazpacho with steeped raisins (£3.95); or a classic like salade Lyonnaise (£4.95); or smoked haddock and bacon quiche (£5.95). There is also the Victoria tapas plate (£8.95) – very popular. Mains are steady dishes well executed. Appleton pork chop with black pudding potato pancake and choucroute (£10.95); Charolais sirloin steak with onion gravy and chips (£16.95); grilled wild salmon with roasted new potatoes, chorizo and aioli (£13.95). These are all examples of those special, simple-sounding dishes that are hard to get right. Desserts are top stuff. It's a pleasure to watch punters savouring buttermilk pudding with poached Yorkshire rhubarb (£4.95), or taunting chocoholics with white and dark chocolate truffle cake (£5.95).

B&B? There are seven simple but comfortable bedrooms.

Further choices

MVH
Eclectic

5 White Hart Lane, SW13
☎ 020 8392 1111

Spooky and eccentric food, but essentially well done. Talent in the kitchen mitigates the wilder flights of fancy.

Glaister's Garden Bistro
Modern British

36–38 White Hart Lane, SW13
☎ 020 8878 2020

Neighbourhood stalwart. Despite its name, a genuine Brasserie feel to the place. Pleasantly informal.

The Depot
Mediterranean

Tideway Yard, 125 Mortlake High St, SW14
☎ 020 8878 9462

This place was once the Council stables. Now it offers a river view and Brasserie food to crowds of happy locals.

Battersea

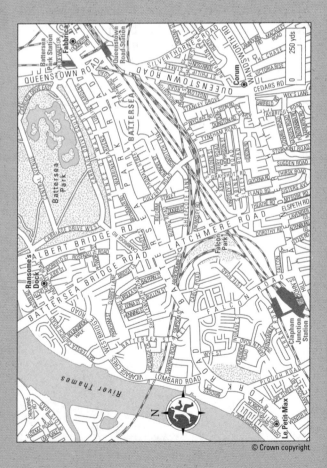

© Crown copyright

Corum

Modern British £17–£35

30–32 Queenstown Rd, SW8 ♿ ☎ 020 7720 5445
Station Clapham Common/BR Queenstown Rd
Open Mon–Fri noon–3pm & 5pm–1am, Sat noon–1am, Sun noon–12.30am
Accepts All major credit cards except Diners ⓦ www.corumrestaurants.com

Corum is an example of a new breed of eatery, (it should really be filed under gastrobar), but whatever it's called, the bar part of the deal is a runaway success. You'll find the gastro part towards the rear where the bar opens out into quite a large dining room that looks as if it is a page torn from the design manual of modern London restaurants. Blond wood floor, tick. Plain walls with modern art, tick. Subtle lighting, tick. Honey-coloured leather chairs, chocolate-leather banquettes, tick. It looks great. Like a thousand other places, but great.

The menu at Corum is an extension of the gastrobar ethos, and the ambition of the kitchen is gradually escalating, with dishes ranging from familiar to ambitious. So you may have to pass over something simple like tomato soup with Parmesan (£4.95) or eggs Benedict (£5.45), to get to foie gras terrine (£7.45) or pan-fried scallops with a Tuscan bread salad (£7.45). The main course dishes are also well-considered: pan-fried seabass comes with Roseval potatoes (£11.95); there may be côte de veau, a serious veal chop served with winter veg, Savoy cabbage and a Dijon cream sauce (£14.95); or something classic like a smoked haddock fishcake with a poached egg (£11.95). At Corum the kitchen brigade know what they're doing – the fishcake is large, light and almost fluffy, and it seems unfair to criticize a lack of ambition when it is patently obvious that these dishes are very popular indeed. Puds (all £5.50) are somewhat predictable, with enough sticky toffee, chocolate and the like for the sweetest of teeth.

✳ It can become very crowded, and favoured locals have been known to "book" their favourite sofa ahead of time.

Fabbrica

Italian £18–£40

153 Battersea Park Rd, SW8 ☎ 020 7720 0204
Station BR Battersea Park **Open** Mon–Fri noon–3pm & 6.30–11pm, Sat 6.30–11pm
Accepts All major credit cards except Diners ⓦ www.fabbricaweb.com

Fabbrica occupies the site that was Metrogusto in the last edition of this guide. This seems to be a very hard address at which to succeed – about all the location has to commend it is proximity to the dogs' home. Fabbrica opened in 2003 and is making a brave attempt. The dining room is modern, light and bright, and there is an almost Scandinavian amount of blond wood on show. The proprietors describe the cuisine as Modern Italian, and dishes are certainly ambitious when it comes to presentation.

The **pricing** is simple – two courses £15.50; three, £19; four, £22.50 – and the menu changes regularly following the whims of the chef and the markets. The format is antipasti, pasta, secondi and pud. From the antipasti a dish of rabbit stuffed with potatoes, sun-dried tomatoes and rosemary is elegant and delicate; or there is beef carpaccio with mustard sauce and a rocket salad; while a scallop and prawn salad with red pepper sauce is fresh and clean tasting – good enough to make you feel that the portion might be a little small. But the egg tagliatelle with a wild boar sauce is rich enough and substantial enough for anyone. Or you could opt for pumpkin gnocchi with smoked ricotta, or tagliolini with tomato and basil. From the mains a fillet of pink sea bream with fennel and dill is as subtle as the delicacy of the fish demands. Osso buco is made with white wine and a mirepoix of carrots which makes it look a tad pallid, but it has enough flavour to charm. Puds may include a solid chocolate tart and the coffee is very good indeed.

✳ The wine list ranges across Italy – some moody bottles at decent prices.

Le Petit Max

Very French £15–£40

Riverside Plaza, Chatfield Rd SW11 ☏ 020 7223 0999
Station BR Wandsworth Town **Open** Daily noon–2.30pm & 7–10pm
Accepts All major credit cards except AmEx & Diners

Le Petit Max opened just prior to Christmas 2003, and at the head of the menu it says "Bienvenue à Battersea". For the eponymous Max Renzland the past fifteen or so years have seen bienvenue à Hampton, Earl's Court, Hampton (again) and Knightsbridge. Battersea is just the latest stop. All of his restaurants have had certain things in common – they have been comfortable places, they have all offered pretty decent value, and they have all been designed for the worship of French provincial food – the kind of honest, satisfying dishes that stem from a love affair with good quality ingredients.

Max will probably be the man who takes your order and his suggestions are worth noting. He may have driven back from France with some fine chickens, or a notable cheese – enter into the spirit of things! Starters will include what has become a signature dish – "Cantabrian anchovies, shallot, butter" (£6.50). Terrific. Or pea and ham soup (£4); or grilled crottin de Chavignol salad (£5.50); or, somewhat incongruously, a rather good Iman Bayeldi (£5.50). Mains are classical in tone – two can share a braised shoulder of milk-fed Pyrenean lamb (£12.50 per person), which comes with a bowl of garlicky haricot beans and makes a stunning dish. Or there's a coq au vin with mash (£9.50). Puds are in the same idiom – rhum baba (£4.50), an outrageously chocolatey pot au chocolat (£4.50). The cooking is accomplished: flavours are huge, as are the portions. The wine list is eclectic and good value. There's a bargain menu du jour – two courses £12.50 and three £16.50. Bienvenue à Battersea indeed!

BATTERSEA

Locals can pitch up on spec. as Max only ever takes bookings for half the tables.

Ransome's Dock

British £22–£50

35–37 Parkgate Rd, SW11 ☎ 020 7223 1611
Station BR Battersea Park **Open** Mon–Fri noon–11pm, Sat noon–midnight, Sun noon–3.30pm **Accepts** All major credit cards ⊛ www.ransomesdock.co.uk

Ransome's Dock is a versatile restaurant – both formal enough for those little celebrations or occasions with friends, and informal enough to pop into for a single dish at the bar. The food is good, seasonal and made with carefully sourced ingredients. Dishes are well cooked, satisfying and unfussy, the wine list is encyclopedic, and service is friendly and efficient. All in all, Martin Lam and his team have got it just right. Everything stems from the raw ingredients: the bread may be from Poilâne, the potted shrimps from Morecambe Bay; they dicker with the Montgomerys over prime Cheddar cheeses. The menu changes monthly, but the philosophy behind it does not. There's an extensive brunch menu at the weekend.

Before rampaging off through the main menu, make a pit stop

at the daily specials; if nothing tempts you, turn to the seven or eight starters. If it's on, make a beeline for the grilled Norfolk smoked eel, with warm buckwheat pancake and crème fraiche (£8.50). It's very rich, very good and very large. There may be Perroche goat's cheese with pear and roast pepper salad (£6.50), or Morecambe Bay potted shrimps with wholemeal toast (£7.50). Main courses are well balanced – Dutch calf's liver (£15.50) may come with spinach and roast garlic mash. Or perhaps Trelough duck breast with Oloroso sherry-braised vegetables (£17.50) tempts? Or there may be a "shorthorn" sirloin steak (£20) with piquillo pepper butter and big chips. Puddings range from the complicated hot prune and Armagnac soufflé with Armagnac custard (£7) to the simple rhubarb fool (£6).

✳ A book-sized wine list, assembled for wine lovers by a wine lover.

Further choices

Adlar
Turkish

50 Battersea Park Rd, SW11
☎ 020 7627 2052

Pleasant Turkish restaurant somewhat out on a limb. Good Turkish sausages. Friendly service.

Le Bouchon Bordelaise
French

5-9 Battersea Rise, SW11
☎ 020 7738 0307

A small and friendly bistro-style restaurant and bar. Sound food and great atmosphere.

Castilla
Spanish

82 Battersea Rise, SW11
☎ 020 7738 9597

A "local" Spanish restaurant. As well as trad tapas there are some interesting main course dishes and a sound wine list.

Jack's Place
British/Steak

12 York Rd, SW11
☎ 020 7228 8519

Old fashioned to the point of appearing retro – this steak house serves good meat.
Interesting wine list!

Lan Na Thai
Thai

2 Lombard Rd, SW11
☎ 020 7924 6090

A high ticket Thai restaurant that specialises in smartly presented elaborate dishes and whizzy cocktails.

Bermondsey

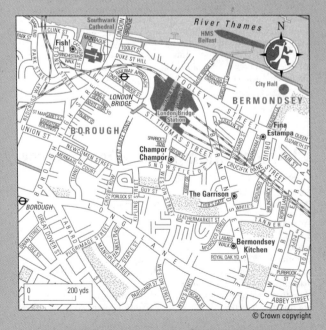

© Crown copyright

Bermondsey Kitchen

Modern British £15–£30

194 Bermondsey St, SE1 & ☎ 020 7407 5719

Station London Bridge **Open** Mon–Fri & Sun noon–3pm & 6–11pm, Sat 6–11pm
Accepts All major credit cards except AmEx ⓦ www.bermondseykitchen.co.uk

When all the old pubs in a neighbourhood have been converted into gastropubs, the next logical development is to start building gastropubs, from scratch. The Bermondsey Kitchen was at the forefront of this trend but it still clings stubbornly to the gastropub ethos; there is a daily changing (and commendably short) menu, prices are very reasonable and the bar is busy with local trade.

The presentation of the dishes here is gratifyingly straightforward; there is a welcome absence of towers and complication, and plenty of strong flavours. Among the starters you may find poached mussels with anchovy aioli (£4.50); a bruschetta featuring wild mushrooms sautéed in garlic butter (£5); or a plateful of fine charcuterie – Serrano ham, lomo, chorizo, and salchichon – (£4.50). Main courses are split among two fish, veggie and two meat. The imaginative vegetable accompaniments and side dishes are worthy of special mention – sprout tops with Seville orange butter; harissa-fried potatoes; celeriac remoulade (all £2.50). There may be Longhorn rib-eye steak with cinnamon and pumpkin mash (£13); chicken breast with braised chicory, vine tomato and basil sauce (£12.50); grilled tuna with warm pepper, mange tout and black-olive salad with salsa verde (£13). Puds, trad and satisfying, include hot chocolate pudding (£4.50) and tiramisù (£4), and there are carefully chosen British cheeses on offer (£4.50). The wine list here will please almost everybody as bottles range from sound and cheap to mid range and interesting.

✳ Stunning rare breed meats from "The Ginger Pig" farm, North Yorkshire.

Champor Champor

Asian Eclectic £30–£50

62 Weston St, SE1 & ☎ 020 7403 4600

Station London Bridge **Open** Mon–Sat 6.15–10.15pm (lunch by appointment)
Accepts All major credit cards except Diners ⓦ www.champor-champor.com

You are unlikely to stumble into Champor Champor by accident as this brightly painted, genuinely eccentric, little restaurant is marooned on the barren shores of Weston Street. The two proprietors describe the food as "creative Malay-Asian" and the chef – Adu Amran Hassan - not only handles the presentation of the dishes but also the interior design. He has had a busy year. In the spring of 2004 the resto emerged from a major expansion after taking over the

shop next door, but it still only seats forty. The food is tough to categorize, but the presentation is sophisticated and stylish and all the flavours are agreeably upfront.

The menu changes with the seasons and offers two courses for £19.90 and three for £24.90. To start, there may be baked pigeon breast in roti chanai parcel with a Malay curry sauce; steamed tilapia with turmeric leaf and crab and coconut bisque; or cassava cake with banana crisps and a wild-mushroom sauce. Do not be disheartened by the unfamiliarity of these dishes – ingredients are carefully matched and flavours work well. Main courses are equally eclectic: masala lamb fillet, is served with an aubergine mousse and an onion and wasabi sauce; or how about duck wontons served with a mandarin and palm sugar sauce and a duck liver sambal? This is well-judged adventurous cookery. Even the desserts are suitably exotic – "chocolate slice, roast parsnip and honey ice cream", touches several bases! The wine list is also refined but fairly priced, and there is a range of moody Asian beers.

✳ A "private room/members' lounge" in the basement opened summer 2004.

Fina Estampa

Peruvian £15–£30

150 Tooley St SE1 ☎ 020 7403 1342
Station London Bridge **Open** Mon–Fri noon–2.30pm & 6.30–10.30pm, Sat 6.30–10.30pm
Accepts All major credit cards ⊛ www.finaestampa.co.uk

While London is awash with ethnic eateries, Fina Estampa's proud boast is that it is the capital's only Peruvian restaurant (if you discount Nobu p.251). The husband and wife team running this place certainly tries hard to enlighten the customers, and bring a little downtown Lima to London Bridge. With its fresh cream-, gold- and coffee-coloured interior, Fina Estampa has a warm and bright ambience, upbeat music, and the attentive, friendly staff add greatly to this vibe.

The menu is traditional Peruvian, which means there's a great emphasis placed upon seafood. This is reflected in the starters, with such offerings as chupe de camarones (£7.95), a succulent shrimp-based soup; cebiche (£6.95), a dish of marinated white fish served with sweet potatoes; and jalea (£9.50), a vast plate of fried seafood. Ask for the salsa criolla

– its hot oiliness is a perfect accompaniment. There is also causa rellena (£5.95), described as a "potato surprise" and it is exactly that: layers of cold mashed potato, avocado and tuna fish served with salsa – the surprise being how something so straightforward can taste so good. Main courses – the fragrant chicken seco (£10.95), chicken cooked in a coriander sauce; or the superb lomo saltado (£13.95), tender strips of rump steak stir-fried with red onions and tomatoes – are worthy ambassadors for this simple yet distinctive cuisine. Perhaps most distinctive of all is the carapulcra (£11.95), a spicy dish made of dried potatoes, pork, chicken and cassava – top choice for anyone seeking a new culinary adventure.

 To drink? The unfortunately named Pisco sour (£3.50).

Fish!

Fish £25–£50

Cathedral St, SE1 ☎020 7407 3803
Station London Bridge **Open** Mon–Sat 11.30am–11pm, Sun noon–10pm
Accepts All major credit cards ❼www.fishdiner.co.uk

The Fish! Group of restaurants has been through a turbulent time. The majority of the chain has fallen by the wayside but this restaurant which was the first site is still plugging away trying to convert Brits into fish-lovers. The feel is large and airy due to the glass walls and there's a courtyard for alfresco eating, plus bar seating for armchair chefs who like to watch the real ones at work.

The good intentions of the place, however, are still apparent. The restaurant is a "GM free zone", and the claim is that all cod comes from sustainable fisheries in Icelandic waters. There's a lengthy printed list of fishy contenders, a number of which will be available depending on what the market has come up with. You select your favourite from those available; choose whether you want it steamed or grilled and then opt for salsa, Hollandaise, herb butter and garlic butter, or red wine fish gravy to go with it. Create your own combo. The choice ranges from organic salmon (£9.95); through sea bream (£12.95); to Dover sole (£19.95) by way of a dozen others. Portions are large and the fish is fresh. The left side of the menu offers starters like prawn cocktail (£6.50) and Thai crabcakes (£5.95), while main dishes include fishcake (£9.95); tuna burger with chips (£10.95); or fish and chips with mushy peas (£11.95). If you like a traditional approach to fish, Fish! won't disappoint. Puddings include stalwarts like bread-and-butter pudding, apple crumble or chocolate tart (all at £4.95). The house white, a Sauvignon (£13.95), is light, crisp and fairly priced.

 The children's menu offers "spaghetti tuna Bolognaise". What would they say in Bologna?

The Garrison

90 Bermondsey St, SE1 & ☎ 020 7089 9355

Station London Bridge **Open** Mon–Sat 12.30–3.30pm & 6.30–10pm,
Sun 12.30–4.30pm & 6.30–9.30pm 6–11pm
Accepts All major credit cards except Diners ⓦ www.thegarrison.co.uk

The Garrison may be unique in that it is a gastropub which opened on a site that was formerly … a gastropub! This place was once the Honest Cabbage until, in August 2003, it was reborn under new management as the Garrison. There is now a row of cramped banquettes plus some tall counters with bar stools. It's a lively place and the menu divides into three sections – good value bar snacks such as Welsh rarebit or whitebait; a brunch menu at the weekends; and the pukka menu which is short and to the point.

You'll get to pick from four starters (unless you import a fish finger sarnie from the bar snacks list) and half a dozen mains. They will probably be fairly ambitious dishes like seared foie gras, roasted mango brioche and aged balsamic (£7); shellfish bisque, crab and tarragon wonton (£4.50); or a game terrine with toast and pickles (£5.25). But you could also look under the heading "salads" – feta with spiced breadcrumbs (£6); Gorgonzola, pear, pink grapefruit and chicory (£6). Mains are equally sophisticated – grilled bream, roast fennel, ratatouille dressing (£13.50); roast magret of duck, spiced apricot, shallot and thyme jus, fondant potato (£13.50); or twice baked goat's cheese soufflé shallot and Parmesan cream (£6.80). For pud there is a cheeseboard (£6.50 but from Neal's Yard), sticky toffee pudding (£4.25); chocolate fudge brownie with crème fraiche (£4); and rather good home made ice creams (£4.50) – the caramel ice cream gets three stars as does the malted milk, with the white peach sorbet getting an honourable two stars.

✳ Movies are shown downstairs, Sat, Sun & Mon.

BERMONDSEY

Bloomsbury

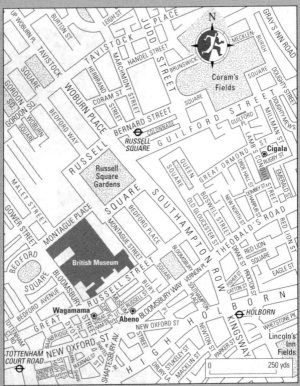

© Crown copyright

Abeno

Japanese £10–£35

47 Museum St, WC1 & ☎ 020 7405 3211

Station Tottenham Court Road **Open** Daily noon–10pm **Accepts** All major credit cards

Abeno claims to be Europe's only specialist okonomi-yaki restaurant, and it may well be. London has plenty of teppan-yaki restaurants – where the chef cooks gourmet morsels in front of you on the hotplate – but okonomi-yaki hasn't swept to popularity, perhaps because even the finest okonomi-yaki looks a bit like roadkill. Imagine a sloppy pizza crossed with a solid omelette then layered with odds and ends. Then imagine it being assembled and cooked on the table in front of you. Abeno is saved by the gentle and friendly service, the freshness of the ingredients, the charm of the cooks, and the low, low prices.

You could try yaki-soba, a fried noodle dish with chicken (£7.75). Or soba-rice, a natty combination of rice and noodles

that's all the rage in Kansai – try it with pork and kimchi (£10.95). You could even try the upscale teppan-yaki fillet steak (£16.80). But you're here for the okonomi-yaki. The base is cabbage, egg and dough, with spring onions and tempura batter; all this is piled onto the hotplate. You specify whether you want deluxe or super deluxe, trad or wholemeal base, and off they go. Try tofu, corn and extra spring onion (£6.80 or £8.80), or spicy Tsuruhasi – kimchi and an extra egg (£7.30 or £10.30). Or Abeno special – pork, bacon, konnyaku, asparagus, squid, prawn and salmon, topped with an egg (£19.80). And there are nice side dishes that will serve as starters, such as ika itame – squid with garlic and soy (£3.20), or miso soup (£2.20). Set menus take the angst out of ordering.

BLOOMSBURY

✳ Keep your elbows well away from the hotplate unless you find the smell of scorching appetising.

Cigala

Spanish/Tapas £18–£30

54 Lamb's Conduit St, WC1 ☎ 020 7405 1717

Station Russell Square **Open** Mon–Fri noon–12.45pm, Sat 12.30–10.45pm, Sun 12.30–9.30pm **Accepts** All major credit cards ⊛ www.cigala.co.uk

The chef-proprietor Jake Hodges – one of the founders of Moro (see p.107) – has here settled into a regime of straightforward Iberian dishes. This is the place to try rabbit, ox tongue, patatas bravas and poached meats, as well as old favourites like the eponymous cigalas na brasa – langoustines with Romesco sauce. Look out for simple dishes. Strong flavours. Fresh ingredients. Real passion.

The tapas menu has grown here and now offers a good all-day option. There is also a set lunch deal – two courses £15 and three for £18. The main menu changes daily. It is dependent on the markets and what the chef can find that looks good. This makes for seasonal dishes – a huge plus. You might start with sopa de marisco (£4.50) – seafood soup. Or rinones Jerezana (£5.50) – kidneys pan-fried with Fino. Or piquillo rellenos (£6) – peppers stuffed with tuna and mayonnaise. All these dishes are simple, well seasoned and have good combinations of flavour. Mains deliver in much the same fashion. Fabadas Asturianas (£13) is a rich, comforting bean stew with good, spicy chorizo, lamb and rashers of fat bacon. Delicious. Paella de cerdo (£16.50 per person, minimum two people, takes thirty minutes) is the real deal, made with pork and chorizo. Puddings lie in wait: arroz dulce (£4.50) is a goodly rice pudding. The wine list doffs its cap to a selection of sherries, and features a good range of well-chosen Spanish wines. The cooking here is very adept and Mr Hodges has the sense to stick to simple, unpretentious dishes and simple, unpretentious presentation.

As is traditional, there's a free tapas with every drink.

Wagamama

Japanese/Chinese £8–£17

4 Streatham St, WC1 ☎ 020 7323 9223
Station Tottenham Court Rd **Open** Mon–Sat noon–11pm, Sun 12.30–10pm
Accepts All major credit cards 🌐 www.wagamama.com

Wagamama is as good a canteen as you'll find, serving simple and generally rather good food at very reasonable prices, which may explain why it has grown into such a large chain so quickly. What it's not is a place for a relaxed or intimate meal. The basement interior is cavernous and minimalist, and diners are seated side by side on long benches. At regular eating times you'll find yourself in a queue lining the stairway – there are no reservations. When you reach the front, you're seated, your order is punched into a hand-held computer and that spurs the kitchen into action. There's beer and wine available, as well as free green tea.

Dishes arrive when they're cooked, so your party will be served at different times. Most people order a main dish – noodles in soup, fried noodles or sauce-based noodles – or a rice dish. Side dishes can also be pressed into service as a starter: yasai yakitori (£4.25) is chargrilled chicken with the ever-popular yakitori sauce, while gyoza (£3.95) are delicious, fried chicken dumplings. The mains include a splendid chilli beef ramen (£8.50) – slivers of sirloin steak in a vat of soup with vegetables. Also good is the yasai katsu curry (£6), which is boiled rice with a light curry sauce and discs of deep-fried vegetables; and yasai chili men (£6.25), a vegetarian "everything-in" dish with courgette, ginger, mushroom, carrot, peas, tomato, tofu and so on, plus ramen noodles. If this all sounds confusing, that's because it is. To enjoy Wagamama you'll need to go with the flow.

Wagamama: "Willfulness or selfishness: selfishness in terms of looking after oneself, looking after oneself in terms of positive eating and positive living".

Brick Lane,
Spitalfields &
Bethnal Green

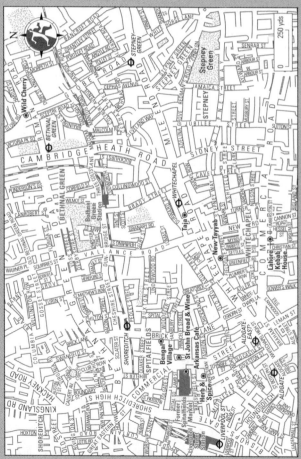

© Crown copyright

Arkansas Café

North American/Steak £12–£30

Unit 12, Old Spitalfields Market, E1 ☎ 020 7377 6999
Station Liverpool Street **Open** Mon–Fri noon–2.30pm & Sun noon–4pm
Accepts Mastercard & Visa

As you approach the Arkansas Café the glow from its steel-pit barbecue invites you in. Bubba Helberg and his wife Sarah claim that they serve the best barbecue this side of the pond, and they may just be right. Their food is fresh and simple, and Bubba chooses his own steaks from Smithfield Market to ensure that the meat is marbled through for tenderness. He marinates and smokes his own brisket and ribs, and his recipe for the latter won him a soul-food award back home. His secret home-made barbecue sauce is on every table.

Decor is spartan – clean-scrubbed tables, canvas chairs and paper plates. It's folksy but fun. There are no starters, and "No fries". Any of the steaks – Irish steak platter (£10.50), bison rib-eye steak platter (£14.50) – are good bets, chargrilled with Bubba's special sauce and served with seasonal vegetables. Note that the price is genuinely market-sensitive and can rise and fall. Corn-fed

BY APPOINTMENT TO HIS EXCELLENCY THE AMERICAN AMBASSADOR PURVEYORS OF PULLED PORK, PIGS AND RIBS THE ARKANSAS CAFÉ·LONDON

French chicken (£7.25) is tender and full of flavour, and a side order of chilli (75p) provides a spicy sauce-like accompaniment. Most of the other dishes on the menu are platters or sandwiches, the latter including choices like chargrilled Barbary duck breast sandwich (£6.25); free-range pork sandwich (£6); beef brisket Texas-style sandwich (£7), which comes meltingly tender and smoky; and, of course, hot dog (£4). Puddings (all £2.50) include New York-style lemon cheesecake and New Orleans pecan pie. They are as sweet and as solid as they should be. The wine list is short and to the point, but the beer list is long.

✱ Bubba will be happy to bring his travelling barbecue to your party, except for the fourth of July when he's usually booked by the American Embassy.

Bengal Village

Indian £10–£25

75 Brick Lane, E1 ♿ ☎ 020 7366 4868
Station Aldgate East/Liverpool St **Open** Daily noon–midnight
Accepts All major credit cards ⊛ www.bengalvillage.com

Brick Lane becomes ever more sophisticated. Where once all was BYO restaurants serving rough-and-ready curries at bargain-basement prices to impoverished punters seeking

Brick Lane Touts

Brick Lane is one of the few areas where competition is so fierce that there are restaurant touts. These enthusiastic individuals usually get paid £1 a customer by the resto, and having promised you all manner of discounts are never to be found when the bill arrives. Do not be swayed by their blandishments.

chilli and all things familiar, there's now a growing crop of slick new establishments serving Bangladeshi cooking. The Bengal Village is one such place. There's a blond wood floor and modernist chairs, but it's about more than just design. The menu touches all the bases: trad curryholics can still plough their way through more than a hundred old-style curries – korma, Madras, vindaloo – but now they can also try some more interesting Bangladeshi dishes, too.

Bucking what seems to be becoming the trend, starters are not the best dishes at the Bengal Village. The onion bhajis (£2.10) are, well, onion bhajis, and the chicken tikka (£2.30) is no more than sound. Move

straight along to the Bangla specialities. Bowal mas biran (£6.95) is boal fish that has been deep-fried with a rich sauce. There are four shatkora curries, the shatkora being a small green fruit that has a delightful bitter citrus tang and goes very well with rich meats – lamb shatkora (£6.95), for example. Then there are ureebisi dishes, traditionally made with the seeds of a large runner-bean-like plant – try chicken ureebisi (£5.95). There are also some interesting vegetarian options: chalkumra (£5.75), subtitled "ash-ground", is made with a pumpkin-like gourd. Or the marrow kofta (£5.75), a curry with large and satisfactorily dense vegetable dumplings floating, or rather sinking, in it.

✱ Bhug mas bhuna (£7.95) "A large fish spotty like a leopard found in Bangladesh".

Herb & Spice   Indian £7–£15

11a Whites Row, E1 ☎020 7247 4050
Station Aldgate East/Liverpool St **Open** Mon–Fri 11.30am–2.30pm & 5.30–11.30pm
Accepts All major credit cards

Do not let the tiny, rather cramped and garish dining room put you off this treasure of a curry house on Whites Row, a small road just off Commercial Street and tucked in behind Spitalfields. A loyal clientele from the City means that to secure one of the 22 seats you'll probably have to book! What sets Herb & Spice apart from the pack is that the dishes are

freshly cooked and well prepared, and yet the prices are still reasonable. When the food arrives it will surprise you: it's on the hot side, with plenty of chilli and bold, fresh flavours.

It's not often that the poppadoms (55p) grab your attention. They do here. Fresh, light and crisp, they are accompanied by equally good home-made chutneys – perky chopped cucumber with coriander leaf, and a hot, yellowy-orange, tamarind-soured yoghurt. The kebabs make excellent starters: murgi tikka (£2.75) – chicken, very well cooked. Or shami kebab (£2.75) – minced meat with fresh herbs. Also gosht tikka (£2.75) – tender lamb cubes. For a main course you might try the excellent murgi biryani (£6.95), chicken cooked with saffron rice and served with a good, if rather hot, vegetable curry. Or there's bhuna gosht (£4.95), a model of its type – a rich, well-seasoned lamb curry with whole black peppercorns and shards of cassia bark. Murgi rezalla (£6.95) is chicken tikka in sauce; it's much hotter and comes with more vegetables than its cousin, the chicken tikka masala. The breads are good, too: from the decent naan (£1.65) to the shabzi paratha (£1.95), a thin, crisp wholemeal paratha stuffed with vegetables.

* For a real tongue-trampler, try the dhal shamber (£2.75), very hot and very, very sweet indeed.

Lahore Kebab House   Indian £5–£18

2 Umberstone St, E1 ☎ 020 7481 9737

Station Whitechapel/Aldgate East **Open** Daily noon–midnight **Accepts** Cash or cheque only

For decades, the Lahore has been a cherished secret among curry-lovers – a nondescript, indeed dowdy-looking kebab house serving excellent and very cheap fare. Recent years, however, have seen a few changes, and now the "Original" Lahore Kebab House is bent on world domination, with branches springing up all over London. Thankfully, the food at the original in Umberstone Street is still good and spicy, prices are still low, and the service brusque enough to disabuse you of any thoughts that the smart round marquetry tables and posh shopfront are signs of impending mediocrity. What they do here, they do very well indeed.

Rotis (50p) tend to arrive unordered – the waiter watches how you eat and brings fresh bread as and when he sees fit. For starters, the kebabs are standouts. Seekh kebab (75p), mutton tikka (£2.50) and chicken tikka (£2.50) are all very fresh, very hot and very good, and served with a yoghurt and mint dipping sauce. The meat or chicken biryanis (£6.50) are also splendid, well spiced and with the rice taking on all the rich flavours. The karahi gosht and karahi chicken (£6) are uncomplicated dishes of tender meat in a rich gravy. And on Friday there is a special dish – lamb chop curry (£6). Also noteworthy is the masala fish (£6). The dal tarka (£5) is made from whole yellow split peas, while sag aloo (£5) brings potatoes in a rich and oily spinach purée. For dessert try the home-made kheer (£2), which is a special kind of trad rice pudding with cardamom.

* BYO by all means – but with hot food, lassi (£2) is more cooling.

New Tayyab

Indian £5–£18

83 Fieldgate St, E1 ☎ 020 7247 9543

Station Whitechapel/Aldgate East **Open** Daily 5pm-midnight
Accepts Cash or cheque only ⊛ www.tayyabs.co.uk

The Tayyab group has come a long way since those first days in 1974. After the initial café came the sweet shop, and then the New Tayyab took over what was once the corner pub. So no.83 was transformed from a scruffy converted pub into a smart new designer restaurant. Now there's art on the walls, smart lighting and the chairs are leather and chrome. Miraculously the food remains straightforward Pakistani fare: good, freshly cooked and served without pretension. And more miraculous still, the prices have stayed lower than you would believe possible. Booking is essential and service is speedy and slick. This is not a place to um and er over the menu.

The simpler dishes are terrific, particularly the five pieces of chicken tikka (£2.40), served on an iron sizzle dish alongside a small plate of salady things and a medium-fierce, sharp, chilli dipping sauce. They do the same thing with mutton (£2.40), or there's a plate of four large and splendid lamb chops (£4.20). Sheekh kebabs (70p) and shami kebabs (60p) are bought by the skewer. There are round fluffy naan breads (60p), but try the wholemeal roti (40p), which is deliciously nutty and crisp. The karahi dishes are simple and tasty: karahi chicken (£4.20 normal portion, £8 large) is chicken in a rich sauce; and karahi aloo gosht (£4.20) is lamb with potatoes in another rich sauce, heavily flavoured with bay leaves. Or there's karahi mixed vegetables (£3.50). A list of interesting daily specials includes dishes such as the trad mutton curry nihari (£4.80), which is served every Monday.

✳ Despite having been a pub Tayyab is unlicensed – remember to BYO.

St John Bread & Wine

British £20–£50

94–96 Commercial St, E1 ☎ 020 7247 8724

Station Liverpool Street **Open** Mon-Sat 8am–11pm, Sun 8am–10.30pm
Accepts All major credit cards except Diners ⊛ www.stjohnbreadandwine.com

This place is younger brother to St John in nearby Clerkenwell (see p.108), and in 2004 – like its older sibling which has won twice before – it won best British Restaurant at the Tio Pepe ITV London Restaurant Awards. It's a utilitarian room with small tightly packed tables and chairs, the whole place is dominated by an open plan bakery and kitchen and wafts from the racks of cooling bread will boot your tastebuds into life. The food is honest here. Simple. Delicious. Very good value.

The menu has a time line running down the side of it –

8am means an Old Spot bacon sandwich (£4.80) or porridge and prunes (£4). By lunchtime at noon you'll find oysters (£2 each); game broth (£6); pickled herrings roast shallots and goat's curd (£6.20); or you could splash out on langoustines and mayonnaise (£9.20). The menu changes with the seasons and what is available at market so perhaps there'll be braised cuttlefish (£6.70) or red mullet served with chicory and anchovy (£13.20)? Maybe pigeon with mushy peas appeals (£12.80)?

Beside the timeline for 7pm there's roast Large Black pork with fennel (£14). All these dishes are supported by fabulous bread, and a fairly forgiving selection of wines. You shouldn't expect anything elaborate or fancypants, but you can be sure of big flavours and intriguing combinations of taste and texture. Puds are good – meringue, pomegranate and cream (£6); baked cheesecake with Marc (£6). When feeling Proustian, take half a dozen Madeleines home with you (£3).

✳ London's most civilised elevenses? "Seed cake and a glass of Madeira (£6.80)".

Taja

Indian £7–£18

199a Whitechapel Rd, E1 ☎ 020 7247 3866

Station Whitechapel **Open** Mon–Wed & Sun 11am–midnight, Thurs-Sat 11am–12.30am
Accepts All major credit cards

Taja's exterior of black and white vertical stripes certainly jolts the eye. Venture in and you find a dining area seating sixty across two floors. The counter is ultra-modern in stainless steel and the seating has recently been upgraded from stools to comfy chairs. On the ground floor, large windows look out onto the hurly-burly of passing traffic just inches away. The food tastes very fresh, and is markedly cheap. Taja is a genuine rarity – a thoroughly modern Bangladeshi restaurant. The menu is both enlightened and lightened, with a host of vegetarian dishes balancing old favourites.

Start with that great test of a tandoor chef, chicken tikka (£2.25). At Taja you get half a dozen sizable chunks of chicken, cooked perfectly – not a hint of

dryness – with the obligatory salad garnish (a waste of time) and a yellowish "mint sauce". Or try chotpoti (£2.25), described as "chickpeas and potatoes with spices, served with a tamarind chutney". Move on to a biryani of mixed vegetables, lamb, or chicken (all £4.95); a good-sized portion comes with a dish of really splendid vegetable curry by way of added lubrication. There are also a host of curry house favourites. Chicken bhuna (£4.45) is an outstanding choice, with a really fresh sauce, hot but not too hot, and with lots of fresh herbs. The naan breads – plain (£1.95), peshwari or keema (both £2.15) – are large, thick-rimmed and very fresh, as a naan should be. The meal deal is a good one – four courses for £6.95 either vegetarian or non-vegetarian.

 Architecture students may spot that this place was converted from a public toilet!

Wild Cherry

241 Globe Rd, E2 ☎020 8980 6678

Station Bethnal Green **Open** Mon11am–4pm, Tues–Fri 11am–7pm, Sat 10am–4pm
Accepts All major credit cards except AmEx & Diners

Wild Cherry is a vegetarian restaurant that, as the mission statement by the door proclaims, "exists firstly to provide fresh home-cooked vegetarian meals for the local community". It's part of the London Buddhist Centre around the corner and was once a soup kitchen for workers and devotees. It's a bright, clean, self-service venue with modern wooden tables and Arne Jacobsen chairs.

A blackboard lists the daily menu and you choose from selections like miso and aramé soup (£2.30); cream cheese and spinach and polenta with roast vegetables (£5.25); chickpea and spinach curry with coriander and coconut served with basmati rice (£4.95); and hot quiche of the day (Stilton and celery) with two salads (£4.95). There's a choice of three different salads every day – maybe beetroot, carrot and ruby chard with orange hazelnut dressing (£2.95 or £4.25), and there's always a quiche and two hot dishes. Baked potatoes include a choice of comforting fillings like humus (£3), grated cheddar (£3.25) and tzatziki (£4.25). Salads (large mixed £4.25, regular mixed £2.95, single scoop £1.50) include choices like aramé rice; ruby chard, cherry tomato and fresh chive; mixed leaf; Moroccan chickpea with rocket; and coleslaw with vegan mayonnaise. Puddings include chocolate and beetroot cake (£1.80); prune and honey cake (£1.50). Choose from fourteen different teas (80p or 90p), ten of them herbal, plus Free Trade coffee (£1.10 per mug, £1.80 per cafetière), and a choice of soya or cow's milk. The portions here are huge, it all tastes wholesome and it's amazing value.

✳ There are usually wheat-free, gluten-free and sugar-free options.

Further choices

Aladin
Indian

132 Brick Lane, E1
☎020 7247 8210

Brick Lane resto just like Brick Lane Restos used to be! Sound curries at sound prices.

Les Trois Garcons
French

1 Club Row, E1
☎020 77613 1924

High camp and high drama in this pub that has been transformed into a French restaurant. Pricey.

Brixton, Dulwich & Herne Hill

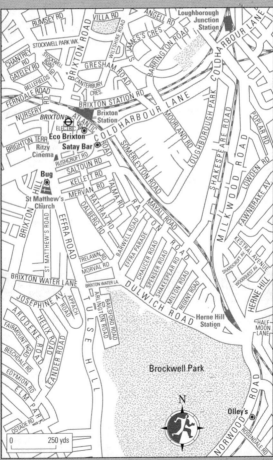

© Crown copyright

Bug

Modern International £15–£40

The Crypt, St Matthews Church, Brixton Hill, SW2 ⚬ ☎ 020 7738 3366
Station Brixton **Open** Tues–Sat 5–11.30pm, Sun 1–9.15pm
Accepts Mastercard, Switch & Visa 🌐 www.bugbrixton.co.uk

Bug lurks in the crypt of a converted church. Hardened Presbyterians may feel a little peculiar eating, drinking and making merry in such circumstances, while the less puritanical may even enjoy the thought that it's a short step to the Bug Bar, the trendy club-bar in the neighbouring crypt, and scarcely any further to the nightclub upstairs. Despite its underground and rather gothic location in the main dining area the atmosphere is anything but crypt-like, and the service verges on jolly, plus there's a slick and trendy private dining room called the Cocoon Room.

Traditionally, the menu has always been mostly vegetarian here, with a fish dish or two to vary the pace, but for some years now meat dishes have been gaining ground. Starters vary: smoked trout fritters, wasabi mayo, pickled cucumber (£3.75); tabbouleh, white-bean puree, caraway bread (£4.25); or pan-fried squid, wilted pak choi, and tomato chutney (£4.25). On the main course list, there's crispy Cantonese mock duck served with pancakes, cucumber, and Oriental dipping sauce (£9); also swordfish steak with wok-fried vegetables (£9.50); wild-boar sausages, spring onion and garlic mash, apple and thyme gravy (£9.95); or braised lamb shank, horseradish-crushed new potatoes, rosemary jus (£9.95). There's a short list of puds – chocolate fondant, vanilla ice cream, prune and Armagnac compote (£4.50). There's a Sunday lunch deal: two courses £13.50 and three, £17, featuring nut roast, organic chicken breast or organic rib-eye steak with all the trimmings.

✳ Wherever possible Bug uses organic produce and British, organic and free-range meat.

Eco Brixton

Pizza £8–£20

4 Market Row, Brixton Market, Electric Row, SW9 ☎ 020 7738 3021
Station Brixton **Open** Mon, Tues & Thurs–Sat 8am–5pm
Accepts All major credit cards except AmEx & Diners 🌐 www.ecorestaurant.com

If you're in Brixton Market around noon, Eco is a must for your lunch break. You may have to share a table, (and then after queuing among the shuffling shoppers), but you can always study the menu while you wait. Formerly Pizzeria Franco, now Eco Brixton, this place has the same menu as its sister, Eco, on Clapham High Street, but the Brixton branch closes at 5pm. It's small and popular, so things can get hectic. Still, the service is friendly, the pizzas crisp and the salads mountainous. Plus there is an identically priced takeaway menu.

All the famous pizzas are here, including a pleasingly pungent Napoletana (£5.90) with the sacred trio of anchovies, olives and capers, and quattro stagioni (£6.90), packed full of goodies. But why not try something less familiar, such as aubergine and sun-dried tomato (£6.50)? Or enjoy la dolce vita (£6.70), where rocket, mushrooms and Dolcelatte all vie for attention? Or even the amore (£6.70), with its French beans, artichoke, pepper and aubergine? Perhaps even one of the calzone (£6.90 or £7.20)? It's a difficult choice.

For a lighter meal – lighter only because of the absence of carbohydrate – try a salad. Tricolore (£6.20) is made with baby Mozzarella, beef tomato, avocado and olives. Side orders such as the melted cheese bread (£3.25) and mushroom bread (£3.75) are highly recommended. For sandwiches, Eco also impresses. Focaccia is stuffed with delights like Parma ham and rocket (£6.25) or Mozzarella and avocado (£5.80). You could also go for starters, but at lunch they seem a little surplus to requirements.

> ✱ Brixton was the first market in London to be lit by electricity, hence the address.

Olley's

Fish & Chips £15–£30

67–69 Norwood Rd, SE24 &. ☎020 8671 8259
Station BR Herne Hill **Open** Mon & Sun 5–10.30pm, Tues–Sat noon–10.30pm
Accepts All major credit cards except Diners ⓦ www.olleys.info

Olley's is a famous fish and chip shop. It is partly famous because it has won various awards, and partly because of proprietor Harry Niazi's tireless publicity offensive. Olley's is just across the road from Brockwell Park, and in the summer of 2004 expanded into yet another shopfront to enlarge the dining room to a whopping ninety-seater. There is a separate area devoted to takeaway.

The list of starters has been trimmed and tidied. You can opt for fresh grilled sardines, (£3.85); prawn cocktail (£3.85); or battered calamari (£3.50). On to more serious matters – the chips are good here. Niazi believes in pre-blanching, and when done well this technique guarantees chips that are fluffy inside and crisp outside. The mushy peas (£1.50) are commendable and so are the wallies (45p) – which non-Londoners will know better as gherkins. The fish is a triumph: fresh, white and flaky inside, crisp and golden outside (obviously the fryer knows his craft). Adding £2 worth of chips to each, the leader board reads as follows: cod (£8.25); plaice (£8.75); haddock (£8.95); salmon (£9.55); monkfish (£9.95); swordfish (£9.95);

halibut (£11.50); and hake (£9.95). You can also choose to have your fish grilled, or steamed, which is the best way when it comes to seabass (£12.95 with chips) or Dover sole (£18.25). Desserts are steady and there is a whole menu of liqueur coffees. If you have the temerity to ask for a fish and large chips, the plateful that arrives is so large that the staff must be taking the proverbial.

✳ Another guide describes the mushy peas here as "the best in London".

Satay Bar

Indonesian £16–£32

447 Coldharbour Lane, SW9 & ☏ 020 7326 5001
Station Brixton **Open** Mon–Fri noon–5pm & 6–11 pm, Sat & Sun 1–5pm & 6–11pm
Accepts All major credit cards except AmEx & Diners ⊛ www.sataybar.co.uk

The Satay Bar is a lively resto and bar tucked away behind the Ritzy cinema. The interior has had a lick of paint and is now grey and gold, the background music is as loud as ever – party, party, party! If you are old and grizzly this may not appeal but otherwise settle in, relax and take a look at the art. Should you like one of the many paintings adorning the walls, buy it – they are for sale.

Dishes are Indonesian with the chilli factor toned down (for the most part) to accommodate European taste buds. The menu is a testing one – at least when it comes to pronouncing the names of the dishes – but the food is well cooked, service is friendly and efficient, and the prices are reasonable. Your waiter will smile benignly at your attempt to say udang goreng tepung (£6.45) – lightly battered, deep-fried king prawns served with a sweet chilli sauce. Obvious choices, such as the chicken or prawn satay (£5.95), are highly rated. Or try the chicken wings with garlic and green chilli (£5.75). The hottest dishes are to be found among the curries. Even though styled "medium", kari ikan (£6.95), a red snapper-based, Javanese fish curry, packs a punch, while the rendang ayam (£5.95), a spicy chicken dish, is only cooled by the addition of a coconut sauce. For something lighter, the mee goreng (£5.25) is a satisfying dish of spicy egg noodles fried with lamb, prawns and vegetables; or there's gado-gado (£4.95), a side dish of bean curd and vegetables with spicy peanut sauce, which is almost a meal in itself.

✳ Go for rijstaffel, a multi-course, colonial Dutch, Indonesian feast; minimum two people (£13.95 per person).

Camden Town

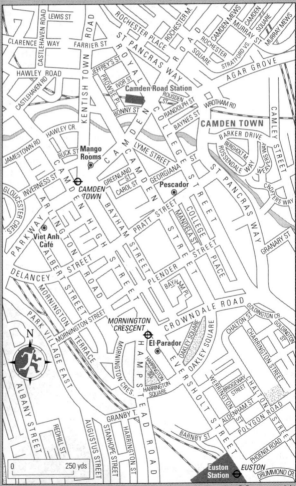

© Crown copyright

El Parador

245 Eversholt St, NW1 ☎ 020 7387 2789

Station Mornington Crescent **Open** Mon–Thurs noon–3pm & 6–11pm, Fri noon–3pm & 6–11.30pm, Sat 6–11.30pm, Sun 6.30–10.30pm **Accepts** All major credit cards

El Parador is a small, no-frills Spanish restaurant and tapas bar, slightly stranded in the quiet little enclave around Mornington Crescent, between King's Cross and Camden. It serves very tasty tapas at very reasonable prices and has a friendly, laid-back atmosphere, even on busy Friday and Saturday nights. Try a glass of the dry Manzanilla (£3) to start or accompany your meal. It's a perfect foil for tapas.

As ever with tapas, the fun part of eating here is choosing several dishes from the wide selection on offer, and then sharing and swapping with your companions. Allow at least two or three tapas a head – more for a really filling meal – and go for at least one of the fish or seafood dishes, which are treats. Highlights include chipirones salteados (£4.50), baby squid pan-fried with sea salt and olive oil; or salteados de gambas (£5), nice fat tiger prawns pan-fried with parsley, paprika and chilli. Carnivores shouldn't miss out on the jamón serrano (£5), delicious Spanish cured ham; or the morcilla de Burgos (£4.60) – sausages that are a cousin of black pudding. The vegetarian tapas are particularly good here. Try pure de patatas del Parador (£3.80), mash with pan-fried pepper and Manchego; and tortilla Espanola (£3.50), a classic Spanish omelette. Desserts keep up the pace: marquesa de chocolate (£3.60) is a luscious, creamy, home-made chocolate mousse; flan de naranja (£3.20), a really good orange crème caramel. It's worth checking out El Parador's strong selection of Spanish wines as there are some good value bottles.

✳ The al fresco tables hidden behind the resto are sought after and should be booked in advance.

Mango Room

10–12 Kentish Town Rd NW1 ☎ 020 7482 5065

Station Camden Town **Open** Tues–Sat noon–3pm & 6pm–midnight, Sun 6pm–midnight **Accepts** Mastercard & Visa

Mango Room is an engaging place, although it does make you wonder why everyone in this part of London is striving so hard to be laid-back. This restaurant describes itself as offering "traditional and modern Caribbean cuisine". It's a homely place, the staff are gentle and the cooking is reliable. If there's a fault to be found, it would be that the spicing and seasoning is somewhat tame, as if the act has been cleaned up a little. But no matter, the Mango Room is very full, and everyone seems to be having a great time, in a laid-back, Camden-cool kind of way.

Traditional starters are the most successful, like the salt-cod fritters with apple chutney (£5), or crab and potato balls (£4.50) – the exception to the under-spiced rule. Ebony wings, marinated in chilli pepper, garlic and soya with a hot and sweet dipping sauce (£4) is a nice dish but not a hot one. For a main course, "Camden's famous curry goat with hot pepper, scallions, garlic, pimento and spices" (£9.50) is subtitled "A hot, spicy, traditional dish", which it isn't. But it is very tasty – with plenty of lean meat, and well presented. For fish-eaters there is Creole snapper with mango and green peppercorn sauce (£10). The side dishes are excellent – plantain (£2.50), rice and peas (£2), white- and sweet-potato mash (£2.50), and a very good, dry and dusty roti (£2.50). The cooking is consistent and the kitchen makes a real effort with the presentation. Puddings are good – the mango and banana brûlée (£4) sports an exemplary hard top.

✳ The Mango Room's special rum punch (£4.50) is sweet enough to class as a dessert.

Pescador

Portuguese/Fish £15–£45

23 Pratt St, NW1 ☎ 020 7482 7008
Station Camden Town **Open** Tues–Fri 6–11pm, Sat 1–11pm, Sun 1–10pm
Accepts All major credit cards except AmEx & Diners

Venture into Pescador and you might as well be in Portugal, which is a good thing ... always presuming that you like fish. The dining room is a plain, cream-painted room that is slowly being overwhelmed by a tidal wave of knick-knacks themed around fish and fishermen. The tables are small and close together and, while the lady of the house takes charge of the till behind the bar, a flotilla of waiters bustles about. This is a busy place and you should book.

Starters range from the simple – pasteis de bacalhau (£3.80): small, fluffy, fried rissoles of potato and salt cod, very good indeed – to all manner of luxurious seafood: giant prawns (£5.90 each), clams (£6), mussels (£4.50). One attractive option is to share a main course portion of sapateira (£16) between two. This is billed as "a crab served with toast", and that's what you get – spread the toast with the brown meat. As is the way with good fish restaurants, there is always a daily special and this might be a large, fresh sea bream that is priced according to the market and can be served in fillets or left on the bone, depending how confident you are feeling. Plainly grilled, very fresh fish is always delicious, and there is also halibut (£10.50), scabbard fish (£9.80), squid (£11.80), sea bass (£16.80) and skate (£10.90). If you like rich food and plenty of it, opt for the arroz de marisco (£13.50). You get a large casserole full of shellfish chowder thickened with rice but left sloppy like a very loose risotto. Tremendous.

❋ Order the crisp, dry Alvarino vinho verde, it will help you blend in!

Viet-Anh Cafe

Vietnamese £15–£40

41 Parkway, NW1 ☏ 020 7284 4082
Station Camden Town **Open** Daily noon–4pm & 5.30–11pm
Accepts Mastercard & Visa

Authentic, it says on the card, and authentic it tastes on the plate. Viet-Anh is a bright, cheerful cafe with oilcloth-covered tables, run by a young Vietnamese couple. They cook and give service that's beyond helpful. In complete contrast to the occasionally intimidating feel of some of the more obscure Chinese restaurants, this is a friendly and welcoming place. If there is anything puzzling or unfamiliar, you have only to ask.

Vietnamese vegetarian spring rolls (£3) and Vietnamese chicken pancake (£3) are classic starters. The former are crisp, well seasoned, and flavoured with fresh coriander; the latter are a delight – two large, paper-thin, eggy pancakes stuffed with vegetables and chicken, and served with large lettuce leaves. You take a leaf, add a slice of the pancake, roll it up, then dip it in the pungent lemony sauce and eat. Hot and cold, crisp and soft, savoury and lemony – all in one. Ordering prawn sugar-cane stick (£5.50) brings large prawns skewered on a piece of sugar cane. Eat the prawn then chew the cane. Pho chicken soup (£4.95) is made with slices of chicken and vegetables plus flat rice-stick noodles in broth. Slurp the noodles and lift the bowl to drink the soup. Lemongrass chicken on boiled rice (£4.95) is a more fiery dish – seriously hot. There are over a hundred items on the menu, ranging from £1 to £13, and most are satisfying one-plate meals. Wines come in at around the £15 mark, or try the Shui Sen tea (£1.20) – more fragrant than jasmine tea and just as refreshing.

❋ Beware the industrial size bottles of "Sriracha HOT chilli sauce" – they aren't kidding.

▲ Wagamama: service with a smile

Further choices

Cafe Corfu
Greek

7 Pratt St, NW1
☎020 7267 8088

This Greek restaurant makes a real attempt to steer away from run-of-the-mill Cypriot dishes. Good Greek wines.

Galangal
Thai

29–31 Parkway, NW1
☎020 7485 9933

Smart but practical neighbourhood Thai. All the usual dishes, friendly staff and a buzzy atmosphere.

Wagamama
Japanese/Chinese

11 Jamestown Rd, NW1
☎020 7428 0800

A branch of the noodle-slurping chain – see review on p.48.

Chelsea

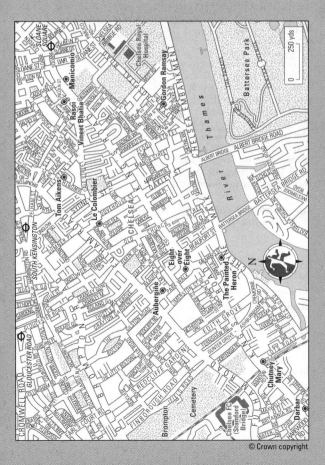

Aubergine

French £40–£125

11 Park Walk, SW10 ☎020 7352 3449

Station South Kensington **Open** Mon–Fri noon–2.30pm & 7–11pm, Sat 7–11pm
Accepts All major credit cards

It's hard to imagine it, but a decade or so ago this neck of the woods was a bleak-ish place to eat out. Aubergine changed all that, and it merits the accolade "old-established". Now it is both familiar enough, and light and airy enough, for even the most discerning of ladies who lunch. The best of everything in season and a talented kitchen make for a busy place, so booking is a must. William Drabble is a very talented chef.

A lunch that comprises terrine of confit chicken and foie gras, followed by breast of duck, braised turnips and thyme, and then coffee parfait with marscapone ice cream, with all the bells and whistles of a serious restaurant and half a bottle of decent wine, doesn't read, look or taste like just £32 worth. Even at full throttle the main dinner menu offers three courses for £55, which is fair for cooking of this calibre. Starters may include Pithivier of wood pigeon and Parma ham with wild mushrooms; or tortellinis of snails, garlic and parsley. Main courses include dishes such as roast John Dory with cod brandade and mushrooms; assiette of duck with prunes; roast veal sweetbread cassoulet of white beans and foie gras. These are well conceived and well executed dishes, beautifully presented. Desserts are equally accomplished – chocolate mousse with bottled cherries; poached pear in red wine. The service is accomplished and unobtrusive; the wine list can test the bravest wallet. The Menu Gourmand at £72 will spin the experience out by presenting seven pixie portions.

✳ Bargain lunch alert! 3 courses, half a bottle of wine, mineral water, coffee, petits fours – £32.

Chutney Mary

Indian £30–£90

535 King's Rd, SW10 ☎020 7351 3113

Station Fulham Broadway **Open** Mon–Fri 6.30–11pm, Sat noon–3.30pm & 6.30–11.30pm, Sun noon–3.30pm & 6.30–10.30pm
Accepts All major credit cards ☻www.realindianfood.com

Chutney Mary is an elegant place to eat, and the dramatic look of the dining room owes a good deal to an able theatrical lighting designer. But the men in the kitchen (headed by chef Rubinath) know their job and turn out refined Indian food. Food so good that in 2003 Chutney Mary won Indian Restaurant of the Year at the London Restaurant Awards. This is not a cheap restaurant but it comes under the heading of "justifiable extravagance".

Start with the crab cake (£9.50) – spankingly fresh crab, loosely bound and top-and-tailed with a potato rosti. Delicious. Or there's the tokri chaat (£6), which is an edible basket filled with various street-food treats and topped with yoghurt and chutney. Or the Konkan crab claws with garlic (£9.50) – huge tender claws swimming in a sea of garlic butter. Vegetarians will enjoy the platter of teen tikki (£6.50) – lotus root and sago, figs and green peas, spiced yoghurt. Mains are equally impressive. Mangalore jheenga (£17.50) are giant prawns, chilli-hot and tamarind-tangy. There's a Goan green chicken curry (£15.35), or there's Kerala pepper-roast duck with a cinnamon coconut sauce (£16.50). The side dishes are worth noting: methi palak saag (£4.50) teams spinach with fenugreek and lotus root. Breads are good here – lacchi paratha (£2.75). The dessert menu (all at £5.50) is also inspired. There is a garam masala brûlée, or a dark chocolate fondant served with orange-blossom lassi. Service is attentive and there is a book-sized wine list backed by a wine cellar that would put many French establishments to shame.

✱ Clock the theatrical "moonlight" – which plays over the tree in the conservatory as night falls – surprisingly convincing.

Le Colombier

Very French £20–£40

145 Dovehouse St, SW3 ☎020 7351 1155

Station South Kensington **Open** Mon–Sat noon–3pm & 6.30–11pm, Sun noon–3.30pm & 6.30–10.30pm **Accepts** All major credit cards except Diners

Viewed from the pavement outside on Dovehouse Street, you can see that Le Colombier was once a classic, English, street-corner pub. But now it's a pub that has a small, glassed-in area in front, covered with tables and chairs. How very Parisian, you might think, and you would be right. This is a French place. It is run by Monsieur Garnier, who has spent most of his career in the slicker reaches of London's restaurant business. With his own place he has reverted to type and everything is very, very French.

The menu is French, the cooking is French, the service is French and the decor is French. The cooking is about as good as you would have found in a smart Routiers in rural France during the 1970s. Starters include such bistro classics as oeufs pochés meurette (£6.30), soupe de poissons (£5.30), and feuilleté d'escargots à la crème d'ail (£6.80). And there are oysters, goat's cheese salad, duck liver terrine, and tomato and basil salad. Listed under "les poissons" there is fletan sauce beurre blanc (£16.90); and coquilles St Jacques a la crème de morilles (£17.50), which is scallops with morel cream sauce. Under "les viandes" there is steak tartare with pommes frites (£14.80); filet de boeuf au poivre (£16.80); and saucisses de Toulouse aux lentilles (£13.20). Under "les grillades" are the steaks and chops. Puddings include crêpes Suzette (£5.80). Both the service and the approach to wine are as French as the menu. For Chelsea, the set menu for lunch and early dinners (two courses and coffee for £15.50; on Sunday £16.50) seems very good value indeed.

✳ "Omelette Norvégienne pour deux" (£12), is also described as "baked Alaska" – something of a geographical conundrum.

Darbar

Indian £15–£50

92–94 Waterford Rd, SW6 &. ☎020 7348 7373
Station Fulham Broadway **Open** Mon–Sat 11.30am–3pm & 6–11.30pm
Accepts All major credit cards ⊛www.darbarrestaurant.net

Darbar opened towards the end of 2003 and, with its designer frontage and large frosted glass windows, looks quite at home among the high-style furniture and antique shops. The head chef is Mohammed Rais whose c.v. includes time spent in a very famous Indian restaurant in Delhi called Bukhara. Dishes are sophisticated, well balanced and with a good depth of flavour. This place has a confident and modern feel to it.

From the starters it's hard to improve on the traditional

approach of ordering kebabs and bread. The chicken tikka, or murg saunia tikka (£7.50) as it is billed here, is well prepared – large chunks of well spiced juicy chicken retain their juiciness. The raunaq-e-seekh (£6.50), minced lamb kebab, is also good, with an agreeable spiciness, but the salmon-dil-tikka (£7.50) may be the star – great texture. The "selection of breads" (£3.50) includes miniature nans, a paratha and a laachi paratha (the buttery, flaky, one). Main courses range from a whole seabass cooked in the tandoor (£14.50); through rogan josh (£9.50); to anari chap (£9.50), a dish of thin-cut lamb chops served in a rich and smooth gravy – very tender. You should order a "dum" dish, the awadhi ghosht biryani (£11.50) is very good, and the sealed pot means that all the flavours are retained in the rice. The other "must have" is the famous lentil dish, in Delhi known as dal Bukhara, but renamed in Chelsea as dal Darbari makhani (£5.50) – lentils cooked very slowly, the sauce finished with an indecent amount of butter. Darbar is a stylish, modern, Indian restaurant serving good food at Chelsea prices.

There's a keenly priced set lunch at £9.95 for vegetarians and £12.95 for non veggies.

Eight over Eight

Asian Eclectic £30–£70

392 King's Rd, SW3 ☎ 020 7349 9934

Station Sloane Square **Open** Mon–Fri noon–3pm & 6–11pm, Sat noon–4pm & 6–11pm, Sun 1–4pm & 6–10.30pm **Accepts** All major credit cards ⓦ www.eightovereight.nu

The name Eight over Eight derives from some obscure tenet of Oriental numerology – the East seems to have taken the art of "lucky numbers" to another level. This establishment is part of Will Ricker's expanding empire which also includes E&O (see p.258), and which performs a very similar service for the denizens of Notting Hill. Eight over Eight opened in 2003 and the front part is dedicated to a large and busy bar where chic cocktails predominate, while the rear is the dining room and is edged with booths.

The cuisine is described as "Pan Asian", so dim sum jostles futo maki rolls, tempura, sashimi, curries, before the menu leads on to salads, then barbecued and roasted meats. It is an eclectic selection and there is something on the menu to whet any appetite. Start with old favourites such as chilli-salt squid (£6); or pork spareribs (£5.50); or prawn and chive dumplings (£6), none of which are cheap, but all of which are presented very elegantly. The sashimi and roll sushi is fresh, good and sometimes groundbreaking – seared tuna with miso aioli

(£6.50); or beef fillet sashimi, wasabi dressing (£6.50). The curries are well spiced, and the salads most interesting – how does duck, watermelon and cashew salad (£11) appeal? Then maybe lotus-leaf chicken, shitake mushroom and sweet chilli soy (£9.50). Service is slick, drinks range from cocktails to cold beer by way of a serious wine list. But do beware – picking lots of little dishes can result in lots of middling price tags and a rather grown up bill.

Check out the rib of beef bulgogi (£34, minimum two people).

Gordon Ramsay

French £40–£150

68–69 Royal Hospital Rd, SW3 ☎ 020 7352 4441

Station Sloane Square **Open** Mon–Fri noon–2pm & 6.45–11pm

Accepts All major credit cards ✆ www.gordonramsay.com

The Gordon Ramsay Empire continues to expand. After Claridges (see p.248) he added the dining room at the Connaught, and the Grill Room at the Savoy plus Pétrus at the Berkeley to his increasingly large sphere of influence. At head office in Chelsea, his restaurant continues to be packed. Thankfully, the prices are not as high as you might fear. There are two fixed-price à la carte menus at both lunch and dinner (£65 for three courses, £80 for seven), and a steal of a set lunch (£35 for three courses). Even if you add £5 for a glass of good house wine, this offers the more accessible face of truly great cooking – as long as you can get a booking.

The menu here evolves gently. On the main menu, look out for a ravioli of lobster and langoustine poached in a lobster bisque and served with a lemongrass and chervil velouté; or a carpaccio of pigeon from Bresse with shavings of confit foie gras, baby artichokes and a Parmesan salad. This is a stunning dish of unusual delicacy. Or try caramelized slices of pig's foot with veal sweetbreads and a celeriac rémoulade and a salad of green beans – as robust and delicious as you could wish for. And those are just starters! Mains intrigue: fillet of turbot poached in red wine with radicchio and celeriac risotto; saddle of Scottish venison with creamed cabbage, beetroot fondant and sautéed wild mushrooms. Even the desserts fascinate – hot chocolate fondant with milk mousse and ice cream. To order successfully here, just pick a dish or an ingredient you like and see how it arrives; you won't be disappointed.

✳ They claim that reservations can only be made a month in advance. Book ahead or last minute.

Manicomio

Italian £25–£75

85 Duke of York Square, SW3 ♿ ☎ 020 7730 3366

Station Sloane Square **Open** Mon–Fri noon–3pm & 6.30–10.30pm,
Sat (brunch) noon–5pm & 6.30–10.30pm, Sun (brunch) noon–4pm & 6.30–10pm

Accepts All major credit cards except Diners

Manicomio is a comfortable restaurant that manages to bring off a difficult trick. Despite being a new project (it opened towards the end of 2003), it gives the impression of being long established, due to genuine brickwork and middle of the road décor; the dining room was carved out of one end of the Duke of York barracks. There are some seats outside which is great if the weather is clement, dodgy when relying on the space heaters. Service is slick and Italian, which accurately sums up most of the wine list as well.

The cooking is good and the menu broadly seasonal. Manicomio is not a place to look for gentle, peasant Italian fare, as there is an edge of chic to even the simplest dishes here – but this is Sloane Square after all. Starters such as a salad of broad beans and peas with Pecorino (£7.25) is as fresh, as green and as good as you could wish for. Beef Carpaccio (£8.75) is very tender, and with a grand zigzag of mustardy dressing. The focaccia (£1.50 per person) is light and fluffy and almost good enough to make you forgive them for the sin of charging for bread. The pasta dishes are sophisticated: spaghetti with crab, chilli and garlic (£9 or £12); or rabbit and Tuscan sausage ravioli (£6.25 or £9.25) – silky pasta. Main courses are solid: calves' liver with Swiss chard and balsamic (£15.75); pan-fried halibut with ratte potatoes, tomato and black olives (£17.25); or grilled leg of lamb with aubergine and pepperonata (£16.25). Puds are trad: tiramisù (£5); lemon tart with pistachio and iced milk (£5.50).

CHELSEA

✳ Manicomio translates as "madhouse".

The Painted Heron

Indian £20–£80

112 Cheyne Walk, SW10 ☎ 020 7351 5232

Station Sloane Square/Fulham Broadway **Open** Mon–Fri noon–2.30pm & 6–11pm, Sat 6–11pm **Accepts** All major credit cards except Diners ⊛ www.thepaintedheron.co.uk

The Painted Heron is one Indian restaurant that has got the balance between authenticity and modernist reinvention about right. The food here is honest, well spiced, and not too fussily presented. The room is cool and elegant, no flock wallpaper, nothing over the top. Service is sound and like so many modern Indian establishments a lot of effort has gone into the wine list. The head chef Yogesh Datta is an accomplished cook and it is no wonder that the Heron has skewered a very long list of awards.

If you are visiting for lunch prepare yourself to eat alone, there is very little trade except on Friday, which is something worth noting if you want good food and quiet. In the evening this is a busy place so you should book. The à la carte menu changes gradually as dishes come and go. Among the starters may be crab with red onions and chilli in dosa pancake (£6.50); pigeon breasts

roast in the tandoor (£6); and calves' liver in a tandoor marinade with mango (£6.50) – a seriously good dish with melty liver and a grand spike of chilli. Mains are well conceived. The spicing is up-front and enjoyable and, although they are Indian dishes, they are described in European terms – chicken tikka with almonds in tomato and cream curry (£11); scallops in a spiced yogurt curry with mushrooms and spring onions (£12.50); or topside of beef in a Rajasthani red-chilli paste (£11.50) – chunks of pleasantly chewy meat in a rich gravy. From the veg dishes "asparagus, green peas in a fenugreek curry" (£4) is a belter – crunchy greenstuff, creamy methi-flavoured sauce. Breads are terrific.

✳ Delicious European style puds – apple pie with rose syrup (£4).

Rasoi Vineet Bhatia

Indian £40–£100

10 Lincoln St, SW3 ☎ 020 7225 1881
Station Sloane Square **Open** Mon–Sat 7–10.30pm
Accepts All major credit cards except Diners 🌐 www.vineetbhatia.com

This restaurant belongs to Vineet Bhatia and his wife. It is small (eight tables at the back and half a dozen in front), it is classy, and "this time it's personal". Rasoi opened in the summer of 2004 and the now self-employed Bhatia is on tiptop form, the food is Michelin two-star level (if only we could rely on their Francophile inspectors agreeing!). This is Indian food at its finest – simple, intensely flavoured, well spiced dishes with inspired combinations of colour and texture. Service is friendly (this is a small family business) and there is a buzz of excitement about the place. The Menu Gourmand is a long multi-course affair, full of surprises, delicious and wholly satisfying. A great way to spend £65 – how often do you get to say that?

Starters include "assorted sea scallops" (£16) – three scallops, one with chilli and sesame, one with onion seed and one that's particularly fine with a spice crust. Or there's a duck platter (£12): duck kebab, samosa, salad and soup. There's an amazing lobster dish that is either starter or main

▲ Indian artifacts adorn the walls

(£18 or £34) – "Ginger and chilli lobster, spiced lobster jus, curry leaf and broccoli khichdi" … and then the plate is dusted at the table with sour spices and cocoa. It's a perfectly cooked half lobster, the khichdi is like a spicy risotto, and there's the added perfume of cocoa. Bhatia's sauces are inspired – he is a very good cook. Other mains include a lamb shank roganjosh cooked on the bone (£20), and a biryani of pickle-flavoured chicken baked under a flaky pastry lid. The wine list is Chelsea and zips up towards the Chateau Latour.

❋ There's a pudoholics dessert platter (£11).

Tom Aikens

Modern British £35–£100

43 Elystan St, SW3 & ☎ 020 7584 2003
Station South Kensington **Open** Mon–Fri noon–5pm & 7–11pm
Accepts All major credit cards except Diners ⊛ www.tomaikens.co.uk

Tom Aikens and his wife Laura opened their new restaurant in 2003. Then, in 2004 it got its first Michelin star and was named "new restaurant of the year" at the Tio Pepe, ITV London Restaurant Awards. All of which would have been more surprising if he hadn't been the same Tom Aikens who previously gathered a hatful of awards at Pied à Terre. This is a very personal restaurant; it is not open on Saturday and Sunday but when it is Tom tends to be in the kitchen. Service is silky and the food is sophisticated and considered. A very rewarding place to eat.

Setting aside (and you shouldn't!) the set lunch at £24.50; three courses à la carte will set you back £55. Stump up £70, and there's the tasting menu – seven courses and coffee. All dishes are imaginative, well presented and with good assertive flavours. From the starters: braised snails come with snail beignets, red wine cassonade, potato soup and garlic; a roast langoustine comes with truffle macaroni, braised chicken wing, pork belly and haricot beans – a very good dish indeed, the different elements working well together. For main course braised veal shin comes with roast veal sweetbreads, pommes purées, braised onion, and caper and rosemary sauce; John Dory fillets are served with a fennel purée, bouillabaisse potatoes and basil sauce vierge. Puds are also complex and rewarding – chocolate negus with pistachio mousse, pistachio parfait, and pistachio and milk ice cream; or pineapple roast with vanilla and rum, and pineapple jelly. The wine list is extensive, but the charming sommelier is particularly helpful.

❋ The set lunch is a bargain – three courses £24.50.

Chinatown

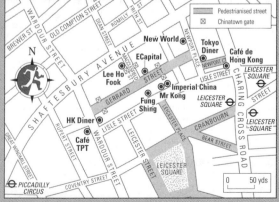

	Pedestrianised street
⊠	Chinatown gate

WARDOUR STREET
BREWER ST
OLD COMPTON STREET
DEAN STREET
ROMILLY
FRITH ST
SHAFTESBURY AVENUE
New World
ECapital
Lee Ho Fook
GERRARD STREET
LISLE STREET
Fung Shing
Mr Kong
Imperial China
HK Diner
RUPERT STREET
WARDOUR STREET
Café TPT
LEICESTER STREET
LISLE STREET
LEICESTER PLACE
NEWPORT PLACE
Tokyo Diner
Café de Hong Kong
NEWPORT CT
LISLE STREET
LEICESTER SQUARE
LEICESTER SQUARE
CRANBOURN
BEAR STREET
CHARING CROSS ROAD
LEICESTER SQUARE
LEICESTER SQUARE STREET
GREAT WINDMILL STREET
PICCADILLY CIRCUS
COVENTRY STREET

N

0   50 yds

Café de Hong Kong

Chinese £4–£20

47–49 Charing Cross Rd, WC2 ☎ 020 7534 9898
Station Leicester Square **Open** Daily noon–11pm
Accepts All major credit cards except Diners

Café de Hong Kong is an engaging place. It bustles along brightly-coloured but spartan, simple with utilitarian booths. There are two dining areas – one on the first floor overlooking the Charing Cross Road and a larger one on the floor above. This is definitely a café. It's full of young Chinese people lingering over spooky soft drinks and eating hearty stuff from large bowls. 2003–2004 saw the opening of several basic Chinese cafés (see Café TPT, below) and they look set to displace the trad Italian pasta pitstops as the cheapest way of fuelling up before going out for the night. No bookings are taken.

To say that the menu is eclectic would be selling it short. The "chef's speciality" is grouper with mango sauce (£5.50) and if that doesn't shock, it is served with "potatoes and vegetables".

Or how about "spaghetti Bolognaise" (£4.20)? You get an oval dish full of spaghetti, topped with some tomatoey meat sauce and then cheese, before being finished in a hot oven. It's O.K. – the kind of cooking you would have expected from an Italian trattoria in about 1970. The menu also offers Russian borscht (£1.50), pork chop curry (£4.20), and some very good meals-in-a-bowl – such as fried noodles with pork (£4.20). And to wash it all down? How about sampling one of the tapioca pearl drinks (£2.80)? A tall glass is filled with crushed ice, various flavourings and a secret spoonful of "pearls" – these are chewy, pea-sized balls of tapioca. You drink your milkshake through a special large-gauge straw and, as you suck up the drink, the pearls shoot into your mouth and rattle around.

✳ "Grouper Gordon Bleu with tartar sauce" (£6.50).

CHINATOWN

Café TPT

Chinese £5–£30

21 Wardour St, W1 ☎ 020 7734 7980
Station Piccadilly Circus **Open** Mon–Sat noon–midnight Sun noon–11.30pm
Accepts All major credit cards except AmEx & Diners

You'll find Café TPT just across the road from HK diner (see p.78) and the look of the two places is very similar. TPT is a busy food factory that is full of happy, predominantly Chinese diners who are tucking into large portions of simple food. The tables in the ground floor

dining room have massive angular wooden stools – not very rump-friendly but you probably won't be lingering over brandy and petit fours as there aren't any!

There are two menus at TPT. There's a big book-like one

which is very similar to every other menu in Chinatown – crispy duck with pancakes (half £13); hot and sour soup (£2.50); deep-fried crispy squid (£8) – all the old familiar dishes, although at agreeably low prices. The paper "placemat" menu is a much more rewarding read. It lists the bargain dishes, congee, noodles, rice dishes and barbecued meats. The fried noodle dishes – such as chicken chow mein (£4.50) are steady; the ho fun dishes (broader noodles) – fried squid with black-bean sauce with ho fun (£8) are much more rewarding. But best of all

are the "pulled noodle" dishes – these are home made, thick and chewy noodles slightly mis-shapen like serious pasta, very filling and rich. Try pulled noodles with beef (£4.50). The barbecued meats are sound here but they will insist on warming them through in the microwave which spoils the texture. The café part of the name is confirmed by the long drinks list. There are all manner of tapioca pearl drinks (see Café de Hong Kong p.75), plus fruit juices and floats – "ice cream with glass jelly and red bean ice". Good fun with the ho fun.

✳ Plain congee (£2) is said to be good for hangovers – a bland, sloppy rice porridge.

ECapital

Chinese £15–£55

8 Gerrard St, W1 ☎020 7434 3838
Station Leicester Square **Open** Daily noon–midnight
Accepts All major credit cards except Diners

This restaurant which opened in the spring of 2002 is settling in nicely and showcases the somewhat neglected cuisine of Shanghai. The chef is David Tam, who won all manner of awards when at Aroma II. The interior is striking: the ceiling is painted deep fuchsia, the walls are a nondescript cream, the lighting is soft – and that's it. For once less really is more. This

is a comfortable, unpretentious place to eat and the food is both delicious and fascinating.

For the nervous, the menu offers a safety blanket of familiar favourites, from crispy seaweed to sweet-and-sour pork; proceed and you'll find a host of good things from Shanghai. Starters include drunken chicken (£5); cold chicken marinated in sweet

Using chopsticks

If you are a novice chopsticker take heart from couple of golden rules:

▶ Always ask for "stick and bowl", then if things get tricky you can use the side of the bowl to push against.

▶ Do not be afraid to use your sticks together like a shovel!

And if all else fails, those little china spoons work well.

wine; or cardboard paper-thin seasoned beef (£5) – slices of slow-cooked beef in a chilli-spiked, savoury marinade. Starters include classic old-fashioned pan-fried dumplings (£2.80), with good crispy bits, and the wonderful thousand-layer pig's ear (£5). A slight exaggeration, as there are just 21 layers, but imagine small strips of agreeably chewy streaky bacon, cut thin, and tasting gelatinous and savoury. The grandstand main course is beggar's chicken (£25). The chicken is seasoned with pickled cabbage and shredded pork, then wrapped in lotus leaves and given a casing of flour and water paste; the entire parcel is baked and, when the casing is smashed at table-side, the fragrant chicken is revealed within. You can also try sea bass West Lake style (£16), or Shanghai braised yellow eel (£12). Exploring this lengthy menu is most rewarding.

✳ Look out for the elite Chinese teas – floral and elegant.

Fung Shing

Chinese £24–£60

15 Lisle St, WC2 ☎ 020 7437 1539
Station Leicester Square **Open** Daily noon–11.30pm
Accepts All major credit cards 🌐 www.fungshing.co.uk

CHINATOWN

Fung Shing was one of the first restaurants in Chinatown to take cooking seriously. Some decades ago, when it was still a dowdy little place with a mural on the back wall, Chinatown's number one fish cook, chef Wu ruled the kitchens. When he died, in 1996, his sous-chef took over. The restaurant itself has changed beyond recognition and now stretches all the way from Lisle Street to Gerrard Street, ever bigger and ever brassier. Even if there has been a slight decline in overall standards, the menu is littered with interesting dishes.

To start, ignore the crispy duck with pancakes (half for £20), which are good but too predictable, and the lobster with noodles (£19 a pound, with noodles £2 extra). Instead try the steamed scallops with garlic and soya sauce (£2.75 each) – nowhere does them better. Or spareribs, barbecued or with chilli and garlic (both £8). The prosaically named "mixed meat with lettuce" (£8.50) is also good, a savoury dish of mince with lettuce-leaf wraps. You could happily order mains solely from the chef's specials: stewed belly pork with yam in hot pot (£9.95); crispy spicy eel (£10.95); roast crispy pigeon (£14); or oysters with bean-thread vermicelli in hot pot (£11.50). Other dishes are good too: perfect Singapore noodles (£6), crispy stuffed baby squids with chilli and garlic (£9.50), and steamed aubergine with garlic sauce (£7.50). The Fung Shing has always been classy but what is unusual, certainly in Chinatown, is the gracious and helpful service. This a restaurant where you can ask for advice with confidence.

✳ Braised double-boiled shark's fin in hot pot (£65).

HK Diner

Chinese £8–£35

22 Wardour St, WC2 ☎ 020 7434 9544

Station Piccadilly/Leicester Square **Open** Daily 11am–4am
Accepts All major credit cards except Diners

HK Diner is a light, bright, busy, modern sort of place, so if you like your Chinese restaurants seedy and "authentic" you will almost certainly walk past with a shudder. "It looks more like a burger bar, so how can it possibly…" Pre-judging this place would be a major mistake, however, as the food is very good, and there is no iron rule that slickness means rip-off. Prices are not cheap, but they are not over-the-top either, and the prospect of getting decent food very late at night (HK stays open until 5am at the weekend) is a beguiling one. Service is attentive, you don't wait long for food, and the tables turn over at a ferocious pace.

The menu offers all the Cantonese favourites, from very good salt-and-pepper spareribs (£6.50) to grilled dumplings (four for £4) and steamed scallops on the half shell (£2.50 each). For main course, deep-fried squid with salt, pepper and garlic (£8.50) is as light, crisp and un-rubbery as you could wish, or there's steamed crab with Sao Sing wine (£13.50). Fried beef with chilli and black-bean sauce (£6.50) is rich and delicious, as is honey-barbecued pork (£6.50). The Singapore noodle (£4.90) is a model of its kind. From the vegetable dishes, choose the fried snow pea shoots with minced garlic (£7) – if you love garlic. This is the one to guarantee that even good friends will keep their distance for the next couple of days. The simple dishes, such as fried noodles with mixed meat (£4.90) or fried noodle with mixed seafood (£6.50), always hit the spot.

✳ Try the "pearl" milkshakes – flavoured milk plus tapioca!

▲ Gerrard Street, Chinatown's main drag

Imperial China Chinese/Dim Sum £15–£50

White Bear Yard, Lisle St, WC2 ☎020 7734 3388

Station Leicester Square **Open** Mon–Sat noon–midnight & Sun 11.30am–10.30pm
Accepts All major credit cards except Diners ⓦwww.imperial-china.co.uk

Imperial China should really be called "Phoenix" something or other as this large, smart and aspirational Chinese restaurant is a re-make of what was once China City. It has certainly become more grandiose. There are various different dining rooms spread over three floors, some are dedicated to Karaoke, and the one on the ground floor seems to have been modeled on James Bond's idea of a cocktail bar – it's not often that you see a baby grand piano in a Chinese restaurant, stranger still to have a pianist tinkling the ivories while you're the one playing chopsticks.

The dim sum here have a growing reputation – the excellence of the dim sum at Hakkasan (p.154) seems to have stung Chinatown into action. Imperial City offers fried pork and spring-onion buns (£2.20);

stewed goose web in black-bean sauce (£2.20); preserved egg and sliced fish cheung fun (£3) as well as most dim sum favourites. There are also some interesting options on the main menu: starters such as lotus root and straw mushrooms (£4); sliced preserved pork knuckle with jelly fish (£7); and simple soups such as hot and sour (£3), or encouragingly, "soup of the day – Chinese clear soup" (£3). From the lengthy list of mains, salt-baked chicken appeals (£22 whole, £11 half); as does shredded pork with ginger and aubergine (£6); stir-fried scallop with lily bud (£9); or deep-fried fillet of eel with chilli (£18). Imperial China tries to be a grown-up sort of restaurant and the pricing reflects this ambition, but there are some interesting dishes, and providing you relish the over-the-top styling it makes a good venue..

✱ Hop along for "steamed custard dumplings in 'rabbit shape' (£2.20)".

CHINATOWN

Lee Ho Fook Chinese £5–£15

4 Macclesfield St, W1 ☎020 7734 0782

Station Leicester Square **Open** Daily 11am–11pm **Accepts** Cash only

The older, regular customers of this small Chinese barbecue house are beginning to feel slightly uneasy. Ten years ago the place was scruffier, the menu shorter, and there were fewer tables. Change is always threatening, and where once there was just a Chinese chef chopping meat and dishing it

out, the menu now lists such extravagances as "appetisers" and set meals. But the old style dishes are still to be had and prices have only crept up a little. Sit down, enjoy a cup of Chinese tea, splash a dollop of the chilli sauce onto the pile of rice topped with barbecued meat placed in front of you, and pick up your chopsticks. This is good, simple, cheap eating.

Choose from lean pork loin, crisp fatty belly pork, soya chicken or duck (all £4.10). You can also mix and match – half pork, half duck, say – or order a "combination" of mixed roast pork, soya chicken and duck with rice (£5). Some choose to order the meats without rice – perhaps a whole duck (£23) or a portion of soya chicken (£5.50). Try adding a plate of crisp vegetables in oyster sauce (£3.80) to your order. And,

before the main event, perhaps a bowl of won ton soup (£2.20), or the even more substantial won ton noodle soup (£2.80). Also attributable to the march of progress is the series of noodle dishes now listed – soup noodles and ribbon noodles (ho fan) – the most expensive of which is the "chicken, and duck leg with noodle" (£6). This establishment continues to do a simple thing very well, which is not as easy a trick to pull off as it sounds. There's also a thriving takeaway trade.

 This place is hard to find – look for the corner of Dansey Place and Macclesfield Street.

Mr Kong

Chinese £8–£28

21 Lisle St, WC2 ☎ 020 7437 7341
Station Leicester Square **Open** Daily noon–3am **Accepts** All major credit cards

You have to wonder whether the eponymous Mr Kong flirted with the idea of calling his restaurant King Kong – despite its marathon opening hours, at all regular mealtimes it's full of satisfied customers who would support such an accolade. Going with a party of six or more is the best plan when dining at Mr Kong, as that way you can order, taste and argue over a raft of dishes and if any really hit the spot you can always order a second portion by way of re-enforcement.

Sad to say, but the trend in Chinatown is for restos to abandon some of their more obscure menu items in favour of safety first. Mr Kong is teetering on the brink. The food is good and the menu still sprawls across a vast number of pages, but it is

shorter than it once was. Take it as read that the old favourite dishes – baked spareribs with chilli and salt (£5.50); braised belly pork with preserved vegetables (£6.50); fried duck with bitter melon (£5.50) – will be consistently good. For a more adventurous time a good tip is to look out for "hot pot" dishes – these are casseroles that come to the table in clay pots. Or look on the Chef's special menu – deep-fried oysters in batter (£7.50); sautéed mixed seafood with fresh mango (£9); crispy beancurd with vegetables (£6.50); sautéed dragon whiskers (pea shoots) with dried scallops (£11). Portions are generous and, even when dishes contain exotic ingredients, prices are reasonable. Just ignore the decor, which despite occasional refurbs remains resolutely ordinary.

 Try the deep-fried pig's intestine with spicy salt (£8.50) – crispy-crunchy-piggy!

New World

1 Gerrard Place, W1 ☎020 7734 0396

Station Leicester Square **Open** Daily 11am–midnight **Accepts** All major credit cards

CHINATOWN

The New World seats between four hundred and six hundred people, depending on how many functions are going on at any one time. This is one of the largest restaurants in Europe, but when you arrive you invariably have to wait in a sort of holding pen just inside the door until the intercom screeches with static and you are sent off to your table. The menu, leather-bound and nearly twenty pages long, features everything you have ever heard of and quite a lot you haven't. In any case, you don't need it – go for the dim sum, which are served every day from 11am until 6pm.

The dim sum come round on trolleys. First, catch the eye of a waiter or waitress with a bow tie, to order drinks, and then you're at the mercy of the trolley pushers. The trolleys are themed: one has a lot of barbecued meat; another is packed with ho fun (broad noodles); another with steamed dumplings; another with soups; another with cheung fun (the long slippery rolls of pastry with different meats inside). A good mix would be to take siu mai (£2.60) and har kau (£2.60) from the "steamers" trolley, then char sui cheung fun (£3.30) – a long roll with pork. Follow this with some deep-fried won ton (£2.20), little crispy parcels with sweet sauce. Or perhaps try something exotic like woo kwok (£2.20) – deep-fried taro dumplings stuffed with pork – and something filling such as char sui pow (£2.20), steamed doughnuts filled with pork. Or perhaps nor mai gai (£3.50) – a lotus-leaf parcel of glutinous rice and meats. If you arrive after 6pm, you're on your own: there are literally hundreds of dishes on the main menus.

✳ Dim sum trolleys are a great way to introduce small children to Chinese food.

Tokyo Diner

2 Newport Place, WC2 ☎020 7287 8777

Station Leicester Square **Open** Daily noon–midnight

Accepts Mastercard & Visa, no cheques

Tokyo Diner offers conclusive proof that you needn't take out a second mortgage to enjoy Japanese food in London. This is fast food, Tokyo-style. The place was actually set up by a Nipponophile Englishman, but the kitchen staff are all Japanese and its Far Eastern credentials bear scrutiny. The décor is crisp and minimalist, and if you don't know sushi from sumo, you'll be glad of the explanatory notes on the menu. When your food arrives, pick a set of chopsticks, snap them apart – it's recommended that you rub them together to rid them of splinters – and get stuck in.

Top seller is the soba noodle soup (£5.10) – thin brown buckwheat noodles in a soya broth. It's pleasant, filling and very popular with the drop-by lunchtime trade. Don't be afraid of slurping it, slurping is OK. Or try the set lunch in a bento box of rice, noodles, sashimi and your choice of teriyaki, all for around £11.50. Other bento favourites include the ton katsu bento (£11.50), which is a kind of superior breadcrumbed pork escalope. If you don't have appetite enough for a full-on bento box, skip the curries – they're a bit like school food – and head straight for the sushi and sashimi. They too come in "sets": try the nine-piece nigiri set (£8.90), which is very good value, or the hoso-maki set (£4.90), which comprises six pieces of salmon, three pieces of cucumber and three pieces of pickled radish. To wash it all down, the Japanese beer Asahi (£1.99) is good, or there's complimentary Japanese tea. For a special treat, try the rich, sweet plum wine (£2.99 for 125ml), which is surprisingly moreish.

✳ Japanese style, the Tokyo Diner does not accept tips.

Further choices

New Diamond
Chinese

23 Lisle St, WC2
☎ 020 7437 2517

Sound Chinese food in a restaurant still scruffy despite a recent facelift. Much loved by chefs due to its 3am closing time.

Poons & Co
Chinese

26–27 Lisle St, WC2
☎ 020 7437 4549

Established in the early 1970s there is now a short chain of Poons restos. Specializes in rather obscure wind-dried meats.

Wong Kei
Chinese

41–43 Wardour St, W1
☎ 020 7437 8408

Somewhat perversely Wong Kei lives off its old reputation as being home to London's rudest waiters. Good for roast meats and for one-bowl noodle dishes.

Chiswick

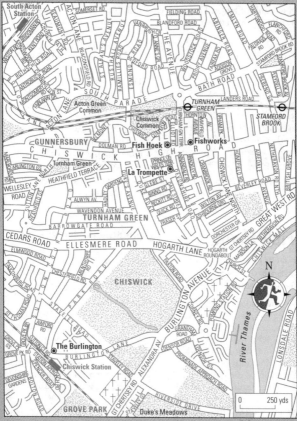

The Burlington

Modern British £20–£35

1 Station Parade, Burlington Lane, W4 ☎ 020 8995 3344

Station BR Chiswick **Open** Mon–Fri 6.30–10.30pm, Sat noon–2.30pm & 6.30–10.30pm
Sun noon–2.30pm & 7–10pm **Accepts** All major credit cards except AmEx

Hurrah! In spring 2004, Redmond and Pippa Hayward – who run Redmond's (see p.32) opened a bistro in affluent Grove Park. The look isn't aggressively designery, but the newly painted room is clean and fresh. There are thirty or so seats in the main dining room, bolstered by a few tables in a conservatory out the back, and an area of pavement in front of the restaurant that will take a few outdoor tables. The service is friendly and efficient.

The food is very good. Strong flavours, quality ingredients, well presented. The king of the starters is the Burlington platter which is a one-plate anti-pasti trolley: roast peppers, olives, salt-cod brandade, creamy celeriac remoulade, slow-roast belly pork, chorizo, a coffee cup of mushroom and rosemary soup, black pudding, smoked salmon, duck-liver parfait, gravlax (£8.50). Simple and excellent. Or there's a salad of artichokes and green beans with wild mushrooms and hazelnut dressing (£5.25 or £6.95). Mains range from pan-fried bream fillet with fennel and orange salad, new potatoes and tarragon sauce (£14.50); to perfectly cooked calves' liver with a lemon and thyme risotto (£10.95). Or try a grandstand dish such as roast marinated pigeon breasts, soft thyme polenta, black pudding, caramelised endive, seared foie gras and Port jus (£12.50) – a very good, very rich combo. Hayward has a knack for bringing out light, bright herbal flavours – the thyme polenta is stunning. Puds are stalwart: dark chocolate tart with rosemary and caramel ice cream (£5.20); blood-orange-and-vodka jelly with coffee Madeleines (£5.20).

✳ The wine list is a model of its type – fifty bins, a quarter under £20 a quarter over £35, the rest somewhere in between.

Fish Hoek

South African/Fish £15–£60

6–8 Elliot Rd, W4 ☎ 020 8742 0766

Station Turnham Green **Open** Tues–Sat noon–2.30pm & 6.30–11pm, Sun noon–3pm &
6–10.30pm **Accepts** All major credit cards except AmEx & Diners

At the end of 2001, Pete Gottgens opened this restaurant dedicated to South African fish. By 2003 it had proved so successful that he was able to close down his other carnivorous restaurant and concentrate full time on fish. Due to the efficiency of the air-freight industry, fish can be landed and iced in South Africa and then pitch up in W4 in about the same time as they would take to get from Aberdeen. This restaurant is a light and airy place and there's a special menu for lunch or early dinner – two courses £11.50, three £16.50.

The menu changes daily and features an impressive array of South African fish – 25 or so choices, and nearly all can be had as half or full portions. Try out three half-portions and live a bit! Grilled Cape swordfish loin, Eastern Transvaal pepperdews, carrot and cucumber salsa (£8.50 or £16.50); peri-peri grilled sardines with sautéed potatoes (£7.75 or £15.50); pan-fried swartkurper fillets, fine beans and courgettes (£8.75 or £17); Aghuilas hottentot, baked whole with new potatoes (£18). The names and provenance are as exotic as the fish themselves. Some non-South African fish stray onto the list – there might be grilled, line-caught mackerel fillets with sweet potato mash (£8.25 or £15.50), Cornish, hand-picked, white crab meat salad (£8 or £15.50) – but the stuff from SA is well worth trying, as are the monster crustacea called queen tiger prawns (£16 or £30). Fish Hoek is a pleasant and informal restaurant where they take a good deal of trouble over simple fish cookery.

CHISWICK

✳ Look at the black-and-white photo to the right of the toilet door: the small boy trotting beside his father is now proprietor of Fish Hoek.

Fishworks

Fish £15–£50

6 Turnham Green Terrace, W4 ☎ 020 8994 0086

Station Turnham Green **Open** Tues–Sat noon–2.30pm & 6–10.30pm, Sun noon–3pm
Accepts All major credit cards except Diners ⓦ www.fishworks.co.uk

There's something spooky about this part of Chiswick; as well as a splendid array of food shops they now have two fish restaurants (see Fish Hoek, opposite). One neighbourhood fish restaurant would be impressive, but to have a choice is remarkable. Fishworks is the London end of a chainlet that links branches in Bath, Bristol and Christchurch, and the vibe is right. Inside is a pretty, modern dining room with a gardeny bit at the rear. Service is friendly and attentive, the wine list is interesting and not too rapacious; all in all a very satisfying place.

There's a longish menu and a very long list of specials on a blackboard. From the starters, perhaps the roast shellfish with garlic and olive oil (£8.50 or £15.90) appeals. Or there may be fresh Dartmouth crab salad with tarragon mayonnaise (£7.50 or £14.90). Or how about steamed River Fowey mussels with wine and parsley (£6.90 or £10.90)? Alternatively, try the grilled tuna (£13.90), or the "skate with black butter and capers" (£14.90). There is a serious fruits de mer (£45 for two, £60 if you add a lobster). And there are "whole fish – for the table", such as a wild sea bass for two (£18 per person). Vegetables are simple and good, a dish of buttered spinach leaves (£1.95) is outstanding. The bread is good. This is a comfortable place where the fish are both skillfully chosen and skillfully cooked. The wine list is eclectic and there are some interesting bottles at accessible prices. Start with half a bottle of cold Manzanilla San Leon (£12.50), and look out for the unusual Pazo Ribeiro (£17.75) from Galicia – dry, white and zingy..

✳ The fishmonger's counter is open 8.30am – 10.30pm.

CHISWICK

La Trompette

French £15–£30

5–7 Devonshire Rd, W4 & ☎020 8747 1836

Station Turnham Green **Open** Mon–Sat noon–2.30pm & 6.30–10.30pm, Sun 12.30–3pm & 7–10pm **Accepts** All major credit cards

La Trompette has yet to see its fifth birthday, but it is securely embedded in the hearts of Chiswickians. This state of affairs isn't a great surprise as Trompette is a thoroughbred from the same stable as Chez Bruce (see p.97), The Glasshouse (see p.30) and The Square (see p.252). The dining room is comfortable with a good deal of light oak and chocolate leather on show. The food is very good, the wine list is comprehensive, the pricing is restrained and the service is on the ball.

The prix fixe arrangements are straightforward: lunch is £21.50 for three courses, (rising to £25 on Sunday); dinner is £32.50 for three courses (£42.50 if you add an extra cheese course – and you should). The head chef is Ollie Couillard, who served time at both Chez Bruce

and The Square. He is a very good cook, and his menu changes on a day-to-day basis. Presentation is simple but elegant. Starters may include such delights as thinly sliced rump of veal with chips cooked in duck fat, rocket and meat juices; or grilled red mullet with aioli, chorizo and saffron beurre blanc; or cream of leek and potato soup. Mains are rich and satisfying. In the appropriate season you might be offered crisp sea bream with olive-oil mash, red peppers and aged balsamic vinegar; or sauté of calf's sweetbread and kidney with shallot purée, salsify, garlic and parsley; or duck magret with foie gras, parsnips, griottine cherries and Port sauce. Puds range from classics such as citrus fruit trifle to indulgent chocolate profiteroles. Enjoy!

✳ Trompette won "Most exceptional restaurant wine list" at the 2004 London Restaurant Awards.

Further choices

Andy's Kebab House
Turkish

3–4 Bedford Park Corner, Turnham Green Terrace W4 ☎020 8994 3953

A gloriously old-fashioned kebab house serving Turkish Cyrpriot dishes in time-warp surroundings. Steady stuff.

The Devonshire House
Gastropub/Modern British

126 Devonshire Rd, W4
☎020 8987 2626

A modern gastropub with ambition. Decent cooking from a chef who served time with Marco Pierre White.

The City

© Crown copyright

1 Lombard Street, The Brasserie

French £35–£80

1 Lombard St, EC3 & ☎020 7929 6611
Station Bank **Open** Mon–Fri Full breakfast 7.30–10.30am, 11.30am–10pm
Accepts All major credit cards Ⓦ www.1lombardstreet.com

The Brasserie at 1 Lombard Street was formerly a banking hall and the circular bar sits under a suitably imposing glass dome. This is a brasserie in the City, of the City, by the City and for the City. The brasserie menu is a model of its kind, long but straightforward with a range of dishes that is up to any meal occasion. It delivers on pretty much every front; serving satisfying dishes made with good fresh ingredients, both stylish and unfussy at the same time. The bar, meanwhile, is like any chic City watering hole – loud, brisk and crowded, with simultaneous conversations in every European language. There is a smaller, 40-seater room at the rear, set aside for fine dining at fancy prices.

The Brasserie menu changes every couple of months to satisfy the band of regulars, and there are daily specials in addition. The starters can be ambitious, such as seasonal game terrine (£8.25), or simple, like Scotch broth (£6.50), while further down the menu there will be some even more comfortable options such as soft-boiled free-range egg (£8.95 or £14.95) served with smoked haddock, and spinach gratin. There's enough listed under shellfish and crustacea to fuel even the wildest celebrations, including griddled scallops with black pudding, leeks and brown butter (£22.50), and casserole of mussels and clams (£8.75 or £14.50). The Classics section has coq au vin à la Bourguignon (£16.50); the Meat section lists steak, sausages, and liver. Puds triumph – there's an indulgent warm chocolate fondant (£6.75) and there's something on the wine list to suit most tastes.

✳ Caviar is a "brasserie" dish here – 50g of Beluga served with blinis, steamed potatoes and sour cream (£120).

Barcelona Tapas Bar

Spanish/Tapas £12–£30

1a Bell Lane, E1 ☎020 7247 7014
Station Aldgate **Open** Mon–Fri 11am–11pm **Accepts** All major credit cards
Ⓦ www.barcelona/tapas.com

At the start of the East End, not a hundred yards from the towering buildings of the City, you find yourself among the market stalls of Petticoat Lane and Middlesex Street. On one of the less salubrious corners you'll see a banner bearing the legend "tapas". Note that the arrow points down. Descend the stairs into a cramped basement which seats about twenty and you're in the Barcelona – one of London's best tapas bars. The range of snacks wouldn't be sniffed at in Barcelona or Madrid, and it includes a fair few Catalan specialities, including the classic tomato- and garlic-rubbed bread – a good accompaniment to any tapas session.

You'll find a number of tapas lined up in typical Spanish style along the back half of the bar – these are just a few of the selection on offer. The Barcelona has a vast (in more ways than one) menu, written in Spanish and Catalan with English translations. Many are simple, such as Serrano ham (£8.50), queso Manchego (£4.95), or aceitunas (£2.95) – olives – and rely on the excellent quality of the raw ingredients. More skill is involved in creating the paellas; the paella Valenciana (£11.95 per person) is particularly good. And there is also a chicken brochette (£6.95). Unusually for such a small place with such a huge choice, there's no need to worry about freshness. There is a bigger, smarter, newer and less charming Barcelona nearby, and the apparent lull between ordering and receiving your dish may be because the girl is running around the corner to the other kitchen to fetch a portion.

✳ Gambas al ajillo (£6.95) – for the kind of breath that gets you elbow room in a rush-hour tube.

Café Spice Namaste

Indian £20–£60

16 Prescott St, E1 & ℡ 020 7488 9242
Station Aldgate East/Tower Hill **Open** Mon–Fri noon–3pm & 6.15–10.30pm, Sat 6.15–10.30pm **Accepts** All major credit cards Ⓦ www.cafespice.co.uk

During the week this restaurant is packed with movers and shakers, all busily moving and shaking. They come in for lunch at 11.59am and they go out again at 12.59pm. Lunchtimes and even weekday evenings the pace is fast and furious, but come Saturday nights you can settle back and really enjoy Cyrus Todiwala's exceptional cooking. The menu, which changes throughout the year, sees Parsee delicacies rubbing shoulders with dishes from Goa, North India, Hyderabad and Kashmir, all of them precisely spiced and well presented. The tandoori specialities, in particular, are awesome, fully flavoured by cunning marinades.

Start with a voyage around the tandoor. The murg kay tikkay (£4.95 or £9.95) tastes as every chicken tikka should, with

yoghurt, ginger, cumin and chillies all playing their part. Or there's venison tikka aflatoon (£6.75 or £12.95), which originates in Gwalior and is flavoured with star anise and cinnamon. Also notable is the papeta nay eeda na pattice (£4.25) – a potato cake perked up with egg, coconut, green peas and Parsee-style hot tomato gravy. For a main course, fish lovers should consider the patra ni machchi (£13.25) – pomfret stuffed with green coconut chutney. Choose meat and you should try the dhaansaak (£11.75) which is a truly authentic version of the much-misrepresented Parsee speciality; it is served with a small kebab and brown-onion rice. Breads are also excellent, and some of the accompaniments and vegetable dishes belie their lowly status at the back of the book-sized menu. Try baingan bharta (£4.95) – an aubergine classic.

 Be sure to read the weekly changing "specials menu".

The Don

Modern European £30–£75

20 St Swithin's Lane, EC4 ☎ 020 7626 2606

Station Bank **Open** Mon–Fri noon–3pm & 6–10pm **Accepts** All major credit cards

George Sandeman first took over the cellars at 20 St Swithin's Lane in 1798. And very fine cellars they are too, complete with an ornate black iron "Capital Patent Crane" for lowering barrels into the depths. Now it is home to The Don restaurant and bistro, which takes its name from the trademark portrait of Sandeman port's "Don" which has been re-hung, with due ceremony, at the gateway to this hidden courtyard. The lofty room on the ground floor makes a striking restaurant, while the vaulted brick cellars make a grand backdrop for the Bistro.

The feel of the smart ground floor restaurant is sophisticated – this place is aiming directly for the fine-dining market, and the strategy seems to be working. The food is accomplished. Starters range from a Mediterranean fish soup with croutons, rouille and Gruyère cheese (£5.90); through a terrine of foie gras, with a prune and Cognac dressing and toasted brioche (£9.95); to scallops baked "en croute" with lime and vanilla (£8.95). Mains may include Shetland salmon in leaf spinach, preserved lemon and sauce Jacqueline (£13.95); rack of young New Zealand venison on pancetta with a Reblochon and potato gateau (£17.25); and a well judged dish of calf's liver with braised chicory and champ potatoes (£15.75). The kitchen knows its stuff: strong flavours and good combinations. Puds are comforting – dark chocolate tart with eau de vie Mandarine sorbet (£5.75); hazelnut pistachio parfait (£5.50). And hurrah, there are savouries, including a delicious French rarebit (£7.75) of grilled Reblochon on toasted potato and garlic bread.

 There is a grand private room in the cellar adjoining the Bistro.

The Place Below
Vegetarian £6–£15

St Mary-le-Bow Church, Cheapside, EC2 ☎020 7329 0789
Station Bank/St Paul's **Open** Mon–Fri 7.30am–3.30pm (lunch 11.30am–2.30pm)
Accepts All major credit cards except AmEx & Diners ⓦwww.theplacebelow.co.uk

The Place Below is a vegetarian restaurant, and yes it is in the crypt of the St Mary-le-Bow Church. But persevere: it has a splendidly low worthiness rating. Wander into the wonderfully elegant Wren church and look for the staircase down to the crypt – you'll see that the resto is split into two halves. The first has an open kitchen at one end and acts as coffee shop and servery – good pastries and breakfast buns. The other side is the restaurant proper which is open at lunch (with prices a pound or two cheaper between 11.30am and noon). Choose from the daily changing menu, push a tray along the canteen-style rails, and the chefs will fill a plate for you.

The menu is reassuringly short and the dining room is lofty, with the large, central communal dining table being the only one with a tablecloth. There are a couple of soups, a hot dish, a quichey option, a salad of the day, good trad puds and that's about it. The soups are hearty, such as leek and potato with Thai flavours; or spicy lentil and chickpea with harissa (both £3.10). The salad of the day (£7.50) can be triumphant: crisp green beans, a rich savoury dollop of wild rice, shredded carrot with sesame seeds, and plenty of fresh leaves. Or how about a hot dish such as Emmental and white wine hotpot with root vegetable mash (£7.50)? The field mushroom, fennel and Gruyère "quiche of the day" (£7) is also well made. There are always puddings puddings such as a marzipan and cranberry cake, or passion fruit syllabub with lavender shortbread (both £2.80). Good cooking, great value.

✳ BYO, and no corkage charged – a winning combination.

THE CITY

Prism
Modern British £35–£80

147 Leadenhall St, EC3 ♿ ☎020 7256 3888
Station London Bridge **Open** Mon–Fri 11.30am–3pm & 6–10pm
Accepts All major credit cards ⓦwww.harveynichols.co.uk

Prism, part of the Harvey Nichols plan for world domination, is still an expensive City restaurant, but since the last edition of this guide the menu has become shorter and prices have been reined in – this is a trend that needs encouragement. Eating here is rather like being inside a towering, white-painted cube; it's very slick, and very much a lofty ex-banking hall. The food is a well-judged blend of English favourites and modernist influences. There is the obligatory (for the City) long bar and the obligatory suave service.

Starters are well executed: Cornish crab and mango salad, with coriander and mild curry dressing (£9); or Sudtirol speck with a salad of roast artichokes (£10); or terrine of ham hock, foie gras, and Puy lentils sauce gribiche (£10); or a risotto made with peas and crisp Carpegna ham (£8). When it comes to main courses, the menu splits into three fish, three meat and a veggie. So there are dishes such as Glenarm organic salmon, served with a fresh herb risotto (£20), as well as more adventurous offerings such as seared Canadian halibut, celeriac and Bramley apple purée and curly kale (£20). The meat side offers roast cutlet of Dutch veal, braised onion and chargrilled polenta (£22); and roast rump of English lamb, cassoulet of cannellini beans (£20). Veggies can look forward to a cannelloni of ricotta and spinach, red pepper coulis and shaved truffle (£14). Puddings include chestnut and chocolate mousse with Swiss meringue (£6.50) and the wine list has some high-ticket numbers.

✳ Welcome back old friend – Muligatawny soup (£5).

Refettorio
Italian £15–£60

Crowne Plaza Hotel, 19 New Bridge St, EC4 ☎ 020 7438 8052
Station Blackfriars **Open** Convivium: Mon–Fri noon–8pm.
Dining room: Mon–Fri noon–3pm & 6–10pm **Accepts** All major credit cards

Refettorio is something very unusual. What we have here is something completely new! It opened in March 2004 within the Crowne Plaza hotel just to the north of Blackfriars bridge. The resto is the brainchild of Giorgio Locatelli (see p.240) and the menu stems from his love of top-quality, artisan-produced Italian foods. The first thing to note is that the same menu, and the same prices, apply whether you eat in the less formal Convivium or end up at the tables with tablecloths.

As you walk into the room there is a counter with a slicing machine and a glass-fronted refrigerator – the contents of which would put any London deli to shame. The menu starts with an epic list of about thirty Italian cheeses and a similar number of regional salamis and cured meats. The idea is that you graze your way to a full tummy. If the choice intimidates, opt for the pre-selected combos – cheeses (£9.50 or £10.50), salamis (£12.50 or £14.50). Otherwise, standouts are the lardo di collonata (£2.50), the salami di cinghale (£3) – made from wild boar, and an implausibly creamy Gorgonzola (£2.50). Then there's a section of fritti: arancini (£5) are good, deep-fried spheres of saffron rice stuffed with cheese. The pasta dishes are very good – tagliolini gratinata (£8 or £12) is green pasta, baked under unbelievably good cheese and ham sauce. Main courses are trad veal chop (£19.50) or seabass in white wine (£19). Puds range from well made tarts to Italian delicacies such as pastiera (£6). The wine list is long and Italian. The service is slick and Italian. This place is good and Italian.

✳ Puds are wonderful, especially the chocolate-and-chilli tart (£6).

THE CITY

Rosemary Lane

French/Californian £18–£60

61 Royal Mint St, E1 ☎ 020 7481 2602

Station Tower Hill/DLR Tower Gateway **Open** Mon–Fri noon–2.30pm & 5.30–10pm, Sat 5.30–10pm **Accepts** All major credit cards 🌐 www.rosemarylane.btinternet.co.uk

The restaurant called Rosemary Lane opened in a converted pub during 2003. The prime mover is a Californian chef called Christina Anghelescu and her menus show an agreeable reliance on seasonal produce, while displaying the same dogged determination to use only the best quality ingredients that we associate with Alice Waters and the other West Coast stars. The menu changes every six weeks or so. The dining room looks like a lick-of-paint-makeover of a dodgy saloon bar – which is just what it is. Service is slick, in a Gallic sort of way.

The food is good. Dishes are pleasantly light, and presentation just about manages to stay elegant without tipping over the edge into elaborate. In the winter starters may include oxtail ragout ravioli served with celeriac cream, and sage flavoured port reduction (£8) – good clear-cut flavours. Or there might be Devon crab served in the shell with creamy spinach,

orange caviars and cresses (£10); or a forest mushroom savoury pudding, watercress soup and salad of watercress and Parmegiano (£7). Mains are considered combinations – seabass en papilotte, truffled fennel beurre blanc, caramelised chicory (£15); a French rabbit daube, toasted brioche, roast winter vegetables, and sherry glaze (£14); or slow-roast poussin, warm salad of Puy lentils, lardons and figs and a creamy tarragon white wine sauce (£14). Puds are good (all £6). There's a bitter chocolate shortbread truffle tart; and the "satsuma curd sandwich" – a somewhat tongue-in-cheek description but a pleasant surprise. As befits the city location there's a grown-up wine list with some good stickies.

✱ There is a good set lunch offer: £14 for two courses, £17 for three.

Searcy's Restaurant

Modern European £25–£55

Level 2, The Barbican Centre, Silk St, EC2 & ☎020 7588 3008
Station Barbican **Open** Mon–Fri noon–2.30pm & 5.30–10.30pm, Sat 5–10.30pm
Accepts All major credit cards Ⓦ www.searcys.co.uk

This comfortable restaurant is hidden deep within the bowels of the Barbican Centre, and in its infancy suffered a bit from the "unfindability" syndrome which afflicts anything protected by the tangle of multi-level walkways. The food has gone from simple to complicated and back again as Searcy's have tried to find the perfect offering. But the company, being under the wing of Richard Corrigan, has the expertise, and the menu now reads well – short and simple.

The deal is a simple one – two courses for £19 and three for £23 – and the menu is written in confident style with just five starters, five mains and five puds. Short menus are generally good news as they imply seasonal ingredients. The starters don't shy away from luxury items, although there are occasionally supplements such as an extra £3 for a warm salad of langoustine with morels, which doesn't sound unfair on what is potentially a £19 meal. Otherwise there may be a ballotine of guinea fowl with truffle; or cauliflower soup with seared scallop and truffle oil. Mains range from best end of lamb with confit turnip; to fillet of wild seabass with citrus risotto and fennel sorbet; or poached loin of veal with a herb crust and glazed carrots. Puds offer a serious warm dark chocolate and banana ganache pudding with vanilla ice cream; and for the lighter palate an exotic salad with lemon balm and a lychee sorbet. There is an extensive wine list but one which does not forget the need for economies – Trebbiano delle Marche, £5 a glass.

✱ There's a short but imaginative snack menu in the lounge bar.

THE CITY

Thai Square City
Thai £15–£45

136–138 The Minories, EC3 ♿ ☎020 7680 1111
Station Aldgate/Tower Hill **Open** Mon–Thurs noon–10pm, Fri noon–11.30pm
Accepts All major credit cards except Diners

It is claimed (mainly by PRs) that this is Europe's largest Thai restaurant, but it may well be true. In a vast room decorated with temple bells, Buddhas, pots, carved panels, teak, wooden flowers and gold-mosaic rooftop dragons, friendly staff greet customers with a genuine smile. Downstairs there's a 100-seater cocktail bar with a 4–7pm happy hour. On Thursday and Friday, the basement turns into a club with a 2am drink and dancing license.

The lengthy menu lists both familiar favourites and more novel ideas. Toong thong (£4) is a dish of minced prawn and chicken in purse-like little sacks, and very moreish. Tod man poo (£5), or Thai crab cakes, will satisfy connoisseurs seeking this favourite, and tom yam kung (£4.50) will delight lovers of the classic lemongrass soup. Moo ping (£5), or barbecued pork served with a sweet and incredibly hot sauce, is tender and good. The menu suggests that it's especially good with sticky rice (£1.75), and it is. Six Thai curries (all £6.25) offer a choice of red or green and different main ingredients. There are the classic noodle dishes such as pad Thai (£6.90). Other treats include Chu-chee lobster (£16.00), which is deep-fried lobster with special curry paste, coconut milk and lime leaves. The wine list starts gently, threads its way through some decent choices at around the £15–20 mark, then rockets to cosset City boys with a Château Cheval Blanc St Emilion at £245. Puddings include banana with coconut syrup and sesame seeds (£3.50), Thai egg custard (£3.00), and ice creams and sorbets (£3.00).

✱ There's a bargain "Lunch Express" midday menu (noon–4pm), with set meals from as little as £6.50.

Clapham &
Wandsworth

Chez Bruce

2 Bellevue Rd, SW17 ☎020 8672 0114

Station BR Wandsworth Common **Open** Mon–Thurs noon–2pm & 7–10.30pm, Fri noon–2pm & 6.30–10.30pm, Sat 12.30–2.30pm & 6.30–10.30pm, Sun noon–3pm & 7–10.30pm **Accepts** All major credit cards ✆www.chezbruce.co.uk

Bruce Poole's comfortable little restaurant has weathered the storm attendant on being singled out for Michelin stardom with admirable aplomb. Chez Bruce still stands for honest, unfussy, earthy, richly flavoured food. The menu boasts old-fashioned dishes that never pander to the latest gastro-trend and makes use of less fashionable ingredients – such as pig's trotters, rabbit or mackerel. Prix fixe three-course menus offer lunch for £21.50 Mon–Fri; £25 Sat; and £29.50 Sun. A three-course dinner is £32.50 Mon–Sun. A bargain indeed.

The menu changes from day to day. The kind of starters you can expect are cream of fennel soup with wild mushroom pastillas; Middle White pig's head croquettes with sauce gribiche and red-wine jus; grilled mackerel with smoked eel,

Savoy cabbage and mustard. Or there might be a classic lurking – perhaps vitello tonnato. Main course dishes are deeply satisfying. You might find pot au feu of duck with bread sauce and foie gras; or crisp fillet of bream with artichokes, gnocchi and red pepper compote; or rolled pork belly with glazed root vegetables and aligot. This is one of the last strongholds of offal (perhaps the reason why this restaurant is the favourite haunt of so many off-duty chefs?). Look out for sweetbreads, or perhaps calf's liver. The Michelin star has led to the wine list being extended and refined and it's now winning prizes of its own. The sweets here are well executed classics: proper crème brûlée; rhubarb and champagne trifle. No wonder Chez Bruce is heavily booked every evening. Go for lunch instead – it'll make your day.

✻ **The cheeseboard is outstanding here.**

Coromandel

2 Battersea Rise, SW11 ☎020 7738 0038

Station BR Wandsworth Town **Open** Daily 11am–3pm & 6.30–11pm **Accepts** All major credit cards

The Coromandel Coast (bottom of India, on the right) has lost out in the publicity war with the Malabar Coast (bottom of India, on the left). This restaurant flies the flag for "Southern Indian and Sri Lankan cuisine the traditional

way" and offers a menu that runs all the way from South Indian vegetarian dishes – dosas and so forth – to Keralan dishes, chilli-rich Chettinad dishes from Tamil Nadu, and Sri Lankan specialities. Spread over two floors, the dining room is brightly painted, modern and busy. The pricing is about the same as at the other restaurants hereabouts, which makes for a bigger bill than at most local curry houses.

On the menu you will find that some of the dishes vary from day to day. There will always be soup of the day (£4.45), but some days this will be a spicy lentil concoction, sometimes a pepper soup and sometimes a tomato rasam. It's one way to keep the kitchen from getting bored. There are also Sri Lankan favourites such as devilled chicken (£5.95), and mutton rolls (£4.95) – dry curried lamb rolled in bread. Main course stars include the seafood moilee (£11.95), kingfish, prawns and scallops in a cashew gravy, Kanara style; Chettinad chicken (£6.95), the really hot one; or there may be a special only served at the weekend, such as Mysore venison (£13.95). The vegetable dishes are good – cadju curry (£7.95) is made with cashews and is rather surprising, if only because the nuts have been cooked until quite soft. Coromandel's breads are also worth investigating, as is their lemon rice (£2.50).

✳ If you want dishes authentically hot, you'll need to ask.

The Freemasons

Modern British/Gastropub £15–£35

2 Northside, Wandsworth Common, SW18 ☎ 020 7326 8580
Station BR Clapham Junction **Open** Mon–Sat noon–3pm & 6.30–10pm, Sun 12.30–4pm & 6.30–9.30pm **Accepts** All major credit cards except AmEx & Diners

This pub has gone full circle. First it became a bar called the Roundhouse, then it was a Livebait fish restaurant, and now

it is the Freemasons once again. It opened towards the end of 2003 and the décor is "standard gastropub": sofas (tick); mis-matched dining chairs (tick); big pictures (tick); scruffy-comfortable look (tick). You can eat anywhere in the pub, but the dining area is somewhat raised and overlooks the open kitchen. The food is good, dishes avoid most of the horrors of elaborate presentation, flavours are strong and there are some interesting combinations of taste and texture.

Start with the plate of decent home-made hommus with bread (£3.50) to take the sting out of your appetite while you study the menu. Starters might include tempura soft-shell crab on crisp polenta with avocado and pickled radicchio (£7); a whole buffalo mozzarella (very good milky mozzarella), with plum tomatoes, rocket and pesto (£6.50); and a salt-cod and cassava fishcake (£5.50) – a competitive fish cake, but it's hard to spot any cassava. Mains are substantial and well thought out: a grilled lamb steak comes with a light and fluffy herb cous cous and chickpeas in a ratatouille sauce (£9.25); pan-fried wasabi salmon comes with egg noodles and a tamarind sauce (£9.75); a large piece of roast pork belly arrives very crisp and gnarled, pleasantly chewy, with a dollop of decent mash and some chilli sauce (£9.75). The lemon and vanilla cheesecake (£4) does its job. The Timothy Taylor's Landlord bitter is well kept, and there is a short, gently priced wine list. Service is friendly.

✳ Occasional flights of fancy: "crocodile and duck rillette".

Gastro

Very French £18–£40

67 Venn St, SW4 ☎ 020 7627 0222

Station Clapham Common **Open** Daily 8am–midnight **Accepts** Cash or cheque only

Gastro was one of the pathfinders in the steady march to trendiness in Cla'am, and where once all was favouritism for regulars, and a no-bookings policy, now you may need a reservation to get in. The food is still unabashed about its Frenchness, but there are competing eateries up and down Venn Street, and Gastro is no longer streets ahead.

The staff are French and the menu lists all the Gallic favourites, which tend to be inexpensive and generously portioned. Think yourself back to your last French holiday and enjoy. Under hors d'oeuvres you'll find a pukka soupe de poisson (£4.95) with the classic trimmings. Ordering seafood is straightforward: oysters are sold in sixes (£6.90); mussels arrive à la marinière (£7.40); and crabe mayonnaise (£9.95) is exactly that – a whole crab and mayonnaise. No arguments there! The mains will also cosset any Francophile tendencies you may have: carré d'agneau grillé au pain d'épice (£13.95), rack of lamb with gingerbread crust; andouillette frites sauce moutarde (£9.40), that deadly French sausage made from pigs' chitterlings; or an authentic entrecôte grillé, sauce Béarnaise, frites (£13.50). And there is always boudin noir pommes purées (£10.45) – black pudding, apples and mash. Fish dishes are well represented: try lotte et ventrêche (£14.25) – monkfish with bacon. For puds think patisserie, and good patisserie at that. The wine list has perked up of late and Gastro offers a "cassoulet menu" on Monday nights – cassoulet, salad, glass of wine £15.95.

✳ "At Gastro the chefs will never cook meat more than medium". You have been warned!

Gourmet Burger Kitchen

Burgers £14–£24

44 Northcote Rd, SW11 & ☎020 7228 3309

Station BR Clapham Junction **Open** Mon–Fri noon–11pm, Sat 11am–11pm, Sun 11am–10pm **Accepts** All major credit cards except AmEx & Diners ⓦwww.gbkinfo.co.uk

On the face of it, the words "gourmet burger kitchen" do not make easy bedfellows. "Gourmet" contradicts "burger", and "kitchen" has an unnervingly homely ring to it. But taken as a whole phrase you can see the intention. "There are burgers here", the proprietors seem to want us to know, "but not those thin, mass-produced ones. Our burgers have flair and originality, but they are not high falutin' burgers; everything is hand-made and good." Anyway, GBK will do for now. The room is cramped and dominated by a large counter behind which there seem to be serried ranks of waitresses and chefs. Everything is pretty casual – you go up to the bar, order and pay, and then your meal is brought to the table.

The menu starts at the "classic – 100 percent Aberdeen Angus

Scotch beef, salad and relish" (£4.95). It also offers the blue cheese burger (£6.60), which adds the tang of Stilton to the main event; the chilli burger (£5.90); the avocado and bacon burger (£6.90); the Jamaican (£6.80), with mangoes and ginger sauce; the pesterella (£6.90), with fresh pesto and mozzarella; lamb (£6.90); venison (£6.95); chicken, bacon and avocado (£6.95); and chorizo (£6.95). Or, for vegetarians, there is even a "burger" made from Portabella mushroom (£6.30); aubergine and goat's cheese (£6.90); or falafel (£5.90). The fries are good and the side salad is excellent, with good fresh leaves and a perky dressing. The Gourmet Burger Kitchen has a good feel to it, and the food is top quality. Despite the dread word "gourmet", prices are not out of reach.

✱ Try the Kiwiburger (£6.70) – topped with beetroot, egg, pineapple, cheese, salad and relish.

Gurkhas Diner

Indian £12–£30

1 The Boulevard, Balham High Rd, SW17 & ☎020 8675 1188

Station Balham **Open** Daily noon–2.30pm & 6–11pm **Accepts** All major credit cards

In the autumn of 2003 new proprietors took over an electrical goods shop on the Boulevard and turned it into Gurkhas Diner, a restaurant offering something a bit different – Nepalese food. Gurkhas is anything but a diner.

The light and spacious room has a parquet floor and this is a restaurant where your napkin comes in a stylish napkin ring and there are over-size wine glasses. Great efforts have also been made with the presentation of the dishes on the plate and there's a good deal of "arranging" and "sauce drizzling" going on, which is largely superfluous given the interesting and well cooked food.

From the starters dayalu (£2.90) is a simple potato cake made with lentils, and served with a fine grained, spicy, sesame sauce. The nakasee (£3.25) is also good – a bamboo skewer of chicken with another delicious sauce. Or there's bhutuwa (£3.25), which is a stir-fry made with chunks of highly seasoned chicken liver. Main courses include a series of dishes made in the "chuli" which is a charcoal-fueled beehive oven. Gurkhali chicken (£5.75) is very good, with a green marinade and strong flavours. Khasi tang (£6.75) is a large lamb shank served on the bone with rich gravy, while "sherpa hot" (£5.75) is a dish that looks as if it has come from Lancashire – lamb curry is topped with discs of potato, giving a new credibility to the term hotpot. Vegetable dishes are also attractive; rato farsi (£3.50) is a mild curry made with pumpkin. Gurkhas Diner deserves your support for daring to do something different, and also for the genuine smiley welcome.

✳ Dudilo kera is the Nepalese for banana fritter.

Metro Garden Restaurant & Bar

Modern British £16–£40

9 Clapham Common South Side, SW4 ☎ 020 7627 0632

Station Clapham Common **Open** Mon–Fri noon–4pm & 6–11pm, Sat & Sun noon–11pm
Accepts All major credit cards except AmEx & Diners

As you emerge from the southern exit of Clapham Common tube station Metro is facing you – which is presumably how the place came by its name. Over the last couple of years the charming "secret" garden has become such a widely known secret that in 2004 the proprietors bit the bullet and changed the name to include it. As you'd expect of any establishment thoughtful enough to provide blankets for the dogs of Sunday brunchers lingering over the newspapers in the secluded garden – the Metro Garden restaurant and Bar has become something of a neighbourhood favourite.

The food is interesting but mercifully wholehearted. Start with sautéed lambs' livers, sage and thyme polenta, caramelised baby onions, balsamic reduction (£5.25); or pan-roast scallops, butterbean and sage purée and crisp pancetta (£6.75). Or perhaps the deep-fried salt-and-pepper squid on wilted greens appeals (£4.95)? Main courses include enough brave combinations of taste and texture for the adventurous diner, and the kitchen casts the net widely for inspiration – rare tuna fillet may come with a lemon thyme and pink peppercorn crust, alongside Parmesan mash and rocket (£13.95); or a Moroccan style merguez stew might be teamed with apricot cous cous (£12.95); or roast duck breast with pak choi, juniper and honey jus (£13.50). Puds are mainstream: ginger and caramel cheesecake with candied orange (£4.95); coffee panacotta with mint pesto (£5.25); lemon tart with raspberry coulis (£3.50). The service is slick but friendly, the wine list sound rather than adventurous.

✳ Chocoholics will demand the Bailey's and chocolate mousse with chocolate cookie (£5.95).

Tabaq

Indian £16–£35

47 Balham Hill, SW12 ☎ 020 8673 7820
Station Clapham South **Open** Mon–Sat noon–2.45pm & 6–midnight
Accepts All major credit cards ⓦ www.tabaq.co.uk

The owners of Tabaq used to drive up from the suburbs to work in a smart West End restaurant, and on the way they would travel along Balham Hill and past Clapham Common. They had set their sights on having a restaurant of their own, smarter than the usual curry house, somewhere they would serve traditional Pakistani specialties. So when signs went up outside number 47 they took the plunge. They named their restaurant after the tabaq – a large serving dish – and set about dishing up authentic Lahori fare. Over a decade later they have a shelf full of awards and a restaurant full of loyal customers to show for it.

The menu comes with a multitude of sections: starters, grills, seafood, chicken curries, specialties, rice, breads and natural vegetables. To start, go straight for the tandoor and grill section, which features some of the best dishes on the menu. Seekh kabab Lahori

(£6.25) is made from well seasoned minced lamb. Or try the masala machli Lahori (£6.25) – fish in a light and spicy batter. As an accompaniment, order a naan-e-Punjabi (£2.50) – a heavy, butter-rich bread from the tandoor – with kachomer (£1.95), a kind of coarse-cut Asian salsa. At this stage of your meal you may well be tempted to choose simply from the salan, or chicken curries. There's murgh taway ka makhani (£8.50) – this sauce is thought to be a buttery ancestor of chicken tikka masala – or murgh palak (£7.25), chicken and spinach. Desserts include one item you do not immediately associate with Pakistani cuisine – baked Alaska (£12), which serves two and must be ordered in advance.

✳ A whole steamed roast lamb, to feed twelve, 24 hours' notice (£140)!

Tsunami
Japanese £15–£45

Unit 3, 1–7 Voltaire Rd, SW4 ♿ ☎020 7978 1610
Station Clapham North **Open** Mon–Fri 6–11pm, Sat noon–3pm & 6–11.30pm
Accepts All major credit cards except AmEx & Diners

The dining room at Tsunami is surprisingly large, and elegant in a minimalist, Japanesey sort of way. All the staff are helpful and friendly, and the kitchen bustles away in full view through a long serving hatch. The restaurant is at the end of Clapham High Street that is nearest to Brixton, and it is very much an area in transition. Scruffy shops gave way to trendy bars and in turn these are gradually being supplanted by ambitious restaurants, of which Tsunami is the perfect example.

The food is very good, the presentation on the plate is quite outstanding, and the bill is not over-the-top. For once all those pretty-as-a-picture arrangements seem to stem from a genuine love of the beautiful. Order a few starters to share. The kataifi prawns with creamy spicy sauce (£5.95) is very good – plump prawns in crispy overcoats. Or there's sunkiss sashimi – seared with hot olive oil and dressed with ponzu: salmon or scallop (£5.95). Or the kawari age (£4.95), tempura made with black cod. Best of all is the tuna tataki (£9.95), which is a sashimi made with seared tuna and dressed with a sharp ponzu dressing. Each slice is raw in the middle and firm around the edge – very delicious indeed. The tempura is light and crisp – asparagus; carrot; pumpkin (all £1 for two pieces). From the main dishes, an old favourite, hira unagi – grilled marinated eel (£9.95) – comes with rice and miso soup; "prime Scottish fillet beef" (£12.95) comes with balsamic teriyaki soy; and the now ubiquitous black cod comes with sweet miso (£16.50).

✳ Oyster shooter (£5.50) – sake, oyster, ponzu, momji daikon, raw quail egg yolk and spring onion.

Clerkenwell & Smithfield

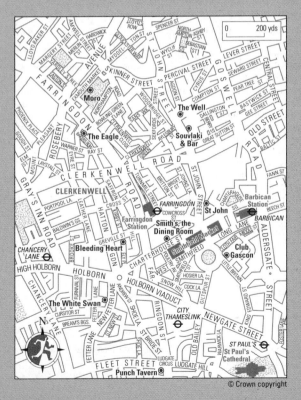

© Crown copyright

Bleeding Heart Restaurant

Modern British £30–£80

Bleeding Heart Yard, off Greville St, EC1 ☎ 020 7242 2056
Station Farringdon/Chancery Lane **Open** Mon–Fri noon–2.30pm & 6–10.30pm
Accepts All major credit cards ⊛ www.bleedingheart.co.uk

Just a glance around the deeply traditional basement rooms at Bleeding Heart Yard will tell you instantly what kind of a place this is. The clientele is from the City, the menu is written with City superiority and the wine list is priced for City wallets. And that's the pukka, suit-wearing, claret-loving kind of City folk. Even during a glorious summer these paneled dining rooms will still be packed, and booking is doubly necessary should the forecast veer towards the windy and rainswept. There's an accessible dinner offer – three courses for £24.95.

The menu changes seasonally and dishes form a bridge between classical French cooking and its Modern British descendants. Starters may include lightly smoked foie gras pressé with roasted apple and a Pourpier salad (£9.95); warm asparagus with creamy goat's cheese quenelle (£7.95); or a millefeuille of fresh crab and confit tomato (£6.95). The mains range from dishes such as fillet of halibut in red wine with a polenta galette and prune and red-wine sauce (£17.25); to rack of Welsh lamb with sweet-potato purée and rosemary jus (£18.95). The owners of the Bleeding Heart empire – restaurant, bistro, tavern, crypt, plus The Don restaurant (see p.90) – also have interests in the antipodes, so New Zealand venison is often featured. There's always Stilton cheese on offer and sound, trad puds (all £5.95). The wine list is formidable. According to the Wine Spectator, this place has "one of the most outstanding restaurant wine lists in the world".

✳ According to the New Yorker, Bleeding Heart Yard is "bleeding hard to find".

Club Gascon

Very French £45–£90

57 West Smithfield, EC1 ☎ 020 7796 0600
Station Farringdon **Open** Mon–Thurs noon–2pm & 7–10pm, Fri noon–2pm & 7–10.30pm, Sat 7–10.30pm **Accepts** All major credit cards except Diners

It's hard to believe it, but Club Gascon opened as long ago as 1998. This place still seems new and still seems fresh, although a cabinet full of awards testifies to how amazingly successful it has become. If you want a booking, they advise calling two or three weeks ahead, though you may strike lucky with a cancellation. Pascal Aussignac is chef here, and his cooking is an authentic taste of southwestern France. The menu is set out in sections and the portions are larger than some starters but smaller than most mains, the idea being that you indulge in your very own dégustation, trying several dishes – which isn't the cheapest way of eating.

The sections are "La route du sel" (cured meats and charcuterie); "Le potager" (vegetables and cheese); "Les foies gras"; "L'océane" (fish and shellfish); "Les pâturages" (mainly duck, game and cassoulet). There are forty different dishes so it's important to spread your ordering. Here are some promising combinations: three "pousse en claire" oysters with seaweed tartare (£9.60); warm Gascon pie of duck and chanterelles (£7.80); roast foie gras "lemon lemon" (£9.50); royal of hare with smooth and crispy parsnips (£13.50); old-fashioned cassoulet Toulousain (£9.50). Or maybe roast John Dory, crunchy baby fern and oxtail reduction (£13.50) appeals? Or the home-made "confit" French fries with fleur de sel (£4)? The problem with eating like this is that you can hit on a dish that is amazing and therefore too small. You must have the confidence to order a second or even third serving.

✱ Don't be daunted, opt for the Tasting Menu – five courses, five glasses of wine (£60).

The Eagle   Mediterranean/Gastropub £10–£30

159 Farringdon Rd, EC1 ☎ 020 7837 1353

Station Farringdon **Open** Meals served Mon–Fri noon–3pm & 6.30–10.30pm, Sat 12.30–3.30m & 6.30–10.30m, Sun 12.30–3.30pm **Accepts** Mastercard, Switch & Visa

For most of its lifetime The Eagle was merely a run-down pub in an unpromising part of London. Then in 1991 it was taken over by food-minded entrepreneurs who transformed it into a restaurant-pub turning out top-quality dishes. They

were pioneers: there should be a blue plaque over the door marking the site as the starting place of the great gastropub revolution. The Eagle has remained a crowded, rather shabby sort of place, and the staff still display a refreshing full-on attitude. The kitchen is truly open: the chefs work behind the bar, and the menu is chalked up over their heads. It changes daily, even hourly, as things run out or deliveries come in. The food is broadly Mediterranean in outlook with a Portuguese bias, and you still have to fight your way to the bar to order and pay.

The menu changes like quicksilver but you may find the likes of the famous caldo verde (£5) – the Portuguese chorizo and potato soup that takes its name from the addition of spring greens. There may be a grilled swordfish with peppers, mint, new potatoes and balsamico (£12.50); or a delicious and simple dish such as roast spring chicken with preserved lemons, potatoes, mustard leaves and aioli (£10.50); or cuttlefish stew with chilli, garlic, parsley, onions and broad beans (£12.50); or a rib-eye "tagliata" with green beans, and mixed leaves, radishes and horseradish (£14). To finish, choose between a fine cheese – perhaps Wigmore served with rhubarb jam and toast (£6.50) – or the siren charms of those splendid, small, Portuguese, cinnamony custard tarts (pasteis de nata), at £1.20 each.

✳ Bife Ana (£8.50), a marinated steak sandwich, has been on the menu since day one.

Moro | North African/Spanish £20–£50

34–36 Exmouth Market, EC1 & ☎ 020 7833 8336
Station Farringdon **Open** Mon–Fri 12.30–2.30pm & 7–10.30pm, Sat 7–10.30pm
Accepts All major credit cards ⓦ www.moro.co.uk

This modern, rather stark restaurant has slipped effortlessly from being new and iconoclastic to occupying a place on the list of London's "must visit" eateries. In feel it's not so very far away from the better pub-restaurants, although the proprietors have given themselves the luxury of a slightly larger kitchen. This has also become a place of pilgrimage for disciples of the wood-fired oven, and as the food here hails mainly from Spain, Portugal and North Africa, it is both Moorish and moreish. You'll probably have to book.

The à la carte changes every fortnight. There's usually a soup, and it's usually among the best starters. How does cauliflower, yoghurt and coriander soup (£3.50), sound? Or you may be offered starters such as pan-fried calves' sweetbreads and artichoke hearts with cardamom (£6.50); blood orange, crisp bread and feta salad (£5.50). Main courses are simple and often traditional combinations of taste and textures. As with the starters, it's the accompaniments that tend to change rather than the core ingredients. Look out for wood-roasted brill, braised sweet-and-sour leeks with red pepper and walnut sauce (£16.50); or charcoal-grilled lamb with roast squash, cumin chickpea puree (£16.50); or perhaps charcoal-grilled sea bass with wilted escarole and lentils (£16.50). Do not miss the splendid Spanish cheeses (£5.50) served with membrillo – traditional quince paste. And there's no excuse for avoiding the Malaga raisin ice cream (£4.50), or the serious bitter chocolate, coffee and cardamom truffle (£5).

✳ There is a grand list of moody sherries.

The Punch Tavern
Modern European £7–£18

99 Fleet St, EC4 ☎ 020 7353 6658

Station Blackfriars **Open** Mon–Fri breakfast 7–11.30am, lunch 11.30–3pm, "platters" 3pm–11pm **Accepts** All major credit cards except Diners

The rather strangely named "Club Mangia" at the Punch Tavern is a genuine attempt to do something different with the concept of the gastropub. The aim was to discard some of the restauranty baggage and make more of the pubby aspects. The Punch Tavern is an elegant old place – stunning tiles, plenty of history. Now it serves food from breakfast right through – unfussy, cheap and welcoming. In the evening the menu is reduced to platters served at the bar; the breakfasts are serious; the home-made cakes are very good indeed. The lunch service works in a novel way: the Tavern staff set up a table in the middle of the bar with three hot dishes and a straightforward salad bar of about twenty options. Pay £5.50 (or £3.75 to take out) and then help yourself. Rough and ready? Certainly! Popular? Definitely!

The lunchtime dishes are unpretentious – there is always a veggie option such as a green vegetable curry or a cauliflower cheese, and there's usually something classical such as a boneless coq au vin or chili con carne. There are also a few "specials" which you can order at the bar: paninis, club sandwiches (£5.50), chicken Caesar salad (£7.50), or maybe a simple pasta dish (£7.50). In the evenings the "platters" range from a cheeseboard (£7.50) – Vacherin, Camembert, Roquefort, Valencay – to a meat platter (£7.50) of Serrano ham, salami, duck pate. Step outside the Tavern and you are surrounded by a huge sprawl of office buildings; inside, you are in a more down-to-earth place – a home to decent workmanlike food and great value.

✳ Delicious cakes, particularly the chocolate brownie.

St John
British £30–£70

26 St John St, EC1 ☎ 020 7251 0848

Station Farringdon **Open** Mon–Fri noon–3pm & 6–11pm, Sat 6–11pm
Accepts All major credit cards ⓦ www.stjohnrestaurant.com

One of the most frequent requests, especially from foreign visitors, is, "Where can we get some really English cooking?" Little wonder that the promise of "olde English fare" is the bait in so many London tourist traps. The cooking at St John, however, is genuine. It is sometimes old-fashioned and

makes inspired use of all those strange and unfashionable cuts of meat that were once commonplace in rural Britain. Technically the cooking is of a very high standard, while the restaurant itself is completely without frills or design pretensions. You'll either love it or hate it.

The menu changes every session but the tone does not, and there's always a dish or two to support the slogan "nose to tail eating". Charcuterie, as you'd imagine, is good: a simple terrine (£6) will be dense but not dry – well judged. Or, for the committed, what about a starter of crispy pig's skin and dandelion (£6)? Or celery soup (£5.20)? Main courses may include calf's liver and swede (£14.80), or oxtail and mash (£14.80). Maybe there will be a dish described simply as "fennel and Berkswell cheese" (£14); perversely, in this den of offal, the veg dishes are a delight. Puddings are traditional and well executed: custard tart and rhubarb (£5.80), or a slice of strong Lancashire cheese with an Eccles cake (£6). Joy of joys, sometimes there is even a seriously good Welsh rarebit (£5). St John has won shedloads of awards, and booking is a must. Whatever your feelings about meat and offal cookery, be assured that St John serves food at its most genuine.

Anthony Bourdain claimed the roast bone marrow and parsley salad (£6.20) as his "Desert Island Dish".

Smiths, the Dining Room

Modern British £15–£30

67–77 Charterhouse St, EC1 & ☏ 020 7251 7950

Station Farringdon **Open** Café: Mon–Fri 7am–11pm, Sat & Sun 10am–5pm Restaurants: Mon–Fri noon–3pm & 6–11pm, Sat 6–11pm (top floor), Sun 12.30–3.30pm & 6.30–10.30pm **Accepts** All major credit cards ⦿ www.smithsofsmithfield.com

Calling Smiths of Smithfield an ambitious project is like saying that pyramid building calls for a large workforce. Rebuild a Grade II listed warehouse in ultra-modern-meets-Blade Runner style and, hey presto, you have two restaurants, two bars, private rooms, kitchens and whatever, spread over four floors. On the ground floor there's a bar and café serving drinks and practical, sensible food. The "top floor" is a 70-seater where they pay particular attention to quality meat with good provenance. On the second floor is the 130-seater "Dining Room". The culinary mainspring here is an enlightened buying policy – quality, quality, quality.

The Dining Room is a large space around a central hole which looks down onto the smart bar area. Eating here is rather like sitting at the centre of a deactivated factory. The menu is divided into Larder, Starters, Soups, Mains, Grills, Daily Lunch Market Specials, Sides, and Sweet Tooth. The way the prices are expressed, however, is coy and irritating – Larder "all at 4 3⁄4 Pounds"; "Sides 2 1⁄2 Pounds". Bah humbug. But the starters are simple and good: grilled mushrooms and Taleggio on toasted sourdough (£4.75); Portuguese-style salt-cod fritters (£5.75); foie gras and chicken liver parfait (£4.75). Main courses may include crisp belly of pork with mashed potato and green sauce (£10.75); roast cod with roast salsify and Hollandaise (£10.75). The lunch specials are from the comfort-eating school, and feature such delights as cottage pie (£9.50). Puds are good. Try chocolate and pear Pithivier (£4.50).

✳ Bacon, egg, beans, sausage, mushrooms, black pudding, tomatoes, bubble and toast (£6.50). In the café.

Souvlaki & Bar

Greek £7–£30

140–142 St John St, EC1 ☎ 020 7253 7234
Station Angel/Farringdon **Open** Mon–Sat 10am–11pm
Accepts Mastercard, Switch & Visa ⓦ www.therealgreek.co.uk

This was the first of the small chain planned by the team at The Real Greek (see p.202). Souvlaki opened during spring 2003 and has been busy from day one, partly because the food is cheap and top-quality, and partly because the tone of the place is perfectly in tune with the mood of the times. The bar with its open kitchen dominates the room and there are a series of high, narrow island tables with stools. As it says on the menu, "Souvlaki & Bar offers Real Greek street food. Regional wines, beers and ouzos complement the flavours", and the good-value Greek wines will convince you.

The menu is very short. There are ten mezedes, among them dolmades (£2.95); taramosalata (£3.80); gigandes plaki (£2.95), a trad bean stew; and htipiti (£3.20), which is a delicious mishmash of cheese, red peppers and roast red onions. The bread is terrific: round, Greek flatbreads, lightly oiled and then crisped on the grill. Then there is the souvlaki. In Greece souvlaki changes with the seasons, so that from November until the end of May it is made from pork and for the rest of the year it is made from lamb. That's the way it is here – £4.75 buys you a flatbread with a splosh of yoghurty tzatziki and some tomato and pepper purée and then a skewer of pork. It is rolled tightly and wrapped in greaseproof paper. For £9.25 you can have a "double" (two of them, unsurprisingly). The same kind of thing made with chicken is (£4.75 or £9.25). Non-souvlakists will find crevettes with a warm potato salad (£6.95), and grilled pork cutlets (£5.90) to stop them going hungry.

✳ Try the splendid "Ouzo Mohito" cocktail, a superstar mixologist meets the Real Greek.

The Well   Modern British/Gastropub £25–£65

180 St John St, EC1 ☎ 020 7251 9363

Station Angel/Farringdon **Open** Mon–Fri noon–3pm & 6–10.30pm, Sat (brunch) 10.30am–5pm & 6–10.30pm, Sun (brunch) 10.30am–5pm & 6–10pm.
Accepts All major credit cards ⓦ www.downthewell.co.uk

The Well is a buzzy bar-cum-gastropub where the diners, staff and owner, Tom Martin, all appear to be friends having a good time. Scrubbed tables and old church chairs give a fresh, accessible feel to this corner venue, which is open as a bar throughout the day and as a restaurant during kitchen hours. A couple of daily specials on a blackboard complement the modern mixed menu, which appears to be geared to everyone's favourite dishes rather than any particular cuisine.

The menu changes regularly, but starters may include bread, garlic and sage soup (£4.50); "pint o' prawns" with mayonnaise (£6.50); or seared chicken livers with a balsamic reduction and mixed leaves (£5.95). Main courses are equally eclectic. Bison sausages come with herb mash and gravy (£9.95); or there may be saddle of rabbit cooked in grain mustard with borlotti beans and Savoy cabbage (£12.50); or chargrilled rib-eye steak (£14.50), which comes with grilled tomatoes, flat mushrooms and French fries. Fish dishes get good representation: pan-fried skate wing with potato and leek compote and brown butter (£13.50), or fillet of salmon with risotto cake and seafood saffron sauce (£13.95). The desserts (all £4.50) range from the classic – chocolate brownies with vanilla cream, or whisky bread-and-butter pudding with custard – to the more adventurous, such as cranberry and cinnamon crème brûlée. British cheeses (£7.50) are from the admirable Neal's Yard Dairy. The wine list ranges from a respectable house red or white at £12.50 to Dom Perignon – for the Clerkenwell-heeled.

✳ Takes its name from the well that served the clerken hereabouts, and led to the name of the area.

The White Swan   Modern British £25–£60

108 Fetter Lane, EC4 ☎ 020 7242 9696

Station Chancery Lane **Open** Mon–Fri noon–3pm & 6–10pm
Accepts All major credit cards except Diners ⓦ www.thewhiteswan.com

The White Swan opened just before Christmas 2003 and is one of a new breed of gastropubs. These places are not content to knock out homely food in homely surroundings; their aspirations are tuned to a world of fine dining where there is little room for junkshop tables and mismatched cutlery. Downstairs the pub ethic dominates with real ale and decent bar food, upstairs there's the dining room. The seating is luxurious beige leather, the ceiling is mirrored, there's a cheese trolley. "It's a pub Jim, but not as we know it."

The food is blisteringly good. The presentation is simple but elegant and flavours are well matched. For cooking of this quality prices are very reasonable. The main menu features six starters and six mains: three courses £22 and two courses £18. Start with courgette and mint soup, or a leek and Lancashire risotto. Or something seasonal such as purple sprouting broccoli, focaccia, and Hollandaise sauce. On to the mains: grilled calf's kidney with bacon and mustard; rib-eye with Roquefort butter; or a dish described as "roast cod with boulangère potatoes, pancetta and rosemary lemon sauce" – a very decent chunk of cod wrapped in boulangère potatoes and then the whole thing swaddled in pancetta. Very satisfying. Puds are good, the "blood orange marmalade sponge pudding with custard"

has a real tang. Having a go at the extensive cheeseboard attracts a hefty £5.50 supplement but it is worth it to see so many fine British cheeses. Service is slick and the wine list has some decent bottles at the cheap end. This is a really good place to eat.

✳ Daily specials such as "half a dozen Irish rock oysters with a champagne granita (£9)".

Further choices

Cicada
Pacific Fusion

132 St John St, EC1
☎020 7608 1550

Part bar, part restaurant, all busy. An unusual menu is loosely based on South East Asia. Sister to E&O (see p.258).

Coach & Horses
Gastropub/Modern British

26–28 Ray St, EC1
☎020 7278 8990

A decent gastropub where the cooking emphasises seasonal ingredients. Won an award in 2004.

Covent
Garden

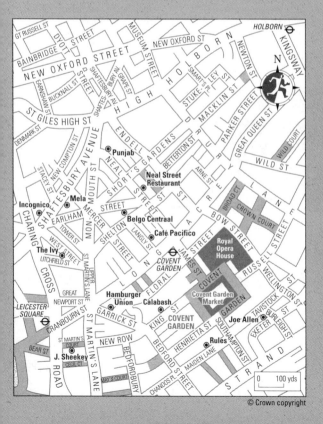

© Crown copyright

Belgo

Belgian £8–£35

50 Earlham St, WC2 ☎020 7813 2233

Station Covent Garden **Open** Mon–Wed noon–11pm, Thurs–Sun noon–11.30pm
Accepts All major credit cards ✪www.belgorestaurants.com

The Belgians invented mussels, frites and mayonnaise, and Belgo has done all it can to help the Belgian national dish take over London. The Belgo group's flagship restaurant is a massive metal-minimalist cavern accessed by riding down in a scissor-powered lift. Turn left at the bottom and you enter the restaurant (where you can book seats); turn right and you get seated in the beerhall, where diners share tables. With 95 different beers, some at alcoholic strengths of 8–9 percent, it's difficult not to be sociable, or perhaps to while away a few minutes pondering the age-old question … name six famous Belgians.

A kilo of classic moules marinières served with frites (£11.95) has fresh mussels that have clearly been cooked then and there. Other options include classique (£11.95), with cream and garlic; Provençale (£12.50), with tomato, herbs and garlic; or even Thai (£12.50), which comes with a Thai curry sauce. And there's plenty for the non-mussel eater. Start with a salade Brabaçonne (£5.95) – a warm salad including bacon, black pudding and duck confit. Or the cheese croquettes (£5.95), made with Orval beer. Move on to carbonade Flamande (£9.50) – beef braised in Geuze beer with apples and plums, and served with frites; or wild boar sausages made with Chimay beer (£8.95) and served with Belgian mash. Desserts include, among many others, traditional Belgian waffles with dark chocolate (£4.50). Belgo delights in special offers: there's a £5.95 lunch, and a deal called "beat the clock", where the prices shift downwards in relation to how early you eat.

✱ The "32 stick" – 32 shot glasses of fruit schnapps £59.50 – "great to share between two!"

Café Pacifico

Mexican £15–£30

5 Langley St, WC2 ☎020 7379 7728

Station Covent Garden **Open** Mon–Sat noon–midnight, Sun noon–11pm
Accepts All major credit cards ✪www.cafepacifico-laperla.co.uk

The salsa is hot at Café Pacifico – both types. As you are seated, a complimentary bowl of searing salsa dip with corn chips is put on your table. As you eat,

hot salsa music gets your fingers tapping. The atmosphere is relaxed and you're soon in the mood for a cold beer; fortunately there are several

Mexican beers, a good selection of wines and dozens of cocktails. But Pacifico's tequila list is the highlight with more than sixty varieties, including some very old and rare brands.

The menu is a lively mixture of old-style Californian Mexican and new Mexican, so while favourites such as fajitas, flautas and tacos dominate, there are also some interesting and unusual dishes. Portions are generous and spicy, and many main courses come with refried beans and rice. Try nachos rancheros (£8.25 or £7.25 vegetarian) for starters, and enjoy a huge plate of corn chips with beans, cheese, guacamole, onions, sour cream and olives. Excellent for sharing. Taquitos (£4.95) – filled fried baby tacos – are good, as are smoked chicken quesadillas (£6.25), flour tortillas with chicken, red peppers and avocado salsa. Main courses include degustación del Pacifico (£9.95), which includes a bit of almost everything. There's the chimichanga del mar (£9.75), a seafood- packed, deep-fried, rolled tortilla; burrito especial (£9.75), a flour tortilla filled with cheese, refried beans and a choice of roast beef, chicken or ground beef, covered with ranchero sauce; or Cuervo swordfish steak asada (£14.95), grilled fish with a tequila and sun-dried tomato salsa.

* Yes, they do have a bottle of mescal with a worm in it.

Calabash

African £10–£25

Africa centre, 38 King St, WC2 ☎ 020 7836 1976

Station Covent Garden **Open** Mon–Fri 12.30pm–2.30pm & 6–10.30pm, Sat 6–10.30pm **Accepts** All major credit cards except Diners

The Calabash, deep within the bowels of the Africa Centre, is at once worthy, comfortable and cheap. The same complex features a splendidly seedy bar, a live music hall, and African arts and crafts for sale. The menu struggles bravely to give snapshots of the extraordinary diversity of African cuisine: they manage dishes from North, East and West Africa, as well as specialities from Nigeria, Ivory Coast, Senegal and Malawi. So if you're looking for a particular dish you may be out of luck. However, if you want a cheerful atmosphere, a small bill, and wholesome, often spicy and usually unfamiliar food, the Calabash is worth seeking out.

Starters include familiar dishes like avocado salad (£2.40) and hummus (£2.30) along with interesting offerings such as aloco (£2.50), which is fried plantain in a hot tomato sauce. Those with an enquiring palate will pick the gizzards (£3.25), a splendid dish of chicken gizzards served in a rich, spiky pepper sauce. Grilled chicken wings (£2.95) are less exotic but very good nonetheless. Main courses are identified by origin. From Nigeria comes egusi (£7.25) a rich soup/stew with spinach, meat and dried shrimps, thickened with melon seed. Yassa (£6.75) is grilled chicken from Senegal, while doro wot (£7.20) is a pungent chicken stew from

Ethiopia, served with injera, the soft and thin sourdough bread. Nyama yo phika (£8.10) is a beef stew made with potatoes and sweet peppers and from Malawi. Drink whichever of the African beers is in stock at the time you visit.

✱ "Chicken" (£6.75), is superb fried chicken served with a ferocious hot sauce. Eat your heart out Colonel.

Hamburger Union

Burgers £8–£20

4–6 Garrick St, WC2 ☎ 020 7379 0412

Station Leicester Square **Open** Mon–Thurs 11.30am–10pm, Fri & Sat 11.30am –10.30pm & Sun 11.30am–10pm **Accepts** All major credit cards except AmEx & Diners ⓦ www.hamburgerunion.com.

With some dishes simpler is always better, and one of those dishes is the hamburger. Rather than getting fancy, purveyors of hamburgers should get real. Everything starts with decent meat and at Hamburger Union they take their meat very seriously indeed. This is a burger resto that has a respected butcher as consultant! The meat comes from an organic and free-range herd in Oxfordshire and the meat is properly hung; the burgers are freshly made on the premises. The restaurant occupies two shop fronts: the one on the left is the takeaway part of the operation and also where you order, pay and then go on through to the very modernist dining room. You take a ticket with you and pop it into the metal stand on your table, so that the waitress can find you when your drinks are ready and your meal is cooked.

The menu is short. There are burgers (£3.95 or £6.75 for a double); cheeseburgers (£4.50 or £7.45); bacon cheeseburgers (£5.50 or £8.45) – some veggie options, and a notable fillet steak (£6.95 or £9.95). Adherents to the Dr Atkins fad can have their burger "protein style" which means that the kitchen replaces the bun with a couple of lettuce leaves. The straightforward burger is very good – juicy, it is cooked as requested and comes on an Italian-style bun with some red onion, mayo and lettuce. The chips (£2) are described on the menu as "proper chips, never frozen" and that is what they are. There are reasonably priced drinks (house red at under £12 a bottle) and a suitably sticky and unctuous malted milk (£3.25).

✱ "Cocktail shakes" (£3.95) – Baileys, Tia Maria or Crème de menthe.

Incognico

French £17–£70

117 Shaftesbury Ave, WC2 ☎020 7836 8866

Station Covent Garden/Tottenham Ct Rd **Open** Mon–Sat noon–3pm & 5.30m–midnight
Accepts All major credit cards

The Nico in question was Nico Ladenis, a respected chef who, sensibly enough, has retired to the south of France leaving his London restaurants in the capable hands of his daughter. This is a very French sort of place and when you are talking about a particular kind of retro French cooking, the French have few equals. The dining room is comfortable and done out in dark-brown tones, the only cavil being that some of the tables are packed in a bit tightly, so that you could whisper in a loved one's ear and still share the billing and cooing with your neighbours.

The cooking is very sound here. The menu is a long one and, while not actually being old-fashioned per se, there are enough old favourites to please the stickiest stick-in-the-mud. Starters such as stuffed artichoke heart Hollandaise (£8.50), six deep-fried oysters (£12.50), and terrine of foie gras (£16.50) all strike a chord. As do mains: ossobuco (£16.50), delightfully rich and served with Parmesan risotto; goujons of calf's liver

✳ Hurrah for the pichet! 50cl of potable red wine for £8.50.

(£16.50); skate with capers (£15.50); entrecôte Béarnaise (£16.50). Puddings (all £6.50) carry on the theme: pear tart; crème brûlée; lemon tart. And the cheese selection weighs in at a rather savage £10.50. Your wallet may also wince at the wine list. The set menu (available at lunch and 5.30–7pm) changes daily and is an outstandingly good deal. You get three courses with two choices per course and the dishes are appealing – spinach gnocchi and red-pepper sauce; shoulder of lamb with white beans; prune and Armagnac tart – £12.50 well spent.

COVENT GARDEN

The Ivy

British £30–£70

1 West St, WC2 ☎020 7836 4751

Station Leicester Square **Open** Daily noon–3pm (Sun 3.30pm) & 5.30pm–midnight
Accepts All major credit cards ⊛www.caprice-holdings.co.uk

The Ivy is a beautiful, Regency-style restaurant, built in 1928 by Mario Gallati. It has

been a theatreland and society favourite ever since and never more so than today. The staff, it is said, notice recessions only because they turn fewer people away. That's no joke: The Ivy is booked solid, and behaves like a club even if it isn't one. To get a booking it helps to proffer the name of at least a B-list celebrity. If your heart is set on a visit, try booking at off-peak times a couple of months ahead, or at very short notice, or ask for a table in the bar area. It's also less busy for weekend lunch – three courses for a bargain £19.50 plus £1.50 service charge, with valet parking thrown in.

And once you're in? Well, first off, whether you're famous or not, the staff are charming and unhurrying. Second, the food is pretty good. The menu is essentially a brasserie list of comfort food – nice dishes that combine simplicity with familiarity. You might start with spiced pumpkin and coconut soup (£5.75), or the risotto of wild mushrooms (£10.75 or £15.75), or the eggs Benedict (£6.25 or £12.50). Then there's deep-fried haddock (£15.25), grilled pork sausages (£10.75), and well-made versions of classic staples such as the Ivy hamburger with dill pickle (£9.50), shepherd's pie (£12.50), and salmon fishcakes (£11.75). Even the vegetable section is enlivened with homely delights like bubble and squeak (£2.75). For dessert you might turn to chocolate pudding soufflé (£7), rhubarb fool (£5.75), or finish with a savoury – herring roes on toast (£4.75).

✳ Eye up the art – works by: Howard Hodgkin, Peter Blake, Tom Phillips and Patrick Caulfield.

J. Sheekey

Fish £20–£70

26–32 St Martin's Court, WC2 ☎ 020 7240 2565
Station Leicester Square **Open** Mon–Sat noon–3pm (Sun 3.30pm) & 5.30pm–midnight
Accepts All major credit cards ⊛ www.caprice-holdings.co.uk

Sheekey's is one of a handful of restaurants which had shambled along since the war – World War I. Then, in the late 1990s, it was taken over by the team behind The Ivy and Le Caprice (see p.117 and p.266). After a good deal of redesign and refurbishment, it emerged from the builders' clutches as J. Sheekey, with much the same attitudes and style as its senior siblings, but still focused on fish. The restaurant may look new, but it certainly seems old, and its series of interconnecting dining rooms gives it an intimate feel. The cooking is accomplished, the service is first-rate, and the fish is fresh – a good combination.

The long menu presents a seductive blend of plain, old-fashioned, classic fish cuisine, such as lemon sole belle meunière (£17.75), with more modern dishes like whole roast gilthead bream with herbs and olive oil (£16.25). There are always handwritten dishes on the menu, "specials" which change on a weekly basis. To start with, there are oysters, crabs and shellfish, plus everything from jellied eels

(£6.25) and devilled whitebait (£6.50), to seared rare tuna (£9.50). Main courses, like pan-fried wing of skate with capers and brown butter (£14.75), or Cornish fish stew with celery heart and garlic mayonnaise (£19.75), are backed up by classics such as fillet of cod (£17.50) and Sheekey's fish pie (£9.75). Puddings range from spotted dick with butter and golden syrup (£5.25) to wild strawberry and champagne jelly with Jersey cream (£10.50). As well as smart wines there are plenty of options at the cheaper end of the list for sensible drinking.

※ Set menu bargains: the weekend lunch, £15.75 for two courses, £20 for three.

Joe Allen   North American £16–£40

13 Exeter St, WC2 ☎020 7836 0651

Station Covent Garden **Open** Mon–Fri noon–12.45am, Sat 11.30am–12.45am, Sun 11.30am–11.30pm **Accepts** All major credit cards except Diners ⓦ www.joeallen.co.uk

By some inexplicable alchemy, Joe Allen continues to be the Covent Garden eatery of choice for a wide swathe of the acting profession. It is a dark, resolutely untrendy place that dishes up American comfort food. If your heart is set on a Caesar salad, chilli con carne or eggs Benedict, this is a great place to come. Joe Allen has a splendid attitude to mealtimes: the à la carte runs all day, so you can have lunch when you will. There's a lunch and pre-theatre menu offering two courses for £14 and three for £16 (noon–4pm), plus a brunch menu on Saturday and Sunday – £17.50 for two courses and £19.50 for three, including a glass of champagne or a Bloody Mary.

The food is the kind of stuff that we are all comfortable with. Starters include smoked salmon with new potatoes, chives and sour cream (£7.50), buffalo mozzarella, tomato and basil salad (£6.50), and black-bean soup (£5). They are followed on the menu by a section described as "salads/eggs/sandwiches" in which you'll find some of Joe Allen's strengths: Caesar salad (£6 or £8); roast chicken salad (£9); and eggs Joe Allen (£9), a satisfying combination of poached eggs, potato skins, Hollandaise sauce and spinach. Main courses range from tuna with sesame crust and braised Chinese cabbage (£14), through barbecue spareribs with rice, wilted spinach, black-eyed peas and corn muffin (£13), to pan-fried calf's liver with mashed potato and grilled bacon (£14). And the desserts are serious – go for the brownie (£5.50), with hot fudge sauce as an extra (£2).

 There's a decent hamburger, but you have to be in the know to order one, as it is never on the menu.

Mela

152-158 Shaftesbury Ave, WC2 ☎020 7836 8635
Station Covent Garden **Open** Mon–Sat noon–11.30pm Sun noon–10.30pm
Accepts All major credit cards ⓦwww.melarestaurant.co.uk

Like its newer sibling – Chowki (p.312) – Mela is a restaurant dedicated to India's regional dishes. Mela may even have cracked the great lunch conundrum – Indian restaurateurs find it very difficult to persuade Londoners to eat curry for lunch. There's a "Paratha Pavilion" at lunchtime, which may sound a bit kitsch but lists a variety of delicious set lunches, from the insubstantial at £1.95, to the jolly good at £4.95. Stellar value in WC2. In 2003 the decor was tamed slightly: now it is marginally smarter and marginally less garish. Service is slick and friendly.

At lunch the set meals revolve around bread – which may be made from maize, sorghum, millet, whole-wheat flour, or chilli- and coriander-flavoured chickpea flour. The latter is particularly good. It may come with the dal or curry of the day for just £1.95! Or with a savoury stuffing at £2.95. There may be other breads, too, such as roomalis (large and thin, wholemeal handkerchief bread), puris (fried chapatis), uttapams (rice-flour pancakes) and naans. Dosas come in at £3.95. At these prices you can experiment. The main menu, which is available at lunch but comes into its own in the evening, makes a real attempt to offer genuine regional dishes. Starters range from gosht utthapams (£4.50) – rice pancakes with lamb; to lehsooni whitebait (£3.95). Then tandoor dishes, such as barrah beer kebab (£10.95), lead on to crab moilee (£14,95); or methi murg (£8.50) – a rich chicken dish. There is also an exemplary gosht rogan josh (£9.25). Good stuff.

✱ Cheap, West End and open throughout the afternoon – an unbeatable combo.

The Neal Street Restaurant

26 Neal Street, WC2 ☎020 7836 8368
Station Covent Garden **Open** Mon–Sat noon–2.30pm & 6–11pm
Accepts All major credit cards

Antonio Carluccio is the genial mushroom hunter who is behind the chain of Carluccio's Caffes (see p.151); the Neal Street was his first restaurant and is a much posher affair. This is upscale Italian but it still sticks to a belief in carefully sourced top-quality ingredients and minimal kitchen interference. When so many dishes reflect the proprietor's love of wild fungi and truffles this can make for pricey dining, but the recently introduced regional set menus offer some respite at £21 for two courses and £25 for three. The room is long and the big mirror at the far end makes it seem longer, the walls are (and have been for decades) lined with thumb sticks carved by the patron. A homely look in a serious restaurant.

The head chef is Andrea Cavaliere and the menu changes regularly. There are always specials and they command attention – start with tiny artichokes, deep fried (£7.50), or anything mushroomy. The pasta course is a delight: tortelli di granchio (£13.50), small parcels of crab in a saffron sauce; or tagliolini al tartufo nero (£14.50 or £20.50) – hand cut pasta with truffle sauce and shavings of black truffle. There is also a tempting array of fish dishes: perhaps the goulash of monkfish and skate with Triestine bread (£16.50) appeals? A dish of boneless oxtail braised in red wine and served with sweet and sour baby onions is top stuff – rich and satisfying. Puds are good – from the bitter chocolate, hazelnut and orange cake (£6), to the Campari and passion fruit sorbet (£6.50). The wine list offers a guide to Italy, and the coffee is exemplary.

✳ "Trifolata di funghi del giorno" (£10.50) – mixed sautéed mushrooms of the day.

Punjab

`Indian £16–£38`

80–82 Neal St, WC2 ☎020 7836 9787

Station Covent Garden **Open** Mon–Sat noon–3pm & 6–11.30pm, Sun noon–10.30pm
Accepts All major credit cards ⓦ www.punjab.co.uk

In 1951, Gurbachan Singh Maan moved his fledgling Indian restaurant from the City to new premises in Neal Street in Covent Garden, his plan being to take advantage of the trade from the nearby Indian High Commission. It was a strategy that has worked handsomely. Today, his grandson Sital Singh Maan runs what is the oldest North Indian restaurant in the U.K., though one which has always been at the forefront of new developments – in 1962 the Maan family brought over one of the first tandoor ovens to be seen in Britain. Despite these occasional forays into fashion, the cuisine at the Punjab has always been firmly rooted where it belongs – in the Punjab.

Punjabi cuisine offers some interesting, non-standard Indian dishes, so start by ordering from among the less familiar items on the menu. Kadu puri

(£2.60), for instance, a sweet and sharp mash of curried pumpkin served on a puri; or aloo tikka (£2.60), which are described as potato cutlets but arrive as small deep-fried moons on a sea of tangy sauce; or chicken chat (£2.90), which is diced chicken in rich sauce. To follow, try the acharri gosht (£8.40), or the acharri murgha (£8.30). The first is made with lamb, and the second with chicken. The meat is "pickled" in traditional Punjabi spices and, as a result, both meat and sauce have an agreeable edge of sharpness. Chicken karahi (£7.95) is good, too – rich and thick. The anari gosht (£8.30) combines lamb with pomegranate, while from the vegetable dishes, channa aloo (£4.70) offsets the nutty crunch of chickpeas with the solace of potatoes.

> ✳ Nameless but not tasteless! Benaam macchi tarkari (£8.70), a "nameless fish curry, speciality of chef".

Rules

Very British £32–£70

35 Maiden Lane, WC2 ☎ 020 7836 5314

Station Covent Garden **Open** Mon–Sat noon–11.30pm, Sun noon–10.30pm
Accepts All major credit cards Ⓦ www.rules.co.uk

Rules would be a living cliché but for one essential saving grace – all the fixtures, fittings and studied eccentricities that look as if they have been custom-made in some modern factory are real. Rules is the genuine article, a very English restaurant. Dickens, Betjeman, H.G. Wells, Thackeray, Graham Greene and King Edward VII are just a few of the celebs who have revelled in Rules. The proud boast here is, "We specialize in classic game cookery", and indeed they do, but thankfully the restaurant has become more of a bustling brasserie than the mausoleum it once was.

First of all you should note that Rules is open from noon till late, which is very handy when circumstances dictate a four o'clock lunch. Start with scrambled egg and smoked salmon (£8.95), or a Stilton and watercress soup (£5.95). Go on to game in season, or the occasional specials: maybe Belted Galloway beef or Tamworth suckling pig, sourced from Rules' own estate in the High Pennines. The steak-and-kidney pudding with mash (£15.95) is a banker, as is the roast rib of beef for two (£39.90) and the smoked Finnan haddock fishcake with spinach and poached egg (£15.95). Also noteworthy is the fillet of venison with wild mushrooms and herb mash (£20.95). Puddings, such as treacle sponge, or sticky toffee (all £6.95), are merciless. Why not go for the traditional blue Stilton cheese with celery and a glass of port (£12.95)? Should you face entertaining out-of-town relatives, or foreign visitors in search of something old and English, Rules is a good place to indulge in nostalgia.

> ✳ The no smoking rule applies everywhere but the private rooms.

Crouch End & Wood Green

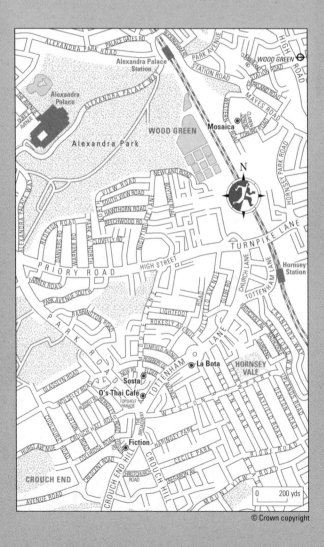

© Crown copyright

La Bota

Spanish/Tapas £12–£30

31 Broadway Parade, Tottenham Lane, N8 ☎ 020 8340 3082
Station Finsbury Park/Turnpike Lane **Open** Mon–Thurs noon–2.30pm & 6–11pm, Fri
noon–2.30pm & 6–11.30pm, Sat noon–3pm & 6–11.30pm, Sun noon–11pm
Accepts All major credit cards except AmEx or Diners

This bustling tapas bar and restaurant enjoys a healthy evening trade, and with good reason. It's a Galician (northwest Spanish) place, and that's always a plus sign, particularly for seafood. Your first decision is a crucial one: do you go all out for tapas (there are thirty on the menu, plus seventeen vegetarian ones, plus another eighteen or so daily specials chalked on a blackboard)? Or do you choose one of the main courses – Spanish omelette, paellas, steaks, chicken, fish and so forth? Perhaps the best option is to play to La Bota's strengths and order a few tapas, then a few more, until you have subdued your appetite and there's no longer a decision to make. In the meantime enjoy the air conditioning – and the house wine at a very reasonable £8.80.

Start with simple things. Boquerones en vinagre (£3.50) brings a plate of broad white anchovies with a pleasant vinegar tang. Jamón serrano (£4.30) is thinly sliced, ruby-red and strongly flavoured – perfect with the basket of warm French bread that is on every table. Then move on to hot tapas: mejillones pescador (£3.80) is a good-sized plate of mussels in a tomato and garlic sauce; chistorra a la sidra (£3.65), a mild sausage cooked in cider; riñones al Jerez (£3.50), a portion of kidneys in a sherry sauce, rich and good. Alas de pollo barbacoa (£3.50) is an Iberian take on chicken wings. Then there's arroz al campo (£2) – rice cooked with saffron and vegetables; chicken riojana (£3.50); and patatas bravas (£2.50), the tasty dish of potatoes in a mildly spicy tomato sauce. Just keep them coming …

✸ If you don't mind looking a squid in the eye, opt for chipirones a la plancha (£3.95) – whole baby squidlets fresh grilled.

Fiction

Vegetarian £20–£40

60 Crouch End Hill, N8 ☎ 020 8340 3403
Station Finsbury Park/Highgate **Open** Wed–Sat 6–10.30pm, Sun 6.30–10.30pm
Accepts Mastercard & Visa

Fiction is strictly vegetarian, although not in the missionary hair-shirt and holier-than-thou style. Rather, the idea is to rediscover the use of indigenous herbs, and to cook, with plenty of wine, dishes that were popular in the days when people ate a lot less meat than they do now. All dishes and wines are marked as vegetarian, vegan and organic, where relevant.

Fiction's menu changes with the seasons. Starters will include a soup, and often it is an original one, such as cumin-spiced roast pumpkin soup (£3.95). Or chunky cheese, sweetcorn and coriander fritters served with salad garnish and a delicious sweet chilli sauce (£4.45) – a bit like Thai crab cakes without the crab. The signature main courses are wood-roasted butternut squash (£10.45) and "The Good Gamekeeper's Pie" (£10.45). The former is described fulsomely as "filled with lemon-garlic button mushrooms"; the latter as "mock duck', chestnuts, leek, shitake mushrooms, and carrots, prepared in an old English marinade of red wines, and baked in a puff pastry pie". Both are very nicely flavoured. There's also a "Fictional" take on Thai red curry (£9.25) – sweet potato, cauliflower, galangal, lemongrass and roast aubergines. Side dishes include roast garlic mash with olive oil (£2.70) and the mini power plate (£3.95) – salad of mixed leaves and freshly sprouted organic legumes and alfalfa. The key pudding is triple chocolate terrine with fresh berry coulis (£3.95), although the agreeably named "tart of darkness" runs it close – a filo pastry case filled with strawberries fried in Balsamic vinegar (£4.35).

✱ You'll find Fiction opposite a hairdresser called Pulp!

Mosaica

Modern British £10–£40

Building C, The Chocolate Factory, Clarendon Rd, N22 &. ☎ 020 8889 2400
Station BR Wood Green **Open** Tues–Fri noon–2pm & 7–10pm, Sat 7–10pm,
Sun noon–3pm **Accepts** All major credit cards

Up in the high pastures of Wood Green there is a straggle of large, run-down buildings called The Chocolate Factory that has been colonized by artists, potters, designers and anyone arty needing cheap, no-frills space. You'll find Mosaica hidden at the heart of Building C, and it is an amazing place – spacious, stylish and comfortable. There is a long bar made up of cinder blocks, topped with a twenty-foot sheet of glass. There's a huge open kitchen. And the two chef-proprietors, John Mountain and David Orlowski, have got the atmosphere dead right – stylish but informal, neighbourhood but sharp. The food is a complete surprise. It's terrific.

The menu at Mosaica is short and changes daily – at lunch the blackboard includes a cheap pasta dish for starving artists. In the evening, starters might include charred asparagus with fried duck egg and Parmesan (£7.25); grilled squid with grilled lime (£8.50); a rabbit

terrine with olives (£7.50); and tuna carpaccio with spring onion and lemongrass dressing (£8.25). Mains range from sea bass fillet with warm potato salad and baby aubergines (£14.95); to grilled rib-eye steak with garlic mash and fine beans (£15.50) – the rib-eye sliced and meltingly tender, the mash rich and not over-gluey.

Or perhaps there's a boneless skate with pancetta and braised endive (£14.95) and an epic dish such as veal T-bone with wild mushroom port wine jus (£15.95). The wine list is short and the service more enthusiastic than polished. But the food is great and the prices forgiving.

✻ Notable puds: chocolate and amaretti biscuit mousse (£6).

O's Thai Café

Thai £12–£30

10 Topsfield Parade, N8 ☎020 8348 6898

Station Finsbury Park **Open** Mon 6.30–11pm, Tues–Sat noon–3pm & 6.30–11pm, Sun noon–10.30pm **Accepts** Mastercard & Visa ⊛www.oscafesandbars.co.uk

O's Thai Café is young, happy and fresh – just like O himself. With his economics, advertising and fashion-design background, and a staff who seem to be having fun, O brings a youthful zip to Thai cuisine. His café is fast and noisy, and the music is played at high volume. But that's not to say the food is anything less than excellent, and it's very good value too. Order from the comprehensive and well explained menu or from the blackboard of specials, which runs down an entire wall.

Of the many starters you can do no better than order the special (£8.95 for two), which gives you a taster of almost everything. Satays are tasty, prawn toasts and spring rolls are as crisp as they should be, and paper-wrapped thin dumplings really do melt in the mouth. Tom ka chicken soup (£3.95)

is hot and sharp, with lime leaf and lemongrass. Main courses include Thai red and green curries – the gaeng kiew wan, a spicy, soupy green curry of chicken and coconut cream (£5.95), is pungently moreish – as well as an interesting selection of specials such as yamneau, aka weeping tiger (£9.50), sliced, spiced, grilled steak served on salad with a pungent Thai dressing. If you like noodles, there are a selection of pad dishes all at £6.50 – stir-fries with a host of combinations of vegetables, soy sauce, peanuts, spiciness, chicken, beef, pork, king prawn or bean curd. Puddings may include khow tom mud – banana with sticky rice wrapped in banana leaf (£1.95), or Thai ice cream (£2.50). There's a wide and varied wine list, with Budweiser, Budvar, Gambrinus and Leffe beers on draught.

✻ There's a discount if you eat early and vacate your table by 8.30pm.

Sosta

14 Middle Lane, N8 ☎ 020 8340 1303

Station Highgate/Finsbury Park **Open** Mon–Fri 7–10.45pm, Sat noon–2.30pm & 7–10.30pm, Sun noon–3pm & 7–10.15pm **Accepts** All major credit cards

During the 1970s, Silvano Sacchi was at the helm of two of London's more fashionable eateries – the Barracuda (a smart Italian fish restaurant in Baker Street) and San Martino (an Italian tratt in St Martin's Lane). Having sold out to a plc, Sacchi retired to Italy with his money and memories. Then a few years ago he dived back into the maelstrom of the London restaurant scene and opened Sosta – it seems to have been busy from day one.

The antipasti range from insalata tricolore (£4.75), a mozzarella, avocado and tomato salad; through carpaccio di spada (£5.95) – fresh swordfish; to tomato bruschetta (£3.50). Onwards to "primi", where you'll find pasta e fagioli alla Veneto (£3.95), a thick pasta and borlotti bean soup, and pasta

dishes such as gnocchi all'aragosta – in lobster sauce (£8.95); papardelle al ragu (£5.65); and tagliolini alla rusticana (£4.95). Pasta dishes cost an extra £2 if taken as a main course. "Secondi" offers five fish and five meat dishes. Orata alla plancia (£10.95) is grilled sea bream. Then there's piccata di vitello al tartufo nero (£14.95), escalopes of veal with black truffle; or tagliata di Angus (£11.95) – fillet steak. Puds are sound (all £3.35): semi-freddo; panna cotto; tiramisù. The wine list has some trad Italian bottles that appeal greatly. At Sosta the service is slick and the tables are close together. The huge pepper mill of the 1970s may have been replaced by a natty modernist Parmesan grater but everyone is attentive in what now seems like an old-fashioned way.

✱ The menu "degustazione" – three courses £11.95 (Tues to Fri nights, & Sat lunch).

Docklands

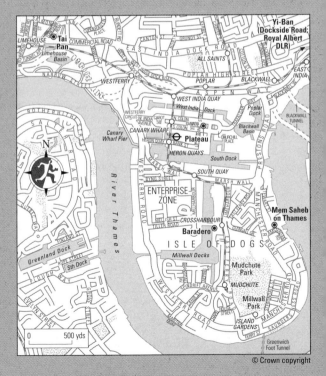

© Crown copyright

Baradero

5 Turnberry Quay, off Pepper St, E14 &. ☎ 020 7537 1666
Station DLR Crossharbour **Open** Mon–Fri noon–11pm, Sat 6–10.45pm
Accepts All major credit cards

Baradero is modern, light, tiled and airy. And, as far as the view of Millwall dock and proximity to the London Arena will permit, you could almost think yourself in Spain. Essentially a tapas bar, it offers main courses too, and both are of restaurant quality. Take a seat at the bar or at one of the well spaced tables, order yourself a bottle of Estrella beer or a glass of Fino sherry, and set about the tapas.

Start with an order of pan con aioli (95p) – good bread with a pot of fearsome but seductive garlic mayonnaise. Or pan con tomate (£1.65) – Catalan-style toast drizzled with olive oil and rubbed with garlic and tomato. Add some boquerones (£3.95) – classic white anchovies, sharp with vinegar and garnished with raw garlic slices; and jamón Serrano (£5.95), a large portion of dark, richly flavoured, dry-cured ham. Then follow up with hot tapas such as croquetas de pollo (£4.25). Whoever would have thought that croquettes could taste so good? Sardinas fritas (£4.50), fresh sardines; or pulpo a la Gallega (£5.50), octopus cooked and seasoned Galician style. Or maybe gambas pil pil (£5.50) – prawns with garlic and a belt of chilli heat. As well as adding new tapas the main courses change each week but feature dishes such as pato con castanes (£12.50), duck breast with port and chestnuts; salmon a la parillada (£10.95), grilled salmon; or chulettas de codero (£12.75), grilled lamb chops with roast vegetables. To keep regulars from getting bored there is live Spanish/Latin music on Friday and Saturday nights 9–11pm.

✳ Enjoy the Zumm – a balletic automatic juicer that seems to wave the whole oranges about before squashing them.

Mem Saheb on Thames

65–67 Amsterdam Rd, E14 ☎ 020 7538 3008
Station DLR Crossharbour **Open** Mon–Fri noon–2.30pm & 6–11.30pm,
Sat & Sun 6–11.30pm **Accepts** All major credit cards ⊛ www.memsahib.com

Mem Saheb on Thames has certainly got an evocative address. "Amsterdam Road" conjures up pictures of old-fashioned docks and wharves, rolling fog banks and cheery East Enders. In practice, this bit of Docklands is a lot like Milton Keynes. The redeeming factor is the river. As the Thames sweeps round in a majestic arc, the restaurant has a superb view across the water to the Millennium folly. Mem Saheb is certainly "on-Thames". As a result there's a good deal of squabbling for the middle table in the non-smoking section (pole position as far as the view is concerned). Ultimately, however, the lucky winner must balance the grandstand view of the Millennium folly with the piped-music speaker that hovers directly above the table.

Start by sharing a tandoori khazana (£8.95), which is a platter of mixed kebabs from the tandoor, including good chicken tikka. Or perhaps some salmon samosas (£3.25)? Also tasty is the kabuli salad (£2.95), a winning combination of chickpeas and hard-boiled egg in a sharp tamarind dressing. Of the main courses, macher jhul (£8.95) is tilapia cooked Bengali-style with aubergine and potato. Rajasthani khargosh (£9.95) is an unusual dish pairing rabbit with a mild sauce and served with garlicky spinach. Konju papas (£7.95) is a prawn curry in the South Indian style – tamarind, mustard seeds and coconut. The breads and vegetable dishes are good, particularly the aloo chana (£4.50) – a simple dish of potatoes and chickpeas. The kitchen is to be commended for avoiding artificial additives and colourings.

> ✳ "Kitchen Curry" (£7.95) – "Each day our chefs cook a different staff curry for themselves. Usually fairly hot, sometimes very hot. Only available from 7pm."

Plateau

Modern British £30–£90

Canada Place, Canary Wharf, E14 ♿ ☏ 020 7715 7100
Station Canary Wharf **Open** Mon–Fri noon–3pm & 6.30–10.30pm, Sat 6–11pm
Accepts All major credit cards ⓦ www.conran.com

Sir Terence Conran's venture into Canary Wharf opened in 2003 and is called Plateau, it juts out from the fourth floor of a giant glass office block and looks out over a square that is surrounded by even larger towers. Visit at night, the view is amazing – spooky in a slightly Bladerunner sort of way, but incredible. Because the other offices tower above you there is no feeling of vertigo until you catch sight of a tiny bus moving round the square below. A couple of upscale operations have had a hard time trying to bring "fine dining" to Canary Wharf, but Plateau looks very assured.

The menu is of stalwart construction. You can have seared foie gras with fig, date and lime chutney (£11); or butternut squash and marscapone ravioli (£7.50); or seared scallops, celery, cranberry sauce (£13.75). Main courses tick a few comfortable boxes: Dover sole with herb crust (£27); braised beef cheeks, purple mash potato (£18.50). Wild seabass comes with crushed potato and pistachio (£20); Aligot (£4.25) translates as pretty desirable mashed potato. The service is sound and unruffled and the wine list is refreshingly egalitarian (in such a lofty and aspirational establishment it's hard not to feel nervous, but before prices wing off into the stratosphere, there is plenty of good drinking at under £25 a bottle and some at under £20). Puds (all £6.50) are sound: chocolate fondant or tart Tatin.

At lunch Plateau is odds on to do good business in a directors, dining room sort of way, but in the evening it is worth a visit purely to gaze out of the window.

> The "bar & grill" shares the view and offers a simpler menu – prix fixe dinner – two courses £16.50.

Tai Pan

Chinese £15–£35

665 Commercial Rd, E14 ☎020 7791 0118

Station DLR Limehouse **Open** Mon–Thurs & Sun noon–11.15pm, Sat 6–11.45pm
Accepts All major credit cards

As Sherlock Holmes fans will know, Limehouse was London's first Chinatown, complete with murky opium dens. Nowadays all it has to boast about is the Tai Pan. This restaurant is very much a family affair – the ebullient Winnie Wan is front of house, running the light, bright dining room, while Mr Tsen commands the kitchen. He organizes a constant stream of well-cooked, mainly Cantonese dishes, and slaves over the intricately carved vegetables, which lift the presentation.

After the complimentary prawn cracker and seriously delicious hot-pickled shredded cabbage, start with deep-fried crispy squid with Szechuan peppercorn salt (£6.90), or fried Peking dumplings with a vinegar dipping sauce (£4.30) – both are excellent. Or try one of the sparerib dishes (£5.40), or the soft-shell crabs (£4.80 each). Alternatively, go for the nicely done, crispy, fragrant aromatic duck with pancakes and the accoutrements (£15.50 for a half). Otherwise, relax and order the Imperial mixed hors d'oeuvres (£8.80 per person, for a minimum of two), which offers a sampler of ribs, spring rolls, seaweed, and prawn and sesame toast, with a carrot sculpture as centrepiece. When ordering main dishes, old favourites such as deep-fried shredded beef with chilli (£5.80), and fried chicken in lemon sauce (£5.30), are just as you'd expect. Fried seasonal greens in oyster sauce (£4.30) is made with choi sum, and is delicious, while the fried vermicelli Singapore-style (£5.10) will suit anyone who prefers their Singapore noodle pepped up with curry powder rather than fresh chillies.

> For a real bargain pay £13.50 and you can eat as much as you like off the menu (minimum two people).

Yi-Ban

Chinese/Dim Sum £10–£30

London Regatta Centre, Royal Albert Dock, E16 ♿ ☎020 7473 6699

Station DLR Royal Albert **Open** Mon–Sat noon–11pm, Sun noon–10.30pm
Accepts All major credit cards except Diners ⊛www.yi-ban.co.uk

If your mission was to find a rather good Chinese restaurant it's unlikely that your first thought would be to go to a barren corner of Docklands and then make your way upstairs to a rowing club bar. Persevere – at one end of the room you'll find Yi-Ban, complete with lots of tables, a license to conduct weddings and friendly staff. But beware this is not an easy place to find – best to navigate yourself to the North West corner of the Albert Dock and start from there. If you turn up at lunch you'll find the room full of happy Chinese customers which is somehow very reassuring.

The room is comfortable in a modernist sort of way, so settle yourself at a large round table. The dim sum are good and cheap: snow pea dumplings

(£2.20) are prawny, green herby numbers; mini glutinous rice rolls are mini and suitably glutinous (£3); the crystal prawn dumplings (£2.20) are good, as are the prawn fun guo (£2.20). The fried options are dry and crisp: sweet and sour wan tun (£2); deep-fried seafood dumplings (£2.50); Vietnamese sugar cane prawns (£2.50). Strangely there are no steamed cheung fun on the menu here but you can indulge any whims for exotica by ordering chicken claws Thai style (£3.50). The lengthy main menu is "standard Chinese sophisticated": steamed scallops (up to £3.50 each depending on how large); baked lobster (the dreaded "seasonal price"); honey spareribs (£5); lemon chicken (£5.90). This is a very pleasant restaurant with a terrific view, smiling helpful staff, and bargain dim sum for lunch – not bad for a converted rowing club bar.

✱ Plane spotters will enjoy the unrivalled view of London City Airport.

Further choices

1802
Modern British

1 West India Quay, Hertsmere Rd, E14
☎0870 444 3886

This is the restaurant attached to the Museum of Docklands, a straightforward menu driven by the seasons.

The Grapes
Gastropub/Fish

76 Narrow St, E14
☎020 7987 4396

Old trad pub marooned in modern Docklands. Allegedly a favourite of Charles Dickens. Now famous for fish and shellfish. Top fish and chips.

Ealing &
Acton

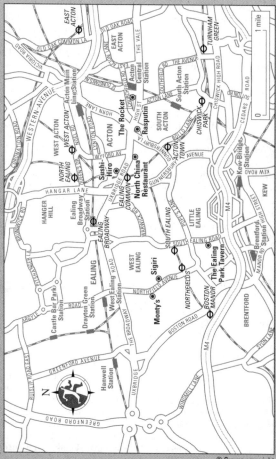

© Crown copyright

The Ealing Park Tavern

Modern British/Gastropub £15–£40

222 South Ealing Rd, W5 ☎ 020 8758 1879

Station South Ealing **Open** Mon 6–10.30pm, Tues–Sat noon–3pm & 6–10.30pm, Sun noon–4pm & 6–10.30pm **Accepts** All major credit cards except Diners

Not so long ago this place was transformed from a lager and football hovel into a tidy pub and eatery, at which time it reverted to its original name – the Ealing Park Tavern. The owners are the people behind another fine gastropub, St John's (see p.197), so it is no surprise that they have made a decent fist of it. It is a handsome place and, like its North London sibling, is founded on the simple premise that hospitality is important. The bar has two or three decent real ales and the wine list is short but gives a fair choice around the £15-a-bottle mark, topping out at £35. The dining room has a tall counter separating it from an open kitchen and the menu is chalked up on a blackboard. What makes the Park Tavern so popular is the food.

The menu is a short one but it is thoughtfully written, changes daily and there is something for everybody. Starters may include a spiced parsnip soup (£4.50); spaghetti vongole (£6); fishcakes with chive crème fraiche (£5.50); or a hearty country terrine (£5.25) – all sound stuff. Main courses are well presented, substantial and seem pretty good value. There might be fish pie (£12); braised lamb shank with a tomato and white bean stew (£11); or slow-roast Gloucester Old Spot pork belly with apple sauce (£11.75). Fish dishes tend to be a good option: how does a whole lemon sole with new potatoes and Hollandaise sauce (£11.50) sound? Puds are comforting and comfortable – orange crème brûlée; treacle tart with clotted cream; chocolate brownie with vanilla ice cream – (all £4.50).

❋ There's a new tapas bar, open daily 5–10pm.

Monty's

Indian £12–£24

54 Northfield Ave, W13 ♿ ☎ 020 8567 6281

Station Northfields **Open** Daily noon–2.30pm & 6–11.30pm

Accepts All major credit cards Ⓦ www.montys.uk.com

Once upon a time, the now-defunct Ealing Tandoori held West London curry lovers in thrall – it was the undisputed first choice. Then, in the late 1970s, the three main chefs left to open their own place, which they called Monty's, on South Ealing Road. As business

boomed, two of the chefs moved on to set up independently. But as all three co-owned the name "Monty's", they all use it, and that is why there are now three different Monty's, all fiercely independent but each with the same name and logo. Unlike many small

Indian restaurants, these are "chef-led", which is why the cooking is classy, the portions are good and prices are fair. This is a restaurant that has a fine grasp of what its customers want.

The trad tandoori dishes are fine, like the tandoori chicken (£5.10 for two pieces). Or there is hasina (£6.95), lamb marinated in yoghurt and served on an iron plate as a sizzler. Breads are delicious – pick between nan (£1.75) and Peshwari nan (£2.50). But the kitchen really gets to shine with simple curry dishes like methi gosht (£7.50) – tender lamb (and plenty of it) in a delicious sauce rich with fenugreek; chicken jalfriji (£7.50); or the very rich moglai chicken (£6.95). Vegetable dishes are also good – both brinjal bhaji (£3.90) and sag panir (£3.90) are delicious. Monty's is one of very few local curry houses to serve perfectly cooked, genuine basmati rice. So the plain boiled rice (£2.10) – nutty, almost smoky, with grains perfectly separate – is worth tasting on its own. Monty's is a good example of the perfect neighbourhood curry house.

✳ Check out the Gurkhali dal (£4.35) – very rich and garlicky.

North China Restaurant

Chinese £15–£30

305 Uxbridge Rd, W3 ☏ 020 8992 9183

Station Ealing Common **Open** Mon–Thurs & Sun noon–2.30pm & 6–11.30pm, Fri & Sat noon–2.30pm & 6pm–midnight **Accepts** All major credit cards ✇ www.northchina.co.uk

The special Peking duck, which always used to require 24 hours' advance notice, is now so popular that the restaurant cooks a few ducks every day regardless. So you don't always have to pre-order. But then you do, because it is so popular that they cannot guarantee that you'll get one unless you order it. The North China has a 24-carat local reputation; it is the kind of place people refer to as "being as good as Chinatown", which in this case is spot-on, and the star turn on the menu doesn't disappoint.

Unlike most other – upstart, deep-fried – crispy ducks, the Peking duck here comes as three separate courses. First there is the skin and breast meat, served with pancakes, shreds of cucumber and spring onion, and hoisin sauce. Then a fresh stir-fry of the duck meat with beansprouts, and finally the meal ends with a giant tureen of rich duck soup with lumps of the carcass to pick at. It is awesome. And the price, £42, is very reasonable, working out at £3.50 per person, per course (based on four people sharing). If you're dull and just want the duck with pancakes, the price drops to £32. So what goes well with duck? At the North China familiar dishes are well cooked and well presented. You might start with barbecued pork spareribs (£4.80), or the lettuce wraps (£3.30 per person, minimum two people), made with prawn and chicken. For a supplementary main course, prawns in chilli sauce (£7.25), although not very chilli, is teamed with fresh water chestnuts and tastes very good.

Singapore fried noodles (£4.20) is powered by curry powder rather than fresh chilli, but fills a gap.

* This place is also good for lobster when available; ginger and onion baked lobster (£22.50).

Rasputin

Eastern European £15–£35

265 High St, Acton, W3 ☎ 020 8993 5802
Station Acton Town **Open** Daily 6–11.30pm **Accepts** Mastercard & Visa

You'll find the Rasputin up at the Ealing end of Acton High Street. This restaurant used to be a dark cave-like sort of room, but after a refurb it is now, in the words of the proprietors, "modern". The menu has moved gently away from what was hitherto an all-Russian affair. All this must be noted before you have made any inroads into the 25 different vodkas, which come both as single shots and – take care here – "by the carafe".

With the menu comes a plate of cucumber, cabbage, green tomatoes and peppers, all markedly salty and with a good vinegary tang. For a starter, try pierogi – rich little dumplings that come stuffed with a choice of potato and cheese, meat, or sauerkraut and mushrooms (all £3.95). The blinis – small buckwheat pancakes – are also good; with smoked trout (£5.50) or, if you enjoy finding a bargain, with Sevruga caviar (£24.95). The Moscovite fish platter (£8.95) is also delicious. At Rasputin they are constantly tinkering with the menu and there usually seem to be several versions extant at once. Hold out for the cabbage parcels (£9.95), which is a simple but satisfying dish of cabbage leaves stuffed with meat and rice, or chicken Kiev made with tarragon butter (£9.90). Fish fans may want to try the salmon fillets in dill sauce (£10.95). Desserts are rather staid – crème brûlée (£3.50) or pancakes filled with a choice of chocolate, walnuts or fruit preserve (£3.50). The Russian tea, served in a glass and holder, is interesting (£2.50): made with tea, lemon and a splash of vodka, it comes with a small bowl of honey alongside for sweetening.

* Serious trenchers only: game mixed grill with cranberry sauce (£14.95).

The Rocket

Italian/Gastropub £7–£45

11–13 Churchfield Rd, W3 ☎ 020 8993 6123

Station BR Acton Central **Open** Mon 7–10.15pm, Tues–Sun 12.30–3.30pm &
7–10.15pm **Accepts** All major credit cards except AmEx & Diners

The Rocket was once a scuzzy bikers' pub where pool tables were the only kind of tables that mattered – fast forward a couple of years to May 2003 when the pub was officially reborn. There is a spacious and comfortable bar to the front, and a spacious terrace for drinking outside in front of it. The refurb has left this Victorian boozer looking pretty good with light-coloured wood floors and deep red walls. The dining room is to the rear and the food is full on and very good. The chefs come from Italy and the menu follows the convention of listing starters, then pasta and risotti, finally mains and puds.

The menu changes monthly and may include starters such as a confit duck leg terrine with winter vegetables (£5.20). Good as this is, it is almost eclipsed by "frico" (£5.95), a fry-up of new potatoes, Asiago cheese and mushrooms served under a pile of rocket. Crispy, melty, rich, self-indulgent – a gloriously simple plateful. There's a good tempered risotto made with porcini and truffle oil (£6 or £10), scattered through with small chunks of potato to soak up the flavours. Pasta dishes are good here. The mains range widely – grilled marlin with sautéed cima di rapa (£13.50); chicken breast stuffed with Montasio cheese and served with a leek and mushroom risotto (£11.95); grilled veal chop with noisette potatoes (£13.95). The wine list has some decent bottles at sensible prices – look for the vibrant Madiran at £22.50. The dessert menu rounds up the usual suspects (all £4.50), from Amaretto tiramisù to ice creams and sorbets.

✳ Lunch specials, choice of three dishes – £6 including a beer.

EALING & ACTON

Sigiri

Sri Lankan £10–£25

161 Northfields Ave, W13 ☎ 020 8579 8000

Station Northfields **Open** Mon–Sat 6.30–11pm
Accepts All major credit cards except AmEx & Diners

On Northfields Avenue there are two or three curry houses, a couple of Chinese restaurants, various cafes, a Thai cooking school and shop, a mixed bag of takeaways and Sigiri – a Sri Lankan restaurant. Sigiri does itself no favours – a ponderous brick façade surrounds the large front window which has that dark, almost one-way glass. From the inside looking out all is light and bright, but from the outside it just looks gloomy. Persevere, as the cooking here is very sound and Sri Lankan food is well worth trying, as it has some interesting flavours and textures.

The star turn among the starters is the appa (or hopper) – these are round, bowl-shaped, rice flour pancakes. They are very delicious and the sides are crisp while the bottom tends to a glorious gooey sogginess. You can have them plain (£1.80), or with an egg cooked in the bottom (£2), or with a kind of coconut milk sludge (£2). Hoppers go well with "sambols" – which are cousins to chutney. They vary from a kind of onion jam (£2), to seeni sambol (£4) which you can have with a sprinkling of small dried fish (better than it sounds) and coconut chutney (£2) – fresh grated coconut with slivers of green chilli. Also good are the cutlets (£3), fishcakes without much fish; and the masala wade (£3) – a crisp and crunchy patty made from various lentils and then deep fried. For main courses there's devilled squid (£6); beef in black pepper (£6), a dry dish with plenty of flavour; or fish seer (£5.50) – fillets of implausibly meaty fish swim in an ocean of light coconut soup. The vegetable dishes are worth a look – mallum (£3.75).

✳ Only a sweet-toothed adventurer would drink the Lion stout.

Sushi-Hiro

Japanese £15–£30

1 Station Parade, Uxbridge Rd W5 ☎ 020 8896 3175
Station Ealing Common **Open** Tues–Sun 11am–1.30pm & 4.30–9pm **Accepts** Cash only

Sushi-Hiro is a very self-effacing sort of restaurant. The sign outside says "Sushi-Hiro, Japanese Gourmet Foods". When you push open the door you find that half the room is given over to a waiting area for takeaway customers, there's a sushi counter with stools and a handful of tables and that's about it. The ceiling is high, the lighting bright, and all is spotlessly clean. It can be bit intimidating, but take heart: all the experts agree that Sushi-Hiro serves some of the best sushi in London.

The menu offers sushi in various guises. You are given a miniature clipboard with a small form to fill in your order and that's when it all gets tricky, as there are fifty or so boxes to tick. The best strategy is to start with the chef's selection of superior nigiri (£12), which brings ten pieces of sushi – tuna, salmon, herring roe, turbot, bass, red clam, scallop, salmon roe, red bream and sweet shrimp. Try them all and then repeat the ones you like the most. The sushi here is very good: the rice is soft and almost warm, the balance between the amount of rice and amount of topping is just about perfect, and the fish is squeakily fresh and very delicious. Or try a piece of very rich eel (£1.80); or mackerel (90p) – a revelation (light and not oily at all). Or go for pickled plum roll (£2.20 for four), made with rice, pickled plum and shiso leaves, which have an addictive flavour. Or try the salty and sticky salmon roe (£1.50). Then round things off with a small bowl of rather splendid miso soup (£1), which comes with a couple of little clams lurking in the depths.

✳ Beware of the "Japanese" opening times, which are "early" by European standards.

Earl's Court

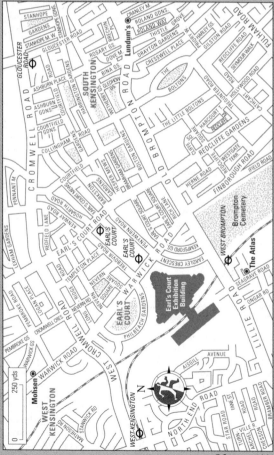

© Crown copyright

The Atlas

Modern British/Gastropub £15–£30

16 Seagrave Rd, SW6 ☎020 7385 9129

Station West Brompton **Open** Mon–Sat 12.30–3pm & 7–10.30pm, Sun 12.30–3pm & 7–10pm **Accepts** Mastercard, Switch & Visa ✆www.theatlaspub.co.uk

The Atlas is part of the great gastropub revolution. This was the first gastropub set up by brothers Richard and George Manners and it works well; so well in fact that by 2004 they had added several more. George is IC the cheffing side: he trained at gastropub headquarters – The Eagle in Farringdon (see p.106). The flavours come mainly from Italy with the occasional North African and Spanish diversion, plenty of upfront flavours, and an identical tone is adopted in all the pubs.

The menus are seasonal, so starters may include asparagus and leek soup with olive oil and shaved Parmesan (£4), and a serious antipasti plate – goat's cheese frittata, pea purée crostini, roast ox tongue with onion marmelade (£7). There are a couple of mid-way dishes that could either be starter or main such as conchiglie with slow-roast vine tomatoes (£5.50 or £7.50). Main courses range from grilled Tuscan sausages, with fennel and black pepper, and baked polenta (£9); through salt-roast loin of pork with thyme and honey (£10.50); to "Caldeirada", a Portuguese seafood stew served with mint and lemon rice (£13). The afters selection is short and to the point – a decent chocolate cake (£4) vies with "Montgomery's cheddar and Gorgonzola" served with pear and grilled bread (£5). The wine selection is also chalked up, and there are some unusual offerings served by the glass, which makes The Atlas a good venue for wine lovers in search of a bit of impromptu tasting. The Atlas is busy, noisy, friendly and young, and the food is good into the bargain. You're likely to end up sharing a table, so get there early.

✳ "Donald's chocolate and almond cake with cream (£4)" is so good that it's found in every pub of the chain.

Lundum's

Danish £15–£60

119 Old Brompton Rd, SW7 ♿ ☎020 7373 7774

Station Gloucester Rd/South Kensington **Open** Mon–Sat noon–11pm, Sun noon–4pm (brunch) **Accepts** All major credit cards

This is a genuine family restaurant – four Lundums work in the business. There's nothing particularly Danish about the room, which is pleasantly light and airy with huge mirrors and a skylight. Late in 2003 the Lundums took over the shop next door and added a few more tables and a bar. The staff proudly produce interesting (and delicious) dill-flavoured aquavit, which they import specially, along with Danish hams, cheeses and all manner of other delicacies. The food is elegantly presented, competently handled and ... Danish. At lunchtime it's trad Danish; in the evening, modern Danish. You cannot help but be swept along by the tidal wave of commitment and charm.

At dinner (£17.25 for two courses, £21.50 for three) the menu, which changes seasonally, reads like a lot of other menus – smoked salmon gravadlax, roast lamb, pan-fried cod. Best, then, to visit at lunch (£12.50 for two courses, £15.50 for three), when there are more Danish dishes on offer. Go à la carte and try the shoal of herrings (£4.50 or £6.25) – simply marinated, or spicy, or lightly curried, or sour with dill. As well as classic open sandwiches (£3.75–£7.75) you can also choose a smorrebrod m/lunt (£6.75–£7.75) of fiskefrikadeller (fish meatballs), or frikadeller (meat meatballs). There are also platters: the Danish (£15.75) comprises herrings, meatballs, plaice and salad; or there's an all-fish platter (£16.75). Or try the Medisterpolse (£10.25) – Danish sausage with red cabbage. Desserts are indulgent and the aquavit deadly.

✱ "Det kolde bord" – trad Danish Sunday brunch buffet – lots to eat; £19.50; booking imperative.

Mohsen

Iranian £8–£25

152 Warwick Rd, W14 ☎ 020 7602 9888

Station Earls Court **Open** Daily noon–midnight **Accepts** Cash or cheques only

Just suppose that you are visiting Homebase on the Warwick Road. As the traffic thunders past, spare a thought for the people who still live here. For, indeed, across the road you will see signs of habitation: two pubs – one a Young's house, the other selling Fuller's beer, and between them Mohsen, a small, busy Persian restaurant. For somewhere in such an obscure location Mohsen tends to be gratifyingly busy. There is nothing better than a loyal core of knowledgeable Middle Eastern customers to keep up standards in a Middle Eastern restaurant.

In the window is the oven, where the bread man works to keep everyone supplied with fresh-from-the-oven sheets of bread. The bread is terrific and the waiters conspire to see that it arrives in relays and never has a chance to get cold. The starters list is largely made up of things to go with the bread. You must have sabzi (£3), a basket containing fresh green herbs – tarragon, flat parsley and mint – plus a chunk of Feta. Eat it with your bread. Or there's maast o mouseer (£2.50), which is a dish of yoghurt and shallots. Or chicken livers cooked with mushrooms (£3). The main courses tend to revolve around grilled meat – joojeh kabab (£9), for example, is a poussin, jointed, marinated, grilled and served on rice. Then there is chello kabab-e-barg (£11), which is outstanding – a tender fillet of lamb flattened and grilled. It's traditionally accompanied by an egg yolk. Look out for the dish of the day; on Wednesday it is kharesh badenjan (£7), a stonking stew of lamb and aubergines.

✱ Drink aromatic Iranian tea (£3) from tiny, gilded glasses.

Edgware Road & Paddington

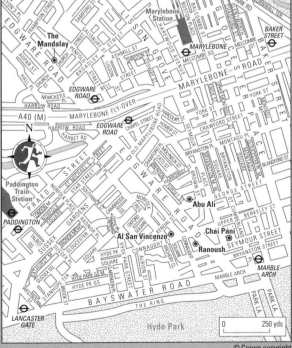

© Crown copyright

Abu Ali

Lebanese £8–£25

136–138 George St, W1 ☎ 020 7724 6338

Station Marble Arch **Open** Daily 9.30am–11pm **Accepts** Cash or cheque only

You can only suppose that, in the Lebanon, going out to eat is man's work. That certainly seems to be the case around the Oxford Street end of the Edgware Road, where you'll find Abu Ali's bustling café. This is an authentic place, the Lebanese equivalent of a northern working man's club, and men gather to smoke at the pavement tables. It's a bit spartan in appearance, but the food is honest and terrific value. Although you are unlikely to find many Lebanese women here, female diners get a dignified welcome. There's nothing intimidating about the place or its clientele.

You will want a selection of starters. Tabouleh (£3) is bright green with lots of fresh parsley, lemon juice, oil and only a little cracked wheat – it even tastes healthy. Hommos (£3) is rich and spicy, garnished with a few whole chickpeas and cayenne pepper. Warak inab (£3) are thin and pleasantly sour stuffed vine leaves, served hot or cold. Moutabal (£3) is also called babaganoush and is a rich dish of aubergine with sesame oil. Kabis is a plate of tangy salt and sour pickles – cucumber, chillies and red cabbage – that comes free with every order. For main dishes there's kafta halabiyeh (£6.50) – minced lamb kebabs with onion and spices. Or there's kafta yogurtliyed (£6.50), which is the self same kebab served with good sharp yoghurt. The plain grilled meats are also good. Try the boned-out poussin – farrouge moussahab (£7.50). To drink, there is mint tea (£2) – a Lipton's teabag and a bunch of fresh mint in every pot – or soft drinks.

✳ Try a bubble pipe (£5); the hard core replace the water with Appletise and ice, for a really sweet and sickly smoke.

Chai Pani

Indian/Vegetarian £10–£18

64 Seymour St, W1H ☎ 020 7258 2000

Station Marble Arch **Open** Daily noon–2.30pm (lunch), 3–5pm (tea), 6–10.30pm (dinner) **Accepts** All major credit cards

Chai Pani means "tea" and "water" – a symbolic offering of Rajasthani hospitality within the home. The name is apt, as not only does this small restaurant, tucked neatly behind Marble Arch, feel welcoming (the décor is almost domestic), but it also serves simple, comforting food that's very fresh and very good. One thing, however, is clear from the menu – the Atkins diet is unlikely to ever penetrate the Shekhawati region of Rajasthan. Potatoes abound, accompanied by aromatic pulse and vegetable dishes (heaving with mysterious ingredients) and breads – soft, crispy, stuffed, plain … you choose. Carb-heavy it may be – but when it tastes this good, who needs meat and two veg?

From the appetizers (all £3.50) choose lauki pakoda – bite-sized dubloons of deep-fried marrow in gram flour, with a mint chutney to die for – or perhaps the wonderful raj kachori, which is a delicate puffed flour shell stuffed with veg and swimming in yoghurt and chutney, though it resembles an ice-cream sundae that's fallen from a great height. Delicious. As for mains, either choose one of the speciality thaali on offer – Desert thaali (£10); Saatvik thaali (£8), a buckwheat puri, aloo in yoghurt gravy, cucumber, raita; or vegan, low-cal or wheat-free thaali (all £10) – Alternatively take your pick from the selections of rice, curry and daal dishes. The aloo matar pulao finds stir-fried rice and peas in a fragrant heap, laced with deadly dried chillies; panchmela subzi is a rich "five vegetable" curry – it's hard to identify all five, but expect pumpkin and … potato. As for the daal, steer toward mangodi kadhi – dried lentil balls drowning in an almost sour soup of yoghurt and gram flour. Much tastier than it reads. The sweets (all £3.50) range from the expected (kulfi, gulab jamun) to the unusual badam halwa – a hot ground-almond cousin of treacle pud.

✱ Pink city – rose lassi with Malibu (£6.50).

The Mandalay

Burmese £6–£16

444 Edgware Rd, W2 ☎ 020 7258 3696
Station Edgware Road **Open** Mon–Sat noon–2.30pm & 6–10.30pm
Accepts All major credit cards

Gary and Dwight Ally, Scandinavian-educated Burmese brothers, have become famous in the Edgware Road desert – the area north of the Harrow Road but south of anything else. The restaurant is bizarre, with just 28 seats, an old sandwich counter filled with strange and exotic ingredients, and greetings and decoration in both Burmese and Norwegian. Gary is in the kitchen and smiley, talkative Dwight is out front. The Ally brothers have correctly concluded that their native language is unmasterable by the English, so the menu is written in English with a Burmese translation – an enormous help when ordering. But the food itself is pure unexpurgated Burmese, and all freshly cooked.

The cuisine is a melange of different local influences, with a little bit of Thai and Malaysian, and a lot of Indian. To start there are papadums (two for £1.20) or a great bowlful of prawn crackers

(£1.90), which arrive freshly fried and sizzling hot (and served on domestic kitchen paper to soak up the oil). Starters include spring rolls (from £1.90 for two) and samosas (£1.90 for four), and salads such as raw papaya and cucumber (£3.90), or chicken and cabbage (£3.90). Main courses are mainly curries, or rice and noodle dishes, spiced with plenty of ginger, garlic, coriander and coconut, and using fish, chicken and vegetables as the main ingredients. The cooking is good, flavours hit the mark, portions are huge, and only a handful of dishes cost over £6.50. Vegetable dishes are somewhat more successful than the prawn ones, but at this price it's only to be expected.

This was one of the first London restaurants to go "No Smoking".

Ranoush

Lebanese £5–£25

43 Edgware Rd, W2 ☎020 7723 5929

Station Marble Arch **Open** Daily 9am–3am **Accepts** Cash only **⊛**www.maroush.com

This branch of Ranoush is part of the Maroush empire which comprises a dozen Lebanese restaurants all over London including the Beirut Express and (as a wild card) Signor Marco, a slick looking Italian eatery at the Marble Arch end of the Edgware Road. This place is a fine, unfussy, late-opening, lively sort of pit-stop that is justifiably popular with late night folk. At the back is the juice bar which gives you the healthy bit, at the front is the kebab servery where towers of meat rotate in front of the gas. In between is a counter packed with all the other items from the encyclopedic menu.

To eat here you need to know what you want, as you start by paying, then take the relevant piece of the receipt to either the kebab men at the front or the juice men at the rear – it's self-service with attitude. The starters are very sound, lots of mezze both cold (£3.90) and hot (around £4): hommos, tabbouleh, and warak ineb are good. The pickles are very good. The main course offerings are large plates of grilled meat, all £10.50 – lamb shawarma; kafta meshwi (minced lamb); and riash ghanam. Best though to opt for the sandwiches (all £3.25): ordering lamb shawarma brings a fresh round of bread wrapped around slivers of grilled lamb and lubricated with a dollop of yoghurt. It arrives wrapped tight in paper and is very difficult to eat without dripping the juices down your clothes. Very good. Variants include chicken shawarma; lahm meshwi (chunks of lamb); soujok (Lebanese spicy sausages). Have a couple, drink some juice, reflect on the night's adventures.

There's a "low calorie platter" – 6 mezze plus 1 skewer of lean meat (£12).

Al San Vincenzo

Italian £35–£65

30 Connaught St, W2 ☎ 020 7262 9623
Station Marble Arch **Open** Mon–Fri 12.15–3pm & 7–11pm, Sat 7–11pm
Accepts Mastercard & Visa

Al San Vincenzo is not a cheap restaurant. But then you'll find it smack bang in the middle of a patch of serious affluence near the bottom end of the Edgware Road. This is a very passionate place with a small dining room and a single-minded chef in the kitchen, which perhaps accounts for the mercifully simple dishes and good seasonal food. The pricing is straightforward: two courses may be had for £28.50 and three courses for £34.50; supplements are rare but some of the more expensive ingredients, such as fresh fish, can bump the price up a bit.

The menu changes to reflect the seasons, but there are usually six or seven starters to choose from. Dishes range from the plain but satisfying, such as deep-fried mackerel with salsa verde; papardelle with grilled wild mushrooms and truffle sauce; to interesting combinations like steamed rock oysters with broad-bean sauce and a Pecorino crust. Flavours are intense and presentation gloriously unfussy. Main courses are in similar vein: wild sea bass baked with fresh herbs and olive oil; risotto with fresh peas, essence of mint and Parmesan; osso buco with mashed potato; or venison all'agrodolce with spinach. The dessert menu ranges from the expected – vin santo with cantucini; lemon tart with a wild berry sauce – to more surprising puds such as fresh dates stuffed with marzipan, rolled in pistachio and served with a bitter chocolate sauce. The wine list covers the mid-ground well, with a well chosen series of Italian wines priced at between £16 and £37.

✳ Oenophiles should look out for the light and bright Vernaccia (£20).

Euston

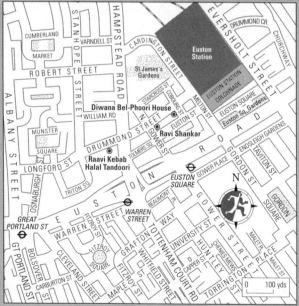

CUMBERLAND MARKET
STANHOPE STREET
VARNDELL ST
HAMPSTEAD ROAD
CARDINGTON STREET
EVERSHOLT STREET
DRUMMOND CR.
CHURCHWAY

ROBERT STREET
St James's Gardens
Euston Station
EUSTON STATION COLONNADE

STARCROSS ST
COBURG ST
MELTON ST
EUSTON SQUARE
Euston Sq. Gardens

Diwana Bel-Phoori House
WILLIAM RD
EUSTON ST
● Ravi Shankar

ALBANY STREET
MUNSTER SQUARE
DRUMMOND STREET
GOWER STREET
TOLMERS SQ
R O A D
EUSTON
ENDSLEIGH GARDENS
TAVITON ST
GORDON ST

● Raavi Kebab
Halal Tandoori
LONGFORD ST
TRITON SQ.
EUSTON SQUARE

BEAUMONT
GOWER PLACE
GORDON SQUARE
MALET ST
MALET PL

OSNABURGH ST
GREAT PORTLAND ST
⊖
E U S T O N
FITZROY ST
WARREN STREET
⊖ WARREN STREET
WAY
G O W E R   S T R E E T
UNIVERSITY ST
HUNTLEY
MALET PLACE

GT PORTLAND ST
BOLSOVER ST
WARREN ST
CLEVELAND STREET
CARBURTON ST
FITZROY SQUARE
GRAFTON WAY
WHITFIELD STREET
FITZROY ST
MAPLE ST
TOTTENHAM COURT RD
CAPPER ST
JAMES MEWS
TORRINGTON PLACE
TORRINGTON ST

N

0   100 yds

© Crown copyright

Diwana Bel-Phoori House

Indian/Vegetarian £7–£20

121 Drummond St, NW1 ☎020 7387 5556

Station Euston **Open** Mon–Sat noon–11.30pm, Sun noon–10.30pm
Accepts All major credit cards

All varnished pine and shag-pile carpets, the Diwana Bhel-Poori House is enough to make the style police wince. Only the Indian woodcarvings dotted around the walls give the game away – that and the heady scent of freshly blended spices. It's a busy place, with tables filling up and emptying at a fair crack, though the atmosphere is convivial and casual rather than rushed. You can bring your own beer or wine (corkage is free) and a full water jug is supplied on each table. This, the low prices (the costliest dish will set you back just £6.75), a chatty menu listing "tasty snacks", and fast, friendly service combine to create a deceptively simple stage for some fine Indian vegetarian cooking. There's even a lunch buffet at £5.95.

Starters are copious, ladled out in no-nonsense stainless-steel bowls. The dahi bhalle chat (£2.50) is a cool, yoghurty blend of chickpeas, crushed pooris and bulghur wheat, sprinkled with "very special spices". The dahi poori (£2.50) is a fragrant concoction of pooris, potatoes, onions, sweet-and-sour sauces and chilli chutney, again smothered in yoghurt and laced with spices. Stars of the main menu are the dosas, particularly the flamboyant deluxe dosa (£5), a giant fan of a pancake with coconut chutney, potatoes and dhal nestling beneath its folds. Also superb is the house speciality, thali Annapurna (£6.75) – a feast of dhal, rice, vegetables, pickles, side dishes, mini bhajees and your choice of pooris or chapatis. There are extras like Bombay aloo (£2.60) but the main course portions are large enough to make them seem pretty ambitious.

✳ Try the Kashmiri falooda (£2.40) – cold milk with china grass and rose syrup topped with ice cream and nuts... drink or dessert?

Raavi Kebab Halal Tandoori

Indian £6–£15

125 Drummond St, NW1 ☎020 7388 1780

Station Euston/Euston Square **Open** Daily 12.30–10.30pm **Accepts** All major credit cards

This small restaurant has been a fixture for more than thirty years, during which time Drummond Street has become one of the main curry centres of London. Competition here is more than just fierce – it is ludicrous – as well-established vegetarian restaurants compete to offer the cheapest "eat-as-much-as-you-can" lunch buffet. It is lucky that vegetables are so cheap. But the Raavi is not just about bargain prices – or vegetables, come to that. It is an unpretentious Pakistani grill house that specializes in halal meat dishes.

The grills here are good but hot: seekh kebab (£2.50), straight from the charcoal grill in the doorway is juicy, well-flavoured and hot; chicken tikka (£2.50) is hot; mutton tikka (£2.50) is hot. The mixed grill (£6.95) brings a bit of everything – everything hot! Lamb quorma (£4.75) is rich with fresh ginger and garlic and topped with a sprinkle of shaved almonds. Chicken daal (£3.95) brings chunks of chicken on the bone, bobbing on a sea of savoury yellow split-pea dhal, and is delicious. Nan breads (90p) are light and crispy. Nihari (£4.95), the traditional Muslim breakfast dish of slow-cooked curried mutton, vies with haleem for the title of bestseller. Haleem (£4.95) is made by cooking some meat, adding four kinds of dhal, a good deal of cracked wheat, and two kinds of rice, plus spices. Cook for up to seven hours, then add some garam masala. The result is a gluey slick of smooth and spicy glop from which any traces of the meat have all but disappeared. And how does it taste? You'd be hard pushed to be more enthusiastic than "not bad".

EUSTON

✳ Beware, the food can be extremely hot here!

Ravi Shankar   Indian/Vegetarian £5–£15

131 Drummond St NW1 ☎020 7388 6458

Station Euston **Daily** noon–10.45pm **Accepts** Mastercard & Visa

As a hotbed of Indian dining, Drummond Street is still a magnet for curryholics and anyone else seeking a good, cheap meal. The Ravi Shankar opened in the 1980s, and its decor is still firmly wedged in an era when plain enough was good enough – even though they have added a smart new wood floor. The Ravi Shankar may look plain, and the seating may not be ultra-comfortable, but the vegetarian food is honest and cheap – something that weighs heavily with the loyal clientele.

The daily specials are impressive – maybe a cashew nut pilau rice and cauliflower curry, served with salad and mint yoghurt chutney for the princely sum of £3.95. There are not many sub-£4 meals left anywhere in London, let alone one that is well cooked and satisfying. The cashew nut pilau is rich and nutty, and the cauliflower curry has been made substantial by the addition of chunks of potato. Or there's vegetable biryani with curry (£4.25), or perhaps aloo palak with chapati (£3.95). And the specials wind onwards to the extravagance of chana bhatura (£4.50) – a delicious fried bread with a chickpea curry. The main menu starters fall into two categories. There are hot snacks from Western India, including samosas (three for £2.30), bhajis (£2.30) and potato bonda (£2.50) – a solid, tasty, deep-fried sphere made from potato and lentils. Then there are cold "snacks and chat", billed as coming from Bombay's famed snack city, Chowpatty beach. Breads are good – treat yourself to an ace stuffed paratha (£1.95).

✳ Try a thali – complete meals from about £3.

Fitzrovia

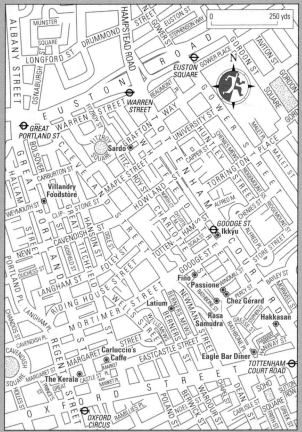

© Crown copyright

Carluccio's Caffe

8 Market Place, W1 ☎020 7636 2228

Station Oxford Circus **Open** Mon–Fri 7.30am–11pm, Sat & Sun 10am–10pm
Accepts All major credit cards except Diners ⊗ www.carluccios.com

FITZROVIA

Antonio Carluccio first ambled across our television screens, in his role as ultra-passionate mushroom hunter. Now branches of Carluccio's Caffe spring up almost as fast as porcini, and the success is well deserved. These are extremely busy restaurants, which makes for a great atmosphere. The downside is the likelihood of a queue at peak times. The front of the premises is a delicatessen-cum-shop, the mid-section is a bar and the rear is a café-restaurant. Commendable effort has been made to incorporate all that is admirable about Continental coffee shops: Carluccio's is open throughout the day, proper meals are available at all hours, the coffee is notably good and children are welcome.

In the morning the temptations are croissants (from £1.20) and coffee: caffè ristretto (£1.20);

cappuccino (£1.80); double espresso (£1.50). All pukka stuff. This segues into the main menu, on which there are always a couple of good soups to be had, such as zuppa di funghi (£3.95) – note the fair price. There's a good "bread tin" (£2.85) with moody Italian regional breads at meal times. There are sound antipasti, including Sicilian arancini di riso (£4.15), which are crisp, deep-fried rice balls filled with mozzarella or ragu. There are salads. Main courses range from calzone (£5,25) to a trad parmigiano di melanzane (£6.75), and from ravioli (£5.95) to osso buco alla Milanese (£9.95). Puds major in ice cream – gelati artiginali (£3.50). For a restaurant serving so many customers, the cooking is very good. Dishes are well seasoned, service is quick and the prices are fair.

❋ On the menu under "Trasporti" – Piaggio Vespa ET2 50cc. (£1,650).

Chez Gérard

8 Charlotte St, W1 ☎020 7636 4975

Station Goodge Street **Open** Mon–Fri noon–11.30pm, Sat 12.30–11pm
Accepts All major credit cards ⊗ www.sante-gcg.co.uk

When the inner prompting shouts for steak frites, Chez Gérard is a very sound option. When it opened, decades ago, this type of French restaurant (where the steak is good and the frites are better) was a novelty: today Chez Gérard feels reassuringly old-fashioned. The emphasis is

moving gently away from steak, but the approach is resolutely Francophile, so you'll find escargots, baked Camembert, and crème brûlée. The bread is crusty, the service Gallic, and the red wine decent. It's not cheap, but the food is generally reliable.

Start with fines de claire oysters (£4.55 for three, £8.95 for six, £13.40 for nine), or, for a real belt of nostalgia, a dozen snails in garlic butter (£5.50). The steaks come in all shapes and sizes – Châteaubriand is for two people (£32.90), while côte de boeuf rib-eye is served on the bone (£15.65). There's a 9oz fillet steak (£18) and an entrecôte (£15.45). There is also the wonderful onglet (£9.55), a particularly tasty French cut of beef. Everything from the grill comes with pommes frites and sauce Béarnaise. Other dishes include confit de canard (£9.45) and filet de Dorade royale (£12.25). But don't kid yourself – you're here for the steak frites. Salads, side orders of vegetables, desserts – including tarte Tatin (£4.75) and a selection of regional French cheeses (£5) – are all in tune with the Gallic ambience. So too are the house wines, which are so good that you can almost disregard the wine list. There is a very sound prix fixe menu available every evening and at Sunday lunch – £13.25 for two courses and £16.50 for three.

✱ Let's hear it for "onglet" – the kindest cut of all.

Eagle Bar Diner American £12–£25

3 Rathbone Place, W1 & ☎020 7637 1418
Station Tottenham Court Rd **Open** Mon–Wed noon–11pm, Thurs & Fri noon–1am, Sat 10am–1am, Sun 11am–6pm
Accepts All major credit cards except AmEx & Diners Ⓦ www.eaglebardiner.co.uk

Unsurprisingly the Eagle Bar Diner is both a bar and a diner. It's a modern looking sort of place with the booths for diners on a slightly raised platform. The bar is purposeful and its

large size gives a clue as to how busy it gets. Everything seems fairly serendipitous as the crowded times for the bar dovetail with the restaurant's peaks, so sometimes it's a bar and sometimes it's a restaurant. The room is comfortable, and service is informal – an agreeably grown-up sort of diner.

The menu sticks to tried and trusted diner fare: Caesar salad (£6.50); add rosemary chicken (£8.95); or with grilled king prawns (£10.50). You can opt for an American breakfast – short stack pancakes or Belgian waffles with bacon and maple syrup (£4.50). There are pasta dishes and sandwiches – hot salt brisket with spicy onions and rocket (£6.75); or "24 hour" tomatoes, grilled pepper, feta, avocado and rocket

(£7.25). But the burgers take centre stage here. An 8oz ground-rump burger (£6.75) comes with onion marmalade, mustard mayonnaise, lettuce, tomato, gherkin and red onion. It comes accurately cooked and well presented. You'll need spuds so choose from a variety of styles (all £2.75): hash browns, herb potatoes, fat chips, or skinny chips. The fat chips are good. The speciality burgers range from Greek (£6.50), made with feta and tzatziki, to South American (£6.80) – with chicken, guacamole and chorizo. Puds are sticky: brownie served warm with ice cream (£4), or cookies and cream ice-cream cake (£4.50). If your sweet tooth is ruling the roost it's worth checking out the shakes and malts.

FITZROVIA

✳ "4oz emu and mountain black pepper burger (£6)".

Fino

Spanish/Tapas £18–£70

33 Charlotte St, W1 (entrance Rathbone St) & ☎ 020 7813 8010

Station Goodge Street **Open** Mon–Fri 10am–3pm & 6–10.30pm, Sat 6–10.30pm

Accepts All major credit cards

Why is it that Spanish food seems so out of place in a slick "new-London-restaurant" setting? Say tapas, and the mind makes an involuntary leap towards cool, tiled, old-fashioned places. Fino opened in the spring of 2003 and majors in tapas, but in a setting that is very modernist indeed. Fino is living proof of its proprietors' admiration for Spain. There's a stylish bar for drinking on the mezzanine and a bar for eating tapas at along the front of the open kitchen downstairs. The food is very sound, and elegantly presented.

There are a good range of classic tapas dishes and some items fresh from the plancha (a no-frills grill). Start with some pa amb tomaquet (£3.50) – a tomatoey, garlicky toast. Add arroz negro (£7.80), a very delicious squid-ink risotto. Also crisp-fried squid (£6.80), delicious with a squeeze of lemon. The croquetas are good – filled with ham (£5.50), or piquillo peppers (£5.50). From the meat section there are milk-fed-lamb cutlets (£9.50) which are impossibly small, tender and with good gravy, and a good portion of jamon Iberico bellota

gran reserva (£15.50) – top ham, melting in the mouth. From the vegetable section there is a dish of chickpeas, spinach and bacon (£6.50) to add a welcome savoury note. From the plancha there are queen scallops (£8.90), squid (£7.20), and clams with sherry and ham (£8.70). In keeping with the smartness of the surroundings the wine list is priced on the merciless side. There are two "set menus" priced at £17.95 per person, and £28 per person (both for a minimum of two) and you will get five or seven courses.

✳ The "lunch express" deal is a good one: £12.95 or £14.95 with dessert.

Hakkasan   Chinese/Dim Sum £30–£120

8 Hanway Place, W1 &. ☏ 020 7927 7000

Station Tottenham Court Rd **Open** Mon–Fri noon–2.30pm & 6pm–midnight, Sat & Sun noon–4.30pm & 6pm–midnight (Sun 11pm) Thurs–Sat bar open until 1am

Accepts All major credit cards except Diners

Hakkasan is as impressive as only the judicious application of a £3,000,000 design budget can ensure. The double-smart cocktail bar is consistently and fashionably crammed. A large dining area sits inside an elegant and ornate carved wooden cage. Top-name designers from the worlds of film and fashion have given their all, and this is a smart and elegant place. The food is novel, well presented, fresh, delicious and, in strangely justifiable fashion, expensive.

The starters are called "small eat" and do not shy away from expensive luxury ingredients. The three-style vegetarian roll (£6) teams a mooli spring roll with a bean curd puff and a yam roll. Live native lobster noodles

with ginger and spring onion (£48) cannot be many people's idea of a "small eat". Or there is grilled Shanghai dumpling (£6). The main dishes are innovative and delicious. Try baked silver cod (£32) with Chinese rice wine, or the stir-fry scallop and prawn cake with choi sum (£10.90). There's also jasmine-tea-smoked chicken (£12.50), and sweet-and-sour organic pork with pomegranate (£9.50) By way of a staple, try the stir-fry glass vermicelli (£7), which enlivens noodles with chicken, crabmeat and fried shallots. The dim sum (served only at lunchtime) are not cheap – prawn puff is £3.90, and sesame prawn toast £8.50 – but there are some very interesting dishes. Try asparagus cheung fun with bamboo pith, dried shitake and cloud ear (£3), rock shrimp shumai (£5.50), or a baked venison puff (£3.90). Whisper it: "These are better dim sum than you'll find in Chinatown!"

✳ 24 hours' notice required for "Monk jumps over the wall" – an abalone seafood soup (£80).

Ikkyu

Japanese £10–£40

67a Tottenham Court Rd ☎ 020 7636 9280
Station Goodge Street **Open** Mon–Fri noon–2.30pm & 6–10.30pm, Sun 6–10.30pm
Accepts All major credit cards

Busy, basic and full of people eating reliable Japanese food at sensible prices – all in all, Ikkyu is a good match for any popular neighbourhood restaurant in Tokyo. What's more, it's hard to find, which adds to the authenticity. Head down the steps and you'll find that the restaurant has had a much-needed lick of paint. It is still an engaging place, if quite obviously tailored to Japanese customers, but the strangeness comes over as politeness, and you won't feel completely stranded. The first shock is how very busy the place is – you are not the first person to discover some of the best-value Japanese food in London.

Nigiri sushi is good here and is priced by the piece: tuna (£2); salmon (£1.70); mackerel (£1.40); cuttlefish (£1.70). Or there's sashimi, which runs all the way from mackerel (£4.50) to sea urchin eggs (£13), with an assortment for £13.50. Alternatively, start with soba (£3.60) – delicious, cold, brown noodles. Then allow yourself a selection of yakitori, either a portion of assorted (£5), or mix and match from tongue, heart,

liver, gizzard and chicken skin (all £1 a stick). You will need many skewers of the grilled chicken skin, which is implausibly delicious. Moving on to the main dishes, an order of fried leeks with pork (£7.50) brings a bunch of long, onion-flavoured greens strewn with morsels of grilled pork. Whatever the green element is, it is certainly not leeks. Or there's grilled aubergine (£3.40), or rolled five vegetables with shrimp (£8.20), which is like a Swiss roll made with egg and vegetable with a core of prawn.

✳ Try shoucho and soda (£3.50); shouchu is a clear spirit that tastes like … clear spirit!

The Kerala

Indian £8–£25

15 Great Castle St, W1 ☎ 020 7580 2125

Station Oxford Circus **Open** Daily noon–3pm & 5.30–11pm
Accepts All major credit cards

At the end of the 1980s Shirref's wine bar was taken over by David Tharakan who sold a good deal of wine and added a short menu of pub food favourites. The big changes came at the end of 1997, when David's wife Millie took over the kitchen and changed the menu. Shirref's started to offer Keralan home cooking, with well judged, well spiced dishes at bargain-basement prices. Since then The Kerala restaurant – which is what it has become – has gone from strength to strength, and achieved a certain notoriety for the great value lunch deals. Such things are not often found this close to Oxford Street.

To start with, you must order a platoon of simple things: cashew nut pakoda (£3.25), potato bonda (£2.95), lamb samosa (£2.95), chicken liver masala (£3.75), mussels ularthu (£3.75). These are honest dishes, simply presented and at a price which encourages experimentation. Thereafter the menu is divided into a number of sections: Syrian Christian specialities from Kerala; coastal seafood dishes; Malabar biryanis; vegetable curries; and special dosas. From the first, try erachi olathiathu (£4.95), a splendid dry curry of lamb with coconut. From the second, try meen and mango vevichathu (£4.95), which is kingfish cooked with the sharpness of green mango. From the biryanis, how about chemmin biryani (£7.45) – prawns cooked with basmati rice? Avial (£3.95) is a mixed vegetable curry with yoghurt and coconut. The breads are fascinating – try the lacy and delicate appams (two for £3) made from steamed rice-flour.

✳ Look out for the "lunch buffet" – a feast for under £7.

Latium

Italian £25–£60

21 Berners St, W1 ☎ 020 7323 9123
Station Goodge Street **Open** Mon–Sat noon–3pm & 6.30–10.30pm
Accepts All major credit cards

The food critics have been grizzling to one another about Latium, a bright new restaurant that opened towards the end of 2003. Some like it and feel that it is fresh, bold and Italian enough for anyone; while the other view is that it is just not Italian enough. As it is located opposite the Sanderson Hotel on Berners Street it seems a little harsh to mark it down for not having a window onto the Trevi fountain. The head chef here is Maurizio Morelli and he was born in Lazio, his cooking has been honed at restos like Ibla and he is very good at his job. His partner is a sommelier and wine importer called Antonio Cerilli which explains why the wine list features so many interesting bottles.

The dining room is gratifyingly plain and the service is slick, The deal is simple: two courses at lunch for £14 or £19.50; three for £18 or £23.50; and four for £22 or £28.50. The menu is broken up Italian style – antipasti; primi platti; secondi; dolce. During the critics' discussions (see above) the term nuova cucina got an airing: the food here may or may not be Roman, and it may or may not be new but it is certainly good to eat. Buffalo mozzarella is wrapped with courgette and served on corn salad with basil oil; stewed baby octopuses come with escarole and chickpea sauce and is very good indeed. Moving on – primi a tagliatelle with a ragout of hare is a well judged dish and the pasta is good. Mains range from roast monkfish wrapped in Parma ham, with girolle mushrooms; to roast venison with polenta and glazed chestnuts. Puds are substantial – a stellar almond and chocolate tart.

FITZROVIA

✳ Choose from an all-Italian wine list that has two hundred bins.

Passione

Italian £22–£55

10 Charlotte St, W1 ☎ 020 7636 2833

Station Goodge Street **Open** Mon–Fri 12.30–2.15pm & 7–10.15pm, Sat 7–10.15pm
Accepts All major credit cards ⓦ www.passione.co.uk

When Passione opened nobody had heard of Gennaro Contaldo, but just about everyone had heard of his protégé, Jamie Oliver, television hero of swathes of Middle England foodies. Gradually, however, Passione has built up a following on its own

merits. Simplicity, an unpretentious feel to the place, seasonal ingredients and talent in the kitchen – these are sure bets when it comes to eating.

You owe it to yourself to have four courses. The menu changes daily, and there is a constant procession of specials. Among the antipasti, there's zuppa di giorno (£9), which sounds so much better than soup of the day, and cinghiale marinato servito freddo con salsa di pesto (£9), marinated wild boar served cold. Then there is pasta and risotto: tagliatelli con capesante e bottarga (£10 or £12) teams scallops with dried tuna roe, while risotto all'accetosella (£9.50 or £11.50) has the tasty tang of

wild sorrel. Mains are rich and satisfying: orata con endiva belga salsina di miele e aceto bianco (£22), is sea bream with endives and a honey and vinegar sauce; involtini di melanzane alla parmigiana (£16.60), a rich dish of baked aubergines with mozzarella; coniglio con rosmarino e patate saltate (£19) is rabbit with rosemary and sauté potatoes. The service is slick here; this is a place where they understand the art of running a comfortable restaurant. Puddings (all £5) are serious stuff, though it has to be said that the delicious gelato Passione, a swirl of zesty limoncello ice with a splash of wild strawberry folded into it, is for all the world a grown-up's raspberry ripple.

✳ Try Contaldo's fabled focaccia – the one that the pukka chap is always banging on about.

Rasa Samudra

Indian/Fish £18–£40

5 Charlotte St, W1 ☎020 7637 0222

Station Goodge Street **Open** Mon–Sat noon–3pm & 6–11pm, Sun 6–11pm
Accepts All major credit cards ⓦ www.rasarestaurants.co.uk

Rasa Samudra represents the "smart fishy" sector in Das Sreedharan's burgeoning portfolio of high-quality South Indian restaurants (see the original Rasa, p.339, and its neighbour, Rasa Travancore, p.340). The food served is sophisticated fish cookery, the kind of stuff that would be more at home in Bombay than in London, consisting as it does of classy South Indian fish dishes – a million miles from familiar curry-house staples.

At first glance the menu may seem heart-stoppingly expensive, partly due to a

strange and exclusively British prejudice that no curry should ever cost more than a fiver, even if made from the kind of top-quality ingredients worth £15 in a French restaurant. All the more expensive choices (often based on fish, always a pricey ingredient) come complete with accompaniments. This makes them substantial enough to allow all but the greediest of diners to dispense with starters, except perhaps for the samudra rasam (£5.95) – a stunning shellfish soup – or the array of pappadoms, papparvardi and achappam (£4), or the banana boli (£4.25), which are plantain fritters with black sesame seeds. Plus, there are some wicked pickles (£3.50). For main course, crab varuthathu (£12.50) – a dish of crab stir-fried with ginger – is well offset by pooris (£2.50) and spicy potatoes (£4.75) as side dishes. Other good choices include konju manga curry (£12.95), prawns cooked dry with turmeric and green mango; and varutharacha meen curry (£11.50) – tilapia cooked with shallots, red chillies and tamarind. The cooking is well judged and the spices well balanced.

✳ Serious gastronauts should opt for the Kerala feast (seafood £30; vegetarian £22.50).

Sardo

Italian £18–£40

45 Grafton Way, W1 ☎020 7387 2521
Station Warren Street **Open** Mon–Fri noon–3pm & 6–11pm, Sat 6–11pm
Accepts All major credit cards ⓦ www.sardo-restaurant.co.uk

Sardo has cut out a niche for itself as a self-proclaimed flagship for Sardinian food. The proprietor, Romolo Mudu from Caligari, acts as front of house. Coupled with plain but fairly uninspired decor, this may make elderly diners feel that they have wandered into a Soho trattoria circa 1980. Take heart, for the food is more interesting than you would expect and is particularly good when you concentrate on the specials, which you'll find on the "menu del mese".

Start with the bresaola di tonno (£9.50), cured tuna sliced finely, or the calamari ripieno (£7.90) – baby squid, stuffed and grilled. As a pasta course perhaps the specials will yield culurgiones di formaggio e patate (£9.50), little pasta parcels filled with potatoes and pecorino cheese. Move on to something simple, but impressive, such as fregola ai gamberi e zucchni (£11.50) – fregola is a Sardinian pasta that comes in small enough pieces to take over the role of rice, and here, comes with prawns and courgettes. Or choose tonno alla griglia (£14.75) – a large chunk of tuna, raw inside, seared outside, spanking fresh and tender as butter. Or maybe salsiccia Sarda (£12) appeals? The proprietor will happily discuss his brother's recipe for these home-made sausages, which have a distinctive aniseed tang. For dessert, go trad Sardinian: sebada (£5) is a puff pastry filled with orange peel and cheese and topped with honey. Or there is a splendid array of five or six different

FITZROVIA

Pecorino cheeses (£6). The wine list includes a page of reasonably priced Sardinian specialities, and there are some distinctive, aromatic whites – note the Vermentinas.

✳ Check out the specials: occasionally this restaurant has the famous mountain prosciutto made from mutton.

Villandry Restaurant

Modern British £22–£55

170 Great Portland St, W1 ♿ ☎ 020 7631 3131

Station Great Portland St **Open** Daily 8.30am–10.30pm
Accepts All major credit cards except Diners

This place is both a foodstore and restaurant and you could end up eating breakfast, elevenses, lunch, tea or dinner. The handsome shop gives onto a modern and rather stark dining room. Passing displays of some of Europe's most extravagant ingredients may jangle the nerves and alarm the wallet, but if you're serious about your food, and you have time to wait for careful preparation, Villandry won't disappoint.

The menu changes daily so you won't necessarily find all – or indeed any – of the dishes mentioned here. But as you'd expect at the back of a foodstore that caters for the well-heeled sector of the foodie faithful, ingredients are scrupulously chosen and prepared with care. At its best, this kind of "informal" menu is surprisingly demanding on the cook – and exact cooking is crucial to ostensibly simple dishes. To start, you might be offered a leek and potato soup with truffle tapenade (£5.75); pigeon salad with noodles, chicory, soy and ginger (£8.25); langoustines and mussels with fish broth (£10.25); or a plate of charcuterie (£7.25 or £12.75). Main courses are often hugely impressive: roast rump of lamb with spiced borlotti beans and spinach (£17.25); pan-fried lemon sole, wild mushrooms and Jerusalem artichokes (£18.50). Desserts may include moist chocolate cake with chocolate sauce (£5.50) and, unsurprisingly, given the array in the shop, there's an extensive if expensive cheeseboard (£11.50), served with terrific walnut and sourdough breads. Wine prices, like the food, are distinctly West End, though there are reasonably priced house selections.

✳ Due to the influence of an American proprietoress there's always a good Thanksgiving party here.

Fulham

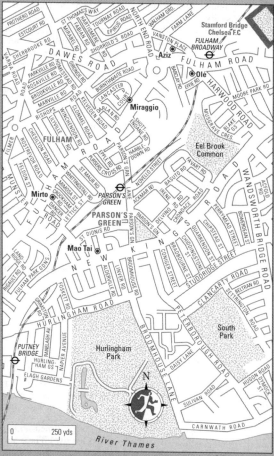

Aziz

Middle Eastern £20–£40

24–32 Vanston Place, SW6 & ☎020 7386 0086

Station Fulham Broadway **Open** Mon–Sat noon–midnight, Sun 10am–midnight
Accepts All major credit cards except Diners

Aziz has a very large and dominant site on Vanston Place, partly because it is neighbour to del'Aziz which is a shop, deli, (and it must be admitted what is virtually another restaurant) – they are all part of the same operation. Proximity to counters laden with good things benefit the vibe, which is helpful, as the restaurant known formally as Aziz looks very posh indeed. There is no hint of Middle Eastern scruffiness here, all is modern, and all is elegant. This presentation carries onto the plate where dishes show up looking very polished. Thankfully flavours are up front, and prices are not that fierce.

The menu splits into a number of sections – you'll find hot, cold and dessert mezze, then starters and main course dishes as well. From the mezze, trad dishes like hummous (£3.50),

and marinated baby aubergine with sumac and chilli (£5) are done well, while hot dishes such as the duck kebab (£6) are fresh and good. And the "freestyle" mezze like date, orange and carrot salad (£3.50) are interesting additions to the canon. "Starters" such as the pastilla of chicken with almonds (£5.50); or the pan-fried marinated chicken livers with cumin and lime (£5.50) are elegant and delicious, though it is hard to say why they are not mezze. Main courses split into tagines, kebabs and fish – monkfish tagine, shellfish broth, saffron, potato and confit of baby fennel (£14.50) is a complex dish well put together. Desserts are particularly fine: chocolate fondant and Moroccan mint tea ice cream (£5.50). The wine list has a good spread and gentle prices.

✱ At Christmas del'Aziz does a good trade in cooked turkeys to carry home. Scrooge would be pleased.

Mao Tai

Chinese £15–£55

58 New Kings Rd, SW6 ☎020 7731 2520

Station Parsons Green **Open** Mon–Fri noon–3pm & 6.15–11.30pm,
Sat 12.30–3pm & 6.15–11.30pm, Sun 12.30–3pm & 6.15–11pm
Accepts All major credit cards ✆www.maotai.co.uk

Mao Tai is much more Chelsea than Chinatown, both in appearance and in the kind of food it serves. It's a pretty restaurant, cleverly lit, well decorated and with brisk, efficient service. The menu has recently undergone reappraisal and the ground has shifted away from the fiery Sichuan influences

to something more suave. Such surroundings – and, to be fair, such food – do not come cheap. Still, you'll leave well fed and well looked after, as both the cooking and service are slick and chic.

Start with steamed scallops (£7.85 for two). These are usually a pretty good indication

of things to come, and at Mao Tai they are well cooked. Salt and pepper prawns (£7.65) are very fresh. Dumplings feature: pork and ginger; prawn, chive and chilli; mushroom and spinach; and pea shoot and prawn (all cost £6.40 for six). The salt and pepper Chesapeake Bay soft-shell crabs (£7 each) in the starters section, are good. From the fish section choose Tianjin turbot steamed on the bone (£15.50) – these are serious restaurant dishes at serious prices. Or perhaps

sirloin strips with lemongrass and cracked black pepper (£12) appeals? Dishes here are made with free-range Angus beef. Onwards to sautéed chicken with orange-blossom honey and pineapple (£8.50), or rabbit with lemongrass and garlic (£8.50). In the vegetable section there's broccoli in oyster sauce (£5.85), and seasonal pea shoots (£8.50). In the face of all these rather exalted prices the Mao Tai feast (£24.70 per person for a minimum of two) may make sense.

✳ "Mao Tai does not use M.S.G."

Miraggio

Italian £15–£40

510 Fulham Rd, SW6 ☎ 020 7384 3142

Station Fulham Broadway **Open** Mon 7–11pm, Tues–Thurs 12.30–3pm & 7.30–11pm, Fri & Sat 12.30–3pm & 7.30–11pm, Sun 12.30–4pm
Accepts All major credit cards except Diners

Bright café-style gingham tablecloths and a simple rustic air belie the quality behind this family-run establishment. Your first sign of this is the appetizing

display of antipasti in the window. There are mouth-watering wafer-thin strips of chargrilled courgette and aubergine, nutty little boiled potatoes with virgin olive oil and roughly chopped flat-leaf parsley, strips of grilled peppers, small and large mushrooms and an aubergine and tomato bake with tiny melted Mozzarella cheeses. It's enough to stop even the most jaded foodie in their tracks.

For starters, choose the antipasti della casa (£7.50) and you'll get the window dishes. Otherwise, try beef carpaccio with truffle oil (£8.50); or melanzana alla Parmigiano (£6.50), baked aubergine rich with cheese. Pastas include the usual suspects: lasagna (£7); and fettuccine with fresh seafood in tomato sauce (£10). There are plenty of meat and fish choices

too, including spigola al forno (£15), baked sea bass; calamari fritti (£12), a dish of perfectly cooked deep-fried squid; and abbacchio al forno (£10.50), roast lamb. If you're not already having spinach with your main course, try a side order of spinaci burro e Parmigiano (£3.50). Popeye would faint with pleasure. Puddings include what is claimed to be the best tiramisù in the area (£4.50); champagne or fruits of the forest sorbets (£2); and zoccolette (£4.50), a home-made profiterole with a Nutella filling. The kitchen is part of one of the dining areas, which is good if you like watching cooks at work.

※ From the "side dishes" – "boiled green beans" would have to be better than they sound.

Mirto

Sardinian £20–£50

839 Fulham Rd, SW6 ☎ 020 7736 3217

Station Parsons Green **Open** Mon–Sat noon–2.30pm & 6.30–11pm, Sun 12.30–3pm & 6.30–10pm **Accepts** All major credit cards except Diners

Mirto opened towards the end of 2003. It's a small, light, friendly restaurant with a Sardinian heart but Metropolitan manners. The menu doesn't feature quite as many regional dishes as Sardo

(see p.159) but the food is fresh and good, and it fits right in on this stretch of the Fulham Road, which is awash with small neighbourhood restaurants. The wine list has a strong contingent of Sardinian bottles but casts its net widely. Service is friendly and professional.

The menu runs through antipasti, pasta, carne e pesce, to dessert. Starters range from pan-fried Pecorino cheese with tomatoes (£6.50); to squid with aubergine fregola and mint (£8) – fregola is a variety of pasta, the size and shape of a grain of sweetcorn. Or there's antipasto Sardo (£8) which is a plate covered in pan carasau (a

Sardinian bread the same dimensions and texture as a poppadom), topped with various hams, salamis and cheeses. The pasta choices are interesting: nettle ravioli with new potatoes thyme and Pecorino (£8); spaghetti with bottarga (£8); or a well made risotto with plenty of razor clams (£8.50) – very delicious, and with a perfect texture. Main courses are well presented. Sea bream comes baked in Vernaccia wine with olives and green beans (£13.50); there are marinated sardines with bay leaf and pinenuts served with baked new potatoes (£12.50); a rack of lamb comes with roast endive (£13). Puds round up biscotti (£6), sebadas (£6.50) and a tiramisu made with pistachios (£5). Beware the eponymous Mirto (£4), a Sardinian liqueur which tastes better in Sardinia.

✳ Traditional roast suckling pig – 24 hours notice.

Olé

Spanish/Tapas £15–£40

Broadway Chambers, Fulham Broadway, SW6 ☎020 7610 2010
Station Fulham Broadway **Open** Mon–Sat noon–3pm & 5–11pm, Sun 6–11pm
Accepts All major credit cards ⊛ www.olerestaurants.com

You can't miss Olé. It's bright and modern with blond wood everywhere, and right opposite Fulham Broadway tube. Olé is a combination bar and restaurant. The bar is open for drinks if you're not hungry and there's the restaurant at the back if you are. This is the sort of place where you may start by going for a drink, and end up eating and being pleasantly surprised by the food. The menu, which changes monthly, is modern Spanish and geared to tapas-style sharing.

The menu is divided into Frias (cold dishes), Calientes (hot dishes) and Ensaladas (salads). For the conventional there are favourites such as jamón Serrano (£5.75), boquerones (£3.90), patatas bravas (£3.20), chorizo al vino blanco (£4.50) and gambas al ajillo (£4.95). The gambas are sweet and hot, with garlic, chilli and olive oil. Tortillas abound here. Instead of just tortilla española (£4.10), there are four more: with pimentos (£4.50), with chorizo (£4.50), with tuna (£4.50) and with a spinach cream filling (£4.20). All are freshly made, and all make pretty good options. Meat-eaters can enjoy tapas such as solomillo de cerdo con verduras al vapor, a la esencia de mostaza (£4.80) which is fillet of pork with steamed vegetables and mustard essence; carne de buey a la plancha con verduras y salsa de tomate y datiles (£4.50), beef fillet with vegetables and date sauce; or pollo a la plancha con surtido de pimientos y crema de ajo (£4.50) – grilled chicken with peppers and cream of garlic. For the sweet of tooth there are eight puddings (all under £4).

✳ Interesting all-Spanish wine list.

Golders Green

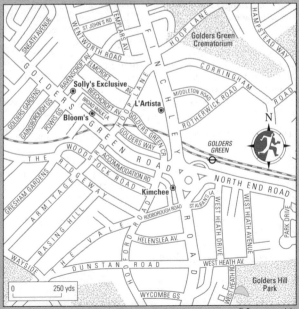

© Crown copyright

L'Artista

Italian/Pizza £15–£25

917 Finchley Rd, NW11 ☎ 020 8731 7501

Station Golders Green **Open** Daily noon–midnight **Accepts** Mastercard & Visa

Situated opposite the entrance to Golders Green tube, and occupying an arch under the railway lines, L'Artista is hard to miss. With its pavement terrace, abundant greenery and umbrellas, this is a lively, vibrant restaurant and pizzeria that exercises an almost magnetic appeal to the young and not so young of Golders Green. Inside, the plain decor is enhanced by celebrity photographs; the waiters are a bit cagey if asked just how many of them have actually eaten here, but the proximity of the tables ensures that you'll rub shoulders with whoever happens to be around you, famous or not.

The menu offers a range of Italian food with a good selection of main courses, such as fegato Veneziana (£8.10), a rich dish of calf's liver with onion and white wine. The trota del pescatore (£7.90) is also good, teaming trout with garlic. But L'Artista's pizzas are its forte. They are superb. As well as traditional thin-crust Capricciosa (£6.80) with anchovies, eggs and ham, or Quattro Formaggi (£6.70), there are more unusual varieties such as Mascarpone e rucola (£6.70), a plain pizza topped with Mascarpone cheese and heaps of crisp rocket, which is actually very good. The calzone (£6.80) – a cushion-sized rolled pizza stuffed with ham, cheese and sausage and topped with Napoli sauce – is wonderful. Pastas are varied and the penne alla vodka (£6.50), made with vodka, prawns and cream, is well worth a try. For something lighter, try the excellent insalata dell'Artista (£5.70), a generous mix of tuna, olives and fennel, with an equally good garlic pizza bread (£3.10).

GOLDERS GREEN

✳ Don't worry about the intermittent Vesuvian tremors – it's merely the Northern Line.

Bloom's

Jewish £12–£30

130 Golders Green Rd, NW11 ☎ 020 8455 1338

Station Golders Green **Open** Mon–Thurs & Sun noon–11pm, Fri 10am–2pm (3pm in summer) **Accepts** All major credit cards ⊛ www.blooms-restaurant.co.uk

Bloom's goes way back to 1920, when Rebecca and Morris Bloom first produced their great discovery – the original veal Vienna. Since then "Bloom's of the East End" has carried the proud tag as "the most famous kosher restaurant in the world". Setting aside the indignant claims of several outraged New York delis for the moment, given its history it's a shame that the East End Bloom's was forced to shut, and that they had to retrench to this, their Golders Green stronghold, in 1965. Nonetheless, it's a glorious period piece. Rows of sausages hang over the takeaway counter, there are huge mirrors and chrome tables, and you can expect inimitable service from battle-hardened waiters.

So, the waiter looks you in the eye as you ask for a beer. "Heineken schmeineken," he says derisively. At which point you opt for Maccabee, an Israeli beer (£1.90), and regain a little ground. Start with some new green cucumbers (90p) – fresh, crisp, tangy, delicious – and maybe a portion of chopped liver and egg and onions (£4.20), which comes with world-class rye bread. Or go for soup, which comes in bowls so full they slop over the edge: beetroot borscht and potato (£2.90), very sweet and very red; lockshen, the renowned noodle soup (£2.90); or kreplach, full of dumplings (£3.50). Go on to main courses. The salt beef (£15.90) is as good as you might expect, and you can try it in a sandwich on rye bread (£8.50). And there are solid and worthy options such as liver and onions (£10.90). You can still order extra side dishes like the dreaded, heart-stopping fried potato latke (£1.90).

✳ London's sweetest vegetable dish? Tzimmas (£2.20) – honeyed carrots.

Kimchee

Korean £18–£40

887 Finchley Rd, NW11 ☎ 020 8455 1035
Station Golders Green **Open** Tues–Sun noon–3pm & 6–11pm
Accepts All major credit cards

Times have changed in Golders Green. In August 2003 a bright and modern Korean restaurant called Kimchee opened on the Finchley Road. It's a charming place with a well-mannered clientele split fifty-fifty between homesick Koreans and adventurous Golders Greenites. Korean food majors in strong flavours, and in dishes that are finished at the table – each table has a barbecue built into the middle of it and your waitress will cook at least part of your meal in front of you.

Start with some pickles: kimchee (£1.90), fermented cabbage with loads of salt and fierce chilli-hot red bean paste, is the most famous. The sliced radish with vinegar (£1.90) is milder and the pickled cucumbers are very good indeed (£1.90). There is also yuk whe (£6.90), the Korean equivalent of steak tartare – shredded raw beef bound together with egg yolk and slivers of pear. This unlikely sounding combination is improbably good. Koon mandoo (£6.50) – large pan-fried dumplings have very good crispy bits. For main course try one of the table-grilled dishes. There's bulgogi (£7.20) –

marinated beef cooked on the metal plate in front of you, or sliced pork (£6.50), or seafood (£7.90). The "pot dishes" are also interesting: a stone pot is heated up until it is sizzling, a layer of rice is then added and on top of that some meat, vegetables, and an egg yolk.

When it arrives at table your waitress mixes it all together, and you get dol bibim bab (£7.20) – instant fried rice cooked by the hot pot. To drink, either stick to Korean beer (£3), or try "soju", a clear spirit served on ice from a mini-bottle (£9.80).

✳ Each table has its own bell push to summon waiters, so the dining room resounds to doorbell chimes.

Solly's Exclusive

Jewish £17–£40

146–150 Golders Green Rd, NW11 ☎020 8455 2121

Station Golders Green **Open** Mon–Thurs 6.30–10.30pm, Sat (winter only), an hour after sundown–1am, Sun 12.30–10.30pm **Accepts** All major credit cards except Diners

What makes Solly's Exclusive so exclusive is that it is upstairs. Downstairs is Solly's Restaurant, a small, packed, noisy place specializing in epic falafel. You'll find Solly's Exclusive by coming out of Solly's Restaurant and going around the side of the building. Upstairs, a huge, bustling dining room accommodates 180 customers. The decor is interesting – tented fabric on the ceiling, multicoloured glass, brass light fittings – while waitresses, all of them with "Solly's Exclusive" emblazoned across the back of their waistcoats, maintain a brisk approach to the niceties of service.

The food is tasty and workmanlike. Start with the dish that pays homage to the chickpea – hoummus with falafel (£4.25), which brings three crispy depth charges and some well-made dip.

Even the very best falafel in the world cannot overcome the thunderous indigestibility of chickpeas, but as falafel go these are pretty good. Otherwise, you could try Solly's special aubergine dip (£3.25), or the Moroccan cigars (£5), made from minced lamb wrapped in filo pastry and deep fried. Solly's pitta (£1.25) – a fluffy, fourteen-inch disc of freshly baked bread – is closer to a perfect naan than Greek-restaurant bread. Pittas to pine for. For mains, the lamb shwarma (£9.75) is very good, nicely seasoned and spiced, and served with excellent chips and good salad. The barbecue roast chicken (£9.50) comes with the same accompaniments, and is also sound. Steer clear of the Israeli salad (£2.75), however, unless you relish the idea of a large bowl of chopped watery tomatoes and chopped watery cucumber.

✳ This is a kosher restaurant, so if you're not fully conversant with the Jewish calendar, check before setting out.

Greenwich & Blackheath

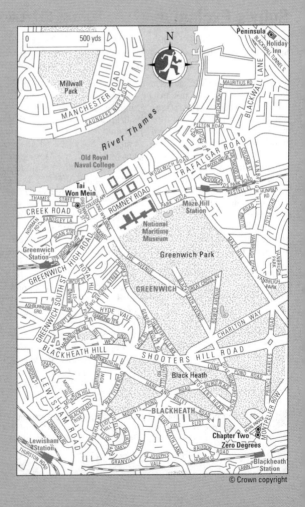

© Crown copyright

Chapter Two

Modern European £18–£50

43-45 Montpelier Vale, SE3 ♿ ☏020 8333 2666

Station BR Blackheath **Open** Mon–Thurs noon–2.30pm & 6.30–10.30pm, Fri & Sat noon–2.30pm & 6.30–11pm, Sun noon–3pm & 6.30–9pm

Accepts All major credit cards ⓦ www.chaptersrestaurant.co.uk

Chapter Two nestles into a small but smart parade of shops just off the heath. A clean, half-clear, half-frosted glass frontage allows you to glimpse the well-dressed diners enjoying themselves within. And when you enter you'll find yourself in a sleek, modern space, with light wood and metal complemented by richly coloured walls, all coming together to set off crisp linen and sparkling glassware. The whole place has a professionally run air, exuding comfort and confidence.

This feeling of competence also embraces the menu. Lunch is £14.50 for two courses, £18.50 for three (£14.50 or £16.50 Sunday); dinner is £16.95 and £19.95 (rising to £23.50 Friday and Saturday). There's nothing particularly unusual or showy on offer, but there's plenty of choice among the reasonably classic, well-thought-out dishes. Among the first courses you may find butternut squash velouté with blue cheese and red onion croquant, or a rolled terrine of confit chicken and ham hock with fruit chutney, or raviolo of crab and white onion purée. Main courses range from the likes of pan-fried salmon, tomato and goat's cheese tart; through slow-roast pork belly with creamed turnips and pan-fried foie gras; to rump of lamb, kidney brochette, and white beans. Portions are generous and presentation is top-class. The puds are mainly tried-and-tested favourites: hot chocolate fondant; vanilla panna cotta; and lemon cream sablé. Chapter Two is a decent local restaurant, service is professional rather than pally, and someone has given the wine list some thought.

✳ You'll find the Michelin-starred Chapter One at Locksbottom in Kent.

Peninsula

Chinese/Dim Sum £8–£35

The Holiday Inn, Bugsby's Way, SE10 ☎020 8858 2028

Station North Greenwich **Open** Mon–Fri noon–11.30pm, Sat 11am–11.30pm, Sun 11am–11pm (dim sum daily until 5pm) **Accepts** All major credit cards

The Peninsula restaurant is in a strange location. Sited on a promontory (defined by trunk roads on two sides and with a major roundabout at its peak), you'll find the Peninsula occupying the ground floor of the Holiday Inn Express hard by the Millennium Dome. The dining room is large and functional, with space for a couple of hundred diners and even on a weekday the dim sum trade is brisk. There are large family tables complete with highchairs and thoughtful Chinese tots chewing chunks of squid. The main menu features all the usual favourite dishes, but it is the dim sum that makes this place stand out.

There are two dim sum menus: a small book-like one on the table, and a list of specials on posters around the rooms – treasure egg puff pastry; or deep-fried yam sandwiched with prawns (both £2.80). From the main menu the cheung fun are sound (even if the flobby white casing is a little robust): you can choose from pork, vegetarian, beef (£2.60) and king prawn (£3.20). Other good choices are the mini spring rolls (£1.90); the paper-wrapped prawns (£2.60); the char sui buns (£1.90); the glutinous rice in lotus leaf (£3.20) comes as one large parcel but is suitably rich, sticky and self-indulgent; the chives dumplings (£1.90) – thin enough to see the green shards through the pastry. The cooking is very sound here, and the prices represent very good value indeed, something you would guess at as soon as you see how exceedingly busy this restaurant is. But the real wonder of the Peninsula is more where it is than what it is. An unexpected find.

✳ From the dim sum specials – snails in curry sauce (£1.90).

Tai Won Mein

Chinese/Noodles £5–£12

39 Greenwich Church St, SE10 ☎020 8858 1668

Station DLR Cutty Sark **Open** Daily 11.30am–11.30pm **Accepts** Cash only

Tai Won Mein's simple signs urge you to "eat fast food" – and the stark interior with its long, low benches reinforces the message. But, while quality is often sacrificed for speed of service, that is certainly not the case here. Good-quality food, together with extraordinarily reasonable prices, mean that this place is always busy. At the weekend, when the nearby markets are in full swing, you must expect to wait for a seat. This will give you a chance to get to know your prospective table-neighbour while you queue.

Table decoration is sparse and your placemat doubles as the menu. Starters include spring rolls (£3.10) and fried spareribs (£3.10). Make sure you ask for the chilli sauce. Main courses are divided into rice, noodles and ho fun (which are a kind of ribbon-like noodle, flatter and softer than the usual); the noodle section is then subdivided into fried noodles and soup noodles. The house special soup noodle (£3.80), served in an enormous bowl, is a steaming vat of egg, prawn, beef, squid, crab meat, mussels, fresh greens and, finally, noodles. Less colourful, but certainly no less satisfying, is pork with noodles in soup (£3.20). The fried noodle dishes are equally imposing – huge plates piled high with such delights as mixed seafood (£3.80). Then there's ho fun with king prawn in soup with vegetables (£3.80), and fried ho fun with roast pork and duck (£3.80). Rice dishes – chicken with curry sauce (£3.20) or ribs with black-bean sauce (£3.20) – are equally popular. Sadly, Tai Won Mein is a pudding-free zone. Good filling meals, fast and cheap!

✳ The house wine costs £8 a bottle – a point in favour of the Chinese beer (£2.10).

Zerodegrees

Italian/Pizza £8–£20

29–31 Montpelier Vale, Blackheath, SE3 ☎020 8852 5619
Station BR Blackheath **Open** Mon–Sat noon–midnght
Accepts All major credit cards except Diners Ⓦwww.zerodegrees-microbrewery.co.uk

0° – as the logotype, napkins, menus and so forth would have it – is a lively fun factory trapped close to the respectable heart of Blackheath. This is a microbrewery complete with plenty of aluminum cladding and stainless steel pipework, and good times are fuelled by beer. When consuming extreme amounts of refreshment, some food becomes vital and this is the need Zerodegrees fulfils.

The menu is an obvious one and has elements from every other drink-fuelled eatery, so expect salads, sausages, mussels, pasta and pizzas. To make things look a little classier there are appetisers such as bruschetta (£2.95), dough balls (£2.20) and somewhat surprisingly, salmon carpaccio (£4.75). The salads are predictable – fusilli pasta salad (£7.95) or classic Caesar salad (£6.95). Mussels (all £10.95) come in kilo pots and in various styles – marinière (with garlic and celery) or Provençale (with tomato and herbs). In similar vein the pasta dishes touch the bases – papardelle with spicy sausage; spaghetti with tiger prawns; linguine with pancetta and clams; tortelloni with spinach and ricotta; and fusilli with black olives (all at £8.95). The pizzas – traditional cheese (£5.50); pepperoni (£6.75); mushroom (£6.75); or mushroom and pepperoni sausage (£7.25) – come from a wood burning oven and are the best ballast on offer to go with the different beers brewed on the premises: a Pilsner; a pale ale; a spooky black lager; a wheat ale and a "special". Zerodegrees is a loud, brash, young place.

Get stuck into the homebrew, there's a happy hour 4–7pm Monday to Friday.

Further choices

Goddard's Pie House
British

45 Greenwich Church St, SE10
☎ 020 8293 9313

Traditional and old established eel and pie shop. Low prices and sound food have survived recent refurbishments.

Mogul
Indian

10 Greenwich Church St, SE10
☎ 020 88581500

Modern looking Indian restaurant with an agreeably traditional menu. All your old favourite curries.

Trafalgar Tavern
British

Park Row, Greenwich, SE10
☎ 020 8858 2437

Large and sprawling pub with dining room. Handy for the more touristy parts of Greenwich.

Hackney & Dalston

Armadillo

Latin American £18–£50

41 Broadway Market, E8 ☎ 020 7249 3633

Station Bethnal Green **Open** Tues–Sat 6.30–10.30pm, Sun brunch noon–4pm
Accepts All major credit cards ⊛ www.armadillorestaurant.co.uk

Armadillo is that rare thing – a small neighbourhood restaurant with an unusual menu and staff who care. Chef-owner Rogerio David, from Brazil, has based his dishes on South American home cooking and in 2004 Armadillo won best American restaurant at the Tio Pepe ITV London Restaurant Awards. The dining room is bright and colourful and, although the menu uses some unfamiliar South American terms, after a couple of the excellent Caipirinhas (a mixture of fierce white spirit called Cachaça, sugar, crushed limes and ice), the friendly explanations from the staff will start to make sense.

To start there may be a Bolivian cheese, onion and chilli pasty served with a green tapenade (£4.50); or fried squid and cassava with sauce criolla (£5); or tilapia in a ceviche made with peppers, red onions and blood oranges (£4.80); or chicken anticucho, potato and black mint crema (£4.70). Mains range from the slightly bizarre – ostrich meatballs, corn cake and watercress (£12) – to more straightforward dishes such as roast suckling pig with Columbian beans and chorizo (£13); sea bream baked in a banana leaf with coconut and ginger sauce and fried plantain (£12.50). Puddings are equally novel. Spicy chocolate ice cream and Amaretti (£3.90) is home-made and delivers what it promises, while pionon with manjar (£3.90), is a kind of Peruvian Swiss roll. Wines are mainly from South America and Spain and are reasonably priced. Or perhaps "Quentão" appeals – a Brazilian spirit, mulled and served with ginger and orange (£3.50).

※ There is a single outdoor table in the courtyard behind – booking essential.

Faulkner's

Fish & chips £8–£25

424 Kingsland Rd, N8 ♿ ☎ 020 7254 6152

Station BR Dalston Kingsland **Open** Mon–Thurs noon–2pm & 5–10pm, Fri noon–2pm & 4.30–10pm, Sat 11.30am–10pm, Sun noon–9pm
Accepts All major credit cards except AmEx & Diners

Faulkner's is a clear highlight among the kebab shops that line the rather scruffy Kingsland Road – it's a spotless fish-and-chip restaurant, with takeaway. It is reassuringly old-fashioned with its lace curtains, fish tank, and uniformed waitresses, and it holds few surprises – which is probably what makes it such a hit. Usually Faulkner's is full of local families and large parties, all ploughing through colossal fish dinners while chatting across tables. It also goes out of its way to be child-friendly, with highchairs leaned against the wall, and a children's menu priced at £4.50.

House speciality among the starters is the fishcake (£1.90), a plump ball made with fluffy, herby potato, or there's prawn cocktail (£3.95). For main courses, the regular menu features all the British fish favourites, served fried or poached, and with chips, while daily specials are chalked up on the blackboard. Cod (from £8.50) and haddock (from £9.75) retain their fresh, firm flesh beneath the dark, crunchy batter, while the subtler, classier Dover sole (from £13) is best served delicately poached. The mushy peas (95p) are just right – lurid and lumpy like God intended – but the test of any good chippy is always its chips, and here they are humdingers: fat, firm and golden, with a wicked layer of crispy little salty bits at the bottom. Stuffed in a soft doughy roll they make the perfect chip butty. Most people wet their whistles with a mug of strong tea (80p), but there is wine on offer, including a Beaujolais Villages (£11) and a Chablis (£17.75).

✳ Real French fish soup imported from Perard in Le Touquet – peppery and dark, (£2.50).

Green Papaya

Vietnamese £15–£35

191 Mare St, London, E8 ☎020 8985 5486

Station BR Hackney Central **Open** Tue–Sat 5–11.30pm, Sun 5–11pm. Closed Monday.
Accepts All major credit cards except AmEx & Diners ⊛www.greenpapaya.co.uk

Among the many Vietnamese restaurants in East London, Green Papaya offers excellent value and a casual café-bar atmosphere. The menu claims, "for a true experience of Vietnamese cuisine". Highest price on the menu is £8 for a main course and the lowest £2.80 for a large bowl of vermicelli, shitake mushrooms, black fungi and kohl rabi soup. Wines are around the £12 – £15 mark for good New World Sauvignons and Shiraz. Cooking is accomplished and makes use of the fresh ingredients and herbs to be found in the many Vietnamese suppliers around. You know they'll never run out of purple basil.

Starters include the usual suspects such as Vietnamese herb rolls with prawns (£3.25), banana flower salad (£3.95), and the eponymous green papaya salad (£2.95). They are fresh, crisp, and delicious. Try the banh tom (£4.95) for a change and experience lightly battered strips of sweet potato and king prawn deep-fried and presented as a nest. Very moreish. There are enough variations of braised, stir-fried and steamed meats, seafood and poultry to satisfy the choosier diner, plus a 10 dish tofu section for vegetarians, although some have fish in them. Slow-cooked lamb cubes with galangal, lemon grass and coconut milk (£5.95) comes in a curiously light-coloured sauce, but the lamb is tender. There are also unusual dishes such as stir-fried kohl rabi with shitake mushrooms and black fungi (£5.00), and stir-fried sweet gourd with bean sprouts and spring onions (£5.00). And of course there's stir-fried morning glory (£5.00).

* Say hello to the china pig in the conservatory out back.

Huong Viet

Vietnamese £8–£25

An Viet House, 12–14 Englefield Rd, N1 & ☏ 020 7249 0877

Station BR Dalston Kingsland **Open** Mon–Fri noon–3.30pm & 5.30–11pm, Sat noon–4pm & 5.30–11pm **Accepts** Mastercard & Visa

Huong Viet is the canteen of the Vietnamese Cultural Centre, which occupies a rather four-square and solid-looking building. The resto has long had a reputation for really good, really cheap food, and regulars have stuck with it through a couple of general refurbishments. But, despite acquiring a drinks license, this place is never going to turn into a trendy bar restaurant. The food has stayed fresh, unpretentious, delicious and cheap, although prices are creeping upwards. The service is still friendly and informal.

Start with the spring rolls (£3.90) – small, crisp and delicious. Or the fresh rolls (£3.50), which resemble small, carefully rolled-up table napkins. The outside is soft, white and delicate-tasting, while the inside teams cooked vermicelli with prawns and fresh herbs – a great combination of textures. Ordering the prawn and green leaf soup (£3.50 or £5) brings a bowl of delicate broth with greens and shards of tofu. Pho is perhaps the most famous Vietnamese "soup" dish, but it's really a meal in a bowl. The pho here is formidable, especially the Hanoi noodle soup, filled with beef, chicken or tofu (£3.90 or £5.50). Hot, rich and full of bits and pieces, it comes with a plate of herbs, crispy beansprouts and aromatics that you must add yourself at the last moment so none of the aroma is lost. The other dishes are excellent too. Look out for mixed seafood with pickled veg and dill (£6.50), which works exceptionally well. You should also try the noodle dishes – choose from the wok-fried rice noodle dishes, or the crispy-fried egg noodles (£3.90 or £5.70).

* This place was once one of Hackney's numerous public bathhouses.

Istanbul Iskembecisi

Turkish £10–£25

9 Stoke Newington Rd, N16 ☎ 020 7254 7291

Station BR Dalston Kingsland **Open** Daily noon–5am **Accepts** All major credit cards

The Istanbul Iskembecisi is just across the road from Mangal II (see below), and at heart they are singing off the same sheet. Despite being named after its signature dish – iskembe is a limpid tripe soup – the Istanbul is a grill house. Admittedly it is a grill house with chandeliers, smart tables and upscale service, but it is still a grill house. And because it stays open until late in the morning it is much beloved by clubbers and chefs – they are just about ready to go out and eat when everyone else has had enough and set off home. The grilled meat may be better over at Mangal II, but the atmosphere of raffish elegance at the Istanbul has real charm.

The iskembe (£2.50), or tripe soup, has its following. Large parties of Turks from the snooker hall just behind the restaurant insist on it, and you'll see the odd regular downing two bowlfuls of the stuff. For most people, however, it's bland at best, and even the large array of additives (salt, pepper, chilli – this is a dish that you must season to your personal taste at the table) cannot make it palatable. A much better bet is to start with the mixed meze (£5.50), which brings a good hummus and tarama, a superb dolma, and the rest drawn from the usual suspects. Then on to the grills, which are presented with more panache than usual. Pirzola (£7.50) brings three lamb chops; shish kebab (£7) is good and fresh; karisik isgara (£8.90) is a formidable mixed grill. For a more interesting option there's arvnavaut cigeri-sicak (£6.50) – liver Albanian style.

※ Isn't it sad that they no longer serve kelle sogus (roasted head of lamb)?

Mangal II

Turkish £6–£25

4 Stoke Newington Rd, N16 ☎ 020 7254 7888

Station BR Dalston Kingsland **Open** Daily noon–1am **Accepts** Cash and cheque only

The first thing to hit you at Mangal II is the smell. The fragrance of spicy, sizzling chargrilled meat is unmistakably, authentically Turkish. This, combined with the relaxing pastel decor, puts you in holiday mood before you've even sat down. The ambience is laid-back, too. At slack moments, the staff shoot the breeze around the ocakbasi, and service comes with an ear-to-ear grin. All you have to do is sit back, sink an Efes Pilsener (£2.50) and peruse the encyclopedic menu.

Prices are low and portions enormous. Baskets of fresh bread are endlessly replenished and there's a vast range of tempting mezeler (starters). The 25 options include simple hummus (£2.50) and dolma (£2.50); imam bayildi (£3), aubergines rich with onion, tomato and green pepper; thin lahmacun (£1.75), meaty Turkish pizza; and karisik meze (£4) – a large plate of mixed dishes that's rather heavy on the yoghurt. The main dishes

(kebablar) themselves are sumptuous, big on lamb and chicken, but with limited fish and vegetarian alternatives. The patlican kebab (£8) is outstanding – melt-in-the-mouth grilled minced lamb with sliced aubergines, served with a green salad, of which the star turn is an olive-stuffed tomato shaped like a basket. The kebabs are also superb, particularly the house special, ezmeli kebab (£7.50), which comes doused in Mangal's special sauce. Afterwards you might just be tempted by a slab of tooth-achingly sweet baclava (£2). Alternatively, round off the evening with a punch-packing raki (£3).

✱ On rare occasions the grilled quails listed on the menu (£8.50) are actually available. And they are good.

Red River

Vietnamese £6–£20

28a Stamford Rd, N1 ☏ 020 7241 2228
Station BR Dalston Kingsland **Open** Mon–Thurs noon–3pm & 6–11pm, Fri noon–3pm & 6pm–midnight, Sat 6–midnight, Sun noon–11pm
Accepts All major credit cards except AmEx & Diners ✇ www.the-red-river.co.uk

Red River – the English translation of the Vietnamese name Sông Hông – is a small and comfortable Vietnamese restaurant tucked away up a side street off the Kingsland Road. Expect the usual rather garish and ornate decorations and a smiling welcome from someone behind the bar. The food is very sound, the prices are very reasonable and the beers are cold. Locals rate Red River very highly, which is all the more remarkable given the profusion of Vietnamese restaurants hereabouts.

The crystal rolls are good here – that pleasant combination of

slightly chewy wrapper, with crisp veg and plump prawns (£2.80 for prawn, £2.20 vegetarian). The "salt n' pepper squid" (£3.50) is dry and crisp and the fried spareribs (£2.50) are good and meaty. After starters the menu goes on to list soups, salads and noodle soups. The Vietnamese crunchy salad with chicken (£2.50) is fresh and well made; Phó Bó (£3.60), the trad Vietnamese noodle soup with beef, is filling as ever. Under seafood there's crispy fried fish with fish sauce (£4), or fish fillet in sweet chilli sauce (£4.80). The poultry and meat section of the menu lists another fifteen or so dishes including a good "slow-cooked" chicken (£4), and lamb with crushed yellow-bean sauce (£3.60). On to the noodle dishes. Rice vermicelli with pork and lemon grass (£4) is good and the crispy noodle with beef is also a good pick (£4). This is a pleasant place, with pleasant, unpretentious food and bargain prices.

✳ In the evening delivery is free for any order over £10.

Sông Quê

Vietnamese £10–£35

134 Kingsland Rd, EC2 ☏ 020 7613 3222

Station Old Street **Open** Mon–Sat noon–3pm & 5.30–11pm, Sun noon–11pm
Accepts Mastercard, Visa, Switch & Solo

Sông Quê has made something of an impact among the cluster of Vietnamese eateries strung out along this section of the Kingsland Road. It's a garish place inside, but proximity to other restos means that if you make the journey and can't get a table here (it's best to book), there are several other establishments offering Vietnamese cooking within walking distance including Viet Hoa (see p.182).

Sông Quê offers a staggering number of dishes. There are 28 starters, 21 noodle dishes, 10 rice dishes, 28 seafood, 13 vegetable dishes and 19 pho or traditional Vietnamese noodle soup dishes – each a meal in itself. Try bo nuong la tot (£5.00): grilled slices of beef wrapped in betel leaf, or goi cuon (£2.70) – fresh rolls of rice paper with zingy fresh herbs. Larger dishes include diep xao hanh gung (£5.50), scallops with ginger and spring onions, as well as the essential rau muong xao loi (£4.50). Translated, but still a puzzle, as

"stir-fried-ong choy with garlic" it's a dish of the most delicious iron-tasting vegetable, a.k.a. water morning glory. Pho

is a must. Each comes with rice noodles, shredded onion and coriander simmered in fresh broth with a separate plate of raw beanshoots, a bunch of basil leaves, Vietnamese parsley and sliced red chillies. Dunk the extra raw vegetables in the hot broth, taking great care with the red chillies. Of the 19 varieties (priced between £4.70 and £5.60), pho ga is chicken, tai nam is rare sliced steak and well done flank, while hu tiu my tho is mixed pork and prawn. Good simple flavours.

✳ If bewildered by the complex menu – vit chien don cuon banh trang (£12 for half) translates as crispy duck with the trimmings!

Viet Hoa Café

Vietnamese £8–£18

72 Kingsland Rd, E2 ☎ 020 7729 8293

Station Old Street **Open** Mon–Fri noon–3.30pm & 5.30–11.30pm,
Sat & Sun 12.30–11.30pm **Accepts** All major credit cards except Diners

The Viet Hoa dining room is large, clean, light and airy, with an impressive golden parquet floor. The café part of the name is borne out by the bottles of red and brown sauce which take pride of place on each table. The brown goop turns out to be hoisin sauce and the red stuff a simple chilli one, but they have both been put into recycled plastic bottles on which the only recognizable words are "Sriracha extra hot chilli sauce – Flying Goose Brand". Apparently this has made all but the regulars strangely wary of hoisin sauce.

For diners wanting to go as a group and share, an appetizer called salted prawn in garlic dressing (£4.95) is outstanding – large prawns marinated and fried with chilli and garlic. From the list of fifteen soups, pho (£5.70) is compulsory. Ribbon noodles and beef, chicken or tofu are added to a delicate broth which comes with a plate of mint leaves, Thai basil and chillies, your job being to add the fresh aromatics to the hot soup – resulting in astonishingly vivid flavours. Main courses include shaking beef (£6.90), cubes of beef with a tangy salad; and drunken fish (£6.90) – fish cooked with wine and cloud-ear mushrooms. Both live up to the promise of their exotic names. There are a good many salad and tofu dishes, including tofu with chilli and black bean (£4.95). Bun tom nuong (£5.95) is a splendid one-pot dish of noodles with chargrilled tiger prawns. Also in one-pot-with-vermicelli territory, you'll find bun nem nuong (£5), which features grilled minced pork, and that old favourite, Singapore noodles (£4.50).

✳ Among the desserts – "fried ice cream" (£2.80).

Further choices

Little Georgia
Georgian

2 Broadway Market, E8
☎ 020 7249 9070

Obscure but friendly restaurant selling equally obscure Georgian dishes which seem to revolve around walnuts.

LMNT
Modern British

316 Queensbridge Rd, E8
☎ 020 7249 6727

Part of Peter Illic's group of restos, all renowned for their awesomely low prices. Sound food and service.

Hammersmith

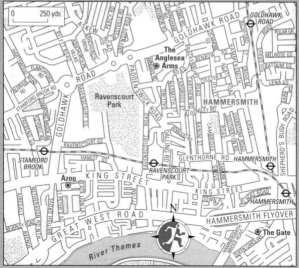

The Anglesea Arms

Modern British/Gastropub £12–£30

35 Wingate Rd, W6 ☎ 020 8749 1291

Station Ravenscourt Park **Open** Mon–Sat 12.30–2.45pm & 7.30–10.45pm, Sun 1–3.30pm & 7.30–10pm **Accepts** Mastercard & Visa

Do not make the mistake of thinking that this establishment is merely a pub. The Anglesea serves very good food indeed, and as well as being one of the very first notable gastropubs it is still one of the shining lights. The menu changes at least twice a day, dishes are crossed out as they run out, but when you've achieved "favoured local" status, you can ask for something simple that's not even on the board. Pitch up early, claim a seat, and not only will you dine well but you'll leave feeling good about the bill.

Who knows what will be chalked up on the blackboard when you visit? The menu is both eclectic and attractive, and prices have an upper limit of about £6 for starters and £13 for mains. You might end up choosing between Cornish mackerel rillette, beetroot,

horseradish and chives (£4.95); an open tart of aubergine, courgette, Feta and mint served with tzatziki (£4.95); and something simple like six Irish oysters, shallot relish and Guinness bread (£7.95). Main courses could be pot-roast stuffed saddle of lamb, white beans, curly kale and rosemary gravy (£10.25), or honest, market-fresh fish dishes like roast fillet of cod, new potatoes, clams, fennel, slow-cooked tomato and dill butter (£12.95). Perhaps, to round things off, a British cheese in perfect condition; maybe Cornish Yarg served with chutney, leaves and water biscuits (£4.95), or a puddingy-type pud such as cherry clafoutis, crème fraîche ice cream (£4.50). This cooking is about as far from the kind of grub you'll be offered in a thousand chain pubs as you can get.

✳ One of very few pubs to offer a range of pudding wines by the bottle, half-bottle and glass.

Azou

North African £10–£30

375 King St, W6 ☎ 020 8563 7266

Station Stamford Brook/Ravenscourt Park **Open** Mon–Fri noon–2.30pm & 6–11pm, Sat & Sun 6–11pm **Accepts** All major credit cards

Azou opened at the very end of 1999, so by London restaurant standards it can now claim to be old-established! It is a small, comfortable, informal North African restaurant where you can enter into the spirit and end up sitting on the floor on a cushion. It is run by husband and wife team Chris and Chris Benarab. The kitchen knows its

business, and the classics – tagines, couscous, grills – are presented with some panache.

The menu is split into various sections. First there is a list of kemia, by way of starters. These are the North African equivalent of tapas and include all the favourites, from dips such as hummus (£3.50) and baba ganoush (£3.95) to bourek (£4) – those little pastries filled with cheese or mince – and "briks" from Tunisia (£4.50), which are deep-fried filo parcels of potato, tuna and egg. One classic that should not be missed is the mechouia (£3.90), which is a salad of grilled tomato and pepper. The main courses are arbitrarily divided up. Under "couscous", vegetarian (£8.90) teams vegetables and chickpeas; "fish" (£12.95) combines fish, shellfish and prawns, or there's "royale" (£15.50), which brings together lamb shank, chicken breast and Merguez sausage. Under "Tagines" there's the tagine el ain (£10.50), lamb shank with prunes, apricots and almonds. From the "Azou Specialities", the tagine romanne (£8.95) appeals – chicken in sweet and tangy pomegranate sauce with almonds, raisins and caramelized onions. These dishes are well made and fairly priced. There's a sound Moroccan wine and an interesting beer from Casablanca.

✳ The ultimate dish at Azou must be ordered in advance. "Mechoul" (£280) is a whole lamb to feed twelve.

The Gate

Vegetarian £16–£36

51 Queen Caroline St, W6 ☎ 020 8748 6932

Station Hammersmith **Open** Mon–Fri noon–2.45pm & 6–10.45pm, Sat 6–11pm
Accepts All major credit cards ⊛ www.gateveg.co.uk

The extraordinary thing about The Gate, which is tucked away behind the Hammersmith Apollo, is that you hardly notice that it's a vegetarian restaurant. This is enjoyable dining without the meat. It's not wholefood, it's not even healthy; indeed, it's as rich, colourful, calorific and naughty as anywhere in town. The clientele is a quiet and appreciative bunch of locals and pilgrims – it's unlikely that anyone could just stumble across this hidden-away, former artists' studio. The airy decor and the high ceiling give it a serene, lofty feel, which may be The Gate's only nod to veggie solemnities.

The short menu changes monthly, but starters are always great. There's usually a tart, such as the leek and trompette tart (£5.25). Also excellent are the sweetcorn fritters (£5.75), which are served with a sweet chilli sauce. Portions are hearty, so it's a good idea to share starters in order to pace yourself and sample all the courses. The mains are generally well executed. Butternut, basil and goat's cheese ravioli (£11) is pan-fried in sage butter and served with purple sprouting broccoli. Or perhaps there's a chipotle-glazed artichoke (£11.25) – poached in chilli and lime-leaf stock before being filled with avocado and Feta cheese. Puddings are splendid: vanilla crème brulée served with strawberry and rose salsa (£5). Those without a sweet tooth should go for the cheese plate (£6). The drinks list is extensive, and the wine section tops out at £28 (except for champagne) and has something for everyone.

✳ Trad meets exotic – pineapple, chilli and passion fruit crumble, served with coconut Anglais (£5.50).

Hampstead &
Belsize Park

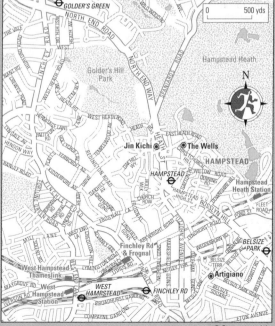

Artigiano

Italian £15–£30

12 Belsize Terrace, NW3 ☎ 020 7794 4288

Station Belsize Park **Open** Mon 7–11pm, Tues–Sat noon–3pm & 7–11pm, Sun noon–3pm & 7–10pm **Accepts** All major credit cards ⓦ www.etruscagroup.com

You'll find Artigiano halfway up a dead-end street in the rabbit warren of Belsize Park. It is a bright, airy restaurant, glass-fronted and with generous skylights. There's more chance of seeing a traffic warden than a passing car and the only disturbance from outside is the rustle of leaves. For such an out-of-the-way place the restaurant is surprisingly big, with more than a hundred covers. It's remarkably busy too, full of thirty-something professionals who've sought it out for the same reasons you have – good food and service, convivial atmosphere, and an escape from the rat race.

The menu is longer than you'd expect, with eight first courses and six pastas followed by as many main courses. There is an admirable tendency to use spanking-fresh ingredients and

to let them be themselves. Antipasti might include insalata mista con erbe fresche (£4.95) – the Italian for a mixed wild leaves salad. Or prosciutto di Parma con melone (£8.50), or bresaola Valtellinese (£8.20) served with a fennel and orange salad. Pastas are home-made and sophisticated. Order ravioli with crab and broccoli (£8.50 or £12), or risotto Milanese con scamorza (£7.95 or £11.45) – saffron risotto with smoked mozzarella. On the "pesci" list there may be sea bass in a parsley crust (£16). Meat-eaters should turn to the costoletta alla Milanese (£16), a veal cutlet with Pont Neuf potatoes; or the petto d'anatra con cavolo rosso (£14) pot-roasted duck with red cabbage. The chocolate and almond semifreddo (£5.50) is seductive and there are home-made ice creams (£4.75).

There's a bargain set lunch: £14.50 for two courses and £16.50 for three, rising to £15 and £18 on Sunday.

Jin Kichi

Japanese £15–£30

73 Heath St, NW3 ☎ 020 7794 6158

Station Hampstead **Open** Tues–Fri 6–11pm, Sat 12.30–2pm & 6–11pm, Sun 12.30–2pm & 6–10pm **Accepts** All major credit cards

Unlike so many Japanese restaurants, where the atmosphere can range from austere to intimidating, Jin Kichi is a very comfortable place. It's cramped, rather shabby and has been very busy for over a decade (tables are booked up even on the quiet nights of the week). It differs from sushi-led establishments in that the bar

dominating the ground floor with the stools in front of it is home to a small and fierce charcoal grill, where an unhurried chef cooks short skewers of this and that.

By all means start with sushi. Ordering the nigiri set brings seven pieces of fresh fish for an eminently reasonable £12.70.

▲ Jin Kichi

But then go for the "grilled skewers". Helpfully enough there are two set meals offering various combinations, and each delivers seven skewers (one combo costs £10.80 and the other £8.50). These make for a very splendid kind of eating as each skewer comes hot off the grill. Be adventurous – grilled skewer of fresh asparagus and pork rolls with salt (£1.60) is a big seller. Grilled skewer of chicken wings with salt (£1.30) is simple and very good, but grilled skewer of duck with spring onion (£1.80) is even better. Grilled skewer of chicken gizzard with salt (£1.10) is chewy and delicious while the grilled skewer of chicken skin with salt (£1.50) is crisp and very moreish. Drink ice-cold Kirin beer served in a frosted glass. The remainder of the menu leads off to fried dishes, tempura, different noodle dishes, soups and so forth, but the undoubted star of the show is the little grill.

✱ Grilled skewer of ox tongue with salt (£1.80) – top skewer!

The Wells
Modern British £15–£45

30 Well Walk, NW3 &. ☎020 7794 3785
Station Hampstead **Open** Daily noon–3pm & 7–10pm
Accepts All major credit cards except AmEx ⓦ www.thewellshampstead.co.uk

As gastropubs spring up all over London the discussion invariably turns to just what defines a gastropub, and one of the places most often used as an example is the Wells. This establishment is smack in the middle of old Hampstead, locals are well heeled and their view of what constitutes a pub is a long way from matters of spit and sawdust. For them the Wells may be a gastropub but for the rest of us it looks like a restaurant. There is a pubby bar downstairs and they do ease off the pedal a bit at lunchtime, but venture upstairs and you are either in a restaurant or the toilets!

Dinner here is priced at £29.50 for three courses (a pretty restauranty price tag). There are a couple of dining rooms, lofty and elegant. The menu changes to take account of the seasons but starters might include watercress soup with poached egg and salted almonds; brochette of scallops with parsnip purée; or a terrine of guinea fowl, foie gras and artichokes served with a fig and walnut chutney – the charcuterie work is done well here. Main courses follow a similar vein. There may be a risotto of wild garlic and white onion with roast ceps; or rack and shoulder of lamb with baby artichokes and ricotta gnocchi; or pan-fried halibut with mussels and pea shoots. Puds range from panna cotta with griottine cherries to apple Tatin with vanilla ice cream. The standard of cooking here is high and dishes are full flavoured, but a gastropub…? Only in Hampstead.

✳ The selection of cheeses from La Fromagerie is worth the £3 supplement.

Further choices

Black & Blue
Steak

205–207 Haverstock Hill, NW3
☎ 020 7443 7744

Decent steaks at this branch of an expanding chain; see review p.256.

Al Casbah
North African

42 Hampstead High St, NW3
☎ 020 7431 6356

Jolly North African restaurant with a good name on the party circuit. Cous cous, and tagines predominate.

Pescador Two
Portuguese/Fish

108 Heath St, NW3
☎ 020 7443 9500

This is the second restaurant of Camden's Pescador; see review p.62.

Weng Wah House
Chinese/Dim Sum

240 Haverstock Hill, NW3
☎ 020 7794 5123

Chinese restaurant with a good reputation, if a slightly old-fashioned feel. There is a bargain set lunch.

Zamoyski
Polish

85 Fleet Rd, NW3
☎ 020 7794 4792

A small friendly Polish wine bar, where the Polish food is helped along by a good deal of vodka. Great atmosphere.

Harrow

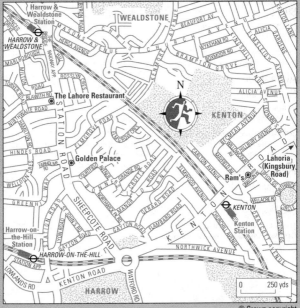

Golden Palace
Chinese/Dim Sum £10–£25

146–150 Station Rd, Harrow, Middx ♿ ☎ 020 8863 2333
Station Harrow on the Hill **Open** Mon–Sat noon–11.30pm,
Sun 11am–10.30pm (dim sum until 5pm) **Accepts** All major credit cards

Even if it were in the heart of Chinatown, you would class the Golden Palace as a seriously busy restaurant. But to find a sophisticated dim sum specialist packing in hundreds of eager customers for a weekday lunch in suburban Harrow is a shock. Inside all is chic and slick, and large tables of young Chinese ladies-who-lunch sit happily alongside families with babies in highchairs. Everyone is eating dim sum and waiters and waitresses rush through with towering steamers. The dim sum here are very good indeed and there's a bustle in the atmosphere that is infectious.

The best strategy is to order several dim sum – some familiar and some exotic – and then repeat those you like best. Most cost just £2.20 a portion, although some stray up to a dizzying £2.80. Bear in mind that most of the dumplings come in threes. Standouts are the crystal prawn dumplings (£2.20) – a thin steamed dumpling full of fresh, almost crunchy prawn, and the prawn and chive dumplings (£2.20) which are similar but with the green of fresh chives showing through the translucent pastry. Deep-fried shredded squid (£2.20) is quite simply the best, tenderest, crispest "Calamari" you have ever eaten. And the truly amazing mini lotus wrapped glutinous rice with meat (£2.50) – two in a portion, open the lotus leaves and find a stunning sticky rice ball with a centre of slow-cooked pork. Rich and intense. The sheer variety of the dishes on offer is impressive, but it is even more unusual to find them all done so well, and at such a reasonable price. Service is brisk but friendly, and the tea is … well, tea!

✳ There is even a page of vegetarian dim sum.

The Lahore Restaurant
Indian £7–£20

45 Station Rd, Harrow, Middx ☎ 020 8424 8422
Station Harrow & Wealdstone/Harrow on the Hill **Open** Daily 11.30am–11.30pm
Accepts Cash or cheque only

The Lahore Restaurant has a BYO drinks policy and an open kitchen, but that's where the trendiness stops. This homely and unpretentious Pakistani eatery serves grilled meats and karahi dishes. The service is friendly, the food fresh, and the prices are extremely reasonable. The room is plain, and a couple of ceiling fans struggle to disperse the fierce heat coming off the grills. There have been some queries about the chilli heat of some dishes – sometimes "hot" doesn't translate as more than "medium" and sometimes it means "eye-watering".

To start order a couple of rotis (60p) and some grilled meats. Chicken tikka (£4) is sound – a good portion, and tandoori chicken wings (six for £5) are great. They're well marinated, perfectly cooked and spicy. Tandoori lamb chops (six for £6) are outstanding – thick-cut, heavy with spice, and juicy. Seek kebabs (two for £1.50) have a welcome belt of fresh chilli and green herbs. It would be quite feasible to make a decent meal of starters and bread, but the curries are very good too, with simple dishes full of flavour, such as karahi jeera chicken (£6). The star turn is the karahi karela gosht (£45.25). The tender, slow-cooked lamb has a rich sauce balanced by the addictive taste of bitter melon. The breads are very good indeed. For an interesting contrast, order a tawa paratha (£1.50) and an onion kulcha (£1.80). The paratha is wholemeal, thick, filling and fried until the outside is flaky-crisp. The onion kulcha is doughy but stuffed with a rich onion mix that includes fresh coriander.

✱ Beware, the off-licence next door shuts at nine o'clock on weekday evenings.

Lahoria

Indian £12–£25

274 Kingsbury Rd, NW9 ☎ 020 8206 1129

Station Kingsbury **Open** Tues–Thurs 6–midnight, Fri & Sat 5.30–midnight, Sun 3pm–midnight **Accepts** Mastercard & Visa

At Lahoria the proprietors re-paint the dining room whenever the mood takes them; the colour varies but it is always bright. Even so, it's a safe bet that nobody comes here for the ambience. There's plenty of competition, with several restaurants clustered on this stretch of road. No matter – this small place is still busy, particularly at the weekend. What makes the Lahoria stand out, is the sheer quality of the food, which combines two admirable attributes – simplicity and goodness.

So, the food: it's fresh, not painfully hot (unless you want it to be) and well balanced. There are a lot of East African Asian specialities, and dishes come by either the plate or the karai (the wok-like cooking utensil). Start with a plate of jeera aloo (£4.95), tasty, rich, soft, fried potatoes with cumin – a sort of Indian pommes Lyonnaise. Or have a plate of masala fish (£4.95) – two fat fillets of tilapia cooked in a fresh green masala. You must try the chilli chicken (£6.25), which is nine chicken wings in a dark-green, almost black sludge rich with ginger, chillies, coriander and a hint of tamarind sourness. Also look out for the mari chicken (£6.25), which is chicken marinated in cracked black pepper. For a main course go for the karai spring lamb (£6.25), served on the bone. It is deliciously rich. Or try a simple classic such as karai masala lamb methi (£6.25). There are 23 vegetarian karai dishes including the delicious karai jinjaro (£4.50), a dish of red kidney beans. And to drink? It's hard to oppose a chilled bottle of Tusker beer from Kenya (£3.25).

✱ The best weekend special is karai boozi ki goat (on the bone, £6.25).

Ram's

Indian/Vegetarian £6–£18

203 Kenton Rd, Harrow, Middx 🚹 ☎020 8907 2030

Station Kenton **Open** Tues–Sun noon–3pm & 6–10pm
Accepts Mastercard & Visa

Anyone in downtown Mumbai will tell you that India's best vegetarian food comes from the state of Gujarat. And one of the leading contenders for the best of Gujarati food is the city of Surat. Since the end of 2001, Londoners have had their very own Surti restaurant – Ram's. The staff rush around, eager and friendly; their pride in both the menu and their home town is obvious and endearing. The menu is a long one and the food is very good.

Gujarati snacks make great starters. Petis (£3.10) are small balls of peas and onions coated in potato and deep-fried. Kachori (£3.10) are the same kind of thing but with mung daal inside a pastry coat. Patras (£3.30) are made by rolling vegetable leaves with a "glue" of chickpea flour batter; the roll is then sliced across, and each slice becomes a delicate and savoury pinwheel. Stuffed banana bhaji (£2.99) is a sweet and savoury combo. The kand (£3.50) is a Surti special – slices of purple potato in a savoury batter. Sev khamni (£3.50) is a sludge of well-spiced chickpeas with coconut, served topped with a layer of crisp sev. Flavours are clear and distinct, and some dishes have a welcome chilli heat. Mains do not disappoint. The famous undhiu (£5) – a weekend special – is a complex dish of vegetables "stuffed" with a Surti spice paste. It combines aubergines with three kinds of potatoes (purple, sweet and white), as well as bananas and peas. The peas pilau (£1.95) is simple and good. The methi parathas (two for £1.75) are dry and tasty. The puris (£1.50) are fresh, hot and as self-indulgent as only fried bread can be.

✳ Try the Surti lemon soda (£1.50).

HARROW

Further choices

The Lahore Kebab House
Indian

248 Kingsbury Rd NW9
☎020 8905 0930

Like Lahoria, this resto is over in Kingsbury, but worth a visit. Cheap and cheerful. Good grilled meats without frills.

Sakonis
Indian/Vegetarian

6–7 Dominion Parade, Station Rd, Harrow, Middx
☎020 8863 3399

Famous for juice and veggie meals, this is part of a chain, see review p.369.

Holloway & Highgate

Lalibela Ethiopian Restaurant

137 Fortess Rd, NW5 ☎020 7284 0600
Station Tufnell Park **Open** Daily 6.30pm–12.30am
Accepts All major credit cards except Diners

Lalibela is remarkable for serving uncompromisingly authentic Ethiopian food and for a genuine understanding of hospitality. There's a slightly harassed but still laid-back feel to the place that's a great comfort to the diner. The unwary can end up seated on low, carved, wooden seats around traditional low tables (so that you can eat with your hands). If your knee joints won't take that kind of punishment, plead for an ordinary table and resign yourself to dripping sauce down your shirt front.

There are a limited number of starters, but they banish any inkling you may have about being in an odd kind of curry house. The lamb samosas (£3.75) have very dry, papery pastry and a savoury, spicy filling – delicious. The Lalibela salad (£3.50) is potatoes and beetroot fried together with a spicy sauce and served hot. Main courses are served traditionally, that is to say as pools of sauce set out on a two-foot-diameter injera bread. Injera is cold, made from fermented sourdough, and thin; tear off a piece and use it to eat with. Portions are small, but the flavours are intense. If you prefer, you can have the dishes with rice or mashed potato. What goes on the injera? Wot, that's what. Doro wot (£8.50) is a piece of chicken and a hard-boiled egg in a rich sauce, while begh wot (£8.95) is lamb with a bit more chilli. Fried fish tibs (£8.95) is a dish of fried fish marinated in rosemary and lemon juice served with a mild chilli and garlic sauce. Try the Ethiopian traditional coffee (£5.50), which is not only delicious, but comes with its own mini-ceremonial.

✳ The Lalibela is a 12th Century Ethiopian church carved in the shape of a cross, from a huge outcrop of solid rock.

Nid Ting

533 Holloway Rd, N19 ☎020 7263 0506
Station Archway **Open** Mon–Sat 6–11.15pm, Sun 6–10.15pm
Accepts All major credit cards

What are restaurants for? Some pundits would have you believe that restaurants are for posing in, some that their mission is to entertain. Nid Ting is a place that feeds people. Lots of them. And it feeds people well, serving good, unfussy Thai food. The dishes here have not been tamed to suit effete Western palates, and you'll get plenty of chilli heat and pungent fish sauce. You'll also get good value and brisk service – both of which obviously appeal, as the place is usually packed. This is a genuine neighbourhood restaurant at ease with its surroundings.

The starters are neat platefuls of mainly fried food: chicken satay (£3.95) is sound, although the sauce is a bland one; a much better bet is the "pork on toasted" (£3.95) – a smear of rich, meaty paste on a disc of fried bread. The prawns tempura (£4.95) are large and crisp, and the peek ka yas sai (£3.95) is very successful – stuffed chicken wings, battered and deep-fried. The menu then darts off into numerous sections: there are hot and sour soups, clear soups, salads, curries, stir-fries, seafood, rice, noodle dishes and a long, long list of vegetarian dishes – all before you get to the chef's specials. From those specials, try the lamb Mussaman curry (£8.75), which is rich and good, made with green chillies and coconut milk. From the noodles, try pad see ew (£5.95), a rich dish made with thick ribbon noodles and your choice of chicken, beef or pork. As a side order, try the som tum (£4.50), which is a pleasingly astringent green papaya salad.

✳ The pla muk kaprow (£6.95), a dish of squid with chilli, garlic and Thai basil is notable.

The Parsee

Indian £15–£40

34 Highgate Hill, N19 ☎ 020 7272 9091
Station Archway **Open** Mon–Sat 6–10.45pm
Accepts All major credit cards ✇ www.theparsee.co.uk

London has had an acclaimed Parsee chef for some years now. His name is Cyrus Todiwala and his main restaurant is Café Spice Namaste (see p.89). Since 2001, however, London has also had what may be the world's best Parsee restaurant and Todiwala is its godfather. Parsees are renowned for their love of food – and for being the most demanding of customers. They start from the admirable standpoint that nothing beats home cooking and complain vehemently if everything is not exactly to their liking. They will be at home in this part of North London.

The food here is very good. Honest, strong flavours; rich and satisfying. Start with the admirable home-style akoori on toast (£3.50) – splendid, spiced, scrambled egg. Or try the masala ma murgh ki kalaeji (£4.25), chicken livers in a typical Parsee masala cooked quickly and served with a roti. Or go for something from the grill such as dhana jeera ni murghi (£4.75 or £9.75) – a superior chicken "tikka" made with ginger and cumin. Main courses include that most famous of Parsee dishes, the dhaansaak (£10.95), a rich dish of lamb and lentils. Then there's the murghi ni curry nay papeto (£9.95) – a distinctive curry made with chicken and potato, cashew nuts, sesame seeds and chickpeas. The breads – roti (£1.25 for two) – are very good, nutty and moreish. The vegetable dishes are good too: koru nay motta murcha (£4.25) is a simple dish made with cubed pumpkin. This is a small, "family" restaurant serving delicious and unfamiliar Indian food. An adventure well worth having.

✳ Save room for the toffee apricot ice cream (£3.75), rich with concentrated Hunza apricots.

St John's Mediterranean/Gastropub £15–£40

91 Junction Rd, N10 ☎020 7272 1587

Station Archway **Open** Mon 6.30–10.30pm, Tues–Fri noon–3.30pm & 6.30–11pm, Sat noon–4pm & 6.30–11pm, Sun noon–4pm & 6.30–10.30pm
Accepts All major credit cards

The rather unprepossessing Junction Road is an unlikely setting for this fine gastropub, where the emphasis is firmly on the gastro. The food is broadly Mediterranean, with a passion for all things rich, earthy and flavoursome. Not only that but the dining room, which lies beyond the pub itself, looks fabulous – all louche, junk-store glamour with its high, gold-painted ceiling, low chandeliers and plush banquettes. There's an open kitchen at one end of the room, while at the other a giant blackboard displays the long menu. The proprietors also own The Ealing Park Tavern (p.134).

As an opening move, the friendly staff bring fresh bread and bottles of virgin olive oil and balsamic vinegar. The menu changes day by day but there will probably be a soup – perhaps carrot and orange (£4.75), or ham, chickpea and spinach broth (£5). Other starters might be a chicken, pork and black pud terrine (£5.50) or chargrilled squid with chorizo (£6). The food is robust and mercifully unpretentious. Main courses range from the traditional – lamb rump with champ and greens (£14) – to the more adventurous, such as monkfish, paella rice, spinach, and chilli (£12). You'll need to take a breather before venturing into pud territory (all £4.50). Pannetone with ice cream; pineapple Pavlova; or a chocolate pistachio and date tart. The intelligent wine list includes a dozen by the glass, with a Cava at £4.25. St John's gets more crowded and more convivial as the night goes on, but it is possible to have a diner à deux; just make sure you're ready to be romantic by 7.30pm, when you might get a table.

✳ At lunch the menu is a touch shorter and a bit cheaper.

Further choices

El Molino
Spanish/Tapas

379 Holloway Rd, N7
☎020 7700 4312

El Molino was set up in 1992 and the tapas are good. Robust Spanish dishes and drinks to match!

Royal Cous Cous House
North African

316 Holloway Rd, N7
☎020 7700 2188

Better than average cous cous establishment; small and comfortable, not too aggressively priced.

Hoxton

© Crown copyright

Carnevale

135 Whitecross St, EC1 ☎020 7250 3452

Station Old Street **Open** Mon–Fri noon–3pm & 5.30–10.30pm, Sat 5.30–10.30pm
Accepts All major credit cards except AmEx ⊛www.carnevalerestaurant.co.uk

HOXTON

This rather strange little restaurant is tucked into an ordinary shop-like space halfway along a scruffy street that's all street market by day and dingy grubbiness by night. Inside is a clean, light but cramped space, full of blond wood tables and chairs, with carefully selected (if not particularly original) prints on the walls and a faux garden to the rear. The interior has been put together in workable form to meet the needs of the customers. Mercifully, the enduring tendency of vegetarian restaurants to litter the premises with hippy references has been brought under control.

Instead, close attention seems to have been paid to the food, which is cooked with care. The menu changes every couple of months, and is not overlong. Starters may range from flageolet bean fritters with marinated red peppers (£4.95); through soup of the day (£2.75); to purple sprouting broccoli with goat's cheese and Kalamata olives (£5.50). They are good enough to be served in many grander establishments. Main courses are equally grounded: potato gratin with fried free-range egg, buffalo mozzarella and wild mushrooms (£11.50); or radicchio and red wine risotto with Parmesan and herbs (£11.50). There is a plentiful list of side orders, though given the size of the portions it is unlikely that you'll need any. If your stamina is up to them, puddings (£4.95) are good, too: try the chocolate and chestnut roulade with passionfruit, or the caramelised blood orange tart. Service is relaxed, coffee is good and there are a number of alternative drinks on offer.

✳ The set menu (noon to 3pm and 5.30pm to 7pm) – three courses, or two courses and a glass of wine, for £12.50.

Cây Tre

301 Old St, EC1 ☎020 7729 8662

Station Old Street **Open** Mon–Thurs noon–3pm & 5.30–11pm, Fri & Sat noon–3.30pm & 5.30–11.30pm, Sun noon–10.30pm **Accepts** Mastercard & Visa

Until recently there was something of a demarcation line between the trendy clubs and restaurants on Old Street, and the more functional throng of Vietnamese restaurants just up the Kingsland Road. But in 2004 Cây Tre opened on Old Street. What is most surprising is that the food is so good, the prices are so reasonable and that the resto has retained that engaging family-run feel that is now getting harder to find on the Kingsland Road.

The menu is fascinating and includes many authentic and complicated Vietnamese dishes. Start with the bò cuôn bánh tráng (£7 per person for two) A griddle is set up on your table for you to grill thinly cut steak; while you're waiting soak rice papers until soft, then add sauce and parcel up the beef with pickles. Also prepared at table is cha cá La Vong (£9), a dish that hails from a notable restaurant on cha cá street in Hanoi. Sliced marinated monkfish is cooked in a frying pan at table on fresh fennel with a shrimp sauce. Another superb starter is the bò lá lôt (£4.50) – parcels of minced savoury beef wrapped in aromatic sapu leaves. From the mains, bò lúc lâc, (£5) – shaking beef – is made with tender rib-eye steak. There is a wide selection of noodle soups including the classic pho (£5), and you can get that most delicious of Vietnamese vegetable dishes, rau muống xào to'i (£4.80) – stir-fried water spinach with garlic dressing. There are two ways to make the most of Cây Tre's charming service and very good food: either opt for one of the "meals-in-a-bowl" and dine quickly, or order up an array of starters and feast.

✳ Try the Vietnamese beer called 333, like the nearby club.

Eyre Brothers

Mediterranean £25–£70

70 Leonard St, EC2 ☎ 020 7613 5346
Station Old Street/Liverpool Street **Open** Mon–Fri noon–3pm & 6.30–11pm, Sat 6.30–11pm **Accepts** All major credit cards

David Eyre will forever be pigeonholed as one of the creators of The Eagle (see p.106) and, as such, a founding father of the gastropub revolution. Which makes it all the more surprising to find Eyre and his brother at the helm of a very large, very swish, very elegant eighty-seat restaurant. Eyre Brothers is on Leonard Street, deep in the trendy part of EC2. There is a long bar and a good deal of dark wood and leather – the overall feel is one of comfortable clubbiness. The food is ballsy, with upfront flavours and textures, and scarcely a day goes by without some dishes falling off the menu and being replaced by new ones.

David's cuisine is hard to categorize – there are a few Spanish and Italian dishes, a lot of Portuguese specialities and some favourites from Mozambique. Starters range

widely, from octopus salad with mussel and chilli vinaigrette (£7); through warm pimentos de picquillo stuffed with duck confit (£7); to fried king scallops with Leon chorizo (£10). You will also be offered jamón Ibérico "Joselito" gran reserva 2001 (£16) – quality is the watchword here. Main courses include grilled Mozambique tiger prawns piri-piri (300g £21) These are large and meaty with a belt of heat from the Portuguese chilli. Or there may be grilled black leg chicken with garlic (£13). Puds are classics with a twist, such as basil and Mascarpone ice cream (£4), or chocolate fondant with almond milk sorbet (£5). This is one place where you can indulge in really good sherry: a rare Manzanilla Passada, a Palo Cortada or an old Oloroso by the glass, or the half-bottle.

> ✳ Ask about the specials available with 24 hours' notice – Portuguese-style suckling pig; Andalusian rabbit with rice.

Fish Central

Fish & Chips £8–£20

151 King's Square, Central St, EC1 ☏ 020 7253 4970
Station Barbican **Open** Mon–Sat 11am–2.30pm & 4.45–10.30pm
Accepts All major credit cards

The Barbican may appear to be the back of beyond – a black hole in the heart of the City – but perfectly ordinary people do live and work around here. Apart from the theatres and concert hall and the proximity to the financial district, one of the main attractions of the place is Fish Central, which holds its own with the finest fish-and-chip shops in town, and indeed a good many snootier restaurants. People tend to be very snobbish about fish-and-chip shops, but Fish Central is just the place to dispel such delusions.

Though at first sight Fish Central appears just like any other chippy – a takeaway service one side and an eat-in restaurant next door – a glance at its menu lets you know that this is something out of the ordinary. All the finny favourites are here, from cod and haddock to rock salmon and plaice (all £5.75), but there's a wholesome choice of alternatives, including grilled Dover sole (£11.90) and roast cod (£8.95) with sautéed potatoes. These dishes are cooked to order, and a menu note prepares you for a 25-minute wait. You can eat decently even if you are not in the mood for fish. Try the Cumberland sausages (£4.95), with onions and gravy. If you think your appetite is up to starters, try the prawn cocktail (£3.25) – the normal naked pink prawns in pink sauce, but genuinely fresh. Chips (£1.50) come as a side order, so those who prefer can order a jacket potato (£1.95) or creamed potatoes (£1.50). There are mushy peas (£1.50), which are, well, mushy, and pickled onion and gherkins (75p).

> ✳ This place has a sound wine list – the house champagne is £22.95.

The Fox

Modern British/Gastropub £17–£35

28 Paul St, EC2 ☎ 020 7729 5708

Station Old Street **Open** Mon–Fri noon–3pm & 6.30–10pm

Accepts All major credit cards except AmEx

It may raise a few eyebrows amongst biologists, but this fox is the direct descent of an eagle – The Fox is sibling to the original gastropub, The Eagle (see p.106). Downstairs it is a grand, pubby sort of pub, with decent real ale and the kind of serious pub food that really appeals. Upstairs is the dining room, which has much in common with the style of the original Eagle: the tables and chairs are an eclectic mix, the cutlery and china are gleefully mismatched, and the whole has a passing resemblance to Steptoe's lair.

The cooking at The Fox is "school of" The Eagle. Dishes are robust, well seasoned, honest and driven by the seasons. The menu changes every day, and while there isn't a huge amount of choice there should be something to please everyone. Pricing is straightforward: two courses cost £15 and three courses £19.75. For starters, a typical choice is between a potato and sorrel soup; smoked trout, dandelion and soft boiled egg; beetroot, Feta and rocket. Note the homeliness of these dishes, their balance and the comfortable combinations of flavour and texture. Main course options may include crab Newberg; cod, peas and escarole; pigeon, bubble and squeak; or gammon and parsley sauce. This food is as sophisticated as it is simple. Finish off with a delicious pud, such as buttermilk pudding with blood orange salad, or chocolate tart, and then a well chosen cheese. With food like this, and a sensibly priced wine list, The Fox makes for a pleasant, good-value and unpretentious place to eat.

✳ There is an agreeable little suntrap terrace, with a few tables for hardened lovers of the alfresco.

The Real Greek

Greek £15–£60

15 Hoxton Market, N1 ☎ 020 7739 8212

Station Old Street **Open** Mon–Sat noon–3pm & 5.30–10.30pm

Accepts All major credit cards ⓦ www.therealgreek.co.uk

This particular Real Greek is called Theodore Kyriakou. And showing off the authentic dishes of his homeland is the difficult mission Kyriakou has embarked upon. Next door to the restaurant is what was once the Hoxton Mission Hall, but now the lofty room has been converted into a busy Mezedopoliou, a bar where you can order a few meze (they cost between £2 and £6 a plateful and the bar is open from noon to 10.30pm) and try a dozen stunning Greek wines by the glass or carafaki. It's a relaxed way to sample some seriously good food. In 2003 The Real Greek set up a third establishment which has become the template for a small chain – The Souvlaki & Bar (see p.110).

The senior restaurant goes from strength to strength. The menu changes with the seasons. The first section is "Mezedes" and each platter has three or four components. One such might include chicken sofrito; courgettes stuffed with mince; tzatziki; and beetroot with yoghurt and walnuts (£8.25). Or there may be a plate with a scallop; a salad of lakerda (a preserved fish); fava; and horta – warm seasonal greens (£8.40). On to "Fagakia": these small dishes could be either starters or sides, such as grilled squid served with a leek and lemon pilaff (£8.40). Main courses are a revelation: duck stuffed with cinnamon spinach (£15.70); roast pork with smoked sausage (£14.90); or kakavia (£9.10) – a full on fish soup served with mayonnaise. Then there is a whole range of Greek cheeses and desserts – the Kymian fig and chocolate pot (£3.25) is outstanding.

✳ Wine lovers will find an amazing list of superb Greek wines – real quality at bargain prices.

Rivington Grill, Bar, Deli

British £18–£40

28–30 Rivington St, EC2 ☎ 020 7729 7053

Station Old Street **Open** Mon–Fri noon–3.30pm & 6.30–10.30pm, Sat 6.30–10.30pm
Accepts All major credit cards

The Rivington Grill, Bar, Deli opened at the very end of 2002. As well as the kind of name that hedges its bets, it has an elegant, high-ceilinged, white-painted dining room, a comfortable bar with high stools for solo diners, and plenty of sofas. The Deli part is to be found in a separate shop just around the corner. The restaurant menu is seasonal and interesting. This food is not Italian, it is not French, it is not fancy and it is not formal. The dishes don't even answer to Modern British. If there is such a cuisine as Ordinary British, then this is it.

On the face of it everything looks simple, but someone in the kitchen has given the dishes some thought and the combinations work well together. There may be Scotch broth (£5.50); a beetroot and goat's cheese salad with walnuts (£7.50); devilled kidneys on toast (£6.75) – lamb's kidneys cooked perfectly and with a well made sharp sauce. Or deep-fried skate cheeks with tartare sauce (£7.50). Main courses also satisfy: hamburger and chips

(£9.50); honey-baked ham with mustard sauce (£12.75); haddock fish fingers and chips with mushy peas (£11.50); roast suckling pig with pumpkin and quince sauce (£14.50). Or Barnsley chop (£15.25) with bubble and squeak – pink lamb, good gravy, nice bubble. Puddings veer from blood orange trifle (£6.25), to steamed chocolate pudding (£5.50). The wine list takes a commendable while to get to £30 a bottle, but then skitters on through a handful of pricey bottles to a £120 Vosne-Romanée. Stick with the middleweights for the best value.

✳ Hurrah! Banana custard (£4.75).

South

Very French £15–£45

128 Curtain Rd, EC2 ☎ 020 7729 4452
Station Old Street **Open** Tues–Sat noon–3pm & 6–10.30pm, Sun noon–3pm
Accepts All major credit cards

South is a small, pretty, modern restaurant with a mint-green exterior and a great deal of blond wood on show inside. It has an open kitchen, pleasant staff and informal atmosphere – all of which means that it slots right into yoof-trendy Hoxton/Shoreditch. Then you read the menu and your perception changes, because South is a very French restaurant that specializes in "cuisine grand-mère", and you'll find a list of old-fashioned seasonal dishes. This is wonderful food with great belts of flavour. This place combines good cooking with reasonable bills.

The menu is uncompromising and changes with the seasons. There may be soupe au pistou (£4.50), or salade de Roquefort, poire et noix (£5.60), and assiette d'hors d'oeuvres (£5.50) – this is so simple and so good. Take a plate and add four mounds: celeriac remoulade (good, creamy and mustardy); dressed grated carrot; tangy mushrooms à la Grecque; and the fourth, dressed beetroot. Or there is langue de veau en gelée (£5.80) – veal tongue in white wine jelly. Mains follow, through roast Pyrenean lamb with spring vegetables (£14.50). to poulet rôti salade pousse d'ail sauvage (£11.90), a really excellent chicken roast to perfection and served with a salad of wild garlic leaves. The puddings are also old friends – croustade des pommes (£5), and a glorious, self-indulgent mousse au chocolat (£5). Meanwhile the wine list keeps faith with this Francophilia and has some interesting bottles from southern France at reasonable prices.

✳ Amazing prix fixe menu – three courses £12.95 (lunch and until 7.30pm).

Zen Satori
Chinese/Indian/Thai £15–£30

40 Hoxton St, N1 &♿ ☎020 7613 9590

Station Old Street **Open** Mon–Wed 11am–3pm, Thurs & Fri 11am–3pm & 6–10pm, **Accepts** All major credit cards except Diners ✆www.zen-satori.co.uk

Zen Satori is the training restaurant of the Asian and Oriental School of Catering, but do not be deceived into thinking that you might end up with an amateurish meal. Granted, the service may be friendly and charming rather than super-slick, but it is easy to prefer it that way. Running down one side of the dining room is a gleaming modern, open kitchen full of bustling cooks – some are students, some are lecturers. Prices are dirt-cheap. The food is fresh, well cooked and well presented. The sooner all these students go out into the world and start spreading this gospel, the better.

The deals are amazing. There are four different set lunches (all £5.95). Pick Thai and enjoy chicken and mushroom tom yum, chicken and coriander cakes, and then beef with lemongrass and French beans – plus a choice of rice or noodles. Order Chinese and get wonton soup, vegetable spring roll, and lemon chicken – plus either rice or noodles. There is a soup, spring roll and green curried vegetables combo for vegetarians. The Indian option teams mulligatawny soup, samosas, and South Indian chicken curry and rice. The curry is a good one – authentically hot, with well balanced spices and a complex array of tastes. In the evening these dishes are available à la carte and will be joined by starters such as sesame prawn toast (£3.50) or chicken tikka (£3.50) – juicy, fresh, large chunks. The wine list tops out at around £15 and there are several decent beers on offer. If you are too mean for the £5.95 set lunch, you'll appreciate the range of "special one plate lunch options" at £4.75.

✳ This school deserves your support: leave a big tip.

Islington & Highbury

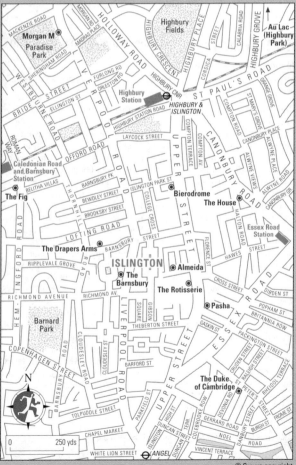

© Crown copyright

Almeida

French £20–£80

30 Almeida St, N1 ☎020 7354 4777

Station Highbury & Islington **Open** Daily noon–2.30pm & 5.30–11pm
Accepts All major credit cards

It may be located in oh-so-trendy Islington, opposite the home base of the Almeida Theatre, and it may be yet another outpost of Sir Terence Conran's sprawling London empire, but spiritually Almeida is stuck in some faintly remembered rural France. The menu at Almeida manages to be a distillation of all that is good about an old-fashioned, gently familiar kind of French cooking and eating. On top of which, the large dining room is comfortable and the service is slick without being oppressive. There is a comprehensive wine list, with a good selection available by the glass.

This is a place to overdose on nostalgia. Bisque de homard (£6.50) is the genuine article; six or twelve escargots à la Bourguignon (£5 or £9.50) provides garlic heaven; there's poireaux vinaigrette, truffe noires (£6.50); cuisses de grenouilles persillés (£8); and best of all, the trolley of charcuterie (£10.50). This chariot is wheeled round to your table and you can pig out on well-made terrines, pâtés and rillettes to your heart's content. Mains carry the theme forward

triumphantly: cassoulet Toulousain (£12.50); steak au poivre (£19.50); whole roast seabass au pastis (£15). Pukka pommes frites (£2.50). For pud there's the tantalizingly named "trolley of tarts" (£6), or petit pot au chocolat (£4.50). With such a single-minded menu, Almeida could have ended up as something of a French resto theme park, but the kitchen is passionate about the classic dishes, and the mood ends up affectionate rather than reverential. No wonder it is busy enough to make booking for dinner a prudent idea.

✱ Lunch, less crowded and just £14.50 for two courses, £17.50 for three.

Au Lac

Vietnamese £8–£25

82 Highbury Park, N1 ☎020 7704 9187

Station Arsenal **Open** Mon–Fri noon–2.30pm & 5.30–11pm, Sat & Sun 5.30–11pm
Accepts Mastercard & Visa

Vietnamese restaurants in London tend to divide into two camps. On the one hand there

are the spartan canteens – no frills, no nonsense and no concessions to non-Vietnamese speakers. And on the other there is a sprinkling of glossy, West End establishments. This branch of Au Lac is hidden away in Highbury and has a dining room that is comfortable in an informal, shabby sort of way, with knick-knacks on the walls. There's now a newer, flashier, branch on the Kingsland Road.

Start with goi cuon (two for £2.20). These are soft rice-flour pancakes wrapped around crunchy veg and large grilled prawns, and they're fresh and light. Then there's goi tom (£6) – you get large steamed prawns, a small pot of hot and spicy sauce, and several large iceberg lettuce leaves. Take a leaf, add sauce and prawn, wrap, eat, enjoy. The deep-fried monkfish

with garlic and chilli (£6) is very good and there are good soups, too. The noodle soups – pho, bun bo and tom hue – come in large portions. They are cheap and tasty, good for eating when alone. For a more sociable, sharing meal, try the chicken with lemongrass and chilli (£4.80). The noodles are also very good – pho xao do bien (£5) is a grand dish of stir-fried rice noodles with fresh herbs and seafood, providing a good combination of flavours and textures. Another very impressive dish is the "minced pork with aubergine in hot pot" (£6.50). Ordering this brings a small casserole whose contents appear almost black. Very dark, very rich, very tasty.

※ If offered special "Vietnamese sake" beware – this clear hooch is a cousin to dry-cleaning fluid.

The Barnsbury

Modern British/Gastropub £10–£30

209–211 Liverpool St, N1 ☎020 7607 5519

Station Highbury & Islington **Open** Mon–Fri noon–3pm & 6.30–10pm, Sat noon–4pm & 6.30–10pm, Sun noon–4pm & 6–9pm
Accepts All major credit cards ✆www.thebarnsbury.co.uk

The establishment now known as the Barnsbury left an incarnation as seedy bar Hourican's behind, and just before Christmas 2002 took on a new role as a rather good gastropub. It has settled in well. The team includes Jeremy Gough, and Kathleen Lynch who runs the kitchen. This is a pleasant, informal, pubby type pub with good food. And wonder of wonders it serves pub food rather than restaurant food. The management have got the menu right, the prices right, the service right and the

ambience right. The Barnsbury deserves its success.

The menu changes day to day and offers seven starters, seven mains and half a dozen puds; the proprietors must be congratulated for not succumbing to the lure of fancy dishes. In the colder months starters will probably include a couple of soups – French onion (£4) or spinach and broccoli (£3.50). Other starters may be a warm Puy lentil salad, chorizo and poached egg (£6); a prawn and crayfish cocktail, with

Mains are "in-your-face-ordinary" and none the worse for that. Steak and Guinness pie (£10.50); chargrilled chump of English lamb, aubergine and coriander pate (£10.50); braised faggots, mushy peas and gravy (£9.50); or grilled whole plaice, garlic, oregano and lemon juice (£10.50). Puddings are also satisfying: chocolate cheesecake; rice pudding brulée; Seville orange cake (all £4.50). The blackboard wine list steers a sensible course between good value at the bottom of the price range and interesting bottles at the top.

pumpernickel bread (£7); or a smoked duck, walnut and pickled cucumber salad (£5.50) – good complimentary flavours.

✳ Corn-fed chicken breast comes with "smoked black pudding" and a tarragon sauce (£10.50).

Bierodrome

Belgian £8–£60

173–174 Upper St, N1 ☎020 7226 5835

Station Highbury & Islington **Open** Daily noon–midnight
Accepts All major credit cards ⊛ www.belgorestaurants.co.uk

Bierodrome is part of the Belgo organisation (p.114), and shares its emphasis on modernist and iconoclastic architecture. The long, low bar is a temple to beer, and with that beer you can eat if you wish. The menu introduces a change of pace from the other branches – yes, there is life after mussels! Here there are sausages with stoemp, along with steaks, duck confit, croquettes and frites. Unsurprisingly the beeriness spreads through the menu – wild boar sausages with beer; roast chickens basted with beer.

It is no surprise that when the Bierodrome first opened they found that the customers were walking off with the beer and wine list. It makes stunning reading, with more than

seventy beers to pore over and ultimately pour out. As you work your way through a series of delicious glassfuls, what you will need is some food. Croquettes make good starters: try the Trappist cheese with piccalilli (£4.50). Wild boar sausages (£8.50) are made with dark Chimay beer and are served with stoemp, a superior kind of mashed potato indigenous to Belgium. Then there are the famous Belgo mussel pots: a kilo pot costs £9.95 and can be had marinière, Provençale, Portuguese or even Thai – the latter cooked with creamed coconut and coriander. Or there's half a spit-roast chicken with frites (£8.50). Steaks include a 6oz sirloin with frites, salad, tomatoes and garlic butter (£10.95), and there's a burger with smoked bacon and Swiss cheese (£8.50). There is an "express" lunch bargain, with a main course for £5.55. As you'd expect from a "beer driven" establishment this place can get lively.

> ✱ Home to London's priciest bottle of beer – containing fifteen litres of La Veille Bon Secours a snip at £635.

The Drapers Arms

Modern British/Gastropub £12–£45

44 Barnsbury St, N1 ☎ 020 7619 0348

Station Highbury & Islington **Open** Mon–Fri noon–3pm & 7–10.30pm, Sat noon–3pm & 7–10.30pm, Sun noon–4pm **Accepts** All major credit cards except Diners

The Drapers started life as an old-fashioned double-fronted Georgian pub and that is pretty much how it has remained, despite the gastropub makeover. There's a bar downstairs and a dining room upstairs, and out the back is a large walled yard that has been paved over and kitted out with tables and chairs, and a pair of huge awnings in case of rain. This "extra dining room" seats another 45 hungry customers, and when the weather is sunny it is a thoroughly charming place.

The menu changes twice daily and reflects the seasons, but starters may include pea soup (£4.80); caramelised onion and goat's cheese tart with rocket and Parma ham (£6.80); roast artichoke, sun-blushed tomatoes with Feta and piquillo peppers (£6.50) or a foie gras parfait with quince jelly and toasted sourdough (£8.50). Or how about a salad of chicken livers, pancetta, frisee and soft poached egg (£5.50)? Among the mains could be lemon risotto with grilled fennel, soft herbs and crème fraiche (£9.50); slow-cooked rabbit with black olives and sherry vinegar (£13.50); deep-fried plaice with pea purée and chips (£12.50); or a 10oz sirloin with chips and Béarnaise (£15.50); as well as monkfish and scallop skewer with cardamom rice (£14.50). The chips (£2.80) are stellar, and side dishes may include welcome combos such as wilted spinach and lemon oil (£3). Puds are sound, and sensibly the kitchen sticks to favourites such as sticky toffee pudding and custard; double-chocolate brownie, hot chocolate sauce and crème fraiche; or nougat glacé with mango and basil (all at £5.50).

> ✱ Good sandwiches and bar snacks.

Duke of Cambridge

Modern British/Gastropub £15–£35

30 St Peter's St, N1 ☎ 020 7359 3066

Station Angel **Open** Mon–Fri 12.30–3pm & 6.30–10.30pm, Sat 12.30–3.30pm & 6.30–10.30pm, Sun 12.30–3.30pm & 6.30–10pm
Accepts All major credit cards ⊛ www.singhboulton.co.uk

In the canon of organic, things don't get much holier than this, the first gastropub to be certified by the Soil Association. Game and fish are either wild or caught from sustainable resources, and the 40-strong wine list is 95 percent organic. As "organic" becomes every supermarket's favourite adjective it is hard to remember that it was tough going in the beginning, and the Duke was there at the start. There's a small, bookable restaurant at the back, but most diners prefer to share the tables in the noisy front bar – the Duke is for the gregarious as well as the organic battalions.

The blackboard menu changes twice daily and is commendably short; you order from the bar. Robust bread with good olive oil and grey sea salt is served while you wait. Starters may include leek and potato soup (£4.50); a pork liver and sage parfait with pickles and toast (£7); or smoked mackerel beetroot and caper salad (£7.50). Main courses are an eclectic bunch: a 7oz chickpea burger comes with grilled bread, tomato salad and yoghurt dressing (£10), while roast cod is teamed with spinach, a mangetout risotto and mussel cream sauce (£13.50). Grilled pork chop comes with horseradish Dauphinoise and Savoy cabbage (£13.50); grilled venison steak is served with braised lentils, green beans, bacon and fig jam (£14.50). Puddings include pear crumble with cream (£5) and a chocolate soufflé cake with crème fraîche and kumquat compote (£5). The wines are well chosen and varied, with a Greek Domaine Spiropoulos Porfyros (£16), and a New Zealand Te Aria Malbec (£21).

✱ Seek out the deliciously light and refreshing Eco Warrior ale brewed by the Pitfield Brewery.

Fig

Modern European £18–£35

169 Hemingford Rd, N1 ☎ 020 7609 3009

Station Caledonian Road **Open** Tues–Sat 7–10.30pm, Sun noon–3.30pm
Accepts All major credit cards except AmEx & Diners ⊛ www.figrestaurant.co.uk

If there were a prize for the best genuinely local restaurant it would go to Fig. This place is small, unpretentious, informal and the food is very good indeed. Chef and co-proprietor Annie O'Carroll has serious form having worked with Peter Gordon. There are about thirty covers at Fig (with the promise of a handful more in the garden at the rear should we get the weather) and the dining room is painted a restful mushroomy sort of brown. Ms O'Carroll plies her trade virtually single-handed, and this pared down kitchen brigade is reflected in a shortness of the menu which changes daily – five starters, five mains and five puds.

Dishes are confident and hearty with upfront flavours. Grilled scallops come with cured salmon, fennel and horseradish breadcrumbs (£6.20) – a brilliant plateful. Or how about scrambled duck eggs on toast with rocket, asparagus and truffle oil (£3.80)? Buttery scramble, crunchy toast, peppery rocket. Or chicken livers, ruby chard, grilled Haloumi and fig Argan oil dressing (£5). Mains range from grilled chermoula bream, with wok-fried pea shoots and yoghurt (£12.50); to grilled lamb with cous cous salad and roast carrots (£12.80). A star dish is the saddle of venison, served with Judion beans, wilted garlic leaves and mushrooms (£13.20). Puds are equally fine – raspberry jellies with ice cream and Turkish delight (£4.50). The wine list is strong at the gentler price levels; service is friendly, and bearing in mind the very few staff involved, the restaurant spins along merrily. A local hero.

✷ There is a real risk that the serious portions here will overwhelm.

The House Modern British/Gastropub £15–£55

63–69 Canonbury Rd, N1 ☇ ☎020 7704 7410

Station Highbury & Islington **Open** Mon 5.30–10.30pm, Tues–Fri noon–2.30pm & 5.30–10.30pm, Sat 5.30–10.30pm, Sun 6–9.30pm (brunch Sat & Sun noon–3.30pm)
Accepts All major credit cards except AmEx & Diners ☻www.inthehouse.biz

As befits a location in one of Islington's smarter enclaves, The House seems more gastro than pub. But what is most unusual about this N1 establishment is that for once aspirations on the menu seem matched by real talent in the kitchen. The House emerged from a lengthy (and seriously expensive) transformation from dodgy local to chic eating house in mid-October 2002 but, despite a dining room that has been busy ever since, service is friendly and unstuffy. There's a menu de jour Tues–Fri: £12.95 for two courses, £14.95 for three.

The kitchen is an open one and before you even get to your food the signs are good – the chefs work quickly, quietly and neatly. On the top of the grill there is an imposing piece of meat warming through: the chargrilled rib of Buccleugh beef, shallot crust, gratin Dauphinoise, green beans, jus gras (£45 for two). Whoever gets to share this particular rib will be thankful that it wasn't straight from fridge to grill. From the starters a parfait of foie gras, chicken livers and Armagnac (£6.95), comes with toasted brioche. There's also a Tatin of red onion, with grilled goat's cheese (£5.95). Mains also hit the spot: braised spiced pork with ginger and pommes cocotte (£13.95), or roast sea bass with piperade (£16). There is also the house shepherd's pie. When talking shepherd's pie a price tag of £10.50 takes some living up to, but it just about delivers. Large chunks of lamb, good gravy, unctuous mash, crisp top. Puds are good – warm gingerbread with clotted cream (£5.50); Valrhona hot chocolate pudding (£5.50). Brunch is big here.

✳ The kitchen will make you a birthday cake if your order it 24 hours in advance.

Morgan M

French £40–£100

489 Liverpool Rd, N1 ☎ 020 7609 3560
Station Highbury & Islington/Holloway **Open** Tues 7–10pm, Wed–Fri noon–2.30pm & 7–10pm, Sat 7–10pm, Sun noon–2.30pm
Accepts All major credit cards except AmEx & Diners

Morgan Meunier is a short, passionate Frenchman. He is also a chef and a very good one. Morgan M is very much his baby: he painted the pictures displayed on the walls, and the large and accomplished front of house team have all worked with him before. The restaurant is in a converted Watney's pub and it is now dark green outside with mint green within. On the wall is a bookshelf displaying a complete set of Michelin guides. Morgan wants a star very badly, and he'll probably get one – the food is certainly good enough. Foodies are already making this resto a place of pilgrimage.

In the main they are right to do so. The style of the place is very French; very haute cuisine dishes are complex and elegant on the plate, but the seasoning is spot on and the dishes work well. Pricing is straightforward: dinner is £30 for three courses, or £39 for the six course Degustation. Starters may include a ravioli of snails in Chablis with poached garlic; or a carpaccio of gently smoked scallops with asparagus coulis and fromage blanc sorbet – very delicate, very fresh

flavours. Onwards to a pavé of turbot topped with a crayfish raviolo, cream of celeriac, champagne velouté; grilled Anjou squab pigeon; or roast fillet of veal with sweetbreads, kidney and a splendidly rich cream and morels sauce. Puds are featured – there's a dark chocolate moelleux (you get to specify dark or plain chocolate) and a raspberry soufflé. The wine list scampers up to a bottle of Margaux at £790 but there's plenty around £30 for mere mortals.

✳ There's a splendid six course veggie menu, "From the garden" £34.

Pasha

Turkish £15–£35

301 Upper St, N1 ☎020 7226 1454

Station Angel **Open** Mon–Thurs noon–3pm & 6.30–11.30pm, Fri & Sat noon–3pm & 6pm–midnight, Sun noon–11pm **Accepts** All major credit cards except Switch

If you picture Turkish food as heavy and oil-slicked, think again. Pasha is dedicated to producing fresh, light, authentic Turkish food that's suited to modern tastes. Dishes are made with virgin olive oil, fresh herbs, strained yoghurts and fresh ingredients prepared daily. Pasha doesn't look like a traditional Turkish restaurant either, being open and airy with only the odd brass pot for decoration.

For anyone new to Turkish cooking the menu is helpful, and so are the staff who will encourage you to eat in Turkish style – with lots of small "meze" dishes. Set menus are popular (minimum two people): £12.95 for twelve meze and £18.95 for the Pasha Feast (ten meze plus main courses, dessert and coffee). Meze may include hummus, tarama, cacik, kisir (a splendid bulgur wheat concoction), falafel, courgette fritters, meatballs and a host of others. Main courses are more familiar but the choice is better than usual. Try kilic baligi (£11.95), fillet of swordfish marinated in lime, bay leaf and herbs, and served with rice; shish kebab (£8.95), the standard lamb kebab; or Izmir kofte (£8.50) – meat balls in tomato sauce. Alternatively try yogurtlu iskender (£8.95) – a trio of shish, kofte and chicken on pitta bread soaked in fresh tomato sauce with fresh herbs and topped with yoghurt. Though meat undeniably dominates the menu, there are five vegetarian and three fish selections. Puddings include the usual Turkish stickies but are light and freshly made. Wines are priced fairly, and there is Efes beer from Turkey (£2.95).

✳ For a tongue-numbing blast of the real Near East, – a shot of raki (£3.95).

The Rotisserie

Rotisserie/Steak £15–£30

134 Upper St, N1 ☎020 7226 0122

Station Angel **Open** Mon & Tues 6–10.45pm, Wed–Fri noon–3pm & 6–10.45pm, Sat noon–10.45pm, Sun noon–10pm **Accepts** All major credit cards ✆www.rotisserie.co.uk

The Rotisserie is buzzing, brightly painted and unpretentious, with a commitment to quality underlying both food and service. Its South African owner makes regular trips to Scotland to lean on the farm gate and make small talk about Aberdeen Angus steers (which, if they did but know it, will soon be visiting his grill), and his menu's claim, "Famous for our steaks", seems well earned. The kitchen also frets about the quality of their chips, which is no bad thing, as the classic combination of a well grilled steak with decent French fries and Béarnaise sauce is one of life's little luxuries.

Rotisserie starters are sensibly simple: a good Caesar salad (£3.95); tiger prawns peri peri (£4.95); grilled mushrooms with garlic and Parmesan (£3.95); chargrilled spareribs (£4.25). Having brushed aside these preliminaries, on to the steaks, all of which are Scottish Aberdeen Angus: 225g rump (£12.95); 300g sirloin (£14.95); 200g fillet (£14.95). All are carefully chosen, carefully hung, and carefully cooked. All of the main courses come with a good-sized bowl of rather good French fries. If you don't want steak, try something else from the rotisserie such as the wonderful crisp-roasted Barbary duck (£12.95) – half a duck with fruit chutney. Or perhaps "simply sausages: with creamed mash and onion gravy" (£8.95). The rest of the menu covers the bases for non-meat-eaters. There's a grilled fish of the day (£12.95), or grilled Mediterranean vegetable skewers with spiced rice (£8.95). Puddings (all £3.95) are sound, and range from pecan pie through the ubiquitous tiramisù, and banoffi pie.

✳ The "monkey gland" sauce is rumoured to include both Coca-Cola and Mrs Ball's Chutney.

Further choices

Brasserie Le Trouvaille
Very French

353 Upper St, N1
☎ 020 7704 8323

Branch of the Soho original; same low prices, same good French food. See review on p.320.

The Fish Shop
Fish

360-362 St John St, EC1
☎ 020 7837 1199

A fish and chip shop turned restaurant. Aspirational menu; comfortable dining with tables laid out over several floors.

Masala Zone
Indian

80 Upper St, N1
☎ 020 7359 3399

Branch of the Soho original, same low prices, same Indian street food. See review on p.314.

Sabor
Pan South American

108 Essex Rd, N1
☎ 020 7226 5551

"Nuovo Latino" newcomer with dishes from Colombia, Brazil, Peru and Argentina. Good ceviche, great salsas and competitive prices.

Wagamama
Japanese/Chinese

N1 Centre, Parkfield, N1
☎ 020 7226 2664

Branch of the reputable noodle chain. See review on p.48.

Kennington & Vauxhall

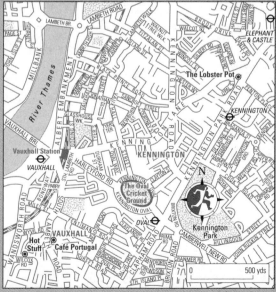

Café Portugal

Portuguese £11–£27

Victoria House, South Lambeth Rd, SW8 ☎ 020 7587 1962

Station Vauxhall **Open** Mon–Sat 8am–11pm, Sun 10am–10.30pm
Accepts All major credit cards except Diners

When setting up a bar, café or restaurant, the first item on any proud new Portuguese owner's shopping list must be the telly. All the televisions in South Lambeth Road seem to be turned up loud, and the one in the bar of Café Portugal is no exception (thankfully, the one in the restaurant half of the operation is not always switched on). Portuguese restaurateurs have all mastered the trick of integrating their establishments with the community and Café Portugal is a laid-back, easy-paced kind of eatery with distinctly dodgy mud-orange décor. The food is workmanlike and appears authentically Portuguese.

To start with you can opt for calamares fritos (£3.70), and sopa do día (£2.20), the soup of the day. Or more interesting dishes like ameijoas a Café Portugal (£3.80), which are clams and must be a step up on that trusty old Portuguese special, avocado with prawns (£3.30). Then there are a dozen fishy options, including lobster, sea bass, Dover sole, monkfish and salt cod. Bacalhau à Gomes de Sá (£9) turns out to be a stunning and gloriously simple dish of salt cod cooked in the oven with potatoes, onions and chunks of hard-boiled egg. For the meat-eater there's carne de porco à Alentejana (£9), another all-in-one, home-cooked kind of meal in which small chunks of pork are served with some clams, chorizo and chopped pickled vegetables, with small cubes of crisp-fried potato scattered over the top. At Café Portugal, puddings are largely pastries and you are doomed if you don't like eggy confections.

✳ Reasonably priced and interesting Portuguese wines.

Hot Stuff

Indian £15–£35

19 Wilcox Rd, SW8 ☎ 020 7720 1480

Station Vauxhall/Stockwell **Open** Mon–Fri noon–10pm, Sat 4–10pm
Accepts All major credit cards ❀ www.eathotstuff.com

This tiny restaurant, run by the Dawood family is something of an institution. It has only a few seats and offers simple and startlingly cheap food to an enthusiastic local following. The food is just what you would expect to get at home – assuming you were part of Nairobi's Asian community. Trade is good and the dining room, though unprepossessing, is welcoming: all soft blues and orange with an array of different-coloured chairs.

The starters are sound rather than glorious, so it's best to dive straight into the curries. There are various chicken curries and lamb curries, all priced at between £3.25 and £5.45. It is hard to find any fault with a curry that costs just £3.25! The most expensive option is in the fish section: king prawn biryani, which costs £7.50 (not much more than you would pay for a curried potato in the West End). The portions aren't monster-sized, and the spicing isn't subtle, but the welcome is genuine and the bill is tiny. Arrive before 9.30pm and you can sample the delights of the stuffed paratha (£1.50) – light and crispy with potato in the middle, they taste seriously delicious. Chickpea curry (£2.60), daal soup (£2.50) and mixed vegetable curry (£2.25) all hit the spot with vegetarians. For meat-eaters, the chicken Madras (£3.40) is hot and workmanlike, while the chicken bhuna (£3.50) is rich and very good. Hot Stuff closes prudently before the local pubs turn out, and part of the fun here is to watch latecomers – say, a party of three arriving at 9.50pm and seeking food. Promising to eat very simply and very quickly may do the trick.

✱ Bring your own alcohol, no corkage is charged.

The Lobster Pot   Very French/Fish £15–£60

3 Kennington Lane, SE11 ☎ 020 7582 5556
Station Kennington **Open** Tues–Sat noon–2.30pm & 7–11pm
Accepts All major credit cards ⓦ www.lobsterpotrestaurant.co.uk

You have to feel for Nathalie Régent. What must it be like to be married to – and working alongside – a man whose love of the bizarre verges on the obsessional? Britain is famed for breeding dangerously potty chefs, but The Lobster Pot's chef-patron, Hervé Régent, originally from Vannes in Brittany, is well ahead of the field. Walk down Kennington Lane towards the restaurant and it's even money as to whether you are struck first by the life-size painted plywood cutout of Hervé dressed in oilskins, or the speakers relaying a soundtrack of seagulls and melancholy Breton foghorns.

These clues all point towards fish. The fish here is pricey but it is fresh and well chosen. Starters range from well made, very thick, traditional fish soup (£6.50) to a really proper plateau de fruits de mer (small £11.50, large £22.50). The main course specials sometimes feature strange fish that Hervé has discovered at Billingsgate. As well as classics like l'aile de raie au beurre noisette (£15.50) – skate with brown butter – there are good spicy dishes, such as filet de thon à la Créole (£15.50), which is tuna with a perky tomato sauce. Simpler, and as good in its way, is les crevettes grillées à l'ail (£18.50), big prawns in garlic butter. The accompanying bread is notable, a soft, doughy pain rustique, and for once le plateau de fromage à la Française (£6.50) doesn't disappoint. The Lobster Pot's weekday set lunch (£11.50 for two courses, £14.50 for three) makes lots of sense. It could get you smoked salmon pate followed by pan-fried plaice goujons and crêpe sauce à la mangue.

✱ Abdicate responsibility and go for the eight course "Menu Surprise" (£39.50) – Hervé's choice, and usually a good one.

Kensington

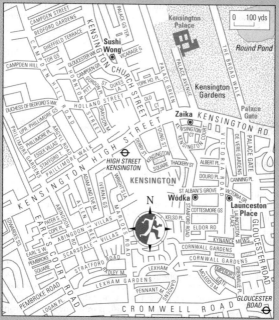

Launceston Place | Modern British £18–£65

1a Launceston Place, W8 ☎ 020 7937 6912

Station High Street Kensington **Open** Mon–Fri 12.30–2.30pm & 7–11.30pm, Sat 7–11.30pm, Sun 12.30–2.30pm & 7–10pm **Accepts** All major credit cards

KENSINGTON

Launceston Place is one of those small, chic streets where you cannot help feeling a pang of envy for anyone rich enough to live in the slick little houses. As the road curves you'll find a sprinkling of high-ticket shops and the Launceston Place restaurant. The restaurant sprawls its way through a nest of rooms and is formal but pleasant. Service is efficient without being in your face and there is a traditional feel to everything. This is a neighbourhood restaurant, but one in a very swish neighbourhood, which makes some sense of the fact that a couple of years after opening here the team went on to create Kensington Place (see p.259) – another resto in tune with its surroundings.

The menu changes every six weeks or so and dishes match traditional combinations with fashionable ingredients in an unstuffy way. Starters range from fish soup with rouille (£6.50), through twice-baked Gruyere cheese soufflé (£8) to marinated duck salad with mango and orange salsa (£8). Mains range from roast cod with mushy peas and fat chips (£17.50); through John Dory with Chardonnay vinegar cream (£17); to meatier offerings such as veal escalope with pancetta and sage (£17.50); or roast chump of lamb with a saffron pea and chorizo risotto (£17.50). The dessert menu ticks all the appropriate boxes: there's steamed orange pudding and custard (£6), or a white chocolate tart (£6.50). The wine list is strong in traditional areas, so think French. The set lunch is much beloved by local ladies-who-lunch – £15.50 for two courses and £18.50 for three.

✳ A three course Sunday lunch is £22.50.

Sushi Wong | Japanese £15–£40

38C–D Kensington Church St, W8 ☎ 020 7937 5007

Station High Street Kensington **Open** Mon–Fri noon–2.30pm & 6–10.30pm, Sat noon–10.30pm, Sun 6–10pm **Accepts** All major credit cards

Sushi Wong is the kind of name you either love or hate but, whichever side you take, it is certainly slick – just like this deceptively sized restaurant. On the ground floor there's a modernist Japanese restaurant-cum-sushi-bar seating about 25 people. The tone of the décor is all brightness and modernity, the service is so low-key that it almost seems timid, but Sushi Wong is a confident and efficient place for all that.

Sushi is delicious here. Ordering the sushi matsu set (£18) brings a round lacquer tray with six pieces of salmon or tuna roll flanked by ten pieces of various sushi – the chef's selection. The fish is fresh, the wasabi strong, the gari delicious and the sushi well prepared. The sushi také (£15.50) combines seven assorted pieces with six pieces of cucumber roll. A good array at a fair price. As well as a long list of individual sushi, there is also a wide range of à la carte starters such as agedashi tofu (£3.90), fried tofu with dashi sauce; tempura soft-shell crab (£7.50); yakitori (£4.50); and gyoza (£4.20), which are steamed dumplings. Mains include tara saikyo yaki (£11.80), broiled cod with miso; steak teriyaki (£12); pork tonkatsu (£9.20); nabeyaki udon (£8.80) – a soupy dish with noodles, chicken, vegetables and prawns – and the Sushi Wong tempura selection (£12.80), which includes king prawns, fish and vegetables. The set menus do make life simpler. Two offer five courses for £22 and one offers six for £26. Finish up with either banana tempura with green tea ice cream (£3.50) or tempura ice cream with fresh fruit (£3.80).

 "Kensington Roll (£4) – inside out crispy salmon and asparagus".

Wódka

Polish £17–£50

12 St Alban's Grove, W8 ☎020 7937 6513

Station High Street Kensington **Open** Mon–Fri 12.30–2.30pm & 7–11.15pm, Sat & Sun 7–11.15pm **Accepts** All major credit cards ⊛ www.wodka.co.uk

Wódka is a restaurant that lies in wait for you. It's calm and bare, and the food is better than you might expect – well cooked, and thoughtfully seasoned. The daily lunch menu represents extremely good value at £14.95, a large proportion of the dishes being refugees from the evening à la carte. Where, you wonder, is the streak of madness that helped the Polish cavalry take on German tank regiments with sabres drawn? On the shelves behind the bar, that's where, in the extensive collection of moody and esoteric vodkas, which are for sale both by the shot and by the carafe.

The soup makes a good starter: Barszcz (£4.90) is a rich, beetrooty affair and comes with little sauerkraut and mushroom parcels called pasztecik. Blinis are also the business: they come with smoked salmon (£7.50 or £11.90), aubergine mousse (£5.50 or £8.90) or 40g of Oscietra caviar (£25.50). A selection (£7.50 or £11.50) will get you all except the caviar. Also good is the kaszanka (£5.90) – grilled black pudding with pickled red cabbage and pear purée. For a main course, the fishcakes (£11.90) with creamed leeks is a firm favourite with the regulars. In line with the Polish love of wild game, when partridge is available it is roasted and served with a splendid mash of root vegetables; wild boar is served with roast baby beetroot and red-wine shallots (£14.90); or there may be braised rabbit with mustard sauce, spatzle dumplings and black cabbage (£13.90). Puddings tend to be of the oversweet, under-imaginative gateaux variety. Opt for the chocolate truffle cake (£4.90).

 "Rowani" – rowan berry vodka, fresh mint, lime and soda (£5.90).

Kilburn, Queen's Park & Willesden

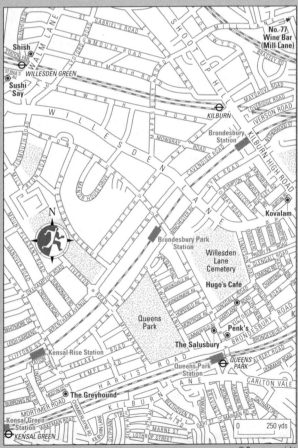

© Crown copyright

The Greyhound

Modern British/Gastropub £15–£35

64–66 Chamberlayne Rd, NW10 & ☎020 8969 8080

Station Kensal Green **Open** Mon 6.30–10.30pm, Tues–Sat 12.30–3pm & 6.30–10.30pm, Sun 12.30–4pm & 6.30–10.30pm **Accepts** All major credit cards except AmEx & Diners

This bit of NW10 is perfect gastropub territory so there were appreciative murmurs when the Greyhound opened in November 2003. It has been busy ever since. There are two long rooms stretching back from the pavement and each has its own front door. On the left, as you look at it, is the bar (previously a rugged Irish bar) and to the right is the dining room (previously a derelict shop). The open kitchen is to the rear of the restaurant and there are a couple of large doors linking drinking with dining. The menu changes monthly but tends to stick with mainstream dishes, simply executed and presented.

The food is sound and the regularly changing menu short and to the point. Starters range from sweet potato and coconut soup (£4.50) to a well made risotto of morcilla and broad beans (£6). Seared tuna comes with a ginger dressing (£6.50); deep-fried oysters come with a Bloody Mary salsa (£8.50); and gnocchi (£5.50) comes with tomato, rocket and goat's cheese. The short list of mains ranges from roast cod with confit potatoes and Brittany artichokes (£13.50); to poached smoked haddock with bubble and squeak, poached egg and Hollandaise (£10.50). Fillet of pork is served with a gratin and cabbage (£10); poached gilthead bream is teamed with olive oil mash (£13); and a grilled rib-eye steak (£14) with green beans, chips and green peppercorn sauce. The wine list is user friendly and avoids merciless smash and grab – there is plenty to be drunk at under £25. Service is friendly and things run pretty smoothly.

✳ The owners of this place used to own the handsome racing greyhound in the painting.

Hugo's

British £17–£35

25 Lonsdale Rd, NW6 ☎020 7372 1232

Station Queens Park **Open** Daily 9.30am–11pm **Accepts** Mastercard & Visa

For many years this resto was known as the Organic Café before it changed hands and was renamed Hugo's. But it would take a very perceptive person to pinpoint any differences other than the name. The kitchen ticks all the right boxes: organic; seasonal; local produce; non-endangered fish; traditional methods; eco-friendly practices. This place is a genuine neighbourhood gem in a semi-private, quiet road with a largish yellow-painted dining room decorated with twisted fig branches and reclaimed chicken-wire light fittings.

The menu changes sporadically and is divided into starters, mains and puds, with the addition of one-course dishes consisting of salads and pastas. But you can mix and match as you wish. The cooking is reasonably classical,

with little that is unnecessarily fancy. Expect a soup – butternut squash and coconut (£4.50) perhaps – or a mixed crostini platter (£5.80). Or grilled goat's cheese with aubergine caviar (£6.50), or maybe an organic smoked salmon platter (£7.50). For main course artichoke risotto comes with smoked Mozzarella (£6.50 or £10.50) and vies for attention with pan-fried fillet of bream with crayfish risotto (£13.50). Braised shank of lamb (£12,80) competes with a stunning organic chargrilled 8oz rib-eye steak, served with hand-cut chips and glazed shallots (£14.80). Puddings are on the heavy side: glazed lemon tart with honey crème fraiche (£4.80); Jack Daniel's pecan chocolate cake (£5.50). The drinks list is short, but there is a range of wines, beers, spirits and juices.

✳ Lunchtime is brunchtime.

Kovalam

Indian £10–£25

12 Willesden Lane, NW6 ☎020 7625 4761

Station BR Brondesbury Park **Open** Mon–Thurs & Sun noon–2.30pm & 6–11.15pm, Sat noon–2.30pm & 6–11.45pm **Accepts** Masterard & Visa

In the 1960s and 1970s, Willesden Lane was something of a magnet for curry lovers, as it boasted a couple of London's first authentic South Indian vegetarian establishments. These places shocked diners, who at that time were "curry and chips at closing time" sort of folk, by serving cheap and honest veggie food. Now Willesden Lane is no longer the cutting edge of

curry, but that did not dissuade some South Indian entrepreneurs from taking over the curry house at no.12 and relaunching it as "Kovalam – South Indian cuisine".

Kovalam is a brightly lit if traditionally decorated restaurant where the best dishes are the specials rather than the curry house staples that creep onto the list. Start with the ghee-roast masala dosa (£4.95), which is large, crisp and buttery, and has a suitably chilli-hot potato heart. The paripu vada with chutney (£2.20) are very good – crisp lentil cakes with coconutty chutney. For your main courses, look closely at the vegetable dishes and the specials: aviyal (£2.75) is creamy with coconut; kaya thoran (£2.75) is green bananas with grated coconut, shallots and mustard.

The koonthal masala (£5.50) is worth trying – it's squid in a very rich sauce sharpened with tamarind. Also try the aaterechi fry (£4.95) – dry-fried cubes of lamb with onion, curry leaves and black pepper; it's very tender and very tasty. Or perhaps the kadachaka kootan? (£3.90). This is a dish of curried breadfruit, heavy with coconut. The breads are good, as are the scented plain rices – lemon (£1.95) and coconut (£1.95).

 Aaterechi is just a South Indian word for lamb, so while Aaterechi Madras sounds cool it's really meat Madras.

No.77 Wine Bar

Modern British £10–£35

77 Mill Lane, NW6 ☎ 020 7435 7787

Station West Hampstead **Open** Mon & Tues noon–11pm Wed–Sat noon–midnight, Sun noon–10.30pm **Accepts** Mastercard & Visa

This rowdy and likable North London wine bar opened its doors in 1982, and by now has survived long enough to match velocities with its clientele. Drawing a veil over a disastrous episode a few years ago when there was an attempt to take the cuisine up market, things now run more smoothly. The food is a kind of refined comfort food and is backed up by an informed wine list that offers great value. The "bits on the side" make great bar nibbles – chilli roast nuts, focaccia, grilled chorizo, marinated fresh anchovies (all £2.50).

Starters range from tempura prawns with sweet chilli sauce (£4.50); or skewered chicken satay, spicy peanut sauce (£4.25); to duck liver pâté with balsamic onions and focaccia toast (£5.75). The soupe de jour has

come down to earth as "soup of today" (£3.95), while for main course, also in keeping with the old spirit, there is a pasta dish of the day (£8.25). But what about the tiger prawn, crab and sweet potato curry (£11.45)? Or cottage pie, chips and gravy (£7.95)? Or chicken breast schnitzel, tomato sauce, sauté potatoes and melted cheese (£9.50)? The polite name for the burger that started life as the "Fat Bastard" is "No. 77 beefburger topped with smoked Cheddar and served with braised capsicum, onions, potato fries and salad" (£8.95). The pud list is littered with familiar faces such as steamed chocolate pudding with chocolate custard (£4.50). Like the menu, the wine list changes as whim and stocks dictate, but the pricing encourages you to try something new.

 Patriotically enough there are usually a couple of rather good English wines on the list here.

Penk's

French £15–£40

79 Salusbury Rd, NW6 ☎020 7604 4484

Station Queens Park **Open** Mon–Thurs noon–3pm & 7–11pm, Fri noon–3pm & 7–11.30pm, Sat 10.30am–3pm & 7–11.30pm, Sun 10.30am–10.30pm
Accepts All major credit cards except AmEx & Diners ⓦwww.penks.com

In 1999 Steve Penk, a former land buyer for a property company, decided to open a "good honest bistro", and after learning his trade at Kensington Place (see p.259) he set up Penk's; It has turned into a model of what a neighbourhood restaurant should be. Penk's is all about bold strokes. The décor is all primary colours, a bright blue exterior giving way to a long thin room painted sunflower-yellow, with space for just thirty diners at wooden tables. Another twenty can fit in a back room suitable for parties, hidden at the end of a corridor lined with wonderful black-and-white prints of the restaurant.

This is a family resto – mum makes the puds, stepdad does the wine list, and sis helps front-of-house. The dinner menu keeps things simple, with starters such as spiced roast tomato soup (£3.95) before moving on to monkfish gratin (£6.25) – something of a signature dish – while "confit aromatic duck with crispy toast and plum chutney" (£5.95) brings a hint of Peking to a taste of France. Salads (£8.95 as a main) are similarly simple yet inventive: pot-roasted tuna teamed with white beans, parsley, lemon, soft-boiled egg, aioli and rocket screams Provence. For main course poached sea bass (£13.95) is an Italianate affair with salsa verde, roast tomatoes and asparagus, served on crostini. Or there's grilled organic pork chop with rosemary (£10.95), while a casserole of cauliflower, pumpkin and spinach with cheesy polenta (£9.95) should gladden any veggie heart. Puds range from sticky toffee pudding with ice cream (£4.95) to the caramelised lemon tart with clotted cream.

✳ Stepdad's wine list is very impressive, and not too aggressively priced.

The Salusbury

Italian/Gastropub £16–£35

50-52 Salusbury Rd, NW6 ☎020 7328 3286

Station Queens Park **Open** Mon 7–10.15pm, Tues–Sat 12.30–3.30pm & 7–10.15pm, Sun 12.30–3.30pm & 7–10pm **Accepts** Mastercard & Visa

The Salusbury has worked hard for its reputation as one of London's better gastropubs. Broadly speaking the pub is a U-shaped space. You go in one door through the bar and continue round the bar to come out in the dining room – a quieter room filled with the kind of tables your mum had in her living room (stripped and scrubbed), and a display of eclectic art lining the walls. If there's one niggle, it's that portion sizes can be daunting. In Yorkshire they call it being "over-faced", but if sound, Italian-accented cooking coupled with excellent value is what rings your bell, you'll like The Salusbury a lot.

The varied menu follows a mainly modern Italian theme rather than the more predictable Modern British bias of so many gastropubs. Starters (and a wave of dishes that could either be starters or mains) may include sautéed prawns with chilli and garlic (£7.50 or £11.50); red onion soup with Pecorino Romano (£4); smoked goose breast with mushroom tartare (£7.50); papardelle with swordfish, black olives and fresh oregano (£7.50 or £10); or artichoke risotto with pesto (£7 or £9.50). There's a practical emphasis on pasta and risotto. Main courses may include monkfish cartoccio with roast peppers and mussels (£14.50); confit leg of duck with lentils (£10.50). Moving on to pud territory, Amaretto, Ricotta and almond pudding (£4.50) vies with sgroppina (£4.50) – a soft lemon sorbet doused in grappa – and pure chocolate tart (£4.50). The wine list is not large, but it is well chosen; service is friendly and un-pushy.

Visit the Salusbury Foodstore (at no 56) – good deli, and pizzas to go.

Shish

Middle Eastern £10–£25

2–6 Station Parade, NW2 ☎ 020 8208 9290

Station Willesden Green **Open** Mon–Fri 11.30am–midnight, Sat & Sun 10.30am–11pm
Accepts All major credit cards except Diners (no cheques) ⓦ www.shish.co.uk

Shish is pretty slick. A large, curved-glass pavement frontage displays a sinuous bar counter that snakes around the dining room, leaving grills, fridges and chefs' stations in the centre. Diners simply take a stool at the counter; it is for all the world like being at a modernist sushi bar. This place owes a debt to Israeli roadside eateries, with its falafel and shish kebabs, but the "concept" (all fast-food missions have to have a suitable "concept") is much more inclusive. The inspiration for Shish is the food of the Silk Road.

Starters are divided into lots of cold mezze and a shorter list of hot mezze. The tabbouleh (£1.95) needs a bit more coriander and parsley. The cucumber wasabi (£1.95) is pleasant pickled cucumber. The red and green falafel (£2.75) are well made – the red variety is engagingly spicy. The hot bread is as delicious as only freshly baked hot bread can be. Kebabs are served in two different ways: either plated with rice, couscous or French fries; or in a wrap. The shish kebabs are really rather good. Mediterranean lamb (£7.75) comes up very tender; apricot and ginger (£7.45)

teams chicken with good tangy apricot flavour; the Persian kofta (£5.75) is made from minced beef and lamb; or there is king prawn shish (£8.45). The portions all seem decent-sized and there are further fish and vegetarian options. Die-hard kebabbers can even insist on a satisfactorily fierce squelch of chilli sauce. This food benefits from being freshly cooked and eaten hot from the grill. It's relatively cheap, too.

✳ Upstairs you'll find "Shish Above": slightly smarter, slightly pricier.

Sushi-Say

Japanese £15–£40

33b Walm Lane, NW2 ☎ 020 8459 2971

Station Willesden Green **Open** Tues–Fri 6.30–10.30pm, Sat 1–3.30pm & 6.30–11pm, Sun 1–3.30pm & 6–10pm **Accepts** All major credit cards except Diners

Yuko Shimizu and her husband Katsuharu run this small but excellent Japanese restaurant and sushi bar. It has a very personal feel, with just ten seats at the bar and twenty in the restaurant, plus a private booth for five or six. Shimizu means pure water, and the cooking is pure delight. The menu offers a full classical Japanese selection, making it a difficult choice between limiting yourself to sushi or going for the cooked dishes. Perhaps adapting the European style, and having sushi or sashimi as a starter and then main courses with rice, brings you the best of both worlds.

Sitting at the sushi bar allows you to watch Katsuharu at work. With a sumo-like stature and the widest grin this side of Cheshire, his fingers magic nigiri sushi onto your plate. In the lower price brackets you'll find omelette, mackerel, squid and octopus (£1.90 per piece). At the top end there's sea urchin, fatty tuna and yellowtail (£2.90 per piece). In between there is a wide enough range to delight even the experts. Nigiri toku (£15.90) brings you eleven pieces of nigiri and seaweed-rolled sushi, and it's a bargain – heavy on the fish and light on the rice. Cooked dishes do not disappoint. Ebi tempura (£10.60) brings you crispy battered king prawns, the batter so light it's almost effervescent, and menchi katsu (£6.50) delivers a deep-fried oval shaped from minced beef and salad. There are set dinners for all tastes, priced from £18.50 to £28.50, and mixed sashimi for £16.50. It's worth trying the home-made puddings, such as goma (sesame) ice cream (£1.90 a scoop).

✳ For experts there's half-frozen sake – Akita Onigoroshi – at £5.50 a glass. Less a slush puppy than a slush mastiff.

Knightsbridge & Belgravia

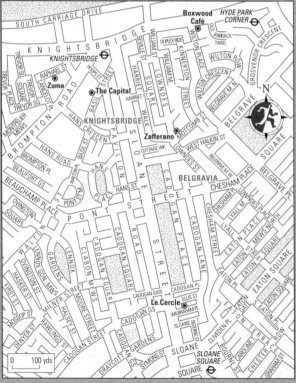

© Crown copyright

Boxwood Café

Modern British £18–£70

The Berkeley, Knightsbridge, SW1 ☎ 020 7235 1010
Station Knightsbridge **Open** Daily noon–3pm & 6–11pm
Accepts All major credit cards except Diners

If the term "café" conjures up images of fag smoke and fried slice, you're better off thinking of this place as Boxwood. When it opened this addition to Gordon Ramsay's stable of hotel eateries was billed as offering simple seasonal dishes in an informal setting. Sure. This is a café in the same way that the Café Royal on Regent Street, or the Union Square Café in New York, is a café. The dining room is more stylish now than it was when it was home to Vong. The tables are well spaced, the chairs are comfortable, the service swarms over you. The standard of cooking is high. Dishes are well presented, and while the prices may not be café prices they are not wildly "Knightsbridge".

The menu is seasonal and changes to suit what is on the market. There may be white onion soup with Parma ham, roast potatoes and chives (£6); or perhaps pickled Arctic herrings with new potato salad (£7.50), or seared beef carpaccio with caviar creme fraîche (£10.50). Mains are also good. Roast cod fillet with mustard crust and piperade (£16); Black Angus grilled rib-eye with Café de Paris butter (£25); or an accurately cooked piece of roast suckling pig with a grain mustard sauce (£15). The wine list has some accessibly priced bottles. The dessert list is a long one and the seasonal theme is carried through. The poppy seed Knickerbocker Glory with roasted apricots and panacotta (£6) is notable, as are the warm sugared doughnuts with espresso sorbet (£6). You do get doughnuts in cafes, but not like these!

✱ Foie gras and veal burger, with port wine onions, cos lettuce, Parmesan and chips (£22.50).

The Capital

French £35–£150

5 Raphael St, SW7 ☎ 020 7589 5171
Station Knightsbridge **Open** Mon–Sat noon–3pm & 6–11pm, Sun noon–4pm
Accepts All major credit cards ⊛ www.capitalhotel.co.uk

The Capital Hotel has quietly gone about its business since 1971. The cooking has always been top-flight, but it took the arrival of a voluble and passionate French chef called Eric Crouillère-Chavot to lift things to the current exalted level. Mr Michelin gives The Capital two stars, putting it

firmly in the top half-dozen restaurants in London, and for once he is right. During the summer of 2004 the old-fashioned dining room and bar got a long overdue re-design. This is not a cheap restaurant. In the evening two courses cost £48 and three £55, while the five-course dégustation menu is

£68. All of which makes the £28.50 three-course lunch a bargain!

Chavot cooks exciting food. Dishes are full-flavoured and elegantly plated. Sometimes presentation strays into the fussy zone beloved of Michelin inspectors, but expect classically rich and satisfying flavours. Starters may include crab lasagna with langoustine cappucino; a millefeuille of veal sweetbreads with field mushrooms and potato gnocchi; or pan-fried duck foie gras "exotic". Main courses carry on in the same vein – pot-roast pigeon, potato and bacon galette with mushrooms; fillet of turbot, truffle gnocchi and mushroom ravioli; or saddle of rabbit "Provençal", white coco beans, deep-fried calamari and a tomato risotto. Puds are elaborate, sculptural and satisfying. Chavot's interpretation of bread and butter pudding may be a pixie portion but it tastes like essence of bread and butter pudding. He may also be offering a praline pear crumble, or an iced-coffee parfait with a chocolate fondant.

✳ The wine list here is both expansive and expensive.

Le Cercle

French £20–£90

1 Wilbraham Place, SW1 ☎020 7901 9999

Station Sloane Square **Open** Mon–Sat noon–midnight, closed Sunday and Monday **Accepts** All major credit cards

Le Cercle opened in the Summer of 2004 and is the first move outside Smithfield for the people who run Club Gascon (see p.105). The restaurant is deep within the bowels of a discreet and exclusive "apartment hotel" which in turn is tucked away up a side street. You come down a flight of steps into a modern double-height room; the wine cellar and the cheese room are on show and there's a long and businesslike bar. It is an all day operation running from lunch through afternoon tea, to bar snacks and dinner. The food is modern, resolutely French and is served in the Club's trademark style of small portions and multiple courses.

The lengthy menu changes seasonally. Sections are themed – "vegetal", "marin", "fermier" and each offers six or seven options. For two people one dish from each section is probably too little food and two dishes is too much. The cooking is of a very high standard. Standouts include crunchy green beans served with pickled chanterelles (£4.25); ravioles de romans parfum de cepes (£3.50); roast John Dory, Noilly Prat and citrus (£5.75); roast veal onglet with shallot sauce (£4.75); crispy black-pudding pie with apple (£4.25); tete de veau sauce ravigote (£3.75); foie gras cercle (£9.50); pan-roasted veal sweetbreads creamy morels (£13.25) – an epic dish, rich and satisfying. But this selection only scratches the surface of a multi-page menu. Puds are good, but careful of the

Provencal (£3.25) – three glasses: green tomato jam; black olive foam; piquillo pepper granita. The wine list majors in the South West and there are numerous offers by the glass.

*From the bar menu: "cheese frenzy" £7.50.

Zafferano

Italian £28–£80

15 Lowndes St, SW1 ☎ 020 7235 5800
Station Knightsbridge **Open** Mon–Sat noon–2.30pm & 7–11pm, Sun noon–2.30 & 7–10pm **Accepts** All major credit cards

It seems old hat now, but when Zafferano opened towards the end of the last Millennium, the combination of modern Italian food and decent value fixed-price menus was a rare and dazzling new development that attracted a host of diners and a number of awards. It is also worth noting that many of those original customers are still regulars and that the two course lunch here is only a fiver more expensive than it was five years ago. Zafferano may have changed chefs but it has kept true to its original values.

The deal is a simple one. At lunch two courses cost £23.50, three £28.50, and four £32.50. Dinner costs £29.50 for two courses, £37.50 for three, and £41.50 for four. Do not think that the "four course" option is merely a bit of Italian whimsy – this is one place where you should go through the card: antipasti; pasta; main and pud. The cooking is good here, the menu is seasonal, and the ingredients carefully chosen. Fortunately the service is slick and the wine list long so the "essence of Italy" mood remains unbroken. Starters may include prosciutto with baby onions; warm octopus salad; buffalo mozzarella with beetroot. Go on to the stunning pheasant ravioli, or the white bean soup with langoustine. Then there may be something simple such as pan-fried calf's liver with balsamic vinegar; or venison medallions with polenta and red wine sauce; or roast John Dory with new potatoes and green olives. Puddings are serious – the tiramisù is formidable, and may even drag you away from the hazelnut parfait with truffle honey.

*The tortino al cioccolato (chocolate fondant pudding) is worth the twelve minute wait!

Zuma

Japanese £30–£120

5 Raphael St, SW7 ♿ ☎ 020 7584 1010

Station Knightsbridge **Open** Mon–Sat noon–2.30pm & 6–10.30pm, Sun noon–4pm
Accepts All major credit cards 🌐 www.zumarestaurant.com

Chef-proprietor Rainer Becker enlisted the Japanese über-design team Super Potato to create this huge restaurant, with the unspoken aim of out-Nobu-ing Nobu (p.251). Judging by the crowds of both celebs and celeb spotters, the plan has worked. The premises that once used to be home to the Chicago Rib Shack is now all stone, rough-hewn granite and unfinished wood. This is a seriously trendy place, and the bar buzzes. The approach to eating is modernist – with Japanese dishes, macrobiotic options and pick-and-mix nibbles portions.

The menu is a long one and complicated to boot. Start by nibbling some edamame, Zuma style (£4.30). These are soya beans that have been boiled in the pod – strip the beans out with your teeth and leave the pods. Or there is tosa dofu (£5.80), which is deep-fried tofu with daikon and bonito flakes, or age watarigani (£8.80), a dish of fried soft-shell crab with wasabi mayonnaise. The sashimi and sushi are exquisite and pricey. The skewers from the robata grill are fresh and appealing. Try satsumaimo no goma shoyo gake (£4.80), sweet potato glazed with sesame; or hotate (£6.80), a scallop with Japanese pepper and black-bean sauce; or tori no tebasaki (£3.80), chicken wings with seasalt and lime. Then there are tempura, seafood dishes and meat dishes. Every dish is presented stylishly, and while prices are high the ingredients are commendably fresh. Nobu fans will be interested to compare and contrast the respective black cod (£21.80) dishes; the Zuma version is marinated and then cooked wrapped in a hoba leaf.

✳ The sake list has over twenty varieties – ask the "sake sommelier" for help!

Further choices

One-O-One
French/Fish

101 William St, SW1
☎ 020 7290 7101

Respected fish restaurant, with accomplished Breton chef – very good fish dishes, although at Knightsbridge prices.

Mr Chow
Chinese

151 Knightsbridge, SW1
☎ 020 7589 7347

High ticket, star spotting, old fashioned Chinese restaurant.

Yo! Sushi
Japanese

Fifth Floor, Harvey Nichols, SW1
☎ 020 7235 5000

Conveyor belt sushi. See review p.322.

Maida Vale

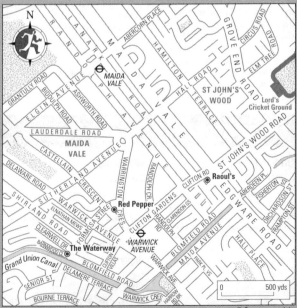

Raoul's

European/Deli £8–£25

13 Clifton Rd, W9 ☎ 020 7289 7313

Station Warwick Avenue **Open** Mon–Sat 8.30am–11pm, Sun 9am–11pm
Accepts All major credit cards (no cheques)

Raoul's **is** a neighbourhood fixture. It looks like a café (albeit a stylish, film-setty, café) and, like a cafe, is open long hours. But this establishment is very W9 and, as a result, Raoul's is more a restaurant that thinks it's a café, rather than the other way around. The waiters are unhurried without seeming world-weary; the room is modern without being aggressively designery. And the menu offers all things to all customers and is backed-up by a blackboard listing daily specials.

The breakfasty **dishes** are good. For a café this place is more eggs Benedict than fried bread but the full English (£6.50) comprises scrambled or fried eggs, bacon, sausage, grilled tomatoes and toast; the American and modernist influences don't become apparent until further down the page – bagels with smoked salmon and cream cheese (£5.40), French toast and maple syrup (£3.95). Sandwiches are modernist on the one hand – ciabatta roll with melted mozzarella, grilled peppers, rocket and sun-dried tomatoes (£5.70) – and trad on the other, with Croque Monsieur (£4.80). Good quality, very fresh ingredients, well presented, exemplary. If you dock here during a main meal time turn to the blackboard; there may be starters such as grilled spareribs (£5.95) and spinach salad (£5.75); then mains such as fettucine with fresh asparagus and truffle oil (£8.95), or a Scotch rib-eye steak with garlic butter and French fries (£12.50). There's a short wine list with economical house wines, and service is cheerful. A very comfortable place.

✱ "All our eggs are free range from Barberino Mugello, Tuscany, Italy".

Red Pepper

Pizza/Italian £15–£35

8 Formosa St, W9 ☎ 020 7266 2708

Station Warwick Avenue **Open** Mon–Fri 6.30-11pm, Sat 12.30-3pm & 6.30-11pm,
Sun 12.30-3.30pm & 6.30-10.30pm **Accepts** Mastercard & Visa

The Red Pepper **is** something of an institution. It may not be the largest restaurant in Maida Vale and it certainly isn't the most elegant – the service hovers on the edge of brusque – and for what is a neighbourhood pizza joint the prices would be high enough to raise an eyebrow anywhere less sleek than W9. But it is packed. Over the years every review of Red Pepper has opened with a complaint that the tiny tables are crammed in too tightly. The waiters have to combine an aptitude for slalom skiing with the skills of a limbo dancer. No matter.

There are **half** a dozen starters, a few pasta dishes, some specials and the list of pizzas. The starters are light and fresh; a spiced crab salad with baby spinach leaves (£7) looks pretty on the plate and is good on the fork as well. Or there's pan-fried goat's cheese with green beans and sun-dried tomato dressing (£6.50); or a bowl of green pea soup with a chargrilled Tiger prawn bobbing in it (£5.50). There are specials, but you should turn your attention to the pizzas. They are large, flat and thin, but not too thin. Toppings are top quality. As well as the usual suspects – Margherita (£6), Napoli (£7.50), stagioni (£9) – the "rossi" (£7.50) is worthy of special mention. The redness comes from tomatoes, red peppers and chilli oil, and the gooey top is nicely piquant. The "primavera" (£9.50) is also very good, topped with San Daniele ham, Parmesan and a handful of rocket. The all-Italian wine list has some interesting bottles at gentle prices – check out the Sardinian reds.

* You need to book for the four pavement tables.

The Waterway

Gastropub £15–£55

54 Formosa St, W9 ☎ 020 7266 3557
Station Warwick Avenue **Open** Daily 12.30–3pm & 6.30–10.15pm
Accepts All major credit cards except Diners ⊕ www.thewaterway.co.uk

Once upon a time the Waterway was marooned at the extreme end of the rough boozer spectrum, after which it was taken over by the people who also run the Ebury (see p.356) and The Wells (see p.188). After a shaky start the dining room towards the rear has developed into a very sound gastropub with comfortable leather banquettes and friendly service. It is still primarily a canalside venue with plenty of room for drinking outside, and both the music and the crowd are loud. But at least now there is good food to be had, albeit at restaurant rather than gastropub prices.

The menu changes regularly but starters may include curiosities such as warm fig and shallot Tatin with watercress and Parmesan (£6.50); or deep-fried calamari with wasabi slaw, coriander oil (£6.95); as well as more trad options like a terrine of ham hock with piccalilli and pea shoots (£6.95); Angus beef carpaccio with pickled shallots and horseradish (£5.85); or Bury black pudding with a poached hen's egg, baby spinach and tomato and spring onion dressing (£5.85). Mains run from chargrilled whole lemon sole with caper and crayfish beurre noisette (£13.75); through braised Welsh lamb shank with pommes Dauphinoise, crispy sweetbreads and beetroot dressing (£14.75); to roasted Scottish salmon with peas à la Francaise £12.50. Puds (all £4.50) are sound rather than awesome. A crème bruleé comes with poached rhubarb; there's bread and butter pudding with crème Anglaise; and hot chocolate pudding with vanilla ice cream. The wine lists touches all the bases and isn't greedy.

* There's a set lunch – two courses for £14.50 and three for £16.50.

Marylebone

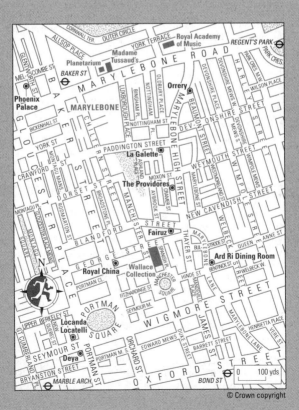

© Crown copyright

Ard Ri Dining Room

Irish £20–£50

At the O'Conor Don, 88 Marylebone Lane, W1 ☎020 7935 9311

Station Bond St **Open** Mon–Fri noon–2.30pm & 6–10pm

Accepts All major credit cards except Diners ⊛www.oconordon.com

The **Ard Ri** dining room is upstairs in the O' Conor Don, a splendid pub run by the O'Callaghan family. While downstairs an ocean of Guinness flows over the bar to the punters, upstairs is quieter, though no less welcoming. There's a fireplace which sports a real fire in season, tables and chairs are mismatched and dark red walls are covered in an eclectic array of pictures – it's a comfortable place in a homely way. Service also has a pleasant gentleness about it.

The food is very hard to pigeon-hole. There are nods to "Oirishness" – "traditional Irish lamb stew" (£12.80), and the French onion soup (£3.80) comes with a Coleeney cheese crouton. Also from the starters, the beetroot home-cured salmon (£4.95) is very good

indeed, cut thickly and with a good flavour (although you probably need to be Irish to understand why it is served with tzatziki). For mains the 100% Irish beef and Guinness sausages (£10.50) are good; there's a roast loin of pork served with black-pudding mash (£11.25); deep-fried fillet of cod comes with a tempura beer batter chips and mushy peas (£11.80). The kitchen does "specials": order for at least two people and 36 hours in advance and you can have a roast leg of lamb, a fore rib of beef or a whole lobster. Puds range from warm apple and potato cake (£4.50) to white chocolate parfait with honeycomb and chocolate chip (£4.50). The wine list is sound, but the Guinness makes the journey up the stairs in perfect condition and is a much more tempting option.

✳ Check out the signed photos on the staircase – there's an actor from the Bill at the bottom and a grinning Bill Clinton at the top.

Deya

Indian £20–£90

34 Portman Square W1 ☎020 7224 0028

Station Marble Arch **Open** Mon–Fri noon–2.45pm & 6–11pm, Sat 6–11pm

Accepts All major credit cards ⊛www.deya-restaurant.co.uk

Deya opened in June 2004 and somewhat implausibly represents a comeback to the resto world for that celebrity restaurateur and thespian Sir Michael Caine, who is a partner. It's a slick affair and when they say Modern Indian, that is certainly what they are striving for, with elaborate presentation, oddly shaped plates and little tasters. The head chef is Sanjay Dwivedi

and his brief is to concentrate on lighter contemporary dishes. The décor is slick, the lengthy wine list is made much of, and service is polished. The elegant bar is a large one that will give some scope for the cocktail mixologist.

There's a two course lunch menu (£14.50) which offers sound value. The standard of cooking is good here but every effort has been made to refine dishes, so some of the familiar classics may seem a bit tamed and unfamiliar. Starters include crab rice (£7), rice topped with crabmeat and accompanied by a crab and sweetcorn samosa; scallops in coconut milk (£8.50) which come with chilli mash; and "salad of tandoori lamb" (£6.50) – a grown-up lamb tikka on a salad made with black-eye beans. Main courses follow the same vein, in that dishes such as rogan josh (£10.50) come in a rich, very smooth gravy; snapper masala (£12.20) presents big chunks of white fish in a tomato gravy; and "butter chicken" (£9.50) is similarly suave and sweet. The breads are good, the tulsi paratha (£2.50) particularly so – strewn with fresh basil. Puddings are given a modernist European twist, so there is a rather good panna cotta made with rosewater and "silky chocolate" (a formidable chocolate mousse).

✳ Tasting menu bargain! Five courses, four wines – £35.

Fairuz

Lebanese £15–£35

3 Blandford St, W1 ☎ 020 7486 8182

Station Bond Street **Open** Daily noon–11.30pm **Accepts** All major credit cards

Squeezed in between two self-consciously hip and groovy Blandford Street eateries, Fairuz happily carries on doing its own thing, which is Lebanese cooking. As you open the front door, jolly souk music, the smell of Eastern spices and the light of the warm, mud-coloured room assault and beguile the senses. This is one of London's most accessible Middle Eastern restaurants.

The menu is set out in traditional style. There's an epic list of mezze, both hot and cold, to start, followed by a selection of charcoal grills. You can leave the selection up to the restaurant and order a set mezza (minimum two people, £17.95 per head), or a set menu (minimum two people, £24.95 per head) which combines a mezza with a mixed grill. The set mezza delivers eight or ten little dishes – plenty for lunch or a light supper. But if you prefer to make your own selection, the menu lists 47 different mezze for you to choose from: cold dishes all cost £4.50; hot dishes £4.95. Particularly recommended are the wonderfully fresh and herby tabbouleh; the warak inab (stuffed vine leaves); the hummous; and makanek (spicy lamb sausages). Even that most dangerously indigestible of delicacies, the falafel, is fine here. Main course grills are generous. Kafta khashkhash (£10.95), lamb minced with parsley and grilled on skewers, is unexpectedly delicate and fragrant, while the shish taouk (£11.95) – chicken marinated in garlic and lemon – really is finger-licking good. Round off your meal with excellent pastries (£4.25), and real Lebanese coffee (£2).

✳ If you can, get there early to secure one of the nook-and-crannyish, tent-like tables.

La Galette

56 Paddington St, W1 ☎ 020 7935 1554

Station Baker Street **Open** Mon–Fri 8.30am–11pm, Sat & Sun 10am–11pm
(brunch 10am–5pm) **Accepts** All major credit cards except Diners ⓦ www.lagalette.com

MARYLEBONE

The proprietors of La Galette have obviously given some thought to the potential of pancakes. La Galette is a bright, modern place with a paint scheme that starts light and gets dark as you travel towards the bare brick wall and the open kitchen at the rear. There's an appealing breakfast served between 8.30am and 4pm, and then there's the main menu, which plunges into the galettes with little more ado.

The hors d'oeuvres are delightful – very simple, and very French. The charcuterie plate (£5.50) teams some saucisson sec with Bayonne,

Jésus and garlic sausage; the vegetarian hors d'oeuvres plate (£4.50) majors in those delightful shredded raw vegetable salads – finely grated celeriac with a good mayonnaise, carrot with a light dressing, pickled beetroot and hard-boiled eggs. And there's a good feist tapenade (£3.50), or there's soup du jour (£3.95). The bread is a good chewy-crusted sourdough. When you feel you can't put off that pancake moment any more, launch into a galette. These large buckwheat pancakes come with a dozen different fillings, and in this instance the use of the word "filling" is not an exaggeration. The "complet" (£6.50), with ham, cheese and a fried egg winking from the centre, is simple and satisfying. Or there's a galette with smoked salmon and fromage frais (£8.50); or naked except for rather good Normandy butter (£3.95). However appealing the galettes, there are still puddies who will proceed directly to the crêpes – "Normandy" comes with caramelized apple and crème Chantilly (£4.95).

✳ A splendid, and extensive list of Breton ciders. Cheap and good.

Locanda Locatelli

8 Seymour St, W1 ⓰ ☎ 020 7935 9088

Station Marble Arch **Open** Mon–Thurs noon–3pm & 7–11pm, Fri & Sat noon–3pm
& 7–11.30pm **Accepts** All major credit cards except Diners ⓦ www.locandalocatelli.com

When Giorgio Locatelli moved here in a corner of the Churchill Hotel, it took about a week for the place to get

booked out. The restaurant opened on Valentine's Day 2002 and by the end of the first week everybody from the Prime

Minister to Madonna had been in to sample the startlingly good North Italian food. The room is elegant and the cooking terrific. Since then business has been brisk. Now there's a phone frenzy at the beginning of each month when everyone struggles to book a table for next month – spontaneous here means five to eight weeks ahead!

There's a splendid basket of mixed breads to keep you busy while you look down the menu. There is a large turnover of

dishes but the cooking is always spurred on by the seasons. There may be antipasti such as wild chicory and caper salad with Parmesan foam (£9.50); cured venison with celeriac and black truffle (£11); or layered potatoes with pancetta and Tallegio cheese (£9.50). Pasta dishes delight: spaghetti (£10.50) comes with octopus; gnocchi with morel mushrooms (£15); or how about a risotto with sausage and peas (£14.50)? Every dish looks elegant on the plate, and combines tastes and textures to their best effect. Main courses may include steamed hake in garlic and vinegar (£17); bollito misto with salsa verde (£23.50); or roast duck with broccoli and spelt (£26.50). The service is slick, and the restaurant has an established and comfortable air. Dolci range from tiramisù (£6.50); to a serious chocolate soufflé (16 minutes, £9). Service runs smoothly and the wine list pays homage to the Italian greats.

✳ Giorgio swears by the medicinal properties of Manni olive oil – take some home for £17.54 per 100ml!!

Orrery
French £40–£120

55 Marylebone High St, W1 ♿ ☎020 7616 8000

Station Baker St/Regent's Park **Open** Mon–Sat noon–3pm & 7–10.30pm, Sun noon–2.30pm & 7–10.30pm **Accepts** All major credit cards ⊛www.orrery.co.uk

There is no doubt that Sir Terence Conran has gone to great lengths to ensure that there is no "formula" in the restaurants within his growing portfolio. But Orrery stands out. This is a very good restaurant indeed, driven by a passion for food. At Orrery they cherish their own network of small suppliers, going for large, line-caught, sea bass above their smaller, farmed cousins, and selecting the best Landes pigeon

and Scottish beef. The service is slick and friendly, the dining room is beautiful, the cheeseboard has won prizes and the wine list is exhaustive. All of the above is reflected in the bill.

Your meal will start well – white onion and thyme soup, truffle emulsion with coco beans and chanterelles (£9.50); or langoustine and frog's legs, wild mushrooms, grilled baby leeks and jus (£16); or partridge mousseline (£12.50). These are sophisticated dishes featuring well judged combinations of flavours. Mains may include roast fillet of halibut, pommes purée, salted grapes and verjus (£24); roast Landes pigeon, polenta galette, foie gras and preserved vegetables (£26); filet of Scottish beef, creamed spinach, bone marrow beignet (£26). Presentation is ultra-chic, flavours are intense – this is serious stuff. Puddings span the range from classics such as fondant of Amedei chocolate, and milk ice cream (£10) to a raspberry soufflé (£9). One way to eat well here is to rely heavily on the set menus: the three-course menu du jour is £23.50. The Menu Gourmand (only for the entire table) brings six courses, coffee and petits fours for £50, rising to £80 when you opt for the specially matched glasses of wine. A stress-free bargain.

✳ Check out the whole roast "Challans" duck for two – £50.

Phoenix Palace

Chinese £12–£45

3–5 Glentworth St, NW1 ☎ 020 7486 3515

Station Baker Street/Marylebone **Open** Mon–Sat noon–11.30pm, Sun 11am–10.30pm
Accepts All major credit cards except Diners

This site was formerly an Indian eatery called the Viceroy of India and it comes as a bit of a shock to find a rather good, large, bright, busy Chinese restaurant marooned this far North, by the stream of traffic intent on dodging the Congestion Charge, as they crawl past Tussaud's. In 2003 the chefs at the Phoenix re-wrote the menu and now it includes a good many more interesting dishes. Thankfully they seem to know what they are doing, so this has become a place to try out something new.

Starters include all the old favourites, such as chicken wrapped in lettuce leaf (£5.50), but try the jellyfish with sesame seed (£8.80); the soft-shell crab with chilli and garlic (£6.50 each); the pork trotters with vinaigrette (£6.80); or chilli potsticker dumplings (£4.80). The menu is a long one and it is worth a careful read as there are some interesting discoveries to be made. Salt-baked chicken (£12 or £24) is a wonderful, savoury roast chicken with juicy meat and crisp skin. There's steamed turbot with Tientsin cabbage and garlic (£28). The fried minced pork patties with salted fish (£8) are very classy, the salt-fish seasoning the pork mix successfully. There's baked crab and salty yolk served with steamed buns (£16.80); eel with pickled mustard green (£12); pork and stuffed beancurd cooked in a claypot (£9.80); venison with yellow chives and celery (£14.50). To find any Chinese restaurant in this out of the way location is a puzzle – to find such a good one is positively inscrutable.

✳ Free delivery, within a mile of the restaurant, of orders above £10.

The Providores

Fusion £7–£22

109 Marylebone High St, W1 &. ☎020 7935 6175

Station Baker St/Bond St **Open** Mon–Fri noon–3pm & 6–11.30pm, Sat & Sun 10am–3pm (brunch) & 6–11.30pm **Accepts** All major credit cards ⓦwww.theprovidores.co.uk

There's only one chef working in London with a 24-carat, bankable reputation for fusion food and that is Peter Gordon, the amiable New Zealander. His showcase is this restaurant which he opened with a consortium of friends. The resto part occupies an elegant room on the first floor. Chairs are comfortable, tablecloths are white and simplicity rules – which is just as well, as the dishes are among the most complicated in town. But what may look like an untidy and arbitrary assemblage on paper becomes wholly satisfying the moment you pop a forkful into your mouth. These dishes all taste fresh, every flavour distinct, and each combination cunningly balanced.

The menu descriptions read like lists: smokey coconut and tamarind laksa with grilled tiger prawn, green tea noodles, crispy shallots chicken-hijiki dumpling, and coriander (£9.50). Puzzled? The rich, creamy, sweet coconut broth is covered with a scattering of crisp bits of shallot and laced with the contrasting textures of ribbon noodles, and tiger prawns. Or how about grilled kangaroo loin on a cassava fritter with spiced quandong relish and Greek yoghurt (£11.50)? Mains may include roast sea bass on white bean and rosemary purée, lemon-braised fennel, lemongrass dressing and wasabi tobiko (£19.30); or roast lamb chump on bonita potatoes with roast beetroot and apple relish (£19.40). Or roast Barbary duck breast on sesame miso aubergines and bok choy with shitake (£19.40). Desserts are equally elaborate: chocolate liquorice 'delice' with soured pink grapefruit, runny cream and chocolate almond wafers (£6.90).

✳ Downstairs there's a walk-in, informal, gentler paced sort of eatery.

Royal China

Dim Sum/Chinese £15–£35

24–26 Baker St, W1 & ☎020 7487 4688

Station Baker Street **Open** Mon–Sat noon–11pm, Sun 11am–10pm
Dim Sum until 4.45pm **Accepts** Mastercard & Visa ⓦ www.royalchinagroup.co.uk

The Royal China Group's first restaurant is on Queensway, and their West End outpost used to be at number 40 Baker Street. In May 2004, however, they moved a few doors down to this new establishment. All the Royal China restos are kitted out in shiny black and gold, very eighties and very glitzy, which makes the more modern, less glossy, rather calmer look of the new dining room all the more welcome. There is a large wall mural in the black and gold idiom but it is no longer oppressive. The dim sum are terrific. There is a long menu featuring much the same array of dishes as you find in every other Chinese establishment, but go before 4.45pm and stick with the dim sum.

Until Hakkasan (see p.154) invented the venison puff, the roast pork puff (£2.20) from Royal China was thought by many to be the best dim sum in town. It is still very good, light, flaky and rich. The

regulars such as steamed prawn dumplings (£2.60) and minced pork dumplings (£2.20) are fresh and well seasoned, and the prawn cheung fun (£3) are well made and commendably thin. Even dishes that sound prosaic like "crispy spring roll" (£2.20) are very good, fresh and crisp with good complementary textures. Also noteworthy are the prawn and chive dumplings (£2.60), and the steamed curry squid (£2.20). Bulk out your order with the glutinous rice in lotus leaves (£3) – a dish that is done very well here. Service is slick and quick and after you've made the choice between Chinese tea (80p) and Tsing Tao beer (£3) try as many different dumplings as you dare.

✱ Try the "pig's skin and turnip in broth" from the specials (£3).

Mayfair & Bond Street

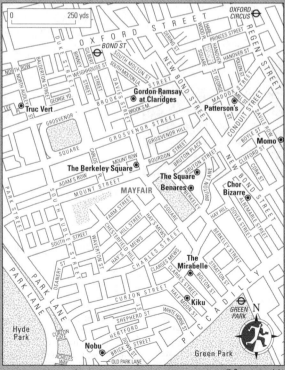

© Crown copyright

Benares

Indian £25–£60

12 Berkeley House, Berkeley Square, W1 & ☎ 020 7629 8886
Station Green Park **Open** Mon–Fri noon–2.30pm & 5–10.30pm, Sat 5–10.30pm,
Sun 6–10pm **Accepts** All major credit cards ⓦ www.benaresrestaurant.com

Atul Kochar is the man who secured one of the first Michelin stars ever awarded to an Indian restaurant in Britain, and in June 2003 he opened Benares to suitable fanfares. It is certainly a classy place: acres of polished stone floors, pools strewn with blossoms and little candles bobbing about. The dining room is modern and stylish. Some of the pricing, and most of the wine list, "goes Mayfair" pretty briskly, but considering the elegance of the setting, the friendliness of the service and the undoubted quality of the cooking, this is a good option as a special occasion Indian restaurant.

When each dish arrives it is beautiful on the plate – lots of influences from smart French chefs but still matching textures with good assertive tastes. Kekdae ki chaat aur tille ka jhinga (£9) is a crab salad teamed with a tangy kumquat chutney and topped with prawns deep-fried in a crisp coat – very fresh, very delicious. The tandoor work is exemplary – lamb chops (£20) are exceedingly plump and tender. A classic dish such as rogan josh (£18.50) is as good as you can get – unless you can find it served on the bone. Or there's hare masala ki machchi (£18.50), which is pan-fried John Dory served with a broth of curried mussels. The vegetable side dishes are most interesting. Pani singara aur faliyon ki subji (£7.50) is superb and an exercise in crunchy textures – water chestnuts and French beans with onion seeds and dried mango. As you would expect in any resto with serious (if unstated) Michelin ambition, there are amuses-gueules before the meal and petits fours to finish.

✳ Two-course lunch £12 and three for £13.95. Tasting menu £35.

The Berkeley Square

French £20–£70

7 Davies St, W1 ☎ 020 7629 6993
Station Green Park **Open** Mon–Fri noon–2.30pm & 6–10pm
Accepts All major credit cards except Diners

This resto was once named The Berkeley Square Cafe, though unfeeling people may have queried the term "cafe" (which was dropped in the summer of 2004) as this elegant and comfortable restaurant, a little to the north of Berkeley Square, serves remarkably good food with unpretentious style.

Chef patron Steven Black's food is ambitious, and pretty on the plate, but his menus are market driven and there's a welcome emphasis on British produce. Service is slick and there is a handful of roadside tables for lunching outdoors on bright days.

The lunch menu offers a choice of three starters, three mains, three puds (one course £13.95, two £16.95, three £19.95) – it's a bargain. Smoked trout and crushed potato terrine with dill crème fraîche; slow-roast belly pork glazed in honey and lavender; poached rhubarb with clotted-cream ice cream. Good dishes, with nicely judged combinations of flavour. The à la carte is a full-on affair (two

courses £36.50, three £42.50 and a seven courses "surprise menu" that must be for the whole table at £47.50). Dishes are appealing – Sennen Cove crab salad with avocado purée, pink grapefruit and peas; shavings of confit foie gras, white asparagus and wild salad leaves; morel mushroom risotto with asparagus and Parmesan; roast loin of Orkney lamb with braised shoulder and Dauphinoise potato; fillet of halibut with brandade fritters, cauliflower and truffle purée; Welsh Black Mountain organic chicken – roast supreme, open herb ravioli of confit thigh, with a carrot and tarragon salad. The wine list is extensive and can get expensive. Puds are elaborate but the ice creams are very good – particularly the black cardamom.

* There's a separate vegetarian menu.

Chor Bizarre

Indian £24–£55

16 Albemarle St, W1 ☎ 020 7629 9802

Station Green Park **Open** Mon–Sat noon–3pm & 6–11.30pm, Sun 6.30–10.30pm
Accepts All major credit cards ⓦ www.chorbizarrelondon.com

Chor Bizarre is something of a novelty, as it's one of a handful of London's Indian restaurants with a "head office" in India. Our Chor Bizarre is a straight copy of the one in the Broadway Hotel, Delhi. Its name is an elaborate pun (Chor Bazaar translates as "thieves' market") and, like the Delhi branch, the London restaurant is furnished with Indian antiques and bric-a-brac. Every table, and each set of chairs, is different, and you may find yourself dining within the frame of an antique four-poster bed. The food is very well prepared and encouragingly authentic. Care is taken over the detail; Chor

Bizarre does, however, carry the kind of price tag you'd expect in Mayfair.

Start with simple things such as pakoras (£5), which are tasty vegetable fritters, or coconut mussels (£6), which come in a coconut fish broth. Kebabs are taken seriously here, too: try gazab ka tikka (£12), a bestseller in Delhi, which is a kind of chicken tikka deluxe. Then, for your main course, choose dishes such as baghare baingan (£8), a Hyderabadi dish combining aubergine, peanuts and tamarind. Or Malabar prawn curry (£15), marinated king prawns with a kick of chilli; or goshtaba (£15), the famous Kashmiri lamb curry – very velvety. Breads are also impressive, including an excellent naan (£2.75); pudina paratha (£3), a mint paratha; and stuffed kulcha (£3). The many imposing set meals are a good way to tour the menu without watching your wallet implode. Try the Maharaja Thali (£24, or £22 vegetarian) – a complete meal on a tray! TV dinners will never be the same again.

✳ Does wine work with Indian food? Charles Metcalfe thinks so: he has devised a striking wine list here.

Gordon Ramsay at Claridge's

French £35–£130

Brook St, W1 ☎020 7499 0099

Station Green Park **Open** Mon–Fri noon–2.45pm & 5.45–11pm, Sat noon–3.30pm & 5.45–11pm, Sun noon–2.45pm & 5.45–10.45pm
Accepts All major credit cards ⓦ www.gordonramsay.com

When Gordon Ramsay took over Claridge's the Mayfair fooderati held their breath. But the dining room is still large, the service is still slick, but the food is much better than it used to be and, it could be argued, better value too. The £30 set lunch here is an even better bargain than the £35 set lunch at Ramsay's Chelsea flagship (see p.70). Unfortunately, like its sibling, Claridge's is booked up far in advance. The à la carte offers three courses for £55.

While Gordon Ramsay has his name over the door, the head chef here is Mark Sargeant. Among the starters may be velouté of cauliflower with a fricasée of wild mushrooms, artichokes and rocket; a smoked eel and celeriac soup with crushed ratte potatoes, crisp ventrêche and poached quails'

eggs; and a tian of Cornish crab with fennel, rocket and herb salad. Presentation on the plate is elegant and seasoning spot-on. Main courses might include roast cannon of Cornish lamb served with confit shoulder (cooked for eight hours), white-bean purée, baby leeks and rosemary jus; pan-fried fillet of dorade with grilled asparagus, globe artichokes and vanilla sauce; braised cheeks of West country pork, cooked with honey and cloves, pommes mousseline, and sautéed foie gras; or fillet of monkfish wrapped in Parma ham on a bed of cèpes risotto, white asparagus and five-spice sauce. The desserts are equally considered: Valrhona chocolate fondant with feuillatine and malt ice cream. This is classy cooking in a classy restaurant in a classy location, but at agreeably accessible prices.

✳ The chef's table seats six comfortably in an air-conditioned alcove overlooking the kitchen.

Kiku

17 Half Moon St, W1 & ☏ 020 7499 4208

Station Green Park **Open** Mon–Sat noon–2.30pm & 6–10.15pm, Sun 5.30–9.45pm
Accepts All major credit cards ⓦ www.kikurestaurant.co.uk

There's no doubt it sounds like a bit of a porky. Kiku is a Japanese restaurant (translates as pricey), deep in the heart of Mayfair (translates as very pricey) and one that serves top-class sushi with a classical ambience – without charging the earth. Your bill will prove it. In helpful, Oriental fashion it lists the huge number of sushi portions you are alleged to have consumed and an average price. For one memorable meal this figure was under £3 per dish. Kiku is laid out around a traditional sushi bar so you can sit and wonder at the dexterity of the knife man. Wander along smack on opening time, snatch a seat at the counter and go for it.

Knowledgeable Japanese folk always start a meal of sushi with tamago (£1.70) – the sweetish, omelettey one which allows the diner to properly assess the quality of the rice. The toro (£5), or tuna belly, is good; the suzuki (£2.90), or sea bass, is good; the amaebi (£2.30), or sweet prawn, is … sweet. Hiramei (£2.70), or turbot, is very delicate. You must have hotate (£2.70), slices of raw scallop, translucent and subtle – very good indeed. From the rolled sushi section, pick the umeshiso maki (£3.20), made from rice with pickled plums and fresh green shiso leaves. Tobiko (£2.70), is slightly advanced and surprisingly good. A successful strategy might be to try a few sushi and then turn to the main menu: perhaps tempura moriawase (£14.50), which is mixed tempura; or sake teriyaki (£9.80), grilled teriyaki salmon. Drink the very refreshing Asahi beer and only venture into the realms of sake if you understand it.

✱ If you suffer from "long menu fatigue system", there are good sushi combinations such as tokujyo nigiri (£30) or jyongiri (£22).

The Mirabelle

56 Curzon St, W1 ☏ 020 7499 4636

Station Green Park **Open** Mon–Fri noon–2.30pm & 6–11.30pm, Sat noon–2.30pm & 6.30–11.30pm, Sun noon–3pm & 6–10pm
Accepts All major credit cards ⓦ www.whitestarline.org.uk

Anyone hoping to open their own restaurant should have lunch at The Mirabelle. It's not just the touch of Marco Pierre White, London's own culinary Rasputin – the whole operation is superlative. Forgive them the mind-numbingly extensive and expensive wine list and concentrate on the

food, which is quite reasonably priced for this kind of cooking. The ingredients are carefully chosen, the presentation on the plate is stunning. The surroundings are elegant, the service attentive and the bar is inviting. Go on, splash out.

Start with a classic: omelette "Arnold Bennett" (£9.50). It's no wonder that Arnold liked these so much – they're rich, buttery and light, made with smoked haddock. Or there's ballottine of salmon Maison Prunier (£8.95). Step up a level for some triumphant foie gras "en terrine" dishes: with green peppercorns, gelée de Sauternes and toasted brioche (£16.95); or

"parfait en gelée" (£9.95). Believe it or not, these two are actually bargains. For a fishy main course, how about an escalope of tuna with aubergine caviar (£14.50)? Or the classical grilled lemon sole served on the bone with sauce tartare (£18.95)? In the meat section, choose from roast venison au poivre with sauce grand veneur (£16.50); or braised pig's trotter with morels, pommes purées and sauce Perigueux (£19.50). Puddings (all at £7.95) are deftly handled. The star is tarte sablée of bitter chocolate. The lunch option is a good one: Monday to Saturday, two lunchtime courses go for £16.50, and three for £19.95; on Sunday three courses cost £19.50.

✳ Surprisingly no one has yet ordered the 1847 vintage Chateau d'Yquem at £30,000.

Momo

North African £30–£50

25 Heddon St, W1 & ☎020 7434 4040

Station Oxford Circus **Open** Mon–Sat noon–2.15pm & 7–10.30pm, Sun 7–10.30pm
Accepts All major credit cards ⊛www.momorestaurant.com

Momo is an attractive and very trendy Moroccan restaurant tucked away in a backwater off Regent Street. For dinner, you usually have to book at least a

week in advance and to opt for an early or late sitting. If you apply for the late shift, be prepared for a noisy, nightclub ambience. The design of the place is clever, with bold, geometric, kasbah-style architecture, plush cushions and lots of candles. Downstairs there's an even more splendid Moorish bar, annoyingly reserved for members only – a shame, as Momo is the kind of place where you could happily carry on the evening, especially if you're booked in for the earlier (7–9pm) dining slot.

The starters include "Momo kemia" (£9.50) which combines méchouia – red-pepper purée, chicken bourek, and briouat au cabillaud (mouth-watering little parcels of paper-thin pastry filled with cod, potatoes and chermoula). Or there is "millefeuille" (£7) made with aubergine and asparagus. For main course, choose from four tagines, which are North African-style stews served in a large clay pot. Try the tagine of chicken with preserved lemons (£14.50) or the tagine of lamb with prunes, quinces and almonds (£15). Alternatively, opt for couscous Méchouia (£32 for two), based around roasted spiced lamb. Or treat yourself to the Fès speciality of pastilla (£10), the super-sweet pigeon pie in millefeuille pastry – a main course that has been relegated to the starters list. Desserts (all around £6.50) include pastries, deep-fried filo parcels of fruit, pancakes and meringues.

Nobu

Japanese £30–£100

19 Old Park Lane, W1 ☎020 7447 4747

Station Hyde Park Corner **Open** Mon–Thurs noon–2.15pm & 6–10.30pm, Fri & Sat noon–2.15pm & 6–11pm, Sun 6–9.30pm **Accepts** All major credit cards

It's hard to know just what to make of Nobu. On the face of it, a restaurant owned by Robert de Niro, Drew Nieporent and Matsuhisa Nobuyuki sounds like the invention of a deranged Hollywood producer. And then there is the cocoon of hype: the restaurant is amazingly expensive, it has a broom cupboard where Boris Becker qualified for his paternity suit. But don't worry, the food is innovative and superb. Ingredients are fresh, flavour combinations are novel and inspired, and presentation is elegant and stylish. See for yourself – the lunchtime bento box, which includes sashimi salad, rock shrimp tempura, black cod and all the trimmings costs just £25.

Chef Matsuhisa worked in Peru, and South American flavours and techniques segue into classical Japanese dishes – some of the dishes here defy classification. There are lists of Nobu "special appetisers" and "special dishes"; the problem is where to begin. Tiradito Nobu-style (£10.50) is a plate of wafer-thin scallop slices, each topped with a dab of chilli, half a coriander leaf and a citrus dressing – delicate and utterly delicious. The sashimi is terrific: salmon (£10.50) is sliced and just warmed through to "set" it, before being served with sesame seeds – the minimal cooking makes for a superb texture. The black cod with miso (£24) is a grandstand dish – a piece of perfectly cooked, well-marinated fish with an elaborate banana-leaf canopy. Other inspired dishes are the rock shrimp tempura (£8.75) and, for dessert, the chocolate and almond parfait with red berry compote (£7.95).

Patterson's

French £15–£65

4 Mill St, W1 ☎ 020 7499 1308

Station Oxford Circus **Open** Mon–Fri 12.30–3pm & 6.30–11pm, Sat 6.30–11pm
Accepts All major credit cards except Diners ⓦ www.pattersonsrestaurant.com

While family-run restaurants serving top-quality, classical, French food are occasionally sighted in France they are as rare as hen's teeth in Mayfair. Patterson's is the exception. Raymond Patterson won his spurs during a fourteen year stint in the kitchens at the Garrick club, and somehow he has persuaded his son to become manager of the new venture, and his wife to work in the restaurant each evening – by day she is a nursery school teacher.

The menu here is littered with those satisfying classical dishes that are so very difficult to do well. A smoked haddock soufflé (£11) served with a chive caviar sauce comes to table towering and quivering, the beurre blanc concoction in a jug to pour into its depths – a stunning dish. Or there may be a ham hock and duck egg ravioli with roast chanterelles (£11). Other starters may include roast foie gras with peach caviar (£13); or a venison and wild-boar terrine with a white-pear cake (£10). These are dishes that put the kitchen through its paces. The mains continue the theme – steamed halibut with crab mousse and fondant leeks (£18); saddle and civet of rabbit with a Swiss chard gateau (£16); or tournedos of beef with foie gras and wild mushroom cannelloni (£20). The puds (all £8) are good: a textbook tart Tatin; an epic white chocolate soufflé with cherry sauce. Patterson's wine list seems unaggressively priced – £28.50 gets you a sound bottle from St Emilion. The service is charming, and there is plenty of both ambition and technical ability in the kitchen. At lunch prices shrink a good deal – starters £5; mains £10; puds £5.

✱ There is sometimes an "oyster lunch" on offer here for just £12: a dozen oysters, cheeseboard and coffee.

The Square

French £30–£130

6–10 Bruton St, W1 ♿ ☎ 020 7495 7100

Station Green Park **Open** Mon–Fri noon–3pm & 6.30–10.45pm, Sat 6.30–10.45pm, Sun 6.30–9.30pm **Accepts** All major credit cards ⓦ www.squarerestaurant.com

The Square is very French: food is terribly important here. And in the gastro premier league – an arena where almost every commentator bows to the supremacy of French chefs and French cuisine – you cannot help a slight smirk that head chef Philip Howard, an Englishman, has got it all so very, very right. At The Square, the finest ingredients are sought out, and then what is largely a classical technique ensures that each retains its essential character and flavour. Eating here is a palate-expanding experience.

This is a very gracious restaurant. Service is suave, silent and effortless. Seasoning is on the button. Presentation is elegant. The wine list seems boundless in scope and soars to the very topmost heights (where mortals dare not even ask the price). In the evening three courses cost £55 (plus a few supplements for serious extravagances). The menu changes on a broadly seasonal basis. Starters are dishes such as lasagne of crab with a cappuccino of langoustines and basil; or oxtail soup with cauliflower foam and black truffle; or assiette of quail. Mains may include fillet of turbot with Beaufort crust; or loin of venison with a tarte fine of celeriac and pear; or roast pigeon from Bresse with stuffed Savoy cabbage leaf. Puddings – such as a fondant of chocolate with malted-milk ice cream – are classics. Howard is an able man and Michelin's two-star measure of his worth is an underestimate. There's also an eight-course "tasting" menu for £75 plus service (for the entire table only). Book now. This is one treat you will never regret.

✱ Lunch – £25 for two courses, £30 for three. Remember, this place has two Michelin stars!

Truc Vert

Modern British £15–£40

42 North Audley St, W1 ☎ 020 7491 9988
Station Bond Street **Open** Mon–Fri 7.30am–9pm, Sat noon–4pm, Sun 9.30am–3pm
Accepts All major credit cards except Diners

Truc Vert is one of those hybrid restaurants. You want it to be a deli, with fine cheeses, artisan chocolate and obscure wild boar salami? Then it's a deli. You want it to be a restaurant, with proper starters, mains and puds? Then it's a restaurant. The Truc is open all day during the week, and it makes a very decent fist of being all things to all customers. The menu comes in two halves. "From the shop" means quiche, salads, chicken from the rotisserie, pâtés, cakes, pastries and cookies. There is also a novel approach to the magnificent cheese counter – you nominate a few cheeses, they make up an elegant plateful, and you are then charged by weight. The same deal works for charcuterie. But despite competition from these instant assortments, the second half of the menu, "From the kitchen", brings main dishes well done and the seasoning spot on.

The menu is rewritten daily, but by way of starter you could be offered a sweet potato and ginger soup (£4.95); saffron crab cakes (£8.25); and baked goat's cheese with artichoke and grilled mixed peppers (£7.75). Mains run the gamut from grilled halibut fillet (£14.50); through penne pasta with roast broccoli, cherry tomatoes and spicy ricotta sauce (£11.90); to grilled lamb cutlets with roast butternut squash, and French bean salad (£14.95). Puds are accomplished – try baked plums with coconut and rum sorbet (£4.75) – but they pale beside the prospect of the epic array of fine cheeses. At lunch the quiches (£4.95), rotisserie chickens (half £9, whole £18), and the selection of pâté with cornichons (£5.95) make the "From the shop" option most appealing.

✱ Un-Mayfair! Pay the shop price and they add £4.50 corkage.

Notting Hill & Kensal Green

© Crown copyright

Assaggi

Very Italian £35–£90

39 Chepstow Place, W2 ☎ 020 7792 5501
Station Notting Hill Gate **Open** Mon–Fri 12.30–2.30pm & 7.30–11pm,
Sat 1–2.30pm & 7.30–11pm **Accepts** All major credit cards

Assaggi is a small, ochre-painted room above The Chepstow pub. It's generally full at lunch and booked well in advance for the evenings. The prices are unforgiving and, on the face of it, paying so much for such straightforward dishes could raise the hackles. But the reason Assaggi is such a gem, and also the reason it is always full, is that selfsame straightforwardness. The menu may appear simple but it is littered with authentic and luxury ingredients, and the cooking is very accomplished indeed. Prepare yourself for a meal to be remembered.

You'll find a dozen starters – with the option to have the pastas as main courses – and half a dozen main courses. Start with pasta, maybe rotolo con asparagi e ricotta al forno (£8.95 or £10.95), or a plate of sensational bufala Mozzarella (£8.75). Or choose grilled vegetables with olive oil and herbs (£8.75). Or there may be a dish such as capesante con salsa alla zafferano (£11.95) – a simple plate of perfectly cooked, splendidly fresh scallops. Main courses are even more pared down: calf's liver (£15.95); a plainly grilled veal chop with rosemary (£18.95); fritto misto (£18.95). But even a humble side salad of tomato, rucola e basilico (£4.75) is everything you would wish for. Puddings change daily and cost £6.25. Look out for panna cotta – a perfect texture – and the beautifully simple dish made from ultra-fresh buffalo Ricotta served with "cooked" honey. To accompany, the short wine list features splendid and unfamiliar Italian regional specialities.

✳ Be careful if offered "specials" made with truffle or wild mushrooms – they are delicious but wallet bruising.

Black & Blue

Steak £12–£40

215–217 Kensington Church St, W8 &. ☏ 020 7727 0004
Station Notting Hill Gate **Open** Mon–Thurs & Sun noon–11pm, Fri & Sat noon–11.30pm
Accepts Mastercard & Visa ⓦ www.blackandblue.biz

Say the words "steak house" to a Londoner and they conjure up a very 1970s image – lots of tartan and red plush, with hapless tourists reaffirming their worst misgivings about British food. It's about time we had a decent chain of steak houses, and Black & Blue may just be a contender. For a start, this establishment, which is part of a lengthening chain, has the very best provenance for its meat. All the steak here comes from Donald Russell of Inverurie – a company that is king of the Aberdeen Angus beef trade.

For a steak house Black & Blue looks smart and modern. There are banquettes, wood panelling, a stylish bar and some rather nice vintage Bovril posters. Starters are predictable. There's a prawn cocktail (£5) – half a dozen large prawns in pink stuff. Or that American abomination, a whole deep-fried onion (£5). Thereafter there's an "all day breakfast", salads, baguettes, two chicken dishes, salmon, prawns and tuna – ignore them all in favour of the steaks. Aberdeen Angus is well-flavoured meat and, commendably enough, when you say rare you get rare. Each steak comes with a very decent mixed salad – steer clear of the proffered dressings – and tolerable fries. There are five steaks: sirloin, rib-eye, fillet, T-bone and a côte de boeuf for sharing. Pricing is straightforward: sirloin 6oz/£12, 10oz/£16; rib-eye 10oz/£17; fillet 6oz/£17, 8oz/£20; T-bone 14oz/£20; côte de boeuf 21oz/£25. There's a small choice of simple desserts: chocolate mousse and lemon tart (both £5) are served with clotted cream. The wine list is not long but is agreeably ungrasping.

❋ There's a very decent hamburger (£8).

The Churchill Arms

Thai £7–£20

119 Kensington Church St, W8 ☏ 020 7792 1246
Station Notting Hill Gate **Open** Mon–Sat noon–9.30pm, Sun noon–8pm
Accepts Mastercard & Visa

The Churchill has nurtured its clientele (who are largely students and bargain hunters) over the years by the simple expedient of serving some of the tastiest and most reasonably priced Thai food in London. The main dining area is in a back room featuring acres of green foliage, but don't despair if you find it full (it fills up very quickly) – meals are served throughout the pub. Service is friendly but, as the food is cooked to order, be prepared to wait – it's worth it. If you really can't wait, pre-cooked dishes such as chicken with chillies (along with that other well-known Thai delicacy, Stilton ploughman's) are also available.

Dishes are unpronounceable, and have thoughtfully been numbered to assist everybody. The pad gai med ma muang hin-maparn (no.15 – £5.85) is a deliciously spicy dish of chicken, cashew nuts and chilli served with a generous helping of fluffy boiled rice. The khao rad na ga prao (no.5 – £5.85), is described as very hot. Not an understatement. This prawn dish with fresh chillies and Thai basil is guaranteed to bring sweat to the brow of even the most ardent chilliholic. For something milder, try the pad neau nahm man hoi (no.17 – £5.85), beef with oyster sauce and mushrooms, or the khao rad na (no.3 – £5.85), a rice dish topped with prawns, vegetables and gravy. Both are good. Puddings are limited in choice and ambition, but for something sweet to temper the heat, try apple pie (£2.50) – a strange accompaniment to Thai food, but surprisingly welcome.

✳ Still a real pub with real beer; seek out a pint of Fuller's London Pride.

Cow Dining Room

Modern British/Gastropub £20–£55

89 Westbourne Park Rd, W2 ☎020 7221 5400

Station Westbourne Park **Open** Mon–Fri 6–11pm, Sat 12.30–3.30pm & 6–11pm, Sun 12.30–3pm & 7.30–10.30pm **Accepts** All major credit cards except Diners

The Cow is something of a conundrum. On the one hand it is a genuine pub – a proper pub, with beer and locals – and on the other, owner Tom Conran has managed to make it something of a meeting place for Notting Hill's smart set. Downstairs all is fierce drinking and cigarette smoke, while upstairs you'll find an oasis of calm and, at its centre, a small dining room. It is a good place to eat. The atmosphere is informal but the food is accomplished. The menu changes on a daily basis and delivers fresh, unfussy, seasonal food.

Starters deliver tried and tested combinations of prime ingredients such as rabbit, white bean and chorizo soup (£4.75); tuna sashimi, spinach oshitashi, soy and wasabi (£9.75); skate wing, capers and beurre noisette (£7.75); or lamb's kidney, black pudding and mustard sauce (£6.75). Main courses cover most of the bases, from goat's cheese and herb ravioli (£7.75 or £14.50); through roast monkfish, ratatouille and pesto (£17.75); to braised milk-fed kid (£16.75); or line caught Cornish cod, spiced chickpeas and gremolata (£13.75). The menu finishes triumphantly with slow-roast belly of "Old Spot" pork with wild mushrooms (£14). Puddings are a suitable mix of the comfortable and the desirable: crème brûlée (£5.25); tart Tatin with vanilla ice cream (£5.25). Or you could go for cheese, which comes with the imprimatur that signifies well-chosen and well-kept cheeses – "Neal's Yard" cheeses with oatcakes (£6.25). The wine list is sound, and if asked nicely your waiter will fetch a pint of De Koninck beer from the bar.

❋ "Cow special" – six Irish oysters and a pint of Guinness, in the bar (£9).

E&O

Asian Eclectic £25–£50

14 Blenheim Crescent, W11 ☎ 020 7229 5454
Station Ladbroke Grove **Open** Mon–Sat 12.15–10.30pm, Sun 1–10pm
Accepts All major credit cards ⓦ www.eando.nu

E&O (it stands for Eastern & Oriental) is geared to non-traditional eating. You're encouraged to abandon the starter and main course convention, and order a mix of small and large dishes to share. Cooking is based on Japanese with added eponymous influences. The venue itself is modern Japanese in feel, and forks, knives, spoons and chopsticks sit in stone pots on the table. Staff are knowledgeable and take trouble to explain if you're unfamiliar with dishes or the spirit of the place. But even more than the taste, it is the presentation of the food that makes it exceptional.

The menu divides into soups, dim sum, salads, tempura, curries, futo maki rolls/sashimi, barbecue/roasts, specials, sides and desserts. Edamame, soy and mirin (£3.00) is a dish of soybeans in the pod to pop and suck out. Fun and delicious. Among the dumplings chicken and snow pea gyosa (£6), and mushroom and chestnut, green tea dumplings (£6) stand out. Chilli-salt squid (£6) is well-seasoned crispy squid served in a Japanese newspaper cone, while baby pork spare ribs (£5.50) come with a sauce good enough to eat with a spoon. In the barbecue/roasts section, black cod with sweet miso (£21.50) is as good as this fish gets. Under curries you'll find sour orange monkfish (£12.50). When you get to the puds you must choose from ices (£5), chocolate pudding (£6.50), which comes with a 20-minute wait, and a shockingly transcultural ginger tiramisù (£6.50). Wines are well chosen and reasonably priced, and there's a selection of six teas (£2.50) served in large Chinese pots.

❋ Can't get a table? Opt for the dim sum served in the bar.

Galicia

Spanish/Tapas £14–£35

89 Westbourne Park Rd, W2 ☎020 8969 3539

Station Westbourne Park **Open** Tues–Sat noon–3pm & 7–11.30pm,
Sun noon–3.30pm & 7.30–10.30pm **Accepts** All major credit cards except Diners

As you walk up the Portobello Road it would be only too easy to amble straight past Galicia. It has that strange Continental quality of looking shut even when it's open. Make it through the forbidding entrance, however, and Galicia opens out into a bar (which is in all probability crowded), which in turn opens into a small, forty-seater restaurant (which is in all probability full). The tapas at the bar are straightforward and good, so it is no surprise that quite a lot of customers get no further than here.

First secure your table then cut a swath through the starters. Jamón (£4.50) is a large plate of sweet, air-dried ham; gambas a la plancha (£6.25) are giant prawns plainly grilled; and pulpo a la Gallega (£5.75) is a revelation – slices of octopus grilled until

bafflingly tender and powdered with smoky pimentón. Galicia does straightforward grilled fish and meat very well indeed. Look for the chuleto de cordera a la plancha (£8.50), which are perfect lamb chops, or lomo de cerdo (£7.75), which are very thin slices of pork fillet in a sauce with pimentón. Or there's the suitably stolid Spanish omelette, tortilla (£5.25). And you should have some chips, which are very good here. Galicia is a pleasant place without pretension. The waiters are all old-school – quiet and efficient to the point of near-grumpiness and the overall feel is of a certain stilted formality. The clientele is an agreeable mix of Notting Hill-ites and homesick Iberians, both of which groups stand between you and that table reservation, so book early.

✱ The wine list is short but has bargains such as a Vega Grand Riserva for just £18.90. Then again, that bin may have run out.

Kensington Place

Modern British £18–£60

201–207 Kensington Church St, W8 ♿ ☎020 7727 3184

Station Notting Hill Gate **Open** Mon–Sat noon–3.30pm & 6.30–11.45pm,
Sun noon–3.30pm & 6.30–10.15pm **Accepts** All major credit cards ◍www.egami.co.uk

The first thing to know about Kensington Place is that it is noisy. The dining room is large, echoing, glass-fronted and noisy with the racket of hordes of people having a good time. The service is crisp, the food is good and the prices are fair. The menu changes from session to session to reflect

whatever the market has to offer, and there is a set lunch that offers a limited choice of three good courses for £16.50 during the week and £18.50 on Sunday. There is also a set dinner that offers three courses for £24.50 or £39.50 to include matched wines.

Rowley Leigh's food is eclectic in the best possible way. The kitchen starts with the laudable premise that there is nothing better than what is in season, and goes on to combine Mediterranean inspirations with classic French and English dishes. Thus you may find, in due season, starters such as carrot soup with risotto and dill (£7), endive, beetroot and orange salad (£6), or omelette fines herbes (£6.50). These are sophisticated dishes, and well-chosen combinations of flavours. Main courses might be steamed mackerel with rhubarb, chilli and mint (£13.50), veal kidneys with agrodolce onions (£17.50), roast white asparagus with pimenton and pepper cream (£17), or roast baby lamb with persillade (£16.50). The dessert section of the menu offers what may be one of London's finest lemon tarts (£6) and some well-made ice creams (£5). There are also traditional favourites with a twist: Beaujolais pears with Financiers (£7), or hot bitter chocolate mousse (£7.50).

✻ This resto has its own, rather good, wet fish shop.

Lucky Seven   North American £10–£28

127 Westbourne Park Rd, W2 ☎ 020 7727 6771
Station Westbourne Park **Open** Mon–Sat 8am–11pm, Sun 9am–10.30pm
Accepts Cash or cheque only

Following the success of the Cow (see p.257), Tom Conran shifted his attention a few hundred yards up the road to a site which was previously a shabby and agreeably seedy little Portuguese café-restaurant-drinking den and set up Lucky Seven, an American diner freshly transplanted to Notting Hill. The kitchen runs across the back behind a high counter and the tiny dining area accommodates 36 people in two sets of booths. There are engraved mirrors. A Pepsi clock. Sally didn't meet Harry here, but doubtless she will soon.

The menu is on a peg-board over the kitchen and it opens with breakfast dishes: two eggs any style (£4.95); with sausage (£5.45); with bacon (£5.54); with Portobello mushrooms (£5.45) – wending its way through omelettes (£4.50) and eggs Benedict (£5.95) to buttermilk pancakes (£4.75). Then there's a section of "soups, stews, salads, sides" before it moves towards "sandwiches and fries". In the evening there's a blue-plate special dish (£6.50 to £8), which ranges from club sandwich to gammon and eggs. For chips choose between "fat" and "French fries" (both £2.25). The burgers are well made, although on the small side for serious trenchers – but, as they start at just £4.95 for the "Classic hamburger", perhaps that is best resolved by ordering two separate Classics or an extra patty (£2.50). In the stews section you will come across such delights as New England clam chowder, and a Cuban black-bean chilli (both £3.95 a cup, £4.95 a bowl). And there are salads – Cobb (£6.95), Caesar (£5) and "Garden of Eden" (£6.25).

✳ "Exterminator chilli" (£3.95 or £4.95) – there's a clue in the name.

Notting Hill Brasserie

Modern British £40–£60

92 Kensington Park Rd, W11 ☎020 7229 4481

Station Notting Hill Gate/Ladbroke Grove **Open** Mon–Sat noon–3pm & 7–11pm
Accepts All major credit cards except Diners ⓦ www.nottinghillbrasserie.com

The Notting Hill Brasserie opened in 2003 and occupies the site that was formerly Leith's Restaurant, offering some c ontinuity for Notting Hillbillies. NHB, as it likes to be called, offers a smart and lively cocktail bar (with piano jazz and blues every evening), as well as the main restaurant. Cocktails range from the traditional, and excellent, dry martini (£8.00) to more exotic offerings such as a Suffering Bustard – dark rum, fresh lime, fresh ginger, topped with ginger beer (£8.00).

Helpfully, NHB's menu features the main ingredient as the first word of each dish, a kind of signature statement. So starters include scallops, sautéed with herb gnocchi and shallots (£11); risotto with herbs, Parmesan and balsamic (£7.50); or veal – sliced rump with caramelized sweetbreads and capers (£7.50). Dishes are well thought through and strongly flavoured. Mains include Red Mullet, pan-fried with confit fennel, saffron crushed potatoes and sardine vinaigrette (£17.50); lamb, roast loin with spring vegetables and globe artichoke puree (£18.50); and "Beef Chateaubriand", which comes roasted in a salt crust, with hand-made chips and sauce Béarnaise (£19.50). This is a single portion Chateaubriand and is offered up to diners intact before the crust is cracked open and the meat served. It's a great way to cook beef and comes with proper chips. Puddings (all at £5.50) include the obligatory chocolate offering in the form of a hot melty-centred fondant, with vanilla ice cream, and an excellent pear millefeuille with anis Anglaise and pear sorbet.

✳ Instead of Irish coffee, try finishing with an Espresso Martini (£8.50).

Nyonya

Malay/Chinese £10–£35

2A Kensington Park Rd, W11 ☎ 020 7243 1800

Station Notting Hill Gate **Open** Mon–Fri 11.30am–3pm & 6.30–10.30pm,
Sat & Sun 11.30am–10.30pm **Accepts** All major credit cards ⓦ www.nyonya.co.uk

Nyonya opened in 2003 and is ultra modern, sensibly cheap, and seriously informal. And all of the above gains added piquancy as the cuisine is downright moody. The French may crow about traditional "cuisine grandmere" but the Straits Malays are just as proud of their "nyonyas" who have much the same credentials. In Nyonya dishes you'll find plenty of coconut cream, some chilli heat, souring from tamarind, and that musty-savoury tang you get from fish sauce or blachan – the seriously stinky shrimp paste.

The room is light and bright, and considering how modern everything looks, the stools are surprisingly comfortable. There are four, long, curved tables so sharing is the order of the day. Service is friendly and the food arrives briskly. Starters include the ubiquitous chicken satay (£5.50) and it is well done here.

The dumplings (£5) are good, especially if you splash out on a small saucer of "sambal blachan" (£2); this is a red sludge made from prawns and chillies, not over-the-top hot but it does add a welcome belt of heat. Main courses come in decent portions. Beef rendang (£7) arrives in a clump, and so it should – this dish should be served almost dry with the coconut sauce reduced to a paste. Up front flavours. A dish of cashew nut prawns (£8.50) is agreeably mild. It's worth ordering the nyonya fried rice (£6.50) which is very rich and sticky and contains a variety of odds and ends – shrimp, chicken, peas, egg. There is also a long list of "hawker favourites" that includes several "meals-in-a-bowl" – a Penang Assam laksa (£7), or Hokkien prawn mee soup (£7.50).

✳ It is hard to oppose a cold Tiger beer (£3) with this kind of spicy food.

Osteria Basilico

Italian £12–£45

29 Kensington Park Rd, W11 ☎ 020 7727 9372

Station Ladbroke Grove **Open** Mon–Fri 12.30–3pm & 6.30–11pm, Sat 12.30–4pm & 6.30–11pm, Sun 12.30–3.30pm & 6.30–10.30pm

Accepts All major credit cards except Diners

Osteria opened 1992, and has flourished ever since. Daytime star-gazing is enlivened by arguments between parking wardens, clampers and their victims, while the traffic comes to a standstill for the unloading of lorries and for a constant stream of mini-cabs dropping off at the street's numerous restaurants. At dusk you get more of the same, with the streetlights struggling to make the heart of Portobello look like the Via Veneto. Inside, pizza and pasta are speedily delivered with typical chirpy Italian panache to cramped, scrubbed tables.

Go easy on the baskets of warm pizza bread, as the antipasti (£6) – various grilled and preserved titbits arranged on the antique dresser – are a tempting self-service affair. Of the other starters, frittura di calamari (£7) and carpaccio di manzo con

pesto, rucola e Parmigiano (£7.50) are both delicious. Specials change daily and have no particular regional influence – perhaps there's a classic such as fettuccine con tartufo bianco, parmigiano e salsa al rosmarino (£13.50). Among the permanent fixtures, spigola alla griglia con olio aromatizzato (£15) is a simply grilled sea bass, carre d'agnello al forno con patate arrosto (£13.50) is roast rack of lamb cutlets with roast potatoes, and filetto di vitello con tortino di patate (£13.80) is veal with a potato cake. Pizzas vary in size depending on who is in the kitchen – perhaps staff with shorter arms throw the dough higher, resulting in a wider, thinner base – but all are on the largish size. Pizza Diavolo (£8) comes with mozzarella and a good, spicy pepperoni sausage.

✳ Montepulciano d'Abruzzo (£15.50) – a pretty decent wine at a pretty decent price.

Tong Ka Nom Thai

Thai £12–£45

833 Harrow Rd, NW10 ☎ 020 8964 5373

Station Kensal Green **Open** Mon–Fri noon–3pm & 6–10pm, Sat & Sun 6–10pm

Accepts Cash or cheque only

At its best, Thai cuisine means intense and distinct flavours – a concept that nearly all of the hundreds of pubs selling Thai grub seem to have mislaid. However the good news is that fresh, cheap and authentic Thai food is alive and well and living on the Harrow Road. Tong Ka

Nom Thai is a small and garish Thai restaurant with a wonderful view of the railway tracks. It is implausibly cheap, the food is very good, and the service friendly.

All the starters are priced at £4. For that, you get six well-spiced tod mun (delightfully chewy Thai fishcakes); or eight popia tod (well-made mini vegetarian spring rolls); or six goong hompha, which are prawns in filo. But the star turn is gai bai toey – six morsels of chicken that are marinated, wrapped in pandan leaf and then fried. They are seriously good. The curries, all at £4, are splendid. Gaeng kheaw wan is a well made green curry which comes with a choice of main ingredients. Other options are a red curry, a yellow curry and a "jungle curry". The house speciality is called "boneless fish fillet" (£5) This is a large hunk of tilapia which comes in a mesmerizing, light, elegant sauce with plenty of holy basil. The sauces here are good – not thickened to a sludge with cornflour, but rich on their own account. You'll need some rice (£1.30) and you should have a noodle dish – perhaps the pad phrik (£4), which is well balanced. At Tong Kanom Thai they serve delicious and authentic Thai food. It is truly remarkable that they can do so at what are almost Thai prices.

✱ This resto is BYO (although they do ask that you buy any soft drinks on the premises).

Further choices

Edera
Italian

148 Holland Park Ave, W11
☎ 020 7221 6090

Stylish Italian restaurant, serving complex and authentic dishes. Good atmosphere and slick service

▲ Edera: slick and stylish

Geale's
Fish & Chips

2 Farmer St, W8
☎ 020 7727 7528

Old style fish and chip restaurant with a dining room, wine list and helpful staff. Just nudges out Costa's on nearby Hillgate Street.

Manzara
Turkish

24 Pembridge Rd, W11
☎ 020 7727 3062

A simple Turkish grill house serving familiar meze seems out of place in W11, but it has a good local following.

Rotisserie Jules
Chicken

133a Notting Hill Gate, W11
☎ 020 7221 3331

Small, familiar restaurant knocking out pretty decent roast chickens with a short list of side orders. Strong takeaway trade.

Piccadilly &
St James's

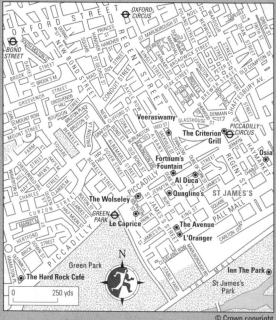

© Crown copyright

The Avenue

Modern British £25–£50

7–9 St James's St, SW1 & ☎ 020 7321 2111

Station Green Park **Open** Mon–Thurs noon–3pm & 5.45pm–midnight, Fri & Sat noon–3pm & 5.45pm–12.45am, Sun noon–3.30pm & 5.45–10pm
Accepts All major credit cards ☻ www.theavenue.co.uk

The Avenue was one of the first banker-led restaurants in London – a bunch of City chums set up the kind of restaurant where they would choose to eat. Now it's part of a sprawling empire, including Kensington Place (see p.259) and Circus (see p.312), to name just two. This is a stark yet stylish barn of a place, entrance is through a glass door (part of a great glass plate fronting the restaurant), and greeting is by designer-clad hosts. Inside it's a very buzzy place with an upbeat atmosphere, dominated by a bar that is much more cocktail than aperitif.

The cooking is well executed and the menu is a fashionable mix of English and the Med. First courses are generally light and bright: chicken consommé and mushroom ravioli (£6.50); escarole, Roquefort and pear salad (£7.50); pickled herring with warm potato pancake and scallion sour cream (£5.50); buffalo mozzarella with radicchio salad and agro dolce sauce (£8.50); or Vietnamese prawn and papaya salad (£8.50). Main courses may include salmon fishcakes with dill butter sauce (£13.50); roast bream with artichokes, red pepper confit and thyme (£16); salt beef with bubble and squeak and charcuterie sauce (£14.50); grilled lamb steaks with soft polenta and slow roast onions (£16.80); or calf's liver with champ and devils on horseback (£15.50). Puddings (all £5.75) range from jam roly-poly with custard; through lemon tart; and flourless chocolate fudge pudding with clotted cream; to chocolate and honeycomb semifreddo. They will appeal to those with a seriously sweet tooth.

✳ Bargain prix fixe menu – £17.95 for two courses, £19.95 for three.

Le Caprice

Modern European £25–£60

Arlington House, Arlington St, SW1 ☎ 020 7629 2239
Station Green Park **Open** Mon–Sat noon–3pm & 5.30–midnight, Sun noon–3.30pm &5.30pm–midnight **Accepts** All major credit cards ☻ www.caprice-holdings.co.uk

Every London socialite worth their salt is a regular at this deeply chic little restaurant, and everyone from royalty downwards uses it for the occasional quiet lunch or dinner. That's not because they'll be hounded by well-wishers or because photographers will be waiting outside. They won't. This restaurant is discreet enough to make an oyster seem a blabbermouth. It's not even particularly plush or comfortable, with a black-and-white-tiled floor, a big black bar and cane seats. What keeps Le Caprice full day in, day out is its personal service, properly prepared food and a bill that holds no surprises.

The much-copied menu is enticing from the first moment. Plum tomato and basil galette (£6.75) is simplicity itself. Crispy duck comes with watercress salad (£9.25), while dressed Dorset crab with celeriac remoulade (£14.25) is very fresh and clean. In season, there are splendid specials – River Spey sea trout with steamed clams and parsley (£18.75). Or perhaps Tamworth pork chop with white asparagus and rosemary butter (£14.50).

Or there may be loin of yellow fin tuna with spiced lentils (£18.25). If you are still up for pudding, try banana sticky toffee pudding (£6.35) or the baked Alaska with cherries and Kirsch (£7.50) to see just what classic English puds are about. In the winter there is an array of more solid rib-stickers. Expense aside, the only trouble with Le Caprice is the struggle to get a table. Try booking well in advance, or go for a last minute table at the bar.

* There is a special vegan and vegetarian menu.

The Criterion Grill French/British £25–£65

224 Piccadilly, W1 ☎020 7930 0488
Station Piccadilly Circus **Open** Mon–Sat noon–2.30pm & 5.30–11pm
Accepts All major credit cards ✇www.whitestarline.org.uk

The Criterion, which is part of Marco Pierre White's empire (see also the Mirabelle p.249, and Chez Max p.326) is one of London's most beautiful restaurants. Covered up and used as a shop for decades (it was once a 24hr Boots branch), happily it is now back to its full-on belle-époque glory. Areas are divided by classical arches, and the impossibly high ceiling is decorated with gold mosaics and flower-like lamps. And a trip to the loos is de rigueur, simply to be able to walk the whole length of the room to view the romantic paintings on the walls. Tables are laid with linen and silver in a modern version of traditional perfection and are set far apart from each other.

The menu features the kind of steady, trad French dishes that have recently swept back into favour: French onion soup

(£7.50); parfait of foie gras (£8.50); moules marinière classique (£8.50); Caesar salad (£7.50). Main courses are created from simple combinations of good ingredients – roast suckling pig with apple sauce (£18.95); smoked haddock glazed with welsh rarebit (£15.50); roast chicken a l'Anglaise with bread sauce (£15.95); grilled lemon sole and sauce tartare (£22.50); slow-roast duck with sage and onion (£16.50). There is also a list of grills entitled "rotis du bouchir" featuring rib-eye Aberdeen Angus steaks in various guises – with escargots and Béarnaise (£15.50). Puddings, which all come in at £7.50, include sticky toffee pudding with vanilla ice cream, creme brulée, and lemon tart. The wine list goes all the way from reasonable to wallet challenging.

* Lunch (until 7pm!) £14.95 for two and £17.95 for three courses.

Al Duca

Italian £20–£40

4–5 Duke of York St, SW1 ☎ 020 7839 3090
Station Piccadilly Circus **Open** Mon–Fri noon–2.30pm & 6–11pm, Sat 12.30–3pm & 6–11pm **Accepts** All major credit cards except Diners ⊛ www.alduca-restaurant.co.uk

This restaurant hit the West End scene in 2000, so in the grand scheme of things it now ranks as a grizzled veteran! You get high-quality, sophisticated food, an agreeable setting, slick service, and all at modest prices – what you get here seems to be far more than you pay for. The formula is a simple one: at lunch, two courses cost £17.50, three cost £20.50, and four £23.50. In the evening, the prices go up to £20, £24 and £28. A three-course dinner for £24 within stumbling distance of Piccadilly? More like this, please!

With this kind of deal its best not to think London – think Italy. Such regularly changing menus are commonplace there. There are six or more starters at Al Duca: dishes such as chargrilled marinated mixed vegetables with balsamic vinegar; or pan-fried wild mushrooms with chicken livers, bacon and crisp polenta. Then there is a raft of dishes under the heading pasta: home-made fettuccine with rabbit ragù and black olives; linguine with clams and garlic; or reginette with peas and bacon. This is followed by an array of main courses: pan-fried salmon with poached potatoes in butter and spinach with balsamic; sea bass; chicken. Finally, six desserts, ranging from a stracchino cheesecake with Acacia honey to a classic almond and pear tart. The standard of cooking is high, with dishes bringing off that difficult trick of being both deceptively simple and satisfyingly rich. Overall there is much to praise here, and the slick service and stylish ambience live up to the efforts in the kitchen.

✱ Try the dessert called seadas, "puff pastry ravioli with ricotta and honey".

Fortnum's Fountain

Very British £15–£40

181 Piccadilly, W1 ⅋ ☎ 020 7973 4140
Station Piccadilly Circus/Green Park **Open** Mon–Sat breakfast 8.30–11am, lunch 11.30am–3pm, tea 3–5.30pm, dinner 5.30–7.45pm
Accepts All major credit cards ⊛ www.fortnumandmason.co.uk

The main entrance to Fortnum's Fountain Restaurant is at the back of

the store, on the corner of Jermyn Street. The Fountain delivers just what you expect given its location – well prepared, very English breakfasts, lunches, teas and early dinners. The ingredients, as you'd expect of London's smartest and most old-fashioned food shop, are top-class. And the Fountain itself is a very pretty room, with classical murals all around.

The Fountain is deservedly famous for its selection of Fortnum's teas and coffees accompanied by cream teas and ice-cream sundaes, and on any given afternoon you will see small children being treated by elderly relatives. The dishes on the Fountain Menu (which serves for both lunch and dinner) reflect the ingredient-buying power of the food department and, sensibly enough, tend to the straightforward. The excellent London smoked salmon with onion bread (£13.50) is a real treat, as is Fortnum's Welsh rarebit on Cheddar bread with grilled tomato, back bacon or poached egg (£9.50). There are also simple classics such as grilled Dover sole with side salad and new potatoes (£24); grilled Aberdeen Angus steak with peppercorn sauce and chips (£16.50); and Highland scramble (£10.25), which teams scrambled eggs with smoked salmon. The restaurant is always busy and, though they turn tables, you will not be hurried. The downside is that there is no booking. That's great for shoppers, but anyone on a schedule should avoid the lunchtime peak. Give breakfast serious consideration.

✳ Pork, lamb and bacon from HRH Prince Charles's little place in Gloucestershire.

The Hard Rock Cafe

North American/Burgers £15–£30

150 Old Park Lane, W1 ☎020 7629 0382

Station Hyde Park Corner **Open** Mon–Thurs & Sun 11.30am–midnight, Fri & Sat 11.30am–1am **Accepts** All major credit cards ⊛www.hardrock.com

The Hard Rock Café is a genuine celebration of rock 'n' roll and this is the original, here since the 1970s. It's also the original theme restaurant, and as such a hard act to follow. The queue out front is legendary. There's no booking and you'll find a queue almost all day long, every day of the year – it kind of adds to the occasion. Once in, there is a great atmosphere, created by full-on rock music, dim lighting and walls dripping with rock memorabilia. The Hard Rock food is not bad, either, predominantly Tex-Mex and burgers.

Scanning the menu is a serious business here – dishes get short but complex essays attached to them – so Tupelo chicken tenders (£5.95) are explained as "boneless chicken tenders, lightly breaded and coated in our Classic Rock (medium), Heavy Metal (hot) sauce or tangy Bar-B-Que sauce. Served with celery and Bleu cheese dressing". The job of copywriter is an important one here. The burgers cover the spectrum from HRC burger (£7.95) to the hickory Bar-B-Que bacon cheeseburger (£9.25). Veggies are catered for by the HRC veggie sandwich (£7.55). There are also Tex-Mex specials such as the grilled fajitas (£12.25), which are a pretty good example of the genre. Further along, among the Smokehouse Specialities, there's the pig sandwich (£7.95) and Bruce's famous Bar-B-Que ribs (£11.95). Puddings are self-indulgent, and the hot fudge brownie (£5.45) elevates goo to an art form. If sweet is truly your thing there's a shooter called "bubblegum" (£5) – Bailey's, blue curacao, banana liqueur!

✳ The "museum and memorabilia shop" is across the road; it used to be a branch of Coutt's bank.

Inn the Park

British £7–£50

St James's Park, SW1 & ☎020 7451 9999
Station St James's Park **Open** Daily 8am–11pm
Accepts All major credit cards ⊛www.innthepark.co.uk

Let's hope that Inn the Park is the shape of things to come. It's no secret that the catering arrangements in London's parks have always been deeply dodgy. The Inn opened during the spring of 2004 and is a revelation. The building is stunning – lots of gentle curves and wood and everything built into a grassy mound like the dwelling of an A-list hobbit. The food is good too – British produce, commendably fresh, unfussy presentation and simply cooked. This place opens for breakfast, then serves snacks, then lunch, then afternoon tea, then dinner. The waiting staff seem friendly and service is slick – which will come as something of a shock to anyone accustomed to the hot-dog-from-a-barrow that used to be the only option.

Breakfast includes boiled egg and soldier (£3.50), a duck egg on sourdough (£3.50), the Great British breakfast (£9.50)

▲ Inn The Park: a bird's-eye view

and "poor knights of Windsor" (£5.50) – French toast or eggy bread to you and I. The tea comes in pots, pots with real leaves in! At lunch and dinner the "proper" cooking is well done: wild garlic and potato soup (£4); jellied ham hock and parsley terrine (£6); oxtail with purple sprouting broccoli (£11.50); seared salmon with a warm salad of potatoes and Denhay bacon (£10.50). There are also home-made ice creams (£4.50) and farmhouse cheeses from Neals Yard (£7.50). The afternoon tea – sandwiches, cakes, scones (£12) is a serious contender, and even the snacks appeal – "plate of British cured and cooked meats with chutneys and pickles" (£8.50). What good, honest food and what a splendid place to eat it.

> ***** The Inn does take bookings, but only for dinner.

L'Oranger
French £30–£90

5 St James's St, SW1 ☎ 020 7839 3774
Station Green Park **Open** Mon–Fri noon–2.30pm & 6.30–11pm, Sat 6–11pm
Accepts All major credit cards

From the outside, L'Oranger looks like a very expensive French restaurant dedicated to expense-account diners. While it's not cheap à la carte, the lunch deal does bring serious cooking within reach. (At lunch you pay £24 for two courses or £28 for three). For your money you can expect modernist cooking of a high standard and lavish use of high ticket ingredients. The saucing leans towards light olive-oil bases rather than the traditional "loadsa-cream" approach.

The "full-on" starters may include leek and potato cappucino, flaked cod and poached egg (£12); ravioli of artichoke with sage and Jabugo ham (£15); confit duck liver, celeriac purée, and apple granité (£17); or grilled Scottish blue lobster with crunchy fennel (£25). For main courses, try roast pigeon, almond purée and a salad of fresh herbs (£23); roast fillet of turbot, salsify and potato gnocchi (£28); rack of lamb with caviar of aubergine and feta cheese (£24); or fillet of wild seabass with artichoke, pink radish and vanilla olive oil (£25). Puddings (£8) are exotic and interesting: poached pear comes with chocolate cremeux and old rum granité; marinated pineapple comes with Java pepper cream and honey ice cream; or there's the L'Oranger soufflé with exotic sorbet. The wine list is encyclopedic, but there's plenty of choice at the lower prices. L'Oranger is refined and elegant with attentive service but a relaxed and unstuffy atmosphere. There's also a secret outside courtyard, which is open at dinner only (weather permitting), and a private function room for twenty.

> ***** Sevruga caviar, a snip at £2 a gram – but a minimum of fifteen grams.

Osia

Australian £27–£100

11 Haymarket, SW1 ☎ 020 7976 1313

Station Piccadilly Circus **Open** Mon–Fri noon–3pm & 5.30–10.45pm, Sat 5.30–10.45pm **Accepts** All major credit cards except Diners ⊛ www.osiarestaurant.com

Osia opened in the spring of 2003, and the man in charge of the kitchen is a genial Aussie called Scott Webster. His food is terrific, presenting original combinations of taste and texture, the service is accomplished and the room comfortable. The bill can end up nerve-racking, but overall it is worth flexing your wallet and trying these dishes. Keep an open mind and open palate, or take advantage of the slightly cheaper set menu offer of £19 for two courses and £23 for three.

The menu starts with the somewhat daunting header, "From the raw bar". In practice this may mean red plum and yellow cherry tomato cocktail with citrus dressing (£5); salt-cured salmon ceviche, dill gherkin and fennel lime oil (£7); or three Colchester rock oysters with watermelon lillipilli vinegar (£7). Onwards to starters: spiced chicken sweetcorn bonbons with mango red onion relish (£7); pan-seared duck liver, date and apple chutney (£8); or salt-and-peppered soft-shell crab with ginger honey mirin dip (£12). Mains look beautiful on the plate and have well-matched, upfront flavours. Try Eucalyptus roasted rack of lamb, wilted warrigal greens, and sweet potato nutmeg mash (£19) – stunning, exotic, herby lamb, fresh-tasting greens. Or Parmesan crumbed seabass fillet, watercress, wilted carrot noodles and dill tomato fondue (£17). Or Barbary-duck-leg confit, white Judion bean stew with olive oil (£16). Puds are outrageous – hot Callebaut chocolate soup with cracked-pepper ice cream (£6). Dive into a pool of molten choccy! The wine list is long on New World, starts at around £18 a bottle and accelerates away.

✳ Hot semolina porridge with stewed fruits and vanilla-bean ice cream (£6).

Afternoon tea

Afternoon tea is a charming institution. Here are three good places to rest your feet and have a cuppa while in the West End:

▶ **The Wolseley** (see p.274). Finger sandwiches, selected teas, and epic cakes.

▶ **Fortnum & Mason** The dining room on the second floor is preferred to the Fountain (see p.268) for classic afternoon tea.

▶ The ground floor room at **Yauatcha** (see p.322). A wild card – moody Parisienne/Oriental cakes and a huge range of China teas. A modernist tea house.

Quaglino's

Modern British £25–£90

16 Bury St, SW1 ♿ ☎ 020 7930 6767

Station Green Park **Open** Mon–Thurs noon–3pm & 5.30–11.30pm, Fri & Sat noon–3pm & 5.30pm–1.30am, Sun noon–3pm & 5.30–11pm
Accepts All major credit cards ⓦ www.conran.com

In 1929 Giovanni Quaglino opened a restaurant in Bury Street which became an instant success. The one thing it had, above all else, was glamour. When Sir Terence Conran redesigned and reopened Quaglino's, more than sixty years later, his vision was essentially the same. The ambience is still impressive – an elegant reception, the sweeping staircase into the bar that overlooks the main restaurant, and the second stairway down to restaurant level. If this kind of thing rings your bell you will be happy here.

The menu is simple, classy and brasserie-style, with very little to scare off the less experienced diner. The plateau de fruits de mer (£34 per person, minimum two people) is as good as you would hope, as is the whole lobster mayonnaise (£29). Fish and chips (£13.50) is served with home-made chips and tartare sauce, and is excellent, while a 42-day-aged Glen Fyne sirloin steak (£22.50) is a treat when served properly cooked, as it is here. Puddings are straightforward and agreeably predictable – blackcurrant parfait (£6.50); apple Charlotte, clotted cream (£6.50). Quaglino's staff can be brusque, but then marshalling large numbers of glamour-seekers is a testing enough job, which would make anyone a little tetchy. You can avoid this altogether by staying in the bar, which offers highlights from the menu – including all the seafood. Furthermore, Quaglino's is open late, which makes it perfect for a genuine after-theatre dinner. There's a prix-fixe menu at lunch and pre- or post-theatre: two courses for £16.50, three for £18.50.

✳ Open daily for afternoon tea, 3–5pm.

Veeraswamy

Indian £25–£60

Victory House, 99 Regent St, W1 ☎ 020 7734 1401

Station Piccadilly Circus **Open** Mon–Fri noon–2.30pm & 5.30–11.30pm, Sat 12.30–3pm & 5.30pm–11.30pm, Sun 12.30–3pm & 5.30–10.30pm
Accepts All major credit cards ⓦ www.realindianfood.com

Veeraswamy is Britain's oldest-surviving Indian restaurant, founded in 1927 by Edward Palmer following a successful catering operation at the British Empire Exhibition. The latest owner is Namita Panjabi, who also owns Chutney Mary (see p.66) and Masala Zone (see p.314). She has swept Veeraswamy into the modern era: the old and faded colonial decor has gone, along with the old and faded dishes. In their place there's an elegant, fashionable restaurant painted in

the vibrant colours of today's India, and an all-new menu of bold, modern, authentically Indian dishes of all kinds.

You'll need to adjust your pattern of ordering. Main dishes come as a plate with rice, and sometimes vegetables too. They're not designed for sharing, and you will definitely need one each. Street food makes great starters: pani puri (£5.25), rich with tamarind; or there's spiced crab cake with fresh plum chutney (£7.50) or mussels moilee (£6.50), which is made from fresh mussels with coconut and ginger. The tandoori dishes could be starters or main – lamb chops (£18) appeals. Other mains are well spiced and have a good depth of flavour. Raan baluchi (£16) is a lamb shank cooked with Kashmiri chillies and rose petals. You could also try the Malabari lobster curry (£21.50), with fresh turmeric and raw mango. There are also vegetarian options, including a veggie thali (£14). As well as a set lunch (£12.50 for two courses, £14.75 for three), there is also a serious "tasting menu" at £31 per person – a starter, thali and dessert.

✳ The King of Denmark used to dine here and bring his own Carlsberg.

The Wolseley — European £25–£75

160 Piccadilly, W1 ♿ ☎ 020 7499 6996
Station Green Park **Open** Daily breakfast 7am–11.30am, tea 3pm–5.30pm, restaurant noon–2.30pm & 5pm–midnight **Accepts** All major credit cards
ⓦ www.thewolseley.com

The Wolseley was one of the most eagerly expected openings of 2003 and it hit the ground running. The two principals are Christopher Corbin and Jeremy King – the men who developed both Le Caprice (p.266) and the Ivy (p.117). The room is tall and theatrical, gloriously dramatic. The atmosphere is "celebrity chic" and the feel of the place owes plenty to middle European grand cafés, as does the menu. One enterprising critic started with breakfast, and then stayed for elevenses, lunch, afternoon tea and dinner – it's probably the one sure way to secure a table for dinner! This place is so busy that it is very hard to get into, but worth it. Try early or late.

The food is good here – unfussy, old-fashioned, and well presented. There are good reports about the breakfast, the cakes and pastries. The main menu has a plat du jour (£12.75) – such as coq au vin on Mondays and cassoulet on Wednesdays. Starters include some nostalgic numbers such as chopped liver (£4.75); steak tartare (£8); and escargots (£9.75 for six). There are salads, such as frisee aux lardons (£7.75); shellfish, including dressed Cornish crab (£13.50); soufflé Suisse (£9.25); eggs bubble'n'squeak (£4.75 or £9.50). Onwards! Nürnberger bratwurst and potato salad (£8.75); grilled Dover sole (£26); a hamburger (£8.50); spit-roast suckling pig

(£13.75). The frites are very good indeed. Among the puds are a Vacherin Mont Blanc (£6), a "fruit bowl" (£5) and serious ice-cream coupes. The wine list is comprehensive. The service is slick and the celebrity count is very high indeed.

> Welcome back "Wiener Holstein" (£15) – veal escalope with anchovies and an egg.

Further choices

Bentley's
Fish/Oysters

11 Swallow St, W1
☎ 020 7734 4756

Old time oyster bar and fish restaurant. Not cheap, but more atmosphere than you can handle.

Destino
Latin American

25 Swallow St, W1
☎ 020 7437 9895

Pleasant and informal, deli and resto open downstairs at lunch time. More ambitious dining room upstairs during the evening.

Fakhreldine
Middle Eastern

85 Piccadilly, W1
☎ 020 7493 3424

Lebanese food as interpreted by a chef with an admiration for French cuisine. Grand view. Sophisticated setting. Beware sophisticated prices.

Wagamama
Japanese/Chinese

8 Norris St, SW1
☎ 020 7321 2755

Branch of the noodle chain. See p.48.

Yo! Sushi
Japanese

Unit 34a Trocadero Centre, Rupert St, W1
☎ 020 7434 2724
Branch of the conveyor sushi specialists. See review p.322.

Primrose Hill
& Chalk Farm

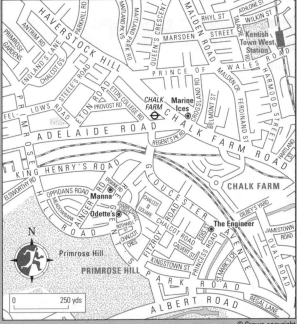

© Crown copyright

The Engineer

Modern British/Gastropub £12–£40

65 Gloucester Ave, NW1 & ☎020 7722 0950

Station Chalk Farm **Open** Mon–Fri 9–11.30am, noon–3pm & 7–11pm, Sat 9am–noon, 12.30–3.30pm & 7–11pm, Sun 9am–noon, 12.30–3.30pm & 7–10.30pm

Accepts All major credit cards except AmEx & Diners ⓦ www.the-engineer.com

The Engineer is now one of London's senior gastropubs – and eating places are spread throughout the building and garden. Wherever you end up sitting, you'll get offered the same menu (which changes every two weeks) and you'll pay the same price. The cooking is accomplished, with good strong combinations of flavours, and a cheerful, iconoclastic approach to what is fundamentally Mediterranean food.

Your hackles may rise at £2.75 for home-made bread and butter, but the bread is warm from the oven, with a good crust, the butter is beurre d'Isigny, and, as they refill the basket after you've scoffed the lot, you end up feeling happier about paying. Starters are simple and good. There's soup (£4) and the price includes the bread mentioned earlier. There may be hommus with warm flatbreads and spicy lamb kofta (£6.25); or something more exotic such as tequila-cured salmon with blinis, horseradish cream and cucumber (£6.75). At lunchtime there are one or two simpler mains than in the evening: toad in the hole with mash and sugar snap peas (£11.25); huevos rancheros (£10.25) with tortilla and black beans. For dinner, expect dishes such as grilled swordfish with lemon-scented fennel and Bloody-Mary sauce (£14.50); risotto cake with butternut squash and Feta cheese (£11.25); or red braised belly pork with steamed baby gem lettuce (£12.50). A side order of baker fries (£2.25) brings thick wedges of baked potato fried until crispy. Desserts hover around £6 – banana Pavlova; custard tart. There is always a decent pint of beer to be had and the coffee is excellent.

❋ The garden is always mobbed in good weather – book early.

Manna

Vegetarian £16–£45

4 Erskine Rd, NW1 ☎020 7722 8028

Station Chalk Farm **Open** Daily 6.30–11pm, Sun 12.30–3pm

Accepts All Mastercard & Visa ⓦ www.manna-veg.com

If your new film – the one where a beautiful American businesswoman meets a tongue-tied but cute Brit aristo, you know the kind of thing – needed an authentic 1970s veggie restaurant for a crucial hand-holding scene, the decor at Manna would fit the bill perfectly. This timewarp sometimes extends to the service, so don't pitch up here

in a hurry, or without a serious appetite – there is no whimsy about the portions here. The cooking is very sound, and if there is such a thing as a peculiarly "veggie" charm, this place has plenty.

The menu devolves into four sections: starters, mains, salads, and desserts. You can also order a selection of any three salads or starters as the "Manna meze" (£14.50), which is a pretty good option given the huge portions. The menu changes regularly but may include starters such as organic Gorgonzola pizzette (£6.75) with red-onion confit and walnuts; or a tortilla tower (£6.50) – spinach, red pepper and potato omelettes layered with smoked Cheddar. Or how about potato bondas stuffed with pink chilli coconut chutney (£5.95)? Salads are complex – grapefruit and avocado, green pea shoots, watercress and baby mustard leaves (£5.95); or perhaps organic warm white bean salad with sage oil and crisp sourdough (£5.95). Mains are an eclectic bunch: whiskey barbecue marinated tofu on roast-garlic mash (£12.50); or Majorcan baked aubergine stuffed with onions and topped with Romanesco sauce (£11.50). Puds are serious: organic chocolate ooze pudding (£6.75) and organic fruit crumble (£5.50) are a challenge to all but the stoutest appetites.

There's a menu code (v) = vegan dishes; (vo) = vegan option; (org) = organic dish; (n) = contains nuts and (g) = gluten free.

Marine Ices

Italian/Ice cream £10–£30

8 Haverstock Hill, NW3 ☎ 020 7482 9003

Station Chalk Farm **Open** Restaurant Mon–Fri noon–3pm & 6–11pm, Sat noon–11pm, Sun noon–10pm; gelateria Mon–Sat 10.30am–11pm, Sun 11am–10pm
Accepts Mastercard, Switch & Visa

Marine Ices is a family restaurant from a bygone era. In 1947, Aldo Mansi rebuilt the family shop along nautical lines, kitting it out in wood with portholes (hence the name). In the half-century since, while the family ice-cream business has grown and grown, the restaurant and gelateria has just pottered along. That means old-fashioned service and home-style, old-fashioned Italian food. It also means that Marine Ices is a great hit with children, for in addition to the good Italian food there is a marathon list of stunning sundaes, coupes, ice creams and sorbets.

The menu is long: antipasti, salads, pastas and sauces, vitello, fegato, carne, pollo, pesce, specialities and pizzas. Of the starters, you could try selezioni di bruschetta (£4.35). Or go for the chef's salad (£5.25), a rocket salad with pancetta and splendid croutons made from eggy bread. Pasta dishes are homemade: mix and match various sauces with various pasta – starters £5.50, mains £6.50, "oven" dishes such as cannelloni and lasagne (both £6.45), then the menu lists nearly every old-style Italian dish you have ever heard of costing between £7.50 and £12. Onwards to a host of pizzas – immense, freshly made and very tasty (£5.45 to £7.25). When you've had your meal, demand the gelateria menu. There are sundaes, from peach Melba (£2.65) to Knickerbocker Glory (£3.95). There are bombe, coppe, cassate and, best of all, affogati (£4.95) – three scoops of ice cream topped with hot chocolate or, even nicer, espresso coffee. Or run amok among fourteen ice creams and eight sorbets (all £1.50 a scoop).

✴ Marine is now run by Aldo Mansi – great grandson of the founder.

Odette's French/Modern European £15–£50

130 Regent's Park Rd, NW1 ☎ 020 7586 5486
Station Chalk Farm **Open** Mon–Sat 12.30–2.30pm & 7–11pm, Sun 12.30–9pm
Accepts All major credit cards except Diners

Odette's is a charming, picturesque restaurant, perfectly attuned to pretty Primrose

Hill. There's a pleasant conservatory at the back (with a skylight open in warm weather) and candles flicker in the evenings. Add ambitious and complex cooking, the odd local celeb, friendly staff, and you have all the ingredients for a very successful local restaurant. In summer, try to get one of the tables that spill out onto the villagey street. As with any long-established place the chef (and the menu) changes from time to time and the trend seems to be towards elaboration.

The food makes commendable use of seasonal produce, so don't expect to find all the dishes listed every time you visit. Starters, if you strike lucky, might include salad of chargrilled asparagus, Parmesan gnocchi and a soft poached egg (£7); dressed Cornish crab with Jersey Royals, and home-made salad cream (£9); or carpaccio of Buccleuch beef with deep-fried oysters (£9). Mains generally include at least one choice each of fish, meat, game and chicken. Steamed halibut comes with pickled cucumber and sliced beets (£17); or there's roast Gressingham duck (£18), with a tortellini of hearts and gizzards, seared foie gras and blood orange. Veggies might go for a tarte fine of Italian white onions and Brie de Meaux (£15). Puddings (all £6.50) are wonderfully indulgent, and include tiramisù parfait with chocolate fritters, and an outstanding mango and stem-ginger sorbet. Odette's has a very long wine list, with something to suit all tastes and purses.

✱ There are good value set menus – £12.50 and £16 weekdays, £15.50 and £19 on Sunday.

Further choices

Belgo Noord
Belgian

72 Chalk Farm Rd, NW1
☎ 020 7267 0718

An outpost of the moules-masters. See review on p.114.

Lemonia
Greek

89 Regent's Park Rd, NW1
☎ 020 7586 7454

Incredibly busy restaurant serving cheerful Greek Cypriot dishes to parties of party people.

Sardo Canale
Italian

42 Gloucester Ave, NW1
☎ 020 7722 2800

New sister restaurant to Sardinian specialist in Fitzrovia; see the review on p.159.

Trojka
Russian

101 Regent's Park Rd, NW1
☎ 020 7483 3765

Somewhat lugubrious Russian Café dishing up home-cooking Russian style – very enjoyable in a low key way.

Putney

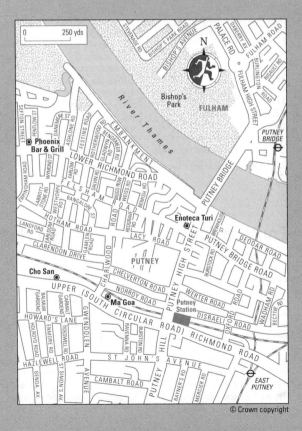

Cho San

Japanese £8–£35

292 Upper Richmond Rd, SW15 ☎020 8788 9626
Station BR Putney **Open** Tues–Fri 6.30–10.30pm, Sat & Sun noon–2.30pm & 6.30–10.30pm **Accepts** All major credit cards

Too many Japanese restaurants use extremely high prices and ultra-swish West End premises to keep themselves to themselves. As a European adventurer basking in the impeccably polite and attentive service, it's hard not to feel a little anxious. What should you order? How do you eat it? Will it taste nice? How much does it cost? If you have ever been assailed by these worries you should pop along to Cho-San in Putney. This small, unpretentious, family-run restaurant opened in 1998 and has built up a steady trade.

This is your chance to try all those dishes you have never had, without wounding your pocket. The sushi is good. The sashimi is good. And a giant boat of assorted sushi and sashimi, with miso soup and dessert, costs £19.90. But why not try some more obscure sushi? The prices of the fancy ones range from £3 to £5.90 for two pieces. Or, if you prefer your fish cooked, choose the perfect tempura cuttlefish (£7.90) – a stunning achievement, its batter light enough to levitate. And then there are always the kushiage dishes, where something is put onto a skewer, gets an egg and breadcrumb jacket and is treated to a turn around the deep fryer. Ordering tori kushiage (£5.60) gets you two skewers, chicken and a chunk of sweet onion. Delicious. Or opt for tempura king prawn (£9.90). Then there are the meat dishes, the fish dishes, the rice dishes, the soba noodles, and the hot sakes, cold sakes and beers. You could eat your way to a good understanding of Japanese food here. Ask the charming, helpful staff and get stuck in.

✳ Yukiguni (sweet red beans) on vanilla ice cream (£3.60).

Enoteca Turi

Italian £15–£65

28 Putney High St, SW15 ☎020 8785 4449
Station Putney Bridge **Open** Mon–Sat 12.30–2.30pm & 7–11pm
Accepts All major credit cards

If you like your Italian food a little more adventurous than the usual, then it is worth making the journey to Putney and Giuseppe Turi's pretty little restaurant. It offers a very genuine and personal version of Italian regional cooking – Turi himself hails from Apulia, and many dishes are based on recipes from this area. Enoteca takes its name from the Italian term for a smart wine shop, so it's hardly surprising that wines feature prominently in the scheme of things. There's a monumental list of more than ninety specialist Italian wines and a separate by-the-glass menu offering eleven Italian regional wines – an excellent way to educate the palate.

As for the food, at lunch there is a shortened version of the dinner menu and dishes are a couple of pounds cheaper. You'd do well to start with asparagus served with Parmesan-coated deep-fried egg (£7.50); or perhaps a plate of antipasto Pugliese (£7.50) – marinated, grilled vegetables served with a fava purée. Among pasta dishes may be ravioli di castagne e ricotta (£8.50 or £10.50); or fettuccine with Pachino tomatoes (£8.50). Main courses may include stinco d'agnello con puree di patate e cipolline, which is lamb shank with spring onion and potato purée (£14.50); or petto d'anatra (£15.50) – duck breast served with new season vegetables and dry marsala sauce. Desserts will test your mettle – go for the torta di cioccolata con nocciole (£5.50), a blockbusting chocolate and hazelnut cake, or perhaps the particularly good, authentic tiramisù (£5). Booking essential even mid week.

PUTNEY

More of a wine bluff than a wine buff ? Check out the wines recommended alongside each dish.

Ma Goa

Indian £14–£30

244 Upper Richmond Rd, SW15 ☎020 8780 1767
Station BR Putney/East Putney **Open** Mon–Sat 6.30–11pm, Sun 12.30–3pm & 6–10pm
Accepts All major credit cards ⊛www.ma-goa.com

Despite the stylish ochre interior, complete with fans and blond wooden floor, despite the café-style chairs and tables, and the computer system to handle bills and orders, the overwhelming impression you are left with when you visit Ma Goa is of eating in somebody's home. This place is as far as you can possibly get from the chuck-it-in-a-frying-pan-and-heat-it-through school of curry cookery. The food is deceptively simple, slow-cooked and awesomely tasty. And it is authentically Goan into the bargain.

The menu is fairly compact: half a dozen starters are followed by a dozen mains, while a blackboard adds a couple of dishes of the day. Shrimp balchao (£4.50) is a starter made from shrimps cooked in pickling spices and curry leaves. Sorpotel (£4 or £7.50) is made from lamb's liver, kidney and pork in a sauce rich with roast spices, lime and coriander. The Ma Goa chorizo (£4.50) is rich, too, with palm vinegar, cinnamon and green chillies. Main courses are amazing. The spices are properly cooked out by slow cooking, which makes lifting the lids of the heavy clay serving pots a

voyage of discovery. Porco vindaloo (£9), sharp with palm vinegar, is enriched with lumps of pork complete with rind. Ma's fish caldin (£9.75) is kind of fish stew with large chunks of fish in a coconut-based sauce. Vegetarians are equally well served. Bund gobi (£3.50 or £6.50) is stir-fried, shredded cabbage with carrots, ginger and cumin, while beringella (£3.50 or £6.50) is an aubergine dish made with pickling spices. The rice here is excellent.

* There are genuine family recipes – "Bella's lamb" (£8), on the menu as lamb kodi (made with cloves, garlic and chilli).

Phoenix Bar & Grill

Italian £16–£50

162–164 Lower Richmond Rd, SW15 & ☎020 8780 3131
Station BR Putney **Open** Mon–Thurs 12.30–2.30pm & 7–11pm, Fri & Sat 12.30–2.30pm & 7–11.30pm, Sun 12.30–3pm & 7–10pm **Accepts** All major credit cards

This restaurant is a member of London's leading family of neighbourhood restaurants, and is related to Sonny's (see p.33). Anyone fancying their chances in what is a cut-throat marketplace would do well to study these establishments. They are all just trendy enough, the service is just slick enough and the cooking is marginally better than you would expect – with competitive pricing. Grub-wise, the Phoenix has a secret weapon: Franco Taruschio (of Walnut Tree fame) didn't much enjoy retirement and he consults at Phoenix to keep himself busy. There's a large, white-painted room inside and a large, white-painted courtyard out front where you can eat alfresco.

The menu here includes some of the famous dishes that made the Walnut Tree a place of foodie pilgrimage. Starters may include a salad of chicory,

pears, walnuts and gorgonzola (£5.75); home-cured bresaola with rocket and shaved Parmesan (£7.50); grilled scallops with organic leaves, tomato and herb oil (£8.50); or pumpkin ravioli with sage cream and Parmesan (£5). Mains range from gnocchi with roast butternut squash and girolles (£11.50); through roast rump of lamb with grilled sweet potato and glazed shallots (£14.50); to spiedino of monkfish and scallops on Piedmontese peppers (£15). Among the puds may be chocolate cake with toasted almond ice cream (£5.25); spumone Amaretto (£5.25); and apple fritters (£5.25). The set lunch and "early bird" dinner (order by 7.45pm and go home by 8.45pm) are grand value at £13.50 for two courses and £16.50 for three.

* Seek out Taruschio's signature dish: vincisgrassi maceratesi – an epic eighteenth-century truffled lasagne (£8.95 or £14.50).

Further choices

Gourmet Burger Kitchen
Burgers

333 Putney Bridge Rd, SW15
☎020 8789 1199

Part of the burger chain. See p.100.

Putney Bridge
French

2 Lower Richmond Rd, SW15
☎020 8780 1811

Architecturally stunning, high-ticket restaurant. Sophisticated French food awarded a Michelin star.

La Mancha
Spanish

32 Putney High St, SW15
☎020 8780 1022

Simple Spanish restaurant serving a good range of tapas. Busy and friendly place.

Queensway & Westbourne Grove

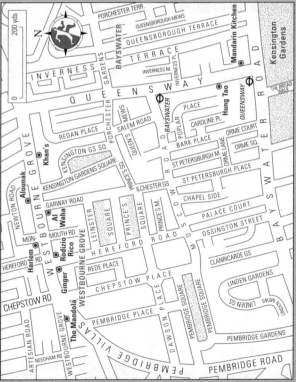

© Crown copyright

Alounak

Iranian £8–£22

44 Westbourne Grove, W2 ☎ 020 7229 0416
Station Bayswater/Queensway **Open** Daily noon–midnight
Accepts All major credit cards

Westbourne Grove has always had a raffish cosmopolitan air to it, which makes it the perfect home for Alounak. Don't be put off by the seedy look – this place turns out really good, really cheap Iranian food. The welcoming smell of clay-oven-baked flat bread hits you the moment you walk through the front door, creating a sense of the Middle East that's enhanced further by the gentle gurgling of a fountain, and the strains of Arabic music.

The sizable contingent of Middle Eastern locals dining here testifies to the authenticity of the food on offer. As an opening move, you can do no better than order the mixed starter (£8.40), a fine sampler of all the usual dips and hors d'oeuvres, served with splendid, freshly baked flat bread. And then follow the regulars with some grilled meat, which is

expertly cooked. Joojeh kebab (£6.90) is melt-in-the-mouth baby chicken, packed with flavour. As you would expect from a Middle Eastern restaurant, lamb dishes feature heavily, and they are simply grilled without fuss or frills. A good way to try two in one is to order the chelo kebab koobideh (£11.10), marinated lamb fillet coupled with minced lamb kebab, which is deliciously rich and oniony. For those with an inquisitive bent there is the innocuous-sounding "kabab tray" (£30 for two), which brings a vast platter best summed up as grilled everything. It's worth looking out for the daily specials, too – especially good on a Tuesday, when they offer zereshk polo (£6.20), a stunning chicken dish served on saffron-steamed rice with sweet-and-sour forest berries.

✳ Round things off with a pot of Iranian black tea (£3).

Ginger

Indian £15–£35

115 Westbourne Grove, W2 ☎ 020 7908 1990
Station Bayswater/Notting Hill Gate **Open** Mon–Fri 5–11pm, Sat noon–midnight,
Sun noon–11pm **Accepts** All major credit cards ⓦ www.gingerrestaurant.co.uk

Given that nearly every curry house on nearly every high street in the land is owned and manned by Bangladeshi businessmen, you might think that Ginger, which serves traditional Bangladeshi food, would be pretty run-of-the-mill. Until you eat there, that is.

This is a restaurant that offers genuine Bangladeshi home cooking. Not the sweet and tomatoey dishes worked up to suit the British palate, but the real deal. Expect lots of fish dishes, and delicious light stews (known as jhols). Plus attentive service, a thoughtful wine list, and some slick cocktails. But, most important of all, the men in the kitchen really know their stuff.

There are some stunning dishes. Start with the shingara (£2.95) – imagine a solid vegetable samosa that has been made with shortcrust pastry, like a deep-fried pasty. The katti kebab (£3.95) is also good (roast lamb in a kind of wrap). The difficult choices continue among the main courses. Surma macher biryani (£8.95) is epic – a fish biryani! Bangladeshis are besotted with fish – try the macher kobiraji (£7.95), which is an aromatic fish curry from West Bengal. Carry on to the raj ash kalia (£10.95), which is a Bengali stir-fry of duck; or the moni puri prawns (£12.95), a dish named after one of the tribespeople of Bangladesh. There are a good many prawn dishes on the menu – try the ajwani chingr jhol (£9.95), which presents king prawns in a thin sauce that is both hot and sour. Lau dal (£3.95) is a revelation: moong lentils cooked with white pumpkin and garlic. The parathas (£2) are very good – flaky and suitably self-indulgent.

Mishti doi (£3.50) is a lurid, set yoghurt. Toothkind it is not.

Harlem

Soul Food £12–£40

78 Westbourne Grove, W2 ☎ 020 7985 0900
Station Queensway **Open** Mon–Sat 10.30am–2am, Sun 10.30am–midnight
Accepts All major credit cards ⊛ www.harlemsoulfood.com

For many years the site at number 78 was occupied by Angelo's, a splendidly seedy Greek establishment that had the great advantage of being a "members only club" and so side-stepped the licensing laws. This made it a place of pilgrimage for many, including a high proportion of lively off-duty policemen. The latest incumbent (which opened during 2003) is Harlem, a bar and restaurant that sets out to bring Soul Food to the Grove. It's a buzzing place, packed with a young crowd and featuring a drinks and cocktails list as long as a first novel. The main bar area is downstairs, while on the ground floor there's another bar and a rather cramped dining area. The food plays a supporting role to the real business of this place, which is partying.

The menu reads well. Among the starters you'll find shrimp hushpuppies (£7.50); gumbo (£5); and pomegranate baby back-ribs (£6), which are cut into tiny pieces and artfully stacked. BBQ wings (£5.50) are on the mild side – more roast chicken than deep South. Fried green tomatoes (£4.50) are good. From the main course options a grilled rib-eye steak, first rubbed with chipotle peppers (£14.50), is a well chosen, accurately cooked piece of meat; and the buttermilk-fried chicken is O.K., although it won't give the Colonel any sleepless nights. Puds (all £5) are an authentically sweet selection – N.Y. baked white chocolate and blueberry cheesecake; chocolate coconut brownies; sweet-potato pie. Harlem is no "destination restaurant" but it's a lively place packed with people drinking and having a good time, much as Angelo's used to be.

✳ If the cocktails don't do it for you the Sam Adams beer (£3) is very good indeed.

Hung Tao

Chinese £8–£20

51 Queensway, W2 ☎ 020 7727 5753

Station Bayswater/Queensway **Open** Daily 11am–11pm **Accepts** Cash or cheque only

It is easy to find the Hung Tao: just look out for the much larger New Kam Tong restaurant, and two doors away you'll see this small and spartan establishment. They're actually part of the same group, as is another restaurant over the road. The reason to choose the Hung Tao above its neighbours is if you fancy a one-plate (or one-bowl) meal.

One of the first items on the menu is the "hot and sour" soup (£2). Uncannily enough, this is hot – with fresh red chillies in profusion – sour, and delicious. There are also a dozen different noodle soups, priced between £4.20 and £5. Then there are twenty dishes that go from duck rice (£4.20) to fried fish with ginger (£7.50). Plus about thirty noodle, fried noodle, and ho fun dishes, priced from £3 to £6. The fried ho fun with beef (£4.20) is a superb rich dish – well-flavoured brisket cooked until melting, on top of a mountain of ho fun. And the barbecued meats displayed in the window are very tasty, too: rich, red-painted char sui; soya duckling; and crispy pork or duck. Towards the front of the menu you'll find a succession of congee dishes. Congee is one of those foods people label "interesting" without meaning it. It is a thick, whitish, runny porridge made with rice, stunningly bland and under-seasoned, but tasting faintly of ginger. Plunge in at the deep end, and try preserved egg with sliced pork congee (£4.50). As well as containing pork, there's the "thousand-year" egg itself, the white of which is a translucent chestnut brown and the yolk a fetching green. Inscrutably, it tastes rather like a cheesy hard-boiled egg.

✳ "Thousand year" eggs are only a hundred days old.

Khan's

Indian £8–£25

13–15 Westbourne Grove ☎ 020 7727 5420

Station Bayswater/Queensway **Open** Mon–Thurs noon–2.45pm & 6–11.45pm, Fri–Sun noon–11.45pm **Accepts** All major credit cards ✆ www.khansrestaurant.com

If you're after a solid, inexpensive and familiar Indian meal, Khan's is the business. This restaurant, in busy Westbourne Grove, is a long-standing favourite with students and budget-wary locals who know that the curries here may be the staples of a thousand menus across Britain, but that they're fresh, well cooked and generously portioned. Just don't expect a restful evening. Tables are turned in a trice, service is perfunctory (this isn't a place to dally over the menu), and it's really noisy. Try to get a table in the vast, echoey ground floor, where blue murals stretch up to the high ceilings – it feels a bit like dining in an enormous swimming pool.

There are some tasty breads on offer. Try the nan-e-mughziat (£1.90), a coconut-flavoured affair with nuts and sultanas, or the paneer kulcha (£1.70), bulging with cottage cheese and mashed potatoes. You might also kick off with half a tandoori chicken (£3.25), which is moist and well cooked, or a creditable chicken tikka (£4.45). For main dishes, all those curry house favourites are listed here – meat madras or vindalu (£3.95), prawn biryani (£5.95), chicken chilli masala (£3.95), king prawn curry (£7.50) – and they all taste unusually fresh. Especially good is the butter chicken (£5.45), while for lovers of tikka masala dishes, the chicken tikka masala (£4.85) will appeal. There's a typical array of vegetable dishes too: bhindi (£3.15), sag aloo (£3.05) and vegetable curry (£3.05). Desserts include kulfi (£3.60) and various ice creams from Haagen Daz (£3.05).

✳ There's a heart symbol on the menu beside "low fat" dishes.

Mandarin Kitchen

Chinese/Fish £17–£x45

14–16 Queensway, W2 ☎ 020 7227 9012

Station Queensway **Open** Daily noon–11.30pm **Accepts** All major credit cards

London has its fair share of French fish restaurants, and there are famous English fish restaurants, so why does it seem odd to come across a Chinese fish restaurant? This is a large restaurant, busy with waiters deftly wheeling four-foot-diameter tabletops around like giant hoops as they set up communal tables for large parties of Chinese who all seem to be eating … lobster.

Whatever you fancy for the main course, start with as many of the steamed scallops on the shell with garlic soya sauce (£2 each or £4.90 for King scallops) as you can afford. They're magnificent. Then decide between lobster, crab or fish. If you go for the lobster, try ordering it baked with green pepper and onion in black-bean sauce (it is priced somewhere over the £15 per pound mark depending on the season), and be sure that you order the optional extra soft noodle (£1.20) to make a meal of it. The crab is tempting, too. Live crabs are shipped up here from the south coast, and a handsome portion of shells, lots of legs and four claws baked with ginger and spring onion is a pretty reasonable £14. Fish dishes require more thought – and an eye to the seasonally changing per-pound prices, which do reflect the gluts and shortages of the fish market. The menu lists "the fish we normally serve" as sea bass, Dover sole, live eels, live carp, monkfish, Chinese pomfret and yellow croaker. Sea bass comes steamed whole. The steamed eel with black-bean sauce is notably rich. The monkfish is meaty and delicious. The squid in chilli and black-bean sauce is good.

* Anyone missing the point could do worse than the veal chop Mandarin style.

The Mandola

Sudanese £12–£25

139–141 Westbourne Grove, W11 ☎ 020 7229 4734

Station Notting Hill Gate **Open** Mon 6–11pm, Tues–Sun noon–11pm
Accepts All major credit cards ✆ www.mandolacafe.co.uk

The food at The Mandola is described as "urban Sudanese", which means forgoing some of the more traditional Sudanese delicacies – strips of raw liver marinated in lime juice, chilli and peanut butter? This would be a small, seriously informal, neighbourhood restaurant but for the fact they have grown and grown, even taking over the shop next door. Thankfully the staff are so laid-back as to make worriers self-destruct on the spot. The restaurant is unlicensed, so everything from fine wine to exotic beer is available (corkage £2) – if you choose to bring it with you.

To start there is a combo of dips and salads, rather prosaically listed as "mixed salad bar" for two (£10.50). There are a few Middle Eastern favourites here, given a twist, and all of them are strongly and interestingly flavoured. Salata tomatim bel gibna (£3.50) is made from tomatoes, Feta and parsley; salata tahina (£3.25) is a good tangy tahini; salata aswad (£4.20) is a less oily version of the Turkish aubergine dish iman bayeldi; salata daqua (£3.50) is white cabbage in peanut sauce; and tamiya (£4.75) is Sudanese falafel. All are accompanied by hot pitta bread. As for main courses, samak magli (£10.50) shows just how good simple things can be – fillets of tilapia are served crisp and spicy on the outside, fresh on the inside, with a squeeze of lime juice.

Lovers of the exotic can finish with the Sudanese spiced coffee, scented with cardamom, cinnamon, cloves and ginger – you get your own flask and coffee set, enough for nine tiny cupfuls, for £4.

✳ Crushed green chilli with lime (£1.75) – like eating molten lead.

Rodizio Rico

Brazilian £22–£40

111 Westbourne Grove, W11 ☎ 020 7792 4035

Station Notting Hill Gate **Open** Mon–Fri 6.30pm–midnight, Sat 12.30–4.30pm & 6.30pm–midnight, Sun 1–11pm **Accepts** All major credit cards except Diners

If you're a lover of smoky grilled meat, Rodizio Rico will come as a godsend. In southern Brazil this restaurant would be seen as pretty run-of-the-mill, but in W11 churrascarias are the exception rather than the rule. Rodizio can be a puzzling experience for first-timers. There's no menu and no prices – but no problem. Rodizio means "rotating", and refers to the carvers who wander about the room with huge skewers of freshly grilled meat from which they lop off chunks on demand. You start by ordering and then help yourself from the salad bar and hot buffet. As the carvers circulate they cut you chunks,

slivers and slices from whichever skewer they are holding. You eat as much as you like of whatever you like, and then pay the absurdly reasonable price of £18 a head.

When you're up helping yourself to the basics, look out for the tiny rolls, no bigger than a button mushroom, called pão de queijo – a rich cheese bread from the south of Brazil. Return to your seat and await the carvers – they come in random order, but they keep on coming. There's lamb, and ham, and pork, and spareribs, and chicken, and silverside beef (called lagarto after a similarly shaped iguana). Then for offal aficionados there are grilled chicken hearts. But the star of the show is picanha – the heart of the rump, skewered and grilled in huge chunks. Taste it and the arguments over the relative merits of rump and fillet are over forever. Brazilians seem to revere the crispy bits, but if you want your meat rare you only have to ask.

✳ South Americans adore impossibly sweet soft drink Antarctica Guarana (£2.20)

Al Waha

Lebanese £16–£50

75 Westbourne Grove, W2 ☎020 7229 0806

Station Bayswater/Queensway **Open** Daily noon–midnight
Accepts Mastercard & Visa ⦿ www.waha-uk.com

Anissa Helou, who has written the definitive book on Lebanese cuisine, nominates Al Waha as London's best Lebanese restaurant. And after cantering through a few courses here you will probably agree with her. Lebanese restaurants are all meze-obsessed, and Al Waha is no exception. What is different, however, is the way in which the chef at Al Waha is obsessive about the main course dishes as well

When you sit down, a dish of fresh, crisp crudités will be brought to the table. It includes everything from some quartered Cos lettuce to a whole green pepper – get the healthy eating part over early. Choosing is then the problem, as there are 21 cold starters and 23 hot ones. Go for balance and include one dish that you have never had before. Hummus (£3.50) is good here; tabbouleh (£4.50) is heavy on the parsley; and the foul moukala (£4.50) is good, despite its name – broad beans with garlic, coriander and

olive oil. From the hot section, try manakeish bizaatar (£4), which is a mini-bread topped with thyme, like a sophisticated pizza. Or there's batata harra (£4.50), potatoes with garlic and peppers. The makanek ghanam (£5) are tiny Lebanese lamb sausages, like very refined cocktail sausages. For main courses, grills predominate, and they are all spanking-fresh and accurately cooked. Good choices include shish taouk (£9.50), made with chicken, and samakeh harrah (£18), a whole sea bass. Star turn is kafta khashkhash (£10) – a superb cylinder of minced lamb with parsley, garlic and tomato. Drink the good Lebanese beer or the very good Lebanese wines.

✱ The "days of the week speciality" (£9.50) are authentic and very good.

Further choices

Four Seasons
Chinese

84 Queensway, W2
☎020 7229 4320

Trad, and very busy, Chinese restaurant thought by some to do the finest roast duck in London.

Tiroler Hut
Austrian

27 Westbourne Grove, W2
☎020 7727 3981

Tirolean cellar, wildly eccentric to the point of becoming chic. Liver dumplings and a cow bell act. Leather trousers and funny hats.

Richmond & Twickenham

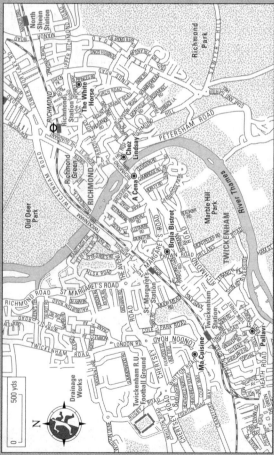

© Crown copyright

A Cena

Italian £20–£50

418 Richmond Rd, Twickenham, Middx ☎020 8288 0108

Station Ricmond/BR St Margaret's **Open** Tues–Sat noon–2.30pm & 7–10.30pm, Sun noon–2.30pm **Accepts** All major credit card except Diners

If you stumble over Richmond Bridge towards Twickenham, A Cena is the first restaurant on the left. This place is more Knightsbridge than Richmond, but seems to have survived those always-difficult first couple of years in some style. There is a bar area to the front that aims to tempt streetwise locals with modish cocktails; all is trendy, all is modern. The menu changes to suit the seasons and the markets, and the food is good – simple in the best kind of way, with clever combinations of flavour and texture. These are straightforward Italian dishes and all the better for that. The only caveat is that portions can be on the small side, especially when viewed in conjunction with their price tags.

Dishes are admirably seasonal – start with the wild-fennel soup (£5.50), or veal sweetbreads with artichokes and Marsala (£8.50). Simple starters like mozzarella di bufala with squashed tomato bruschetta (£7), or Dorset crab salad with almond aioli (£8.50) always appeal. The pasta of the day and the risotto are well made; dishes such as leek risotto with prosciutto (£6.50 or £11.50) vie with fusilli with tomato, basil and Parmesan (£5.50 or £8.50). Main courses read and eat well: baked sea bass with lemon, capers, anchovy and new potatoes (£16.50); veal chop with roast cherry tomatoes and wild greens (£17); polenta fritters with tomato, spinach and Parmigiano (£12.75). The puds are good. The zuppa Inglese (£5) – Italian for trifle, and the baked ricotta cheesecake (£5) are seriously rich, and so they should be.

✳ Try a "Finlay" (£6) – limoncello and prosecco.

Brula Bistrot

French £11–£25

43 Crown Rd, St Margaret's, Twickenham, Middx ☎020 8892 0602

Station BR St Margaret's **Open** Daily 12.30–2.30pm & 7–10.30pm **Accepts** Mastercard & Visa ⓦwww.brulabistrot.com

In 1999, two friends chose St Margaret's as a locale and, as they were called Bruce Duckett and Lawrence Hartley, opened a restaurant called Brula. Within eighteen months the business had become so successful that they had to move across Crown Road into larger premises. Now the Brula Bistrot (the name was enlarged, in keeping with the new premises) is no longer a cramped affair. There are large windows with a profusion of rather elegant stained glass. Thankfully, the food and philosophy have endured – well-cooked French bistro food, limited choice, low, low prices.

Lunch at Brula Bistrot will cost you £10 for one or two courses and £12 for three. Extra veg (should you want any) costs a further £3; an espresso to finish is £1.50. The menu changes on a weekly basis, so you might choose between dishes such as marinated squid salad or braised leeks with hard-boiled egg. Then on to fish of the day with haddock purée or jambonneau with parsley sauce. Finally, your pick of the puds. All very French. Running alongside is "the Bistrot Offers" list (informal à la carte): nine snails with garlic butter (£6.50); celeriac remoulade poached egg, and ham (£6.50); roast lamb chump with pissaladière (£12.50); king scallops with artichoke purée and pancetta (£13.75). The Frenchness even extends to the list of suggested apéritifs at the top of the evening menu: kir (£3.50), or kir royale (£7.50). And, should you spurn these blandishments, the wine list is short and agreeably priced with a good showing under £20.

✳ Have the onglet steak and chips at lunch for a £5 supplement.

Chez Lindsay Very French/Pancakes £7–£28

11 Hill Rise, Richmond, Surrey ☎ 020 8948 7473
Station Richmond **Open** Mon–Sat 11am–11pm, Sun noon–10pm
Accepts Mastercard & Visa

At first glance, Chez Lindsay looks rather like Chicago in the 1920s – all around you people are drinking alcohol out of large earthenware teacups. The cups are in fact traditional Breton drinking vessels known as bolées, the drink is cider, and Chez Lindsay lists a trio of them, ranging from Breton brut traditionnel to Norman cidre bouché. Most people are attracted to this small, bright restaurant by the galettes and crêpes, though the menu also includes a regularly changing list of hearty Breton dishes – especially fish. It's a place for Francophiles – both the kitchen and the front of house seem to be staffed entirely by Gauls, which in this instance means good service and tasty food.

Start with the moules à la St Malo (£6.50), which are cooked with shallots, cream and thyme. Then decide between the galettes or more formal main courses. The galettes are huge buckwheat pancakes, large and lacy, thin but satisfying. They come with an array of fillings: egg and ham (£5.05); scallops and leeks (£8.75); Roquefort cheese, celery and walnuts (£6.95); and "Chez Lindsay" (£6.95) – cheese, ham and spinach. The other half of the menu features a good steak frites (£13.75) and lots of fish and shellfish. The "gratin de Camembert, vivanneau et crevettes" (£11.75) is an interesting dish – a gratin containing red snapper, prawns and Camembert. Or there's the bar grillé (£15.75) – a whole grilled sea bass with salad and new potatoes. Real pud enthusiasts will save themselves for the chocolate and banana crêpe (£4.50).

✳ At lunch, the menu de midi (a salad and a galette) – just £6.50.

Ma Cuisine

Very French £15–£30

6 Whitton Rd, Twickenham, Middx ♿ ☎020 8607 9849

Station BR Twickenham **Open** Daily noon–2.30pm & 6.30–11pm
Accepts All major credit cards except Diners ❂www.mcclementsrestaurant.com

Ma Cuisine is sibling to its near neighbour McClement's and while McC's is upscale and wins Michelin stars, Ma Cuisine is cheerful and wins the tyre people's medal for special value. This is an old-fashioned, bistroey sort of place, even down to the gingham-look table covers and French staff whose first priority is to ensure that you are kept supplied with baguette and butter. The menu is made up of unrepentantly old-school French favourites. So saying, the cooking is adequate and the atmosphere buzzes along.

You don't often see a starter that includes a hunk of foie gras and still costs only £5, but you'll find one here – a fiver marks the upper boundary of the starter prices. "Yorkshire pudding, topped with sautéed foie gras and onion gravy". The foie gras is fine but the rather leathery pudding wouldn't do in Yorkshire! There may also be French onion soup (£3.95); or grilled sardines with garlic butter (£4); or a rather good rillette of skate with olive oil dressing (£4); or a risotto of wild mushrooms (£4). Mains continue the theme – blanquette of rabbit with tarragon sauce (£9); coq au vin (£8.75), slow-cooked chunks of what was once an impressively large bird; cassoulet (£8.75) suffers from a few shortcuts but is suitably filling; sea bream with red wine glaze (£9.50). Puds (all at £3.95) include a tolerable tart Tatin, and a chocolate pot with coffee cream. Amazingly enough the wine list also keeps faith with the mood and a Cab. Sav. from the Languedoc (£13) is workmanlike enough. A deal like this gladdens the hardest heart.

✳ Crepes Suzette (£3.95) – nostalgia on a plate.

Pallavi

Indian £10–£23

1st Floor, 3 Cross Deep Court, Heath Rd, Twickenham, Middx ☎020 8892 2345
Station BR Twickenham **Open** Mon–Fri noon–3pm & 6–11pm, Sat & Sun noon–3pm & 6–midnight **Accepts** All major credit cards ❂www.mcdosa.com

This is a small outpost of an extensive Indian restaurant empire. Pallavi is one of the simplest and the cheapest, and started its days as a large takeaway counter with just a few seats, then moved over the road from the original site to smarter premises. The cooking has traveled well, and still deserves the ultimate compliment – it is genuinely home-style, with unpretentious dishes and unpretentious prices. True to its South Indian roots, there is an impressive list of vegetarian specialities, but the menu features just enough meat and fish dishes to woo any kind of diner.

Start with that South Indian veggie favourite, the Malabar masala dosa (£3.50). This huge, crisp pancake is made with a mixture of ground rice and lentil flour, and is a perfect match for the savoury potato mixture and chutney. Or try the delightfully named iddly (£3.50), a steamed rice cake made with black gram, which is eaten as a breakfast dish in India. The main dishes are simple and tasty, and are served without fuss. For unrepentant carnivores, chicken Malabar (£3.95), or keema methi (£3.95) both hit the spot. But there are also some interesting fish dishes, including the fish moilee (£6.95). Veggies are good too: try parippu curry (£2.20), split lentils with cumin, turmeric, garlic, chillies and onions; or cabbage thoran (£2.50) – sliced cabbage with carrots, green chillies and curry leaves. The pilau rice, lemon rice and coconut rice (all £2.20) are tasty, and parathas are even better – try a green chilli or a sweet coconut paratha (both £2.50).

✳ From the menu, "The soul of Kerala in the heart of Twickenham".

The White Horse

Modern British/Gastropub £12–£35

Worple Way, Richmond, Surrey ☎ 020 8940 2418

Station Richmond **Open** Mon–Sat noon–3pm & 6.30–10pm, Sun noon–4pm & 6.30–9.30pm **Accepts** All major credit card except Diners

All over town, pubs have been torn away from the traditional breweries and transformed into ever trendier gastropubs, but in this instance Fuller's brewery is somewhat ahead of the game. Several years ago it gave a free hand to the management at one of its pubs in Richmond and encouraged them to modernize their approach to the food they offered. A number of chefs have come and gone, but the White Horse is still something of a jewel in Fuller's crown, particularly if you want to eat out. The pub is still a pub – dark decor but with good, large tables that are well spread out. The food and pricing are also spot-on, as is confirmed by a steady trade.

The menu is a short one, and changes twice a day to accommodate whatever is best from the market. There might be breaded calamari with sweet chilli mayonnaise (£5); sautéed field mushrooms with lardons and chorizo (£5.50); home-made crab cakes with Worcestershire dip (£5.50); or chicken liver and wild mushroom pate (£5.50). Main courses are also simple, such as baked fillet of salmon with anchovy mashed potato (£12.50); rib-eye with carrots and broccoli (£13); duck breast with parsnip and sweet potato purée, and apricot jus (£13.50); or penne pasta with roast aubergine, tomato and basil sauce (£8). The wide-ranging wine list tops out while still reasonably priced. What's more, there is the intelligent option of a 250ml glassful of any one of ten different wines (£4.20 – £5.20). Puds are sound: mocha cheesecake with cream (£4.50), or spicy apple and cinnamon crumble (£4.50).

✳ Fuller's "Chiswick" bitter is well worth trying – hoppy and crisp.

Shepherd's Bush & Olympia

SHEPHERD'S BUSH

UXBRIDGE ROAD

STERNE

HOLLAND PARK AVENUE

Abu Zaad

SHEPHERD'S BUSH

BUSH GREEN

Blah Blah Blah

GOLDHAWK ROAD

Patio Bush Bar & Grill

GOLDHAWK ROAD

HOLLAND ROAD

SHEPHERD'S BUSH

The Havelock Tavern

Kensington Olympia Station

The Popeseye

KENSINGTON (OLYMPIA)

Cotto

Olympia

N

HAMMERSMITH ROAD

HAMMERSMITH

0   250 yds

© Crown copyright

Abu Zaad

Syrian £15–£35

29 Uxbridge Rd, W12 ☎020 8749 5107

Station Shepherd's Bush **Open** Daily 11am–11pm
Accepts All major credit cards except AmEx

Abu Zaad bears the trappings of its recent success lightly. The bar has been moved to the back room, and there are now a few more tables. It still serves as a pit stop for coffee and pastries, the cooking arrangements are still dominated by a charcoal grill and a full-sized bread oven. Abu Zaad is a busy place and a friendly one – the food is good and awesomely cheap. The décor teams rich greens with decorative metal panels – very Damascene.

This may be the cheapest place in London to experiment with meze, as (whether hot or cold) most cost about £2. Here £2 will buy you a large portion of makanic (meaty, chipolata-sized sausages); baba ganouj (delicious aubergine mush); or foul medames (boiled fava beans with chickpeas, tomato and lemon juice); or hummus. A stunning haystack of tabbouleh is more expensive at £2.50, but comes with spankingly fresh chopped parsley and mint. Ordering a dish called falafi (£1.50) brings four crisp and nutty falafel. You must try the fattoush (£2), a fresh, well-dressed salad with croutons of deep-fried flatbread. In fact, all meze you order will arrive with a basket of delicious fresh flatbread. The food is described on the menu as "Damascene Cuisine" but most of these dishes are claimed by every Middle Eastern chef. Drink a glass of carrot and apple juice (£1.50) and feel healthy. The menu goes on to list dozens of main courses, from rich casseroles to charcoal grills, and they are all priced at about £4.90. There's a good case for not bothering with a main course here; simply order seven or eight meze between two.

❋ Damascus is the oldest continually inhabited city in the world.

Blah Blah Blah

Vegetarian £16–£25

78 Goldhawk Rd, W10 ☎020 8746 1337

Station Goldhawk Road **Open** Mon–Sat 12.30–2.30pm & 7–11pm
Accepts Cash or cheque only

Blah is an old-time veggie haven, and has décor to match. The floors, tables and chairs are wooden, there are blinds rather than curtains, and the only decorations of note are driftwood and old iron lamps. Add wallpaper music and the echoing noise levels become formidable. Legend has it that an old chap called Paul McCartney was overheard here asking for the music to be turned down. The menu casts its net widely and you can expect dishes with all manner of influences, but all of them reasonably priced and generously portioned.

Generally speaking starters are £4.95 (there are a couple that are cheaper), while mains are £9.95, and puds £4.95. Among the starters might be cream of asparagus soup; plum tomato and mozzarella torte; a Greek salad; and a spicy Indian potato cake filled with curried cauliflower, carrots and peas. Dodging over to the Windies, there may be plantain fritters made with raisins, ginger and sweet potato and served with a tomato, chilli and pineapple sauce. Main courses are similarly eclectic. Stir-fried noodles come with hot Thai sauce; baked tostada is put together with sweet potato gratin, refried beans and a Jalapeno cream sauce; a "Mediterranean" roulade teams baked and rolled potato layers with ricotta and roast peppers, and courgettes served with a creamy spinach sauce and deep-fried leeks; or there could be a Middle Eastern pie filled with new potato, chilli and tomatoes. Puds are rewarding: glazed lemon tart; rhubarb and apple charlotte; roast plum crumble; and the "wicked" chocolate pot.

Unlicensed but BYO is very reasonable: corkage £1.25 per person.

Bush Bar & Grill   Modern British £15–£50

45a Goldhawk Rd, W12 ☎ 020 8746 2111

Station Goldhawk Road **Open** Mon–Sat noon–3pm & 5.30–11.30pm, Sun noon–4pm & 6.30–10.30pm **Accepts** Mastercard & Visa ⓦ www.bushbar.co.uk

The Bush Bar & Grill captures the informal, pacey bustle of a classic brasserie rather well. Service is brisk and with attitude, and the food comes flying out over the pass from an open kitchen that runs the length of the room. The menu changes on a monthly basis and sensibly they have adopted a policy of sourcing as much British produce as possible, and of favouring organic producers. The large dining area is busy and the whole place has an agreeable buzz, as the cocktail bar is open from noon to midnight.

Starters may include roast red pepper and tomato soup (£4.25); or fresh white Cornish crab with spiced avocado (£7.25). Salads range from warm ham hock salad with soft-boiled quails' eggs (£6.25 or £10.50) to Feta, truffle potatoes and French beans (£6.25 or £10.50). Mains range from broad bean and mint risotto

(£9.50) to smoked haddock fish cakes with tartare sauce (£9.50). From the grill there's whole Dover sole with lemon and watercress (£15.50), and Aberdeen Angus rib-eye steak and chips (£15.50) – all the beef here is from Donald Russell of Inverurie. Puddings are sound: chocolate whiskey mousse (£4.50); banana pancakes with rum-and- raisin ice cream (£4.50). The wine list at the Bush Bar & Grill is also extremely encouraging. In such a chic establishment, a reliable house wine (Armit's French Red or White) priced at £11.75 deserves a warm welcome. There's a good-value set menu that runs at lunch and pre-theatre (5.30pm to 7.30pm): £12.50 for two courses and £15 for three. That should tempt them away from the nearby BBC canteen.

 For each adult eating Sunday lunch a child eats free.

Cotto

Modern British £15–£50

44 Blythe Rd, W14 ☎ 020 7602 9333

Station Kensington (Olympia) **Open** Mon–Fri noon–2.30pm & 7–10.30pm, Sat 7–10.30pm, Sun noon–2.30pm **Accepts** All major credit cards ✆ www.cottorestaurant.co.uk

From the outside, Cotto, which stands on a corner site in a residential neighbourhood behind Olympia, is nothing special. Acres of plate-glass frontage reveal a sprinkling of tables around a large central bar area. The room has been redecorated and is now done out in tasteful modern shades: browns, taupe and aubergine. This is a genuine neighbourhood restaurant that is now becoming established and getting to grips with its mission, which is to provide good grub for discerning local residents.

The balance of the menu will strike a chord with foodies. Though the restaurant has an Italian name (cotto means "cooked"), its menu draws from both English and French traditions. It seems that the cooking is firmly rooted in the best of all approaches: treating ingredients with respect and striving to get the most out of each of them. The menu – which changes regularly to follow the seasons – is not long, but there's plenty of variety, and the deal is a simple one: two courses for £17 and three for £19.50. The five starters might include parsley soup with snail croquettes; a house terrine; or a duck-breast salad with pickled vegetables. Main courses usually include a proper vegetarian choice, such as a celeriac and Gorgonzola lasagna, as well as a fish option, like roast cod with braised squid in red wine. Meat dishes may include braised middle neck of lamb with pommes boulangère; or roast saddle of rabbit with Parma ham and cavolo nero. Puddings, such as poached pear and chocolate ice cream, or passion fruit parfait with coconut cream, will please any sugar addict.

 Cheeses are from la Fromagerie, and worth the £3 supplement.

SHEPHERD'S BUSH & OLYMPIA

The Havelock Tavern

Modern British/Gastropub £8–£30

57 Masbro Rd, W14 ☎020 7603 5374

Station Shepherd's Bush **Open** Mon–Sat 12.30–2.30pm & 7–10pm, Sun 12.30–3pm & 7–9.30pm **Accepts** Cash or cheque only ⓦwww.thehavelocktavern.co.uk

The Havelock is one of those pubs marooned within a sea of houses; in this instance it's the sea of houses just behind Olympia. It's a real pub, with a solid range of beers as well as an extensive wine list. The menu is chalked up daily on the blackboard that features the kind of fresh, interesting, wholesome stuff you wish that you could get around to cooking for yourself. The bar seats 75 and during the summer there's a terrific garden complete with vines and a pergola. Service involves stepping up to the bar and ordering what you want, so there's no service charge to bump up what are very reasonable prices indeed.

The menu is different every session, with more "one-hit" dishes served at lunch, when most customers are pressed for time. Starters might be sautéed tiger prawns, rocket, parsley and garlic butter (£7.50); split pea, bacon and mint soup (£4); chorizo, chickpea, snail and tomato stew with crostini (£5.50); or deep-fried buffalo Mozzarella fritters, with roast tomatoes, baby spinach, black olive dressing (£6). Main courses range from steamed fillet of smoked haddock, with creamed lentils (£10.50); to venison, wild mushroom and bacon stew (£11). Or there might be a classic such as chargrilled rib-eye steak, chips and watercress (£12). Puddings are equally reliable – chocolate nemesis, crème fraîche (£4), or the toasted banana bread, butterscotch sauce and vanilla ice cream (£4). A great deal of effort goes into selecting slightly unusual wines for the blackboard wine list. Many of them are offered at bargain prices.

✳ It is said that the Havelock is one of Simon Hopkinson's favourite eateries.

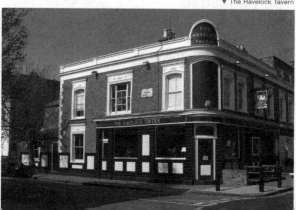

▼ The Havelock Tavern

Patio

Polish £13–£26

5 Goldhawk Rd, W12 ☎ 020 8743 5194

Station Goldhawk Road **Open** Mon–Fri noon–3pm & 6pm–midnight, Sat 6pm–midnight, Sun noon–11.30pm **Accepts** All major credit cards

The ebullient Eva Michalik (a former opera singer) and her husband Kaz have been running this Shepherd's Bush institution for more than a decade, and it's not hard to see why the show is still on the road. At Patio you get good, solid Polish food in a friendly, comfortable atmosphere, and for a relatively small amount of money. And this little restaurant is a people-pleaser – you can just as easily come here for an intimate tête-à-tête as for a raucous birthday dinner. There are two floors; downstairs feels a little cosier and more secluded.

The set menu (available at lunch and dinner) is Patio's trump card. For £13.90 you get a starter, main course, dessert, petits fours ... and a vodka. Starters may include plump and tasty blinis with smoked salmon; wild mushroom soup; Polish ham; and herrings with soured cream. Everything is fresh and carefully prepared. For mains, there's a good selection of meat, fish and chicken dishes – the scallops in dill sauce, when available, are outstanding. Or you might try a Polish speciality such as golabki (cabbage stuffed with rice and meat), which is also available as a vegetarian dish; or chicken Walewska (chicken breast in fresh red-pepper sauce); or sausages à la Zamoyski (grilled with sautéed mushrooms and onions). Be prepared, too, for high-octane puds, such as the Polish pancakes with cheese, vanilla and rum – the fumes alone are enough to send you reeling. Also good is the hot apple charlotka with cream. For those after more variety the à la carte offers further choice, and for not a great deal more money.

✳ There have been sightings of a roving gypsy quartet.

The Popeseye

Steak £18–£80

108 Blythe Rd, W14 ☎ 020 7610 4578

Station Hammersmith **Open** Mon–Sat 7–10.30pm **Accepts** Cash or cheque only

Just suppose you fancy a steak. A good steak, and perhaps a glass (or bottle) of red wine to go with it. You're interested enough to want the best, probably Aberdeen Angus, and you want it cooked simply. The Popeseye is for you. All the meat here is 100% grass-fed Aberdeen Angus and the restaurant is a member of the Aberdeen Angus Society. The dining room is small, and things tend to get chaotic. As to the food, there is no choice: just various kinds of steak and good chips, with home-made puddings to follow. Oh, and the menu starts with the wine list. You choose what you want to drink, and only when that's settled do you choose your steak – specifying, of course, the cut and the size (and they come very big here), and how you want it cooked.

Now – about these steaks. Popeseye comes in 6oz, 8oz, 12oz, 20oz and 30oz (at £10.45, £12.95, £17.45, £22.45 and £32.50), as does sirloin (£12.95, £15.95, £20.45, £25.95 and £38.50), and fillet (£14.45, £18.95, £23.45, £31.95 and £45.95). All prices include excellent

chips, and a side salad is an extra £3.45. Puddings are priced at £4.95 and come from the home-made school of patisserie – such delights as apple crumble, sticky toffee pudding and lemon tart. The wine list is an ever-changing reflection of what can be picked up at the sales and represents good value. There are fine clarets and Burgundies, plus the best of the Rhône, Australia, Argentina, Chile and Spain – and there are also two white wines on offer for people who have lost the plot.

✳ Popeseye is the Scottish name for rump steak.

Further choices

The Cumberland Arms
Gastropub/Modern British

29 North End Rd, W14
☎ 020 7371 6806

Agreeable gastropub, part of a small chain which includes The Atlas; see review on p.140.

Chez Marcelle
Lebanese

34 Blythe Rd, W14
☎ 020 7603 3241

Old fashioned, small, informal, Lebanese restaurant. Marcelle is a master of Lebanese home cooking.

Esarn Kheaw
Thai

314 Uxbridge Rd, W12
☎ 020 8743 8930

Thai restaurant with a good reputation; look out for authentic dishes from Northern Thailand.

The Rotisserie
Steak

6 Uxbridge Rd, W12
☎ 020 8743 3028

Long established, South African steak house. See review on p.214.

Soho

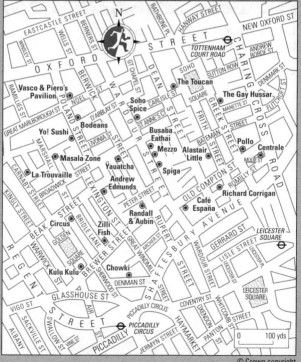

© Crown copyright

Alastair Little

Mediterranean £35–£65

49 Frith St, W1 ☎ 020 7734 5183

Station Leicester Square **Open** Mon–Fri noon–3pm & 6–11.30pm, Sat 6–11.30pm
Accepts All major credit cards

Alastair Little was the chap who led us out of a world where an Italian restaurant was judged by the size of its pepper mills. He championed simple, strong flavours, fresh produce, joyful meals, and although it is a very long while since he was a full-time presence in the kitchen, the flame still burns brightly. In 2003 he finally handed over the reins. The restaurant is still called Alastair Little which in some ways is appropriate because it still serves his kind of food.

Unlike the decor, which has stayed much the same, the menu changes twice a day. Pricing is simple: at lunch £29 buys you three courses; at dinner £38 gets you three courses. The wine list is a largely sub-£30-a-bottle affair, with a sprinkling of more ambitiously priced famous names. The menu runs the gamut but everything is seasonal. So starters may include spinach soup, dhal and rava dosa; sizzling prawns with chilli, garlic and parsley; a salad of seared tuna, artichokes, French beans and quail eggs; and, at something of a tangent, six native oysters with shallot vinegar and spicy sausages. The main courses follow on in similar vein: skate with black butter and capers; pork fillet, chorizo, bacon, white beans and cabbage sprouts; Gressingham duck breast, egg and bacon salad, chips and Béarnaise. To end your meal there are splendid puds, such as a café Liègeoise, or panna cotta with blood orange jelly – and the satisfying alternative of a plate of British cheeses with oatcakes.

✳ There's a serious Bellini on offer here (£7.50).

Andrew Edmunds

Modern British £20–£35

46 Lexington St, W1 ☎ 020 7437 5708

Station Oxford Circus **Open** Mon–Fri 12.30–3pm & 6–10.45pm, Sat 1–3pm & 6–10.45pm, Sun 1–3pm & 6–10.30pm **Accepts** All major credit cards except Diners

Andrew Edmunds' wine bar, as it is called by Soho locals, has been an institution in the area

for over fifteen years – a long time when you consider how speedily so many restaurants

SOHO

come and go. It all started when the lease on the wine bar next door to his print gallery became vacant and he decided that, as he wanted to go on eating there himself, he should take it on. The restaurant now has a loyal band of regulars who like the imaginative bistro-style dishes, strong flavours and bold combinations. It's cosy, dark and very crowded.

The menu changes weekly and combines solid favourites with bright new ideas. Start with parsnip and apple soup (£2.95); or dressed crab (£5.50); or black pudding, caramelized apples and horseradish crème fraîche (£4.50). Main courses may include stalwart and straightforward dishes such as best end of lamb, with haricot beans and thyme purée and roast aubergines (£13.50); confit duck leg with red cabbage and potato wedges (£9.75); roast monkfish with mash and purple sprouting broccoli (£12.50); or an impressive vegetarian option such as vegetable tagine with cous cous, toasted almonds and coriander (£8.25). This is very like stumbling on a neighbourhood restaurant in some affluent suburb, only you are in the very heart of Soho. Puddings include chocolate mousse cake (£4), the ubiquitous tiramisù (£3.75), and nutmeg ice cream (£3.75). Wines are a passion with Andrew Edmunds. The constantly changing, broker-bought list is long and special and, because of his low mark-up policy, there are some genuine bargains.

* Small dining room makes booking essential.

Bodeans

North American £12–£45

10 Poland St, W1 ☎ 020 7287 7575

Station Piccadilly Circus **Open** Mon–Fri noon–3pm & 6–11pm, Sat & Sun noon–11.30pm **Accepts** All major credit cards ⓦ www.bodeansbbq.com

Bodeans is the brainchild of one of the men who set up Belgo (see p.114) It's a fair old leap from Belgian mussels to American barbecue but Bodeans seems to have struck a chord and is a friendly busy place. Upstairs is a kind of diner/deli/sandwich shop. Downstairs is a restaurant. Only somewhere paying serious homage to Americana would have a strident tartan carpet, wall lights made to look like antelope horns and a red-painted ceiling. Even the service is American gushy and there is an authentic "commercial" ring to the place, something that you will either love or hate.

The starters are not very impressive – smoke-fired chicken wings (£3.95) come either hot or mild and are the best of the bunch, or there is clam chowder (£3.95). Cut to the chase and get amongst the real smoky barbecued stuff. Baby back-ribs (£9.95 for a whole slab, £6.50 for a half) are considered by ribologists to be too tender and a bit of a cop-out. The pork spareribs (£12.25 for a whole slab, eleven–twelve ribs; and £7.95 for a half, five–six ribs) are terrific. Mains come with average coleslaw and pretty good beans. Fries (£1.95) are good and crisp. The star dish is the beef back-ribs (£11.95 for a whole slab, five ribs; £7.50 for a half-slab) which are dry and chewy. Very good. There are other delicacies such as Boston Butt (£6.95), a pulled pork sandwich. But only the ribs will stick to your ribs. Puds tread the ice cream and pie route, while to drink there is a flotilla of different Bloody Marys (all £5.50), or beer.

✳ Sat and Sun, one child per adult eats free until 5pm.

Busaba Eathai

Thai £8–£25

106–110 Wardour St, W1 ☎ 020 7255 8686

Station Piccadilly Circus **Open** Mon–Thurs noon–11pm, Fri & Sat noon–11.30pm, Sun noon–10pm **Accepts** All major credit cards except Diners ⓦ www.busaba.com

SOHO

Busaba occupies a West End site that was once a bank – you remember the days when banks were conveniently positioned all over the place? Former customers stumbling into 106 Wardour St would be more than a little surprised by the dark, designery and implacably trendy Thai eatery that is now bedded in. This place serves decent Thai food at low prices, and with consummate lack of pretension. For all the cod philosophy, this is a jolly and energetic restaurant and you will probably have a very good time.

Food, grouped into categories, veers towards one-pot dishes, and vegetarians are particularly well served. If you want starters you need to peruse the side dishes. Choose from such things as po-pea jay (£2.90), which are vegetable spring rolls; or fishcakes (£4.20); or Thai calamari (£4.20), which are not unlike everyone else's calamari.

▲ Busaba Eathai: designery and implacably trendy

There are curries: Mussaman duck curry (£8.80); green chicken curry (£6.90); green vegetable curry (£6.50); and aromatic butternut pumpkin curry (£5.70). You'll find genuine Thai veg, such as pea aubergines, sweet basil and lime leaves, although dishes do tend to be on the sweet side. Or there's phad Thai (£6.10), and thom yam chicken (£6.40). Stir-fries include chargrilled duck in tamarind sauce with Chinese broccoli (£7.80); ginger beef (£6.60); and chargrilled cod with lemongrass and tamarind sauce (£7.80). The power juice phenomenon has reached Busaba. Nam polamai (£2.90) is organic, and combines carrot, apple and celery with dandelion and nettle extract.

✳ Mekhong Thai whiskey, with ice (£3.50).

Café España

Spanish £10–£20

63 Old Compton St, W1 ☎ 020 7494 1271

Station Piccadilly Circus/Leicester Square **Open** Mon–Sat noon–midnight, Sun noon–11pm **Accepts** Mastercard & Visa

Situated as it is, at the heart of Soho's pink strip at the Wardour Street end of Old Compton Street, and nestled among the hard-core shops and video stores, Café España is a remarkably balanced restaurant. From the outside it looks rather small and shabby – not very prepossessing at all, in fact, and much like the more tourist-focused trattorias. But once through the door, tripping over the dessert trolley, you'll be greeted by a friendly maître d' and led up the stairs to join a hubbub of hungry Soho folk with a nose for a bargain.

The menu does give a nod to the trattoria, with a short list of pastas, but it is the Spanish cooking that you should be here for. From the tapas, mejillones a la plancha (£4.40) delivers a hefty portion of mussels, a tortilla Espanola (£4.20) is the size of a saucer, and ordering the jamón serrano (£5.50) brings a decent portion at a price you'd be hard to match wholesale. Chipirones (£4.50), a plate of baby squid, and boquerones (£3.75), the classic white anchovies, are good. For something more substantial, there's plenty of choice, mostly in the form of simple grills. ordering chuletas de cordero a la brasa (£9.95) will bring lamb chops; higado de ternera (£8.95), calf's liver and bacon; and rodaballo a la plancha (£12.95) – grilled turbot. Or there are the traditional Valenciana and marinera paellas (£22, to feed two), though these are slightly less exciting. Service is swift, if a little harassed. To enjoy Café España to the maximum, go mob-handed and allow yourself the luxury of running amok with the tapas selections before pouncing on the paella.

✳ Be warned – the sangria is a dark and dangerous West End concoction.

Centrale

Italian £5–£15

16 Moor St, W1 ☎ 020 7437 5513

Station Leicester Square/Tottenham Court Rd **Open** Mon–Sat noon–9.30pm
Accepts Cash or cheque only

Even by the standards of the surrounding bottom-dollar belly-fillers, Centrale is exceedingly cheap, and by those self-same standards it's beginning to look exceedingly shabby. Cracked vinyl banquettes force you into cosy, chatty proximity with strangers across the narrow red Formica tables. But Centrale still seems effortlessly friendly and also strangely glamorous. Odd, really, when this is basically a place to line your stomach with cheap pasta before going on to a pub or club.

The menu is artless – orange juice (80p) as a starter – and portions are substantial. Appetizers include home-made minestrone (£2), salami (£3.75), and pastina in brodo (£2) – short pasta snippets in a clear, slightly oily soup. There's a fair spread of diner staples to follow, including pork chop (£4.75) and fried scampi (£5), each partnered by an inevitable sprinkling of chips, but the main event here is the pasta. The

✳ BYO – 50p a bottle or £1 for a big bottle!

Bolognese dishes – spaghetti, tagliatelle, rigatoni and ravioli (all £3.75) – are equally dependable, adequately spicy and chewily meaty, as is the lasagne al forno (£4.50). The "specials" include spaghetti vongole (£4.50), and rigatoni Alfredo (£4.25) – a pungent swirl of cream, mushrooms, cheese, tomato and lots and lots of garlic. Rather than a small salad (£1.75), a side order of spinach (£2.25) adds something green to the solid bulk of the pasta. The menu gives up a bit when it comes to dessert, sticking to just three old favourites: banana split (£1.75), apple pie (£1.50) and ice cream (£1.20).

SOHO

you are welcome to bring your own wine

The perfect croissant

There are plenty of good spots for coffee and croissants in Soho. Here are the top three:

▶ Best of all **Maison Bertaux**, 28 Greek St, W1 (020 7437 6007) – old-fashioned charm, stellar croissants and milky French coffee – no espressos here!

▶ Also good **Patisserie Valerie**, 44 Old Compton St, W1 (020 7437 3466) www.patisserie-valerie.co.uk

▶ And **Amato**, 14 Old Compton St, W1 (020 7734 5733) www.amato.co.uk

Chowki

SOHO

2–3 Denman St, W1 ☎ 020 7439 1330

Station Piccadilly Circus **Open** Mon–Sat noon–11.30pm & Sun noon–10.30pm
Accepts All major credit cards 🕸 www.chowki.com

Chowki is masterminded by chef Kuldeep (see also Mela, p.120), and it is a large, cheap restaurant serving authentic home-style food in stylish surroundings. The menu changes every month in order to feature three different regions of India. Thus April 2004 featured the North-West Frontier, Lucknow, and Goa, then by June it was Kashmir, Maharastra, Chettinad. During a whole year Chowki showcases 36 different regional styles of food! All the dishes are authentic and all come with accompaniments. Chowki has 120 seats spread across three dining areas, but you'll still probably have to wait for a table at peak times.

There are three or four starters and three or four mains from each region. When the menu showcased the cuisine of Rajasthan, Hyderabad and Mangalore, starters included epic Rajasthani quail (£4.25); dumplings stuffed with banana from Hyderabad (£2.25); and a dish of prawns marinated in tamarind (£4.25). These would be interesting dishes at three times the price. Mains follow the lead and come with an appropriate vegetable and the correct rice or bread. From Hyderabad comes a sour mutton stew (£8.95). From Mangalore there's a dish of chicken cooked with coconut (£8.50), or a mackerel poached in spice paste (£8.50). All the dishes have the unmistakable stamp of homely cooking – rich, simple, appetizing flavours. Service is friendly, and this is a comfortable, modern place. Finding anywhere this good – and this cheap – within earshot of Piccadilly Circus is little short of miraculous.

✳ The regional feast – three courses (£10.95) or share three different feasts to sample most of the menu.

Circus

1 Upper James St, W1 ☎ 020 7534 4000

Station Oxford Circus **Open** Mon–Fri noon–3pm & 5.45pm–midnight, Sat 5.45pm–midnight **Accepts** All major credit cards 🕸 www.egami.co.uk

When it opened towards the end of the 1990s, Circus was everything a fashionable fin-de-siècle restaurant should be. The decor was cool shades of black and white, there was a de rigueur members' bar downstairs, open till late, and there were spiky "statement" flower arrangements. The service was efficient and good-looking, and the food was very much of the moment. It took little time for Circus to become a destination restaurant for media and design professionals.

A few years and several trends later, Circus has proved that it can stand the test of time.

The menu works hard to offer something for everyone. Tucked in alongside the pan-fried risotto with smoked haddock and soft poached egg (£6.80), and the globe artichoke, ratte potato and Parmesan salad (£5.50), you'll find starters as diverse as spring onion and potato soup (£5.50), or 30g of Sevruga caviar with trimmings (£40). Main courses offer the traditional – roast rump of lamb with Provencal vegetables (£18.50), honey-roast Gressingham duck breast (£18.50) – as well as more modern dishes such as roast ostrich with black-bean rice and kasuindi (£16.80). Everything about this place suggests that whatever you choose will be well executed and pleasing to the eye. The kitchen is obviously at ease, cooking good-quality ingredients properly and with predictable results. This being an expense-account eatery ideal for business lunches and dinners, desserts are often skipped. Which is a shame, as the pastry chefs obviously delight in flights of fancy – Amaretto cheesecake with coffee sauce (£6.30).

* Set lunches and pre- and post-theatre: two courses £12.50, three £15.

SOHO

The Gay Hussar

Hungarian £16–£65

2 Greek St, W1 ☎ 020 7437 0973
Station Tottenham Court Rd **Open** Mon–Sat 12.15–2.30pm & 5.30–10.45pm
Accepts All major credit cards ⊛ www.simplyrestaurants.com

As you walk in off the street, the ground-floor dining room of The Gay Hussar stretches before you: there are banquettes, there are waiters in dinner jackets, there is paneling and the walls are covered with political caricatures. "Aha!" the knowledgeable restaurant-goer murmurs. "How very retro – some chic designer has replicated an entire 1950s restaurant dining room." Not so. Granted, it has been spruced up, and the room is clean and comfortable, but The Gay Hussar is the real thing, right down to the faded photo of a naked Christine Keeler.

Perhaps the politicos like the food, which is solid, dependable, comfortable and tasty. It's also good value: at lunch there is a prix fixe of two courses for £16.50, and three for £18.50. In the evening, dishes get a trifle more complicated. Starters include a fish terrine with beetroot sauce and cucumber salad (£4.90), and hási pástétom (£3.90) – a fine goose and pork pâté. But the most famous (a house speciality that has featured in various novels) is chilled wild-cherry soup (£3.80), which is like a thin, bitterish, sourish yoghurt and is rather good. Main courses are blockbusters. Try the hortobagyi palacsinta (£13.50), a pancake filled with a finely chopped veal goulash and then sealed, deep-fried and served with creamed spinach. Or there are fish dumplings (£11.50), which are served with rice and a creamy dill sauce. Or cigány gyors tal (£13.75), a "gypsy fry-up" of pork and peppers. Puds are also fierce – poppy-seed strudel comes with vanilla ice cream (£4.50); options like chestnut purée (£4.50) have real substance.

✳ Tokaji Aszu, Eszencia – 50cl 1983, £120.

Kulu Kulu

Japanese £12–£30

76 Brewer St, W1 ☎ 020 7734 7316

Station Oxford Circus/Piccadilly Circus **Open** Mon–Fri noon–2.30pm & 5–10pm, Sat noon–3.30pm & 5–10pm **Accepts** Mastercard & Visa

Kulu Kulu is a conveyor-belt sushi restaurant that pulls off the unlikely trick of serving good sushi without being impersonal or intimidating. It is light and airy and there are enough coat hooks for a small army of diners. The only thing you might quibble over is having to sit on the low stools – anyone over six feet tall will find themselves dining in the tuck position favoured by divers and trampolinists. The atmosphere is Japanese utilitarian. In front of you is a plastic tub of gari (the rather delicious pickled ginger), a bottle of soy and a small box containing disposable wooden chopsticks.

The plates come round on the kaiten, or conveyor, and are coded by design rather than colour, which could prove deceptive: A plates cost £1.20, B plates are £1.80, C plates are £2.40, and D plates £3. All the usual nigiri sushi are here, and the fish is particularly fresh and well presented. Maguri, or tuna, is a B; Amaebi, or sweet shrimp, is a C; salmon roe is an A; Hotategai, or scallops, is a C, and very sweet indeed. Futomaki, a Californian, cone-shaped roll with tuna, is a B. The Ds tend to be ritzier fishes such as belly tuna. As well as the sushi, the conveyor parades some little bowls of hot dishes. One worth looking out for combines strips of fried fish skin with a savoury vegetable purée. It counts as an A, as does the bowl of miso soup. For the indecisive, mixed tempura (£8.80) is good and crisp and there's also mixed sashimi (£10). To drink there is everything from Oolong tea (£1.50) to Kirin beer (£2.60).

✳ One of the premium sakes is made in the Rocky Mountains!

Masala Zone

Indian £7–£20

9 Marshall St, W1 ☎ 020 7287 9966

Station Oxford Circus/Piccadilly Circus **Open** Mon–Sat noon–3pm & 6–10,30pm **Accepts** Mastercard & Visa ⓦ www.realindianfood.com

Masala Zone is impossible to pigeonhole. The food is Indian, but modern Indian, with a commendable emphasis on healthy eating – as would be the norm in India, there's a long list

of attractive vegetarian options. The dining room is smart and large, but the prices are low. The fast-food dishes on the menu tend to be the roadside snacks of Bombay. In all, this is an informal, stylish and friendly place, serving food that is simple and delicious.

The gentle informality extends to the menu, which begins with small plates of street food (most around £3). There are sev puris, dahi puris, samosas, a particularly fine aloo tikki chaat. Pick several dishes and graze your way along – at these prices it doesn't matter if there's the occasional miss among the hits. At lunch there are splendid Indian sandwiches, including a large masala chicken burger (£4.75) and a Bombay layered-vegetable grilled sandwich (£3.50). There are also half a dozen curries that are well balanced and richly flavoured – served simply, with rice, they cost between £5 and £6.75. But you should move straight on to the thalis, which are the authentic option. At Masala Zone these are steel trays with seven or eight little bowls containing a vegetarian snack (to whet the appetite), a curry, lentils, a root vegetable, a green vegetable, yoghurt, bread, rice and pickles. You just choose the base curry and a complete, balanced meal arrives at your table. Choose from chicken thali (£8.75), lamb thali (£9.25), prawn thali (£9.25), or vegetarian thali (£7.75).

> Look out for the stretch limo in the mural – it impressed the visiting tribal artists greatly.

Pollo

Italian £6–£16

20 Old Compton St, W1 ☎020 7734 5917

Station Leicester Square **Open** Daily noon–midnight **Accepts** Mastercard & Visa

You won't find haute cuisine at Pollo, but you do get great value for money. As at neighbouring rival, Centrale (see p.311), this is comfort food, Italian-style – long on carbohydrate and short on frills. Sophistication is in short supply, too – the interior design begins and ends with the linoleum floors and tatty pictures. Diners are shoehorned into booths presided over by a formidable Italian mama who tips you the wink as to what you should order. Downstairs there's more space, but you still might end up sharing a table.

The spotlight of Pollo's lengthy menu falls on cheap, filling pasta in all its permutations. Tagliatelle, rigatoni, ravioli, pappardelle, tortelloni and fusilli are all available. Your choice is basically down to the pasta type, as most of them are offered with the same selection of sauces. The tagliatelle marinara (£4.10), with seafood, tomato and garlic is very good, as is the rigatoni puttanesca (£3.90), or the papardelle tonno (£3.90) with tuna and tomatoes. There are several pizzas (all priced at £3.90) – Napoli, funghi, quattro stagioni, or Vesuvio. And vegetarians are very well catered for. Meat-free highlights include tortelloni wild mushrooms (£4.10), spaghetti al pesto (£3.80), and gnocchi Romana (£4) – with cream tomatoes and mushrooms. Other main course dishes include several chicken options and eight omelettes. A bottle of house wine is a bargain at £7.45 and so are the puddings, but after a substantial hit of pasta, the imposing portion of tiramisù (£2.40) is a challenge for even the greediest.

✳ The 1970's starter "Tricolore" is alive and well – avocado, tomato, mozzarella (£2.50).

Randall & Aubin   Modern British £15–£50

15 Brewer St, W1 ☎ 020 7287 4447

Station Piccadilly Circus **Open** Mon–Sat noon–11pm, Sun 4–10.30pm
Accepts All major credit cards

Once a butcher's shop, Randall & Aubin was recast as a sharp restaurant – as its seafood counter and champagne buckets groaning with flowers suggest – but it's also a rotisserie, sandwich shop and charcuterie to boot. Randall's serves good food speedily, to folk without a lot of time. In summer, the huge sash windows were opened up, making this a wonderfully airy place to eat, especially if you grab a seat by the window.

There's an extensive menu. An eclectic choice of starters roams the globe, with soupe de poisson (£3.90), Japanese fishcakes (£5.95), and salt-and-pepper squid with fresh coriander and teriyaki dressing (£7.85). Main courses range from "original" Caesar salad (£6.85), through spit-roast herb chicken (£10.50), and sausage with butter-bean mash and onion gravy (£10.50), to organic sirloin steak with pommes frites (£12.85) – sauce Béarnaise £1 extra. There are also some interesting sides, such as gratin Dauphinoise (£2.85), or zucchini frites with basil mayonnaise (£3.95). If you don't mind crowds, drop in at lunchtime for a hot filled baguette (£6.70 to £7.85). How about a lamb souvlaki, tzatziki and salad baguette (£7.85)? Available also in the evening, the baguettes provide an inexpensive yet satisfying meal. The list of fruits de mer offers well priced seafood, ranging from a whole dressed crab (£11.50), through grilled lobster, garlic butter and pommes frites (half £12.50, whole £25) to "the works" (£26 per head, minimum two people). Puddings all cost £4.50 and range from tarts and brûlées to the more adventurous pear and caramel galette, or chocolate truffle cake.

✳ If you like chewing salty rubber you'll like whelks (£8.50).

Richard Corrigan at the Lindsay House

British £30–£120

21 Romilly St, W1 ☎020 7439 0450

Station Leicester Square **Open** Mon–Fri noon–2.30pm & 6–11pm, Sat 6–11pm
Accepts All major credit cards ⓦ www.richardcorriganatlindsayhouse.co.uk

Even among chefs – not usually held to be overly calm and level-headed people – Richard Corrigan is regarded as something of a wild man. But at Lindsay House his cuisine has gone from strength to strength. The restaurant is split into a series of small rooms, the service is attentive, and the food is very good indeed. The menus are uncomplicated and change regularly to keep in step with what is available at the market. A three course dinner costs £48, while at lunch the line-up is smaller, as is the price – a real bargain at £25 for three courses. There is also an epic seven-course tasting menu for £59.

Only a fool would try to predict which dishes Richard Corrigan will have on his menu tomorrow, but you can be sure that they will combine unusual flavours with verve and style. Starters either surprise (warm potato and goats' cheese terrine) or are lusciously opulent (roast foie gras, potato blini and caramelised apples). There are also intriguing combinations such as tea-roasted sweetbread with aubergine. Main courses follow the same ground rules (or lack of them): squab pigeon with chorizo and black pudding; scallops with pork belly and spiced carrots; or halibut with turnip gratin, steamed cockles and clams. The puddings may include Seville orange tart with chocolate soufflé and buttermilk sorbet. The wine list is extensive and expensive. One thing distinguishes the cuisine at the Lindsay House – Corrigan's love affair with offal. Sweetbreads, kidneys and hearts all end up on the menu – dishes that perfectly illustrate his deft touch with hearty ingredients.

✱ There's now a veggie "Garden" menu (£52), completely offal free!

SOHO

Soho Spice

Indian £8–£28

124–126 Wardour St, W1 ☎020 7434 0808

Station Piccadilly Circus **Open** Mon–Thurs 11.30am–midnight, Fri & Sat 11.30am–3am, Sun 12.30–10.30pm **Accepts** All major credit cards ⓦ www.sohospice.co.uk

During 2003 Soho Spice was taken over by the hot restaurant group who are behind Mela (see p.120) and Chowki (see p.312). It's large – seating a hundred in the restaurant and forty in the bar – and it's busy, with loud music and late opening at the weekends. The decor is based around a riot of colour, and the main menu features contemporary Indian cuisine. What's more, when you order a main course it comes with pulao rice, naan, dhal and vegetables of the day – which makes ordering simple and paying less painful.

On the main menu, starters include seekh kebab (£3.95); achari murgh tikka (£3.95), tikka made with pickling spices; calamari (£3.50), stir-fried spicy squid; masala jhinga (£4.95), deep-fried spicy marinated king prawns; sunhara samosas (£3.50), which are made with chicken; or aloo matar tikki (£3.25), which is a sort of super potato cake. Main courses represent good value, given that the accompaniments are all included. Good choices are the hara murgh ka tikka (£9.95), which is made with chicken and green herbs and chillies; khara masala murgh (£9.95) made with chicken, whole spices and tomatoes; and chamen puralan (£12.50) – king prawns in a thick Keralan sauce. Or how about adrakh ke panjai (£12.95) – a dish of spiced lamb chops? Gentler palates will enjoy the tandoori machli (£12.50) – fresh salmon, marinated and cooked in the tandoor. Desserts offer mango or pistachio kulfis (£2.95) – Indian ice creams made with boiled milk – and that sweetest of comfort foods, gulab jamun (£2.95), which is a dumpling soaked in rose syrup.

For chilli heads – mirch baigan: baby aubergines, bullet chillies (£8.50).

Spiga

Italian/Pizza £15–£35

84–86 Wardour St, W1 ☎020 7734 3444

Station Leicester Square **Open** Mon, Tues & Sun noon–3pm & 6–11pm, Wed–Sat noon–3pm & 6pm–midnight **Accepts** All major credit cards

Spiga has an impeccable pedigree. It comes from the same stable as Aubergine (see p.66), L'Oranger (see p.271) and Zafferano (see p.232), and has that piece of kit which has long identified any Italian restaurant as serious – a wood-fired oven. But despite its credentials eating here is a pleasantly casual affair. The atmosphere is lively – sometimes the music is too lively – and the look is cool. Spiga may have cut the prices but they haven't cut corners: the tableware is the latest in Italian chic.

Menus change monthly, with occasional daily specials, but there's a definite pattern. Starters will get you in the mood. The buffalo Mozzarella (£7 or £9) is served with fresh tomatoes and basil. But the home-made pasta is very good, such as gnocchi verdi di patate con crema di Fontina (£9); or tagliatelle ai calamari e piselli (£9.50), the pasta served with calamari and peas; or tagliatelle pomodoro fresco e basilico (£7.50) – the best kind of fresh tomato sauce. Or consider a pizza – thin crust, crispy and the size of a dustbin lid. Pizza bufala (£9.50) is rich with genuine Mozzarella; pizza Fiorentina (£8.50) comes with tomato, Mozzarella and spinach. Alternatively, main courses offer up chargrilled and pan-fried

dishes: filetto di rombo con patate novelle (£14) teams pan-fried turbot with new potatoes and artichokes, while petto di pollo grigliato con patate al forno (£12.50) is a simple but good chargrilled chicken breast with roast spuds. Pudding highlights include a wickedly indulgent lemon and mascarpone tart (£6) and an excellent tiramisù (£6).

✱ Forget garlic bread, here there's "Gorgonzola bread".

The Toucan

Irish £10–£20

19 Carlisle St, W1 ☎020 7437 4123

Station Leicester Square/Tottenham Court Rd **Open** Mon–Sat 11am–11pm
Accepts All major credit cards 🌐www.thetoucan.co.uk

When they opened The Toucan the proprietors' first priority was to approach Guinness and ask if they could retail the black stuff. They explained that they wanted to open a small bar aimed single-mindedly at the drinking public, just like the ones they had enjoyed so much in Dublin. Guinness replied that, providing they could shift two barrels a week, they'd be happy to put them on the list. Neither party imagined that the regular order would end up at more like thirty barrels a week! It's an impressive intake, but then The Toucan is an impressive place, serving home-made, very cheap, very wholesome and very filling food, along with all that Guinness.

Start with six Rossmore Irish oysters (£6), or the vegetable soup with bread (£2.50). Go on to the steak and ale pie and champ (£5.95), or sausage and champ with onion gravy (£5.95) – champ is a kind of supercharged Irish mashed potato, with best butter playing a leading role alongside the spring onions. It features in a couple of novelty items such as chilli and champ (£5), or garlic mushrooms and champ (£3). And just when you think you have the measure of the place, there's Thai chicken curry and rice (£5.95). The JPs (jacket potatoes, from £3.50) come with various fillings, and there's an array of sandwiches. One thing to bear in mind if you've come here hungry is that there are times when The Toucan becomes so packed with people that you can scarcely lift a pint. At those times, all attempts at serving food are abandoned.

✳ There are eighty different Irish whiskies, including the stratospherically expensive.

La Trouvaille

Very French £20–£55

12a Newburgh St, W1 ☎020 7287 8488
Station Oxford Circus **Open** Mon–Sat noon–3pm & 6–10pm
Accepts All major credit cards ✆www.latrouvaille.co.uk

French haute cuisine has topped the European Champions League for about a century, and, although the English may resent such total dominance, there is a particular kind of French eatery they still adore. At La Trouvaille the proprietors understand the English longing for really French Frenchness; they even know that they should provide one or two dishes that are a step too authentic for most Brits. They know that waiters who would be considered too over-the-top for Allo, Allo are admired here. They know that their clientele want good food at a price that doesn't break the bank.

The set lunch is £16.95 for two courses and £19.75 for three courses plus cheese – very good value for this quality of cooking. Dinner ups the price to £24.50 for two courses, three courses for £29.50. Starters may include watercress soup with goat's cheese, or artichoke vinaigrette, which comes with an improbably large artichoke that is all the better for simple presentation. Main courses stay in character: onglet de "Galloway"; glazed roast duck leg; canon de mouton "Herdwick". Someone in the kitchen has a truly French respect for the integrity of ingredients. So pick bavette frites, sauce Béarnaise and then revel in excellent Scottish beef. When considering the puds – choccy mousse, crème brûlée, roast pears – divert to the weekly cheese plate, which is outstanding. Three cheeses – perhaps a chunk of melting Livarot, a wedge of waxy Brebis, and a richly blued Fourme d'Ambert – plus a little pot of truffled honey.

✳ "Supreme de faisan et choucroute au jus de gin".

Vasco & Piero's Pavilion

Italian £16–£35

15 Poland St, W1 ☎ 020 7437 8774

Station Oxford Circus **Open** Mon–Fri noon–3pm & 6–11pm, Sat 7–11pm
Accepts All major credit cards ⓦ www.vascosfood.com

Very much a family-run restaurant, the Pavilion has been a Soho fixture for the past twenty years. But there's nothing old or institutional about the cooking or decor. Vasco himself cooks for his regulars, and the establishment has long been a favourite with diners who appreciate his food, which is fairly simple but made with top-class ingredients. Dishes are biased towards Umbrian cuisine. Customers include the great and the good, and the Pavilion's modern yet comfortable atmosphere guarantees them anonymity.

There's only an à la carte menu at lunch but in the evening the basic deal is that you choose either two courses for £21 or three for £25. Given the quality, freshness of ingredients and attention to detail, this proves exceptional value. Starters may include roast beetroot, tomato, eggs and anchovies. Or there may be duck salad, mixed leaves and mostarda di Cremona. Pastas, all home-made, are excellent, too, particularly the tagliolini with king prawns and zucchini – perfectly cooked and with a sauce that is prepared from fresh ingredients and tastes like it. For carnivores, however, there is nothing to beat the calf's liver with fresh sage – paper-thin liver that literally melts in the mouth. Piscivores should turn to the scallopine of swordfish with garlic, parsley and cannellini beans, or to the sautéed monkfish with saffron and lentils. Puddings continue the theme – they're simple and top-quality. A panna cotta is gelatinously creamy, a praline semi-freddo is rich and soft as well as being crunchy.

SOHO

❋ The "light" menu offers two courses for £14.50.

Yauatcha

`Dim Sum/Teahouse £15–£25`

15 Broadwick St, W1 ☎ 020 7494 8888

Station Piccadilly Circus **Open** Teahouse Mon–Sat 8am–11.30pm, Sun 9am–10.30pm.
Dim Sum Mon–Sat 10am–11.30pm, Sun 10am–10.30pm **Accepts** All major credit cards

Yauatcha was one of the most eagerly awaited openings of 2004, and when it did open (in late spring) it did so to a gratifying amount of controversy. On the one hand the critics raved (one gave it five stars), and on the other hand the snipers sniped about the concept of a booking only securing your table for ninety minutes. This place is a new, bright, designer take on dim sum from Alan Yau, the man behind Hakkasan (see p.154) and the food is amazingly, blisteringly good. The little dishes here sweep effortlessly to a "best ever" rating, and if you cannot stuff yourself greedily in ninety minutes you should be ashamed.

It is hard to object to tea by way of accompaniment – there's a lady who is a kind of tea sommelier and there are half a dozen regional and specialised Chinese teas (£2.50 to £3 a pot). There are dumplings – all are good, some are amazing, most come three to a portion. Chinese chive dumpling (£3.90) is a delicate green pastry basket with a savoury middle; prawn and enoki mushroom dumpling (£3.90) has a thin, translucent casing; box dumpling (£3) is round and solid, with pastry outer and savoury middle. Five-spice roll (£5.50) is like an über sausage roll, meaty with crisp exterior; pork and spring-onion cake (£3) is ring shaped, with light pastry crust and rich filling; venison puffs (£3.90) – the best puff pastry with a meaty filling. Don't worry, choose what you like and you will not be disappointed. At ground level there is a tea room which offers an appealing combo of fine Chinese teas and super-slick French patisserie – really good, really elegant little cakes.

✳ Try the "Blue" tea called rou gui (£3).

Yo! Sushi

`Japanese £10–£35`

52 Poland St, W1 ☎ 020 7287 0443

Station Oxford Circus/Piccadilly Circus **Open** Daily noon–midnight
Accepts All major credit cards ⓦ www.yosushi.co.uk

This was the first Yo! Sushi to open and so, in the order of things, it is the first one to adopt the "new look". Now all is dark wood and comfortable booths and the somewhat harsh techie feel is no more. In among all this the food has been refined and, while purists may shudder, it continues to be more consistent than the hype would have you suspect.

Plates are marked in lime (£1.50), blue (£2), purple (£2.50), orange (£3), pink (£3.50) and black (£5). When satiated you call for a plate count, and your bill is prepared. You sit at the counter with a little waiters' station in front of you – there's gari (pickled ginger), soy and wasabi, plus some little dishes and a forest of wooden chopsticks. Kirin beer costs £3, a small warm sake £3, and unlimited Japanese tea is £1. You're ready to begin. Yo! Sushi claim to serve more than a hundred sushi, so be leisurely and watch the belt – and, if in doubt, ask. The sushi range from roasted pepper and avocado (both £1.50); through salmon, crabstick and avocado (£2); and tuna, grey mullet and salmon skin (£3); and so on up to yellowtail and fatty tuna – which carry both the warning that they are "as available", and a pink price tag of £3.50. There are about twenty different maki rolls (with vegetarians well catered for), at all prices. The ten different sashimi and five different gunkan all command the higher orange and pink prices. New "specials" broaden the appeal: spider roll (£8.50), tempura soft-shell crab; crispy-duck roll (£8.50); or Alaskan black cod (£8.50) served with white miso.

✱ The basement bar/club Yo! Below has not been changed.

SOHO

Zilli Fish

Italian/Fish £25–£60

36–40 Brewer St, W1 ☎ 020 7734 8649
Station Piccadilly Circus **Open** Mon–Sat noon–11.30pm
Accepts All major credit cards ⓦ www.zillialdo.com

Bright, brittle and brash, Zilli Fish is a part of Aldo Zilli's empire. You can see into the surprisingly calm kitchen through a large window as you walk along Brewer Street. Inside, in a hectic atmosphere, the restaurant serves a modern Italianate fish menu to London's media workers and the rest of the young Soho crowd. Tables are close and everything is conducted at a racy pace. Not ideal for a secret conversation or for plighting your troth, unless you want the whole place to cheer you on.

The starters here are an attractive bunch: pan-fried squid with Thai sauce (£8.90); mussels arrabbiata with bruschetta (£7.50); tuna carpaccio with rocket and Parmesan (£8.70). Then there are the pasta dishes, such as penne arrabbiatta (£8.95) and spaghetti vongole (£12.75) – clams with Italian cherry tomatoes and basil. The menu goes on to feature a modestly entitled section, "What we are famous for". These are dishes like traditional deep-fried cod, chips and tartare sauce (£15.90); spaghettini with whole fresh lobster (£25); and wild salmon stuffed with crab and spinach, and steamed in ginger and soya (£18.50). Or baked sea bass fillet (£18), wrapped in banana leaf and cooked with cherry tomatoes, ginger, garlic, basil, olive oil and lemon dressing. From the side orders the rocket, Parmesan and roast tomato salad (£4) is a winning combination of flavours. Puddings (all £6.50) include a Ricotta and amarena cherry tart with cherry coulis; a home-made tiramisù with Pavesini; and Pecorino and Gorgonzola with honey.

✱ Fried banana spring rolls with white chocolate ice cream.

Further choices

Aperitivo
Italian

41 Beak St, W1
☎ 020 7287 2057

With connections to Assaggi (see p.255), this resto serves Italian food tapas-style: lots of small dishes.

Ed's Easy Diner
Burgers

12 Moor St, W1
☎ 020 7434 4439

Very good, very messy hamburgers. The authentic hand-held experience. Good shakes. Good chips.

The Endurance
Gastropub/Modern British

90 Berwick St, W1
☎ 020 7437 2944

Old market workers' boozer transformed into central gastropub. Sound food, a busy place.

Kettners
Pizza/Burgers

29 Romilly St, W1
☎ 020 7734 6112

One of Soho's oldest restaurants, now selling a sound pizza and a good hamburger. There's a buzzing champagne bar!

Mr Jerk
Caribbean

189 Wardour St, W1
☎ 020 7287 2878

Rough-and-ready Caribbean eatery with surprisingly good food. The eponymous jerk chicken stands out.

Wagamama
Japanese/Chinese

10a Lexington St, W1
☎ 020 7292 0990

Another branch of the ubiquitous noodlers. See review p.48.

◀ Ed's Diner – welcome to Soho

South Kensington

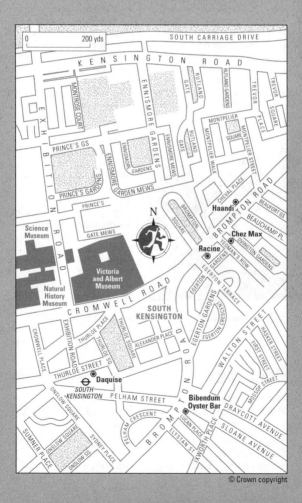

Bibendum Oyster Bar Seafood £12–£30

Michelin House, 81 Fulham Rd, SW3 ☎020 7589 1480
Station South Kensington **Open** Mon–Sat noon–10.30pm, Sun noon–10pm
Accepts All major credit cards 🕸 www.bibendum.co.uk

Bibendum Oyster Bar is one of the nicest places to eat shellfish in London. The 1911 building, a glorious tiled affair that was a former garage for the French tyre people, is Conranized throughout, but the oyster bar is in what looks like the old ground-floor workshop, and they've done precious little to it. On the forecourt stand two camionettes: one a shellfish stall, selling lobsters, oysters and crabs to the Chelsea set; the other a flower stall, with lilies, ginger flowers and roses rather than carnations. Upstairs is Bibendum proper – a very grown up restaurant.

The menu is a shellfish lover's heaven. Here you'll find three different types of rock oyster (£9.50 to £10 per half-dozen) – you can choose your favourite or order a selection to find out the difference. The crab mayonnaise (£9) comes in the shell, giving you the enormous fun of pulling it apart and digging through the claws. Or you can have it done for you in a crab salad (£9.50) – probably just as good, but not nearly so satisfying. If you're really hungry, there's a particularly fine plateau de fruits de mer (£29.50 per head, minimum two people), which has everything: crab, clams, langoustines, oysters, prawns and shrimps, as well as winkles and whelks. There is plenty of choice for those allergic to claw-crushers, simple combinations such as Szechuan chicken salad (£12.80), or grilled tuna with marinated tomatoes (£14). Desserts are simple and delicious – petit pot au chocolat (£6); cheese (£6.50); and the inevitable crème brûlée (£6).

✳ There are six different champagnes available by the half bottle.

Chez Max Very French £15–£65

3 Yeoman's Row, SW3 ☎020 7590 9999
Station Knightsbridge/South Kensington **Open** Mon 6–11pm, Tues–Sat noon–3pm & 6–11pm, Sun noon–3.30pm **Accepts** All major credit cards

This is the latest establishment from which Max Renzland has moved on but left his name behind (see Petit Max, p.38), and it remains under the direction of Marco Pierre

White. The basement room looks the part and oozes bourgeois Frenchness from every pore – bistro glass screens between tables, plenty of dark-red paint and old French posters, tiled floor. The menu is more "classic French Brasserie" than you'll find in most Parisian classic French brasseries, and the whole place has a pleasantly old-fashioned feel to it: Chez Max is more Elizabeth David than Alain Ducasse.

The menu opens with a familiar "signature dish" – Cantabrian salted anchovies, shallot, butter, toast (Les Entrées are all £6.95). There's also soupe de moules Billy By; snails with garlic butter (an extra £2); grilled crottin de Chavignol; and Baltic herring with potato salad. Les Plats are suitably recherché: confit de canard, pommes Sarladaise, Béarnaise (£12.50); Monsieur Max's fishcake (£10.50); sole grillée, sauce tartare (£21.50); braised shoulder of lamb à la Dijonaise, creamed haricots (£15.50). And then there are specials – Aberdeen Angus Châteaubriand, Béarnaise, salade verte and frites (for two £37); poulet noir au vin jaune, with morels and rice (£16.50). Side dishes are sound – gratin Dauphinoise (£2.75). Puds are resolutely old style: rhum baba (£4.50); prune and Armagnac crème brûlée (£5.50); pot au chocolat amer with vanilla ice cream (£5.50). Service is Gallic and efficient and the wine list has suitably French strengths.

✱ What a grand disregard for language: "Chez Max – Eating House Francais".

Daquise

Polish £8–£25

20 Thurloe St, SW7 ☎ 020 7589 6117

Station South Kensington **Open** Daily 11.30am–11pm **Accepts** Mastercard & Visa

Daquise is more old-fashioned than you could possibly imagine. High ceilings, murky lighting, oilcloth table covers, charming service, elderly customers – the full Monty. During the day it serves coffee, tea and rather good cakes to all-comers, breaking off at lunchtime and in the evening to dispense Polish home cooking, Tatra Zwiecka beer, and shot glasses of various vodkas. Several novels have been completed here by penniless writers seeking somewhere warm to scribble – buying a cup of coffee gets you a full ration of patience from the management; all you need supply is a little inspiration. The food is genuine here, and does evolve, albeit at a glacial pace. Portions are serious, but prices are very reasonable, even if you don't take advantage of Daquise's hospitality to wile away the day.

Start with Ukrainian barszcz (£3), rich and red, or the new starter, herrings with bread (£3.80) – the herring fillets are amazingly good. Thick cut, pleasantly salty and with a luxurious smooth texture. Go on to the kasanka (£6.50), a large buckwheat sausage, cousin to black pudding and made using natural skins; the beef stroganoff (£9.50); or the meatballs

(£5.50) served with mushroom sauce and rice. Or, for the fearless, there is giant golonka (£8.80), a marinated pork knuckle which is boiled and served with horseradish sauce. Also, welcome back an old friend, Vienna schnitzel (£9.50) – with a fried egg on top. Side-dishes include an odd kind of sauerkraut (£1.50), served cold and very mild; cucumbers in brine (£1); and kasza (£2), the omnipresent buckwheat.

✳ Daquise, "established in 1947" and much the same today.

Haandi

Indian £12–£40

136 Brompton Rd, SW3 ☎ 020 7823 7373

Station Knightsbridge/South Kensington **Open** Mon–Fri noon–3pm & 6–11pm, Sat & Sun noon–3pm & 6–11pm **Accepts** All major credit cards ⓦ www.haandi-restaurants.com

East African Punjabi restaurants are famous for simple dishes, rich, intense sauces and a welcome belt of chilli heat – the kind of food that hitherto has meant a trek to Southall or Tooting. This is a brave initiative. The management decided to expand an empire based on successful establishments in Nairobi and Kampala by adding the long and narrow space, which, in a bygone age, was a Sloaney haven known as the Loose Box. The decor is curry-house-smart, the room is as light and bright as a nearly-basement can be, and you can see into the kitchen through a curved glass wall. The menu and chefs have been flown in from East Africa. The curries are incredibly rich and become so being reduced gradually rather than being thickened with powdered nuts.

Start with some kebabs. Tandoori fish tikka (£8.50) is made with Tilapia. The chicken malai tikka (£8.80) is also very good. Another star turn from the tandoor is the lamb tandoori chops (£8.90), which are implausibly tender lamb chops, richly spiced, with good crispy bits to gnaw. The curries are also very satisfying. Try the tawa prawn masala (£12.90) – good-sized prawns, which are cooked firm and retain some bite, inhabit a very rich, very strongly flavoured, almost dry masala. Or how about the kake di lamb curry (£8)? This is a trad lamb curry, served on the bone. The vegetable dishes are equally good. Dum aloo Kashmiri (£6.50) is made with potatoes that have been stuffed with cashew nuts, curd cheese and sultanas – implausible but delicious. The breads are excellent – look out for the chilli naan (£1.90).

✳ There are three set lunches – veggie (£7.95); meaty (£9.95) and seafood (£13.95).

Racine

French £18–£50

229 Brompton Rd, SW3 ☎ 020 7584 4477

Station Knightsbridge/South Kensington **Open** Mon–Fri noon–3pm & 6–10.30pm, Sat noon–3.30pm & 6.30–10pm, Sun noon–3.30pm & 6–10pm
Accepts All major credit cards

SOUTH KENSINGTON

Racine goes from strength to strength. It fields something of a foodie "dream team" – chef Henry Harris and front-of-house Eric Garnier – and the food is French. Not just any old French, but familiar, delicious, nostalgic dishes from the glory days of French cooking. The dining room at Racine is dark brown and comfortable. The service is friendly and Gallic. The prices are reasonable, and haven't crept up too much year on year. It's no surprise that this place is busy enough to make booking an imperative.

Henry Harris is a very good cook and his menus are invariably skillfully written. Everything tempts, everything is priced reasonably, and he takes a great deal of trouble to source and buy top-quality seasonal ingredients. To start with, expect simple but glorious combinations such as jambon de Bayonne with celeriac rémoulade (£6.50); pâté de foie de volaille et fines herbes (£5.25); melted Raclette, shallot and cornichons salad (£6.50), or a truly wonderful warm garlic and saffron mousse with mussels (£7) – light and airy, with a triumphant texture and a delicate taste. Mains continue the "classical" theme: roast skate with braised endive and green peppercorn sauce (£13.50); tête de veau with a well made sauce ravigote (£11.50); plus chicken, chops, steak and fish. The dessert menu deals in classics: petit pot au chocolat (£6); strawberries in Beaujolais (£5); and Mont Blanc (£5), which is a rich chestnut purée with meringue and chocolate sauce. The wine list is Francocentric but merciful – even the smart bottles seem reasonably priced.

✳ Two courses for Knightsbridge ladies who lunch £15.50, three £17.50.

Further choices

Cambio de Tercio
Spanish

163 Old Brompton Rd, SW5
☎ 020 7244 8970

Spanish restaurant with less formal deli-diner on the other side of the road. Good cooking.

Ognisko Polskie
Polish

55 Princes's Gate, SW7
☎ 020 7589 4635

Elegant, old, eccentric restaurant in the Polish club. Good bar and a great garden at the rear.

Southall

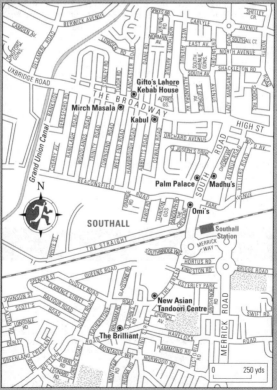

© Crown copyright

The Brilliant

72–76 Western Rd, Southall ♿ ☎ 020 8574 1928

Station BR Southall **Open** Tues–Fri noon–2.30pm & 6pm–midnight,
Sat & Sun 6–11.30pm **Accepts** All major credit cards ⊕ www.brilliantrestaurant.com

The Brilliant is a Southall institution. For more than twenty years the Anand family business has been a nonstop success and it is now a bustling 250-seater. For 25 years before that, the family's first restaurant, also called The Brilliant, was the toast of Kenya. The food at The Brilliant is East African-Asian, and very good indeed. There are changes afoot here. You can see that the Anand family is pulling back slightly and it is to be expected that, as The Brilliant starts hiring chefs from outside, so the menu will go more mainstream. Let's hope that the legendary high standards prevail.

To start with, you must try the butter chicken (£8 half, £16 full). A half-portion will do for two people as a starter. This dish is an enigma: somehow it manages to taste butterier than butter itself – really delicious. There's also jeera chicken (£8 or £16), rich with cumin and black pepper. And chilli chicken (£9 or £18), which is hot, but not quite as hot as it used to be! If you're in a party, move on to the special meal section – these come in two portion sizes, suggested for three people and five people. Methi chicken (£17.50 or £32.50), masaladar lamb (£17.50 or £32) and palak chicken (£17.50 or £32) are all winners. Alternatively, choose among the single-portion curries, which include masala fish (£9), a curry of unimaginable richness with good firm chunks of boneless fish. As well as good rotis (£1), the bread list hides a secret weapon, the kulcha (£1). Hot from the kitchen they are amazing – it's best to order a succession so that they don't go cold.

SOUTHALL

✳ The carrot pickle is very good here.

Gifto's Lahore Karahi

162–164 The Broadway, Southall ♿ ☎ 020 8813 8669

Station BR Southall **Open** Mon–Thurs noon–11.30pm, Fri–Sun noon–midnight
Accepts All major credit cards ⊕ www.gifto.com

There is no more competitive place for an Indian restaurant than Southall, which makes it all the more remarkable that Gifto has not only been busy for so many years, but continues to expand and add yet more covers. Downstairs is a barn of a room with the open kitchen running along one side and serried ranks of tables on the other. There's a newer room upstairs but both are busy and there is often a queue at the door on Saturday or Sunday. Gifto's Lahore Karahi specialises in freshly grilled well spiced meats and simple curries. The food is good, cheap and takes a minimal time to get from chef to diner.

Whatever you add to fill out your order you should start with bread. The stuffed paratha (£2.50) is good – thin and almost flakey, and both the plain naan (90p) and the Peshwari naan (£1.90) are delicious. Accompany them with an order of chicken tikka (£4.40), the seekh kebab (£2.20), or the splendid tilapia fish (£9.90), whole, marinated and cooked in the tandoor. The curries are served in a karahai here and taste very fresh and vibrant. The saag gosht (£6.80) is exemplary, the spinach melting down to make a rich sauce. Also good are the butter chicken (£6.80); the methi chicken (£6.80) rich with fenugreek; and the karela gosht (£6.80) – lamb and chunks of bitter melon in an intensely flavoured sauce. Either drink the various freshly squeezed juices or bring your own supplies of alcohol. Service is quick and efficient and given the large scope of this food factory it hums along smoothly.

* Indian puds are good here – gajrela (£1.60) is a sort of carrot cake.

Kabul

Indian/Afghan £5–£15

1st Floor, Himalayan Shopping Centre, The Broadway ☎020 8571 6878
Station BR Southall **Open** Daily noon–midnight **Accepts** Mastercard & Visa

Find the Himalaya Shopping Centre and wend your way past the silk merchants and the shops selling exotic CDs. Head up the escalator and to the left you'll find the Kabul, which has taken over the space allocated to an entire shop. It's a spacious restaurant with comfortable chairs, dark-blue tablecloths and a series of banquettes running along the wall. The menu splits into two sections: Afghan food and Indian food. Curiosity should compel you to try some Afghan dishes. Portions are very large and prices very competitive.

Start with dumplings – ordering the Afghan starter called mantu gosht (£5.99) brings a dinner plate covered in large savoury dumplings filled with spiced lamb. Ashak are also dumplings and come in meat and non-meat versions. The vegetarian ones (£4.99) are amazingly good, light dumplings with dough so thin that you can see the green leaves of the filling through the skins. Also notable is the showr-na-kath (£1.99), a bowl full of chickpeas in a thin, green, herby, chilli-warmed liquid. Eat them with a spoon, or more sensibly with some of the excellent Afghan nan bread (£1.20). For mains, the quabuli murgh (£5.99) is a large plate of delicious rice pillau made with plenty of sultanas and garnished with shreds of carrot; on top of it is a tender chicken drumstick, and it comes with a bowl of curry with a large minced-lamb cake hidden in its depths. Another winner is the karahi tukham (£2.50), which is a small karahi full of light, buttery, rich and spicy scrambled eggs.

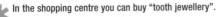 In the shopping centre you can buy "tooth jewellery".

Madhu's

Indian £25–£60

39 South Rd, Southall 📞 ☎020 8574 1897

Station BR Southall **Open** Mon & Wed–Fri 12.30–3pm & 6–11pm, Sat & Sun 6–11.30pm **Accepts** All major credit cards 🌐 www.madhusonline.com

In 2004 both Sanjay Anand, and his restaurant Madhu's collected a hat-full of awards. Following a serious fire and the re-opening in 2003, with chic new décor and a new logo (a red M with a flourish), things have gone very well indeed. The service is slick, the food is very good and the whole operation is polished, from the smart white asymmetric china to the serried ranks of gleaming cutlery. There is even Louis Roederer Crystal on the wine list at £350 a bottle. Take heart: the cooking has not lost its way.

The food here is predominantly East African-Asian, and is well spiced with good, full-on flavours – thank goodness nothing has been toned down. Starters are pricey but portions are good. Try the famous butter chicken (£8): very tender, very delicious, but sadly still dyed a lurid orange. Or there are the lamb chops (four for £8) – well spiced and juicy. Anyone homesick for Africa will relish the mogo jeera (£3), cassava pan-fried with cumin. Main courses also come in large portions. Masala fish (£8) is a hunk of tilapia in a rich tomatoey sauce. The simple dishes are also well made – sag gosht (£8) is a good choice, lamb cooked with fresh spinach and agreeably spicy. The vegetable section also hides some treasures: bhune karele (£6) – a bitter gourd stuffed and then oven-roasted – is a particularly fine and vibrant dish. Breads are good, particularly the bhatura (£1.50), which is a fluffy cross between chapati and doughnut. If you can avoid the allure of the Crystal, you'll find Tusker and Whitecap beers at £3 a bottle. Make sure that they are cold.

SOUTHALL

✳ Nyamah choma (£7), Masai influenced chilli lamb spareribs.

A weekend walk

Southall is a fascinating place, especially on Saturday and Sunday when the streets are crowded; however, be forewarned that parking is in very short supply. There is a multi-story carpark to the South of the Broadway (roughly speaking it's behind the Himalaya Shopping Centre), but it's best to take the train to Southall BR and walk up South Road and along the Broadway. Best buys include the barbecues (you'll need the car to take them home), simple steel troughs like window boxes for around £25; gold jewellery (sold by weight, very good value); and boxes of ripe mangoes – remarkably cheap (four mangoes for £2.50).

Mirch Masala

Indian £10–£25

171–173 The Broadway, Southall, Middx ☎020 8867 9222
Station BR Southall **Open** Daily noon–midnight **Accepts** Cash or cheque only

The original Mirch Masala is still plying its trade in Norbury, South London, the second branch is busy in Tooting, but this imposing establishment in Southall opened in May 2004 and has quickly taken over as the flagship. The other branches were the kind of establishments where customers raved about "food so good" that they could forgive the restaurants any amount of scruffiness. The new resto is a smart affair: new chairs, stone floor, big windows, smart open kitchen. Prices have gone up a little, but the menu is the same and the cooking still tastes fresh and feisty. Be careful to specify how hot you want your dishes to be.

As you sit down you get a poppadum and a plate of cucumber and raw onion. From the starters the best choice is to stick to the "kebabs". Seek kebabs (90p each); chicken tikka (£3.50); and fish tikka (£4); are good. The lamb chops (£5) are very good – good crispy bits and plenty of fresh bread stuffed with onions. The vegetarian dishes are also good here – look out for the karahi butter beans methi (£4), a strongly flavoured dish heavy with fenugreek that was something of a house special in Norbury. There is a new range of "deigi" dishes – a kind of steam roasting, but the simple karahi curries cooked to order are too good to miss. Very fresh, plenty of fresh herbs and clean flavours. Karahi ginger chicken (£6); karahi methi gosht (£6) and, best of, all karella gosht (£6), lamb with bitter melon. The breads are good and the rice dishes sound. Cheap, fresh food, served quickly and without fuss!

✳ The menu motto: "Food extraordinaire. You wish it, we cook it."

The New Asian Tandoori Centre

Indian £8–£18

114 The Green, Southall, ♿ ☎020 8574 2597
Station BR Southall **Open** Mon–Thurs 9am–11pm, Fri–Sun 9am–11.30pm
Accepts No credit cards

On the menu at the New Asian Tandoori Centre it states, "Famous & suitable venue for business & social gathering", and so it is. The NATC is a large, light and airy place. It is made up from three shopfronts and splits into three rooms: on the right there's a seriously busy takeaway operation, in the middle a no-frills canteen and on the left, a smarter dining room complete with a bar and ornamental stonework. This is one time when you can stick to the "middle path" with confidence. Service is friendly and, except for the tandoori dishes, the food arrives briskly.

The menu offers the kind of strongly flavoured food you would expect in a Punjabi cafe. Start with good jeera chicken (£6), rich with cumin, or simple savoury kebabs: chicken (£1) or lamb (90p). Or there's a vegetable pakora (£1.30). The boneless fish tikka (£3.50) is stunning: large, firm-fleshed chunks of fish, well spiced and not at all dried out. With the rather good breads in support – chapatis (60p), bhaturas (60p), naans (80p) – a few starters and grilled meats could easily make a meal. But it would be a pity to miss out on the main course dishes. The menu is split into two halves: vegetarian and non-vegetarian. There is a good bhindi dish (£3.50) of fine soggy aubergines; Bombay aloo (£3); chana dal (£3), a delicious rich yellow chickpea sludge; and a curry made with karela (£3.50) – bitter melon. Meat-eaters will enjoy the butter chicken (£6); the bhuna chicken (£5.50); the economically named lamb curry (£5.50); and the bhuna lamb that is only served on Saturday and Sunday (£5.50).

* "Black label, 1 peg" (£2.50) – a Raj style bargain!

SOUTHALL

Omi's

Indian £5–£12

1–3 Beaconsfield Rd, Southall ☎ 020 8571 4831
Station BR Southall **Open** Mon–Thurs 11am–10.30pm Fri & Sat 11am–11pm, Sun 11am–9.30pm **Accepts** All major credit cards

Omi's is a small, no-frills eatery with a kitchen that seems at least as spacious as the dining area. The explanation for this lies down the street, where you'll find one of Southall's larger banqueting and wedding halls (there is a thriving outside-catering operation). But then Omi's has never been purely a restaurant – until some years ago, the food shared a counter with a van-rental business. In 2004 Omi's fulfilled a long-held dream, and now there is silverware and crockery from Mumbai to set off an elegant new paint job. The restaurant seats fifty with an eighty-seat function room upstairs. But you'll still find tasty, Punjabi/Kenyan-Asian dishes, lots of rich flavours and great value.

The food is cooked by a formidable line-up of chefs in the back, doubtless knocking up dishes for diners with one hand while masterminding the next Indian wedding for eight hundred with the other. There's a constant stream of people picking up their takeaways. The starters are behind the counter: chicken tikka (£3) is good and spicy, while aloo tikki (50p) is a large, savoury potato cake, delightfully crisp on the outside. Or try the masala fish (£3.50), a large slab of cod thickly encrusted with spices. Go on to sample a couple of the specials. Aloo methi (£4) – potatoes cooked with fenugreek – is very moreish indeed, as is the chilli chicken (£5). All the curries are commendably oil-free and thrive on the cook-and-reheat system in operation here. They are best eaten with breads: parathas (70p), rotis (40p) and the mega-indulgent, puffy fried bhaturas (50p) are all fresh and good.

❋ The multi-course set meal (veg or non-veg) is cheap – £5.

Palm Palace

Sri Lankan £10–£20

80 South Rd, Southall ☎020 8574 9209

Station BR Southall **Open** Daily noon–3pm & 6–11.30pm **Accepts** All major credit cards

The Palm Palace may be short on palms, and it is not palatial by any manner of means, but the food is great. This is the only Sri Lankan restaurant among the restaurant turmoil that is Southall, and the menu features a great many delicious and interesting dishes. As is so often the case with Sri Lankan food, the "drier" dishes are particularly appealing, and there is a good deal of uncompromising chilli heat. The dining room had a modest refurb in 2004, and service is friendly and attentive.

Starters are very good here. Try the mutton rolls (£1.50) – long pancake rolls filled with meat and potatoes. Or there's the fish cutlets (£1.50), which are in fact spherical fishcakes very much in the same style as those you find in smart West End eateries, but better spiced and a tenth of the price. Move on to a "devilled" dish: mutton (£4.50), chicken (£4.50) or, best of all, squid (£4.95) – these dishes combine spices with richness very well. There was a time when every curry house in the land featured Ceylon chicken, but here you'll find a short list of real "Ceylon" curries including mutton (£3.95): they're good, if straightforward. Try the chicken 65 (£4.50) – the name is said to refer to the age of the chicken in days, for if it were any younger it would fall apart during cooking; any older it would be tough). The hoppers (Sri Lankan pancakes) are good fun: string hopper (£2.50); egg hopper (£1.25); milk hopper (£1). Try a simple vegetable dish as well. Sag aloo (£2.50) brings fresh spinach and thoughtfully seasoned well-cooked potato.

❋ "Chocolatey, mocha, liqueur-like": Michael Jackson about Lion Stout.

Further choices

Rita's Samosa Centre
Indian

112 Broadway, Southall
☎020 8571 2100

Old, informal, cheap, simple restaurant. Noted for a very good chunk of tandoori fish.

Roshni
Indian

7–9 South Rd, Southall
☎020 8574 3721

A relative newcomer, Roshni is a large, modern restaurant serving the same mix of grills and curries as the other large Southall emporia.

Stoke
Newington

LORDSHIP PARK

LIZABETH WALK

LORDSHIP ROAD

Clissold
Park

N

STOKE NEWINGTON CHURCH ST

Rasa
Travancore

Rasa

Anglo
Anatolyan

DUMONT RD

KYNASTON RD

STOKE
NEWINGTON

Stoke
Newington
Station

STAMFORD HILL

STOKE NEWINGTON HIGH

RECTORY ROAD

BROOKE RD

NEVILL RD

BAXTON ROAD

DARVILLE RD

STOKE NEWINGTON ROAD

STOKE NEWINGTON CHURCH ST

CLISSOLD ROAD

SANDBROOK ROAD

OLDFIELD ROAD

ALBION ROAD

QUEEN ELIZABETH'S WALK

BARBAULD RD

GR

EVERING ROAD

BEATTY RD

AMHURST ROAD

WALFORD RD

FOULDEN RD

BURMA RD

SPRINGDALE RD

BRIGHTON RD

FARLEIGH ROAD

CLISSOLD CRESCENT

ADEN GR

AVENUE ROAD

VINSTON ROAD

MILTON GROVE

SHAKESPEARE WALK

PALATINE RD

ALLEN ROAD

BELGRADE RD

PRINCE GEORGE RD

COWPER ROAD

PRINCESS MAY RD

GREEN LANES

LEONARD RD

HOWARD RD

BRENT RD

HARRETT'S GROVE

Belle Epoque

MATTHIAS ROAD

PELLERIN RD

ARCOLA ST

POETS RD

WOODVILLE RD

BRETT RD

MILLARD CL

STOKE NEWINGTON ROAD

FERNTOWER RD

NEWINGTON
GREEN

ALVINGTON

PYRLAND RD

MILDMAY ROAD

SANDRINGHAM RD

BERESFORD RD

NEWINGTON GREEN RD

MILDMAY GROVE NORTH

WOLSEY RD

Dalston
Kingsland
Station

GROSVENOR AVE

MILDMAY

MILDMAY GROVE SOUTH

KINGSBURY'S WALK

0   250 yds

© Crown copyright

Anglo Anatolyan

Turkish £8–£20

123 Stoke Newington Church St, N16 ☎020 7923 4349

Station BR Stoke Newington **Open** Mon–Fri 5pm–midnight Sat & Sun 1pm–midnight
Accepts Mastercard & Visa

The food is sound at the Anglo Anatolyan, the bills are small, and the tables so crowded together that you get to meet all the other diners. But the most intriguing feature of the restaurant is the large and impressive royal crest engraved in the glass of the front door. Under it an inscription reads, "By Appointment to Her Majesty Queen Elizabeth II, Motor Car Manufacturers". Why? Do the Windsors slip up to Stoke Newington when they feel a new Daimler coming on? Predictably, asking the waiters for provenance doesn't help much: they look at you seriously and confide that they "got the door secondhand".

The food at the Anglo Anatolyan is usually pretty decent. The bread in particular is amazing: large, round, flat loaves about two inches deep, cut into chunks, soft in the middle and crisp on the outside; it is baked at home by a local Turkish woman. To accompany it, start with ispanak tarator (£3.15), which is spinach in yoghurt with garlic, and a tremendous, coarse tarama (£2.95). And also sigara borek (£3.45) – crisp filo pastry filled with cheese and served hot, and arnavut cigeri (£4.15) – cubes of fried lamb's liver. The main courses are more easily summarized: sixteen ways with lamb, one with quails, two with chicken, one with prawn, and two vegetarian dishes. Kaburga tarak (£6.75) is crisp, tasty lamb spareribs; iskender kebab (£7.75) is fresh doner on a bed of cubed bread, topped with yoghurt and tomato sauce; kasarli beyti (£7.75) is minced lamb made into a patty with cheese, and grilled. They are all pretty good.

✳ Printed on the bills is "Another cheap night out." True enough.

La Belle Époque

French/Café Patisserie £15–£15

37 Newington Green, N1 ☎020 7249 2222

Station Dalston Kingsland BR **Open** Tues–Fri 8am–6pm, Sat & Sun 9am–5pm
Accepts Mastercard & Visa

An authentic French café in Stoke Newington? Formidable! Overlooking Newington Green, La Belle Époque showcases the skills of proprietor Eric Rousseau, a prodigious patissier-chocolatier-confiseur-glacier. Before opening La Belle Époque in 2002, he trained in Paris and worked all over the world. Eric is the first baker in Britain to receive France's official 'Artisan Boulanger' certificate. He makes fortnightly trips across the Channel to buy the twenty types of flour that produce dozens of different loaves, including that elusive 'proper' baguette, as well as supplies of chocolate and gourmet goods, including cassoulet and confitures, truffles, foie gras and escargots.

Weekends always see queues of Stokies waiting to take home the hand-made croissants (95p) and other Viennoiserie. But "eating in" at one of the tables in the light and airy shop area, or in the darker backroom for smokers, will show Eric's obsessive attention to detail. Croissants come with Beurre d'Isigny and miniature pots of French jam. Accompany them with a genuine café au lait. Lunch brings a daily changing choice of quiches (£3.15 or £4.15 with a green salad), salads (£2.90), Bouchées à la Reine (£3.65), vol au vents stuffed with mushrooms, or Croques Monsieur (£4.25) – made with the classic béchamel filling, rather than being the usual ham-and-cheese toastie. At tea time, cakes, tarts and gateaux are extravagant in both design and engineering. Eric's signature creation is the 'Belle Époque' itself: Cuban chocolate mousse with a crème brûlée centre filled with Grand Marnier and orange fondant.

✳ There are regular courses for polishing up your baking skills.

Rasa

Indian/Vegetarian £12–£30

55 Stoke Newington Church St, N16 ☎ 020 7249 0344
Station BR Stoke Newington **Open** Mon–Fri 6–11pm, Sat & Sun noon–2.30pm & 6–11pm **Accepts** All major credit cards ⊛ www.rasarestaurants.com

Rasa has built up a formidable reputation for outstanding South Indian vegetarian cooking. As well as great food, the staff are friendly and helpful, and the atmosphere is uplifting. Inside, everything is pink (napkins, tablecloths, walls), gold ornaments dangle from the ceiling, and a colourful statue of Krishna playing the flute greets you at the entrance. Rasa's proprietor and the majority of the kitchen staff come from Cochin in South India. As you'd expect, booking is essential.

This is one occasion when the set meal – or "feast" (£15.50) – may be the best, as well as the easiest, option. But however you approach a Rasa meal, everything is a taste sensation. Even the pappadoms are a surprise: try the selection served with six home-made chutneys (£3). If you're going your own way, there are lots of starters to choose from. Mysore bonda (£2.75) is delicious, shaped like a meatball but made of potato spiced with ginger, coriander and mustard seeds; or there is kathrikka (£2.75), slices of aubergine served with fresh tomato chutney. The main dishes are good too. Cheera parippu curry (£3.75) is made with fresh spinach and toor dal with a touch of garlic; moru kachiathu (£3.90) combines mangoes and green bananas with chilli and ginger. Or go for a dosa (paper-thin crisp pancakes). Masala dosa (£5) is packed with potatoes and comes with lentil sauce and coconut chutney. Puddings sound hefty but arrive in mercifully small portions; the pal payasam (£2.50) is a rice pudding made with cashew nuts and raisins. A fine end to a meal.

✳ Rasa translates as "flavour", "desire", "beauty", or "elegance".

Rasa Travancore

Indian £15–£35

56 Stoke Newington Church St, N16 ☎ 020 7249 1340
Station BR Stoke Newington **Open** Daily 6–11pm
Accepts All major credit cards ⓦ www.rasarestaurants.com

Rasa Travancore is painted glow-in-the-dark Rasa pink, just like the original Rasa, which faces it across the roadway. Rasa Travancore moves the spotlight onto a particular facet of Keralan cuisine: Syrian Christian cooking, and a very welcome move it is too. All the South Indian flavour notes are there – coconut, curry leaves, ginger, chillies, mustard seeds, tamarind – but as well as veggie specialities, Syrian Christian dishes feature fish, seafood, mutton, chicken and duck.

The menu is a long one and great pains have been taken to explain every dish. Apparently the king prawns in konjufry (£4.95) have been marinated in "refreshing spices". Or there's Kerala fish fry (£3.95), a large steak of firm-fleshed kingfish dusted with spice and pan-fried. Very delicious. Travancore kozhukkatta (£3.75) is a sort of ninth cousin to those large, doughy Chinese dumplings – steamed rice outside with spiced minced lamb inside. The main course dishes are fascinating and richly flavoured. Kozhy olthu curry (£5.25) – billed as "a famous recipe from Sebastian's mum"! – is a rich, dryish, oniony chicken curry. Lamb stew (£5.95) is a simple and charming lamb curry. Duck fry (£6.95) is dry-fried chunks of duck with curry leaves and onion. Kappayyum meenum vevichathu (£7.95) is a triumph – a soupy fish curry, delicately flavoured and served with floury chunks of boiled tapioca root dusted with coconut. Excellent accompaniments are the tamarind rice (£2.50), which has an amazing depth of flavour, and the flaky, buttery Malabar paratha (£2).

✳ Travancore kayi curry (£3.90) – "chef Narayonani's signature dish".

Swiss Cottage & Finchley Road

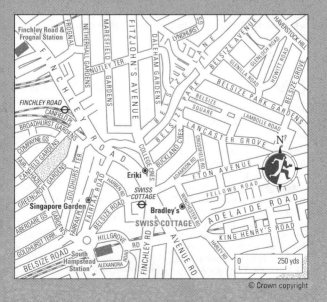

Finchley Road & Frognal Station
FROGNAL
NETHERHALL GARDENS
MARESFIELD GARDENS
CANUTLEY TER.
FITZJOHN'S AVENUE
DALEHAM GARDENS
LYNDHURST
LANE
BELSIZE AVENUE
GLENILLA ROAD
GLENLOCH ROAD
HOWITT ROAD
HAVERSTOCK HILL
BELSIZE GROVE

FINCHLEY
CANFIELD DR
FINCHLEY ROAD
BROADHURST GARDENS
COMPAYNE GS
CANFIELD GARDENS
HAZEL
GREENCROFT GARDENS
ROAD
GOLDHURST TER.
BELSIZE PARK
COLLEGE CRES.
BUCKLAND CRES.
ADAMSON RD.
BELSIZE
SQUARE
BELSIZE PARK GARDENS
LANCASTER GROVE
LAMBOLLE ROAD
CROSSFIELD RD.
ETON AVENUE

Eriki
SWISS COTTAGE
FAIRFAX RD
HARBEN RD.
FAIRFAX PL.
Singapore Garden
ABERDARE GS
GOLDHURST GARDENS
GOLDHURST TERR.
BELSIZE ROAD
South Hampstead Station
ALEXANDRA
HILLGROVE RD
ROAD
BELSIZE ROAD
FINCHLEY RD
AVENUE RD
Bradley's
SWISS COTTAGE
WINCHESTER RD.
FELLOWS ROAD
ADELAIDE ROAD
KING HENRY'S ROAD
HARLEY RD

N

0   250 yds

© Crown copyright

Bradleys

Modern British £16–£60

25 Winchester Rd, Swiss Cottage, NW3 ☎ 020 7722 3457

Station Swiss Cottage **Open** Tue–Fri noon–3pm & 6–11pm, Sat 6–11pm,
Sun noon–5pm, **Accepts** All major credit cards

Bradleys has been an open secret in North London for years – secret in that it's damn hard to find. Make the effort for a great value set lunch and early doors dinner menu (6–7 pm), as well as an innovative à la carte menu and an unusually presented wine list. The set menu offers one course for £8.50, two courses for £12 and three for £16.00. A typical three-course choice could include grilled asparagus, warm jersey potatoes with samphire and lemon dressing, seared beef with Asia spiced salad, raspberry and orange crème brulée. Excellent value and good training for an attack on the à la carte menu in the future.

Cooking is sound and dishes tend to be classic flavour combinations with very well judged twists. For example there's roasted peaches with Bayonne ham, Mascarpone and basil (£7.00); tian of Cornish crab with avocado and tomato vinaigrette (£7.00); and chargrilled squid with Piedmont pepper (£6.50). Mains include wild salmon with Balsamic strawberries, watercress and herb cous cous (£17.00); Barbary duck breast with cherry compote, cabbage and turnip Dauphinoise (£15.50); or wild Sea Bass fillet with peperonata and fennel purée (£18.50). Purists might question strawberries with salmon, or cabbage and turnip in a Dauphinoise, but they work well. Bradleys wine list is divided into quaint sections like 'aromatic', 'medium weight', 'clean and fresh', 'heavyweight', 'old ones' and 'blockbusters'. In the latter section you can find a Vosné Romanée 1er Cru (£63), a Chateau Talbot 1995 (£71) and other fine wine bargains.

✱ Good Sunday Lunch, £16 for two courses, £20 for three, including a Pimms.

Eriki

Indian £20–£45

4–6 Northways Parade, Finchley Rd NW3 ☎ 020 7722 0606

Station Swiss Cottage **Open** Sun–Fri noon–3pm & 6–11pm, Sat 6–11pm
Accepts All major credit cards ☯ www.eriki.co.uk

Eriki is an ambitious, new-style, Indian restaurant. This means that attention has been paid to the design (glowing red walls, heavy wood chairs, blond wood floor), to the menu, which includes a few less familiar regional dishes, and to the prices, which are a tad higher than you might expect – presumably to keep out riff raff. This place is determined to distance itself from run-of-the-mill High Street curry houses. Service is slick and overall Eriki achieves its objective and delivers a polished (if pricey) night out.

The food is good and commendably unfussy, although the starters do get a fairly elaborate presentation. Scallops hariyali (£5.95) arrives in a scallop shell like an old-style coquilles St Jaques – two accurately cooked scallops in a mild creamy sauce. Or there's calamari mirch fry (£5.95), stir-fried squid. Or masala dosa (£3.95). (There is a healthy representation of South Indian dishes on the menu including a good range of veggie options). Classic mains such as koh-e-rogan josh (£7.95) are well spiced and with a good coarsely ground sauce. Murgh Xacutti (£7.95) is

again, well spiced. The duck with tamarind and pink pepper (£8.95) is light and almost a fusion dish. Kumb palak (£5.95), young spinach leaves, teamed with a few button mushrooms, tastes very fresh. And the kali dal (£5.95) – which is a pretty fierce price for lentils – is well made, with mixed pulses and a hefty tempering of butter. Breads are sound, the Malabari tawa paratha (£1.95) being the pick: very flaky, very self-indulgent.

* There's an ambitious wine list to challenge the Indian Ambari beer.

Singapore Garden   Singaporean £15–£35

83a Fairfax Rd, NW6 ☎ 020 7328 5314

Station Swiss Cottage **Open** Sun–Thurs noon–2.45pm & 6–10.45pm Fri & Sat noon–2.45pm & 6–11.15pm **Accepts** All major credit cards ✆ www.singaporegarden.com

Singapore Garden is a busy restaurant – don't even think of turning up without a reservation – and performs a cunning dual function. Half the cavernous dining room is filled with well-heeled, often elderly, family groups from Swiss Cottage and St John's Wood, treating the restaurant as their local Chinese and consuming crispy duck in pancakes. The other customers, drawn from London's Singaporean and Malaysian communities, are tucking into the Teochew braised pig's trotters. So there are both cocktails and Tiger beer. But it's always busy, and the food is interesting and good.

Start with a chiew yim soft-shell crab (£7), which is lightly fried with garlic and chillies rather than annihilated in the deep fryer, like the fresh crab fried in the shell (£15), which does offer exceptional crispy

bits. If you're feeling adventurous, follow with a real Singapore special – the Teochew braised pig's trotter (£10), which brings half a pig's worth of trotters slow-cooked in a luxurious, black, heart-stoppingly rich gravy. Or try the claypot prawns and scallops (£12), which delivers good, large, crunchy prawns and a fair portion of scallops, stewed with lemongrass and fresh ginger on glass noodles. Very good indeed. From the Malaysian list you might pick a daging curry (£6.75) – coconutty, and not especially hot. Or the squid blachan (£9), rich with the strange savoury taste of prawn paste. Or a simple dish such as archar (£4), which is a plate of crunchy pickled vegetables sprinkled with ground peanuts. One option is the mee goreng (£5.50), because this noodle dish is a meal in itself.

* The "healthy alternative": a Steamboat (£31.50 per person, min two) – uber-fondue.

Tooting & Balham

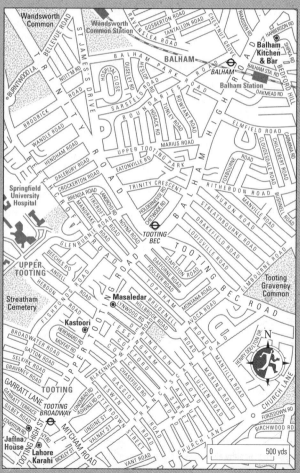

© Crown copyright

Balham Kitchen & Bar

Modern British £15–£50

15–19 Bedford Hill, SW12 & ☎020 8675 6900

Station Balham **Open** Mon–Sat 8am–noon (breakfast), noon–11pm, Sun 8am–noon (breakfast), noon–10.30pm **Accepts** All major credit cards

As a locale SW12 is moving up the social scale so fast that you half expect to see an outbreak of nosebleeds. Perhaps it's all a response to the Balham Kitchen and Bar? The name may be prosaic, but this place is part of the SoHo House Club group – we are talking svelte member's club in Soho, and another SoHo House Club in New York, somewhere so blisteringly trendy that it featured on Sex in the City. The Balham Kitchen is a large bar, but the size doesn't make the slightest difference. Even midweek the place is packed with a spectrum of punters that goes all the way from codgers to city boys by way of elegant parties on a girls' night out.

The menu is carefully constructed along Brasserie lines. The starter section goes from watercress soup (£5); to moules marinière (£6.50 or £9.50); and on to hand-carved Serrano ham (£7). There's a "small plates" section featuring a skewer of black pudding and cheese (£4.50), or perhaps a plate of crispy squid (£4.50) appeals? Then there's "salad and sandwiches" which offers a decent cheeseburger (£8.50) and a well made Caesar salad (£6.50 or £9.50), unfussy and dressed with a cold soft-boiled egg – very classical. Main courses flirt with retro: chicken Kiev (£11); smoked haddock with a rarebit crust (£11.50). A grilled rib-eye steak (£13.50) is served with well made Béarnaise sauce and chips. A duck pot pie with broad beans (£12) is wholly successful, the duck leg sticks up through the pastry crust and the gravy is very decent. The wine list is rather shaded by the array of cocktails but carries on manfully. Service is very crisp.

❋ Good breakfasts, superior brunches at the weekend.

Jaffna House

Sri Lankan £5–£12

90 Tooting High St, SW17 ☎020 8672 7786

Station Tooting Broadway **Open** Daily noon–midnight
Accepts Mastercard & Visa ⓦwww.jaffnahouse.co.uk

Jaffna House is a charming, simple, scruffy place. The food is Sri Lankan, very good, often very spicy and implausibly cheap. At the front there is a basic café and takeaway area, while at the back (the entrance is actually on Coverton Road), you'll find the dining room which is not that much smarter than the café. Service is friendly but there is one trap: in the smart bit there are two menus, one for starters and one for main courses – it is easy to get carried away and order your whole meal from the starters menu.

The starters are good even if there is an emphasis on frying (but thankfully the fried food is well done, dry and crisp). Vadai (65p) are small patties of mixed lentils, fried. Mutton rolls (70p) are delicious – filled pancakes, breadcumbed and deep fried. Vaaipan (65p) are hand grenade sized balls sweetened with mashed banana and fried. Fish cutlets (70p) are similarly shaped, subtly spiced fishcakes. Bridging the gap to the main courses are the "devilled" dishes – mutton (£3.25); beef (£3.25). These are strongly flavoured, dry curries and they are hot. Among the curry leaves and onions there are enough green chillies to make the lips sting. Then the menu romps on through hoppers (£1) to various kotthu (£3.50), which are made with chopped up rotis; a strange Sri Lankan speciality called pittu (a kind of rice flour stodge); dosas and a few curry house staples; plus a long list of tandoori specials. Best to stick with the Sri Lankan dishes and drink cold Lion beer – £3 for a 660ml bottle.

❋ "Toilets behind you" – helpful sign on the corridor wall.

Kastoori Indian/Vegetarian £12–£20

188 Upper Tooting Rd, SW17 ☎020 8767 7027
Station Tooting Broadway **Open** Mon & Tues 6–10.30pm, Wed–Sun 12.30–2.30pm & 6–10.30pm **Accepts** Mastercard & Visa

Anyone who is genuinely puzzled that people can cope on – and indeed enjoy – a diet of vegetables alone should try eating at Kastoori. Located in a rather unpromising-looking bit of town, Kastoori is a Gujarati "Pure Vegetarian Restaurant". The food they serve is leavened with East African influences, and the large and cavernous restaurant is run by the admirably helpful Thanki family – do be sure to ask their advice, and act on it.

First onto the waiter's pad (and indeed first into the mouth, as they go soggy and collapse if made to wait) must be dahi puri (£3.25) – tiny crispy flying saucers filled with a sweet-and-sour yoghurty sauce, potatoes, onions, chickpeas and so forth. You pop them in whole; the marriage of taste and texture is a revelation. Samosas (three for £1.95) are excellent, the onion bhajis (five for £2.75) are also a revelation – bite-sized and delicious, a far cry from the ball-of-knitting served in most High Street curry emporia. Then make sure that someone orders the vegetable curry of the day (£4.85), and others the outstanding cauliflower with cream curry (£4.95) and special tomato curry (£4.95) – a hot and spicy classic hailing from Katia Wahd. Leave room for the chilli banana (£5.25), bananas stuffed with mild chillies (an East African recipe), and mop everything up with generous helpings of puris and chapatis (both at £1.40 for two). The smart move is to ask what's in season, as the menu is littered with oddities that come and go. For example, there's a "beans curry" subtitled "Chef's Choice" (£4.95).

✳ "Thanki Europeenne (£6.25) – the Thanki family's European special."

Lahore Karahi

Indian £10–£22

1 Tooting High St, SW17 ☎ 020 8767 2477
Station Tooting Broadway **Open** Daily noon–midnight
Accepts Cash or cheque only ⓦ www.lahorekarahi.co.uk

Though the bright neon spilling onto the pavement beckons you from Tooting High Street, spiritually speaking, the Lahore Karahi is in the curry gulch of Upper Tooting Road. It's a busy place, and behind a counter equipped with numerous bains-marie stand rows of cooks, distinguishable by their natty Lahore Karahi baseball caps, turning out a daily twelve-hour marathon of dishes. Prices are low, food is chilli-hot and service is speedy. Don't be intimidated: just sit down (don't worry if you have to share a table) and start ordering. Regulars bring their own drinks or stick to the exotic fruit juices – mango, guava or passion – all at just £1.

Unusually for what is, at bottom, an unreconstructed grill house, there is a wide range of vegetarian dishes "prepared under strict precautions". Karahi karela (£2.95) is a curry of bitter gourds; karahi saag paneer (£3.50) teams spinach and cheese; and karahi methi aloo (£2.95) brings potatoes flavoured with fenugreek. Meat-eaters can plunge in joyfully – the chicken tikka (£2.25), seekh kabab (£1.20 for two) and tandoori chicken (£1.75) are all good and all spicy-hot, the only fault being a good deal of artificial red colouring. There are also a dozen chicken curries and a dozen lamb curries (from £4.25 to £4.50), along with a dozen specialities. Those with a strong constitution can try the dishes of the day, like nihari (£5.50), which is lamb shank on the bone in an incendiary broth, or paya (£4.95), which is sheep's feet cooked until gluey. Breads are good here: try the methi naan (£1.50) or the tandoori roti (60p).

✳ Great for takeaway. Try the biryanis.

Masaledar

Indian £8–£20

121 Upper Tooting Rd, SW17 ☎020 8767 7676
Station Tooting Bec/Tooting Broadway **Open** Daily noon–midnight
Accepts Mastercard & Visa

What can you say about a place that has two huge standard lamps, each made from an upturned, highly ornate Victorian drainpipe, topped with a large karahi? When it comes to interior design, Masaledar provides plenty of surprises, and a feeling of spaciousness. This establishment is run by East African Asian Muslims, so no alcohol is allowed on the premises, but that doesn't deter a loyal clientele, who are packing the place out. Along with several other restaurants in Upper Tooting Road, Maseladar has had to expand, and has added another 25 covers. The food is fresh, well spiced and cheap – there are vegetable curries at £3.25 and meat curries for under £5 – and, to cap it all, you eat it in an elegant designer dining room.

As starters, the samosas are sound – two meat (£1.95) or two vegetable (£1.95). Or try the chicken wings from the tandoor (£2.25), or the delicious lamb chops (four pieces £3.75). You might move on to a tasty, rich chicken or lamb biryani (£4.75), or try a classic dish like methi gosht (£4.75) – this is strongly flavoured and delicious, guaranteed to leave you with fenugreek seeping from your pores for days to come. Then there's the rich and satisfying lamb Masaledar (£4.95), which is disarmingly described as "our house dish cooked to tantalize your taste buds". The breads are terrific, especially the wonderful thin rotis (90p). Look out for the various deals that range from "All day lunch platter" to "birthdays, parties, conferences ... private parties of up to 120".

❋ "Fresh passion juice 300ml (£2.50)."

Further choices

Mirch Masala
Indian

213 Upper Tooting Rd, SW17
☎020 8672 7500

One of three Mirch restos selling karahi dishes and grilled meat. See review p.334.

Sakonis
Indian

180 Upper Tooting Rd, SW17
☎020 8772 4774

An outpost of North London veggie and juice giant. See review p.369.

Sree Krishna
Indian

192–194 Tooting High St, SW17
☎020 8672 4250

Tiny, old-established, South Indian restaurant. Some would say tatty, but a good cheap place for veggie dishes.

Tower Bridge

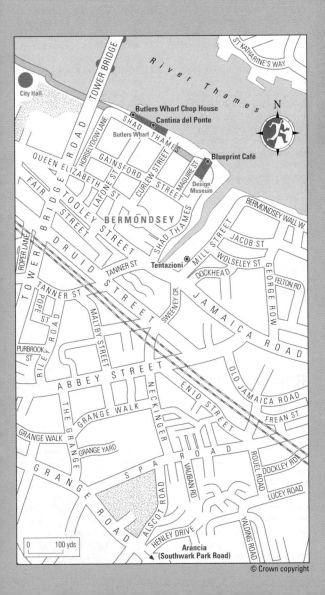

Arancia

52 Southwark Park Rd, SE16 ☎ 020 7394 1751

Station BR South Bermondsey **Open** Tues–Sat 12.30–2.30pm & 7–11pm
Accepts Mastercard & Visa

Gentrification has spread through this part of town; this is yet another area where house prices have climbed beyond reason. Arancia has to live with these changing times. Ten years ago this patch was all pie and mash and car chases, but now, sensible and authentic Italian food is quite acceptable. The proprietors of Arancia are to be congratulated on keeping the food cheap enough to attract the long-term residents, while at the same time good enough to ensnare newcomers.

Starters might include zuppa di spinaci (£3.50), a spinach and mint soup served with bruschetta. Or you might find insalata di baccalà (£4.50), a salad of salt cod and roast peppers. Or tortino di polenta e cipolla (£4.50), a winning combination of polenta cake and caramelized onions. For main course there may be trota al forno (£9) – baked trout spiked with Strega. You can also bank on dishes such as pollo al Marsala (£9.50), boned stuffed roast chicken; salsiccie e fagioli (£9.50), Italian sausages served with cannellini beans; or stufato al frutti di mare (£9.50), a mixed seafood stew with everything in it from mussels to monkfish by way of squid, scallops and cuttlefish. For vegetarians there may be torta al basilico e olive (£9) – a tart made with ricotta basil and olives and served with spinach. The puddings are adventurous: perhaps a rather good chocolate semifreddo (£3.30); or pear and almond tart (£3.50). The pursuit of bargain prices is also the theme of the all-Italian wine list. They are certainly inexpensive wines, and they are all just about drinkable.

✱ Arancia also offers an outside catering service.

Blueprint Café

Design Museum, Shad Thames, SE1 ♿ ☎ 020 7378 7031

Station Tower Hill **Open** Mon–Sat noon–3pm & 6–11pm, Sun noon–3pm
Accepts All major credit cards ⊛ www.conran.co.uk

The Blueprint Café is one of those restaurants that has been quietly going about its business for so long – fifteen years in fact – that it has merged imperceptibly into the background. If the Blueprint had opened in the last month or so it would be attracting rave reviews and people would be mobbing the place. Consider just two points: there's a set dinner (Mon–Thurs & Sat 6–7pm, Fri 6–11pm), £17 for two courses, £21 for three; and there's a second wine list offering twenty wines at under £20. The dining room is modern but unthreatening, and occupies a glass fronted box jutting out towards the river – the views of Tower Bridge are amazing. The food is very good indeed.

The menu changes every day and is market driven. How about nettle and celery soup (£5.50)? Or beetroot, soft-boiled egg and horseradish (£6.50)? Or there might be preserved garlic, tapenade and goat's cheese (£7) – light and lemony goat's cheese on toast, with coarsely chopped olive tapenade, and a whole head of garlic softened and sweetened by slow cooking. Or maybe smoked eel with Jersey Royals and mint (£7.50) appeals? The mains carry on the theme with fresh seasonal dishes: halibut with parsley and anchovy sauce (£18); a tart made with Durrus cheese, potatoes and rosemary (£12.50); beef and parsley pie (£13) – slow-cooked beef in gravy rich with parsley. What a good pie! Poached turbot with morels (£19) successfully teams a huge chunk of plain steamed fish with a cream sauce. Puds range from almond tart (£6.50) to crème brûlée (£6) by way of a very rich choco-laden gateaux, the St Emilion (£7).

✳ The blue binoculars on each table are stolen by the hundred.

Butlers Wharf Chop House

British £15–£60

36e Shad Thames, SE1 ☎ 020 7403 3403

Station Tower Hill/London Bridge **Open** Mon–Sat noon–3pm & 6–11pm, Sun noon–3pm

Accepts All major credit cards ⓦ www.conran.com

Butlers Wharf Chop House – another Conran creation – really deserves everyone's support. For this is a restaurant that makes a genuine attempt to showcase the best of British produce. There's superb British meat, splendid fish, and simply epic British and Irish cheeses. What's more, the Chop House

wisely caters for all, whether you want a simple dish at the bar, a well priced set lunch or an extravagant dinner. The dining room is spacious and bright, and the view of Tower Bridge a delight, especially from a terrace table on a warm summer's evening.

Lunch in the restaurant is priced at £19.75 for two courses and £23.75 for three. The menu changes regularly but tends to feature starters such as potted duck, brandied prunes and toast, or Loch Fyne smoked salmon. Mains will include dishes like fish and chips, and steak and kidney pudding as well as the house specialities such as a flawless roast rib of beef with Yorkshire pudding and gravy. After that you just might be able to find room for a pud like rhubarb crumble tart with vanilla ice cream, even if the sticky toffee pudding is a dish too far. Dinner follows the same principles but is priced à la carte. Thus, there may be starters such as cock a leekie soup (£6.50), and half a lobster mayonnaise (£16.50). Mains might include steak, kidney and oyster pudding (£16); charcoal-grilled veal with butter beans (£17); or halibut with mussel and saffron broth (£17.50). There's also steak and chips, priced by size – from £22 for a 10oz sirloin to £26 for a 12oz fillet.

✱ There's a decent weekend brunch – two courses £13.95, three for £16.95.

Cantina del Ponte   Italian £12–£35

Butlers Wharf, Shad Thames, SE1 ☎020 7403 5403
Station Tower Hill/London Bridge **Open** Mon–Sat noon–3pm & 6–11pm, Sun noon–3pm & 6–10pm **Accepts** All major credit cards ✇www.conran.com

Jostling for attention with the Pont de la Tour, the Cantina del Ponte (its considerably pricier Conran sibling), does not try to keep up, but instead offers a different package. Here you are

greeted with the best earthy Italian fare, presented in smart Conran style. The floors are warm terracotta, the food is strong on flavour and colour, the service is refined, and the views are superior London dockside. Book ahead and bag a table by the window or, better still, brave the elements in summer and sit under the canopy watching the boats go by.

The seasonal menu is a meander through all things good, Italian-style, with a tempting array of first courses, and mains that include pizza, pasta and risotto, not to mention side orders, puddings and cheeses. Simple, classic combos like Mozzarella with aubergines (£5.95) always appeal. Or there's grilled squid with chilli and rocket (£6.95). Veggie dishes such as gnocchi with cherry tomatoes and basil (£5.50 or £10.25) are good, or how about a classic like risotto primavera (£5.50 or £10.25)? Pizzas feature all the old favourites, like quattro formaggi (£7.15), Margherita (£6.25) and Napoletana (£6.75). Main courses range from sea bass with rosemary (£13.95); through lamb steak with courgettes (£13.95); to scallops with pancetta and broad beans (£15.50). Puds veer from tiramisù (£4.95), through torta di cioccolata and noci (£4.50), to panna cotta with rhubarb (£5.25). There are competitive set menus (lunch and pre-theatre), priced at £11 for two courses and £13.50 for three.

✳ Great takeaway pizzas.

Tentazioni

Italian £10–£55

2 Mill St, SE1 ☎ 020 7237 1100

Station Bermondsey/Tower Hill **Open** Mon & Sat 7–10.45pm, Tues–Fri noon–2.30pm & 7–10.45pm **Accepts** All major credit cards ⊛ www.tentazioni.co.uk

This small, busy and rather good Italian restaurant has crept up behind Sir Terence Conran's Thameside flotilla of eateries and is giving them a terrific run for their money. The food is simple, high-quality peasant Italian, with strong, rich flavours. The pasta dishes are good here, as are the stews, and the wine list is interesting. This place has a flexible attitude – most of the starters can be turned into main courses, and the menu changes to reflect the seasons and the markets.

You may find choices such as the ravioli (£8 or £12) – filled with pumpkin and amaretti, and served with butter and sage; or green pappardellle with rabbit and olives (£8 or £12); fresh gratinated mussels on a spicy sauce with garlic crostini (£8); or a simple-sounding dish such as minestrone di verdura con riso (£7). Main courses offer hammer blows of flavour: fillet of lemon sole with mustard grains, porcini mushrooms and smoked oysters (£17); venison stew with juniper, cabbage and bacon (£18); honey-glazed duck breast, green tea lasagna with foie gras and spring onions (£19). Or maybe steer toward a risotto made with beetroot and Prosecco (£12). For pudding it is hard to better the sformatino di ricotta con salsa al caffè (£7), a delicious Ricotta pudding with coffee sauce, although the "chocolate ecstasy" (£7) has many fans. Italian cheeses are also featured – pan-fried Ovinford cheese comes with Abbamele Sardo and Sardinian carrassau bread (£7). There is an interesting wine list that caters to most pockets … especially deep ones!

✳ There's a tempting "Degustazione" five courses for £36.

Victoria

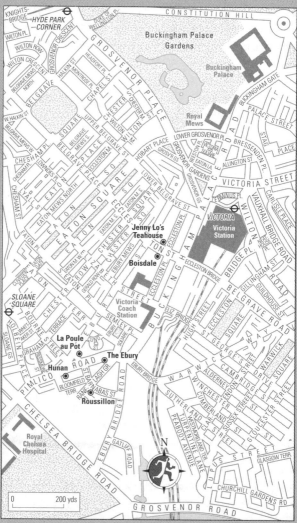

© Crown copyright

Boisdale

15 Eccleston St, SW1 ☎ 020 7730 6922

Station Victoria **Open** Mon–Fri noon–1am, Sat 7pm–1am
Accepts All major credit cards ⓦ www.boisdale.co.uk

Boisdale is owned by Ranald Macdonald, who is next in line to be the Chief of Clanranald, and if that information gives you a premonition of what the restaurant is like you are probably thinking along the right lines. This is a very Scottish place, strong on hospitality, and with a befuddlingly large range of rare malt whiskies. Fresh produce – correction, fresh Scottish produce – rules wherever possible, and it is no wonder that the clubby atmosphere and reliable cooking makes this a haven of choice for local businessmen, who are also likely to be found in the ultra-Scottish back bar, home to the formidable malt whisky collection.

There are various Boisdale menus, one is a two-course menu with choice of five starters and five mains for £17.45 (yes, just like the rebellion!). Starters range from marinated Orkney herring and mini roast Macsween haggis to dill-marinated Scottish salmon. Main courses veer from crofter's pie, to smoked haddock fishcakes, to – you've guessed it – roast Macsween haggis. The à la carte includes a good many luxury ingredients. As well as Lochcarnan smoked salmon from South Uist (£9.90), and Rannoch Moor smoked venison with black truffle dressing (£9.90), there's a rabbit, pigeon and foie gras terrine with pear chutney (£8.50).

Commendably, the mains feature fresh fish of the day, and fresh offal of the day. There are various Aberdeen Angus beef steaks: fillet with Béarnaise sauce and chips (£21), or rib-eye with black truffle, pommes Dauphinoise, spinach and wild mushrooms (£21.50).

✳ Try the "Flying Scotsman" – a two course lunch for £14.

VICTORIA

The Ebury

Modern European £30–£70

11 Pimlico Rd, W1 ♿ ☎ 020 7730 6784

Station Sloane Square/Victoria **Open** Mon–Sat noon–3pm & 6.30–10.30pm
Accepts All major credit cards except Diners ⓦ www.theebury.co.uk

VICTORIA

Downstairs the Ebury is a busy bar which, although it calls itself a Brasserie, serves bistro food and has a crustacea bar. It has come a long way since it was a Pimlico pub, but not quite as far as the upstairs restaurant which is now a very slick affair indeed, and is Chelsea to its roots. The room is elegant, chandeliers have been sighted, the standard of cooking is good here, and the service lives up to its "sharp restaurant" status. The menu changes regularly and is commendably seasonal while also being inventive.

The deal is a straightforward one: two courses cost £25 and three £29.50; things are posh enough here to make you grateful that you know just what you are in for – even though the wine list has enough fire power to blow your wallet away. Starters may include a warm salad of smoked eel, chorizo and planchada beans; ceviche of scallops and salmon with daikon and shiso cress; grilled quail with salad gourmande, mustard and red wine; or a brave dish like duck hearts with Brillat Savarin cheese, wild mushrooms, parsley and garlic butter. Mains also major in carefully chosen goodies – grilled loin of pata negra pork with pig cheeks and sweet-potato purée; grilled Gilthead bream with piperade and fennel gratin; a Pithivier of ceps and celeriac with baby squash and cep cream; or roast halibut with buttered noodles and steamed mussels. Puds range from the familiar: crème brûlée; baked apple with Calvados and cinnamon ice cream; and hot chocolate pudding; to a citrus fruit terrine with yoghurt sorbet.

✳ The selection of cheeses attracts a £3.50 supplement, but it's worth it.

Hunan

Chinese £32–£60

51 Pimlico Rd, SW1 ☎ 020 7730 5712

Station Sloane Square/Victoria **Open** Mon–Sat noon–2.30pm & 6–11.30pm
Accepts All major credit cards

The Hunan is the domain of Mr Peng. As you venture into his restaurant you put yourself into his hands, to do with you what he will. It is rather like being trapped in a 1930s B-movie. You order the boiled dumplings … and the griddle-fried lettuce-wrapped dumplings turn up, "because you will like them more". And most likely you will. Probably ninety percent of Mr Peng's regular customers have given up the unequal struggle, submitting themselves to the "feast" – a multi-course extravaganza, varied according to the maestro's whims and the vagaries of the market, that might include pigeon soup. Or goose. Or a dish of cold, marinated octopus. This fine food and attentive service is matched by the Hunan's elegant surroundings, but be warned – the prices are Pimlico rather than Chinatown, and they continue to escalate.

If you want to defy Mr Peng and act knowledgeable, there is an à la carte at lunchtime. Standouts include hot and spicy beef (£7), sizzling prawns (£8), braised scallops in Hunan sauce (£8) and spicy braised eggplant (£6). However, for all but the strongest wills, resistance is useless and you'll probably end up with what is described on the menu as "Hunan's special leave-it-to-us-feast – minimum two persons, from £30.80 a head. We recommend those not familiar with Hunan cuisine and those who are looking for a wide selection of our favourite and unusual dishes to leave it to the chef Mr Peng to prepare for you his special banquet and allow him to change it as his whim dictates. Many of the dishes are not on the menu."

✳ Even Alexis Gauthier, Roussillon's Michelin-starred head chef (see p.359), leaves it to Mr P.

VICTORIA

Jenny Lo's Teahouse

Chinese/Teahouse £7–£22

14 Ecclestone St, SW1 ☎ 020 7259 0399
Station Victoria **Open** Mon–Fri 11.30am–3pm & 6–10pm, Sat noon–3pm & 6–10pm
Accepts Cash or cheque only

Jenny Lo's Teahouse is the complete opposite of trad, over-designed, Chinese restaurants. This place is bright, bare and stylishly utilitarian. From the blocks of bright colours and refectory tables, this is a somewhat smart, but comfortable, place to eat. And that just about sums up the food too. Service makes you think that you're in the politest cafeteria in the world and the prices don't spoil the illusion. Although portion sizes and seasoning can vary, the food is freshly cooked and generally delicious, which meets with unqualified approval from a loyal band of sophisticated regulars.

The menu is divided into three main sections: soup noodles, wok noodles and rice dishes. Take your pick and then add some side dishes. The chilli beef soup (£7.50) is a good choice: a large bowl full of delicate, clear, chilli-spiked broth is bulked out with yards of slippery ho fun (ribbon noodles like thin tagliatelle), plus slivers of beef and fresh coriander. The black-bean seafood noodles (£6.95) are an altogether richer and more solid affair, made from egg noodles with prawn, mussels, squid and peppers. Rice dishes range from long-cooked pork and chestnuts (£6.50), to gong bao chicken with pine nuts (£6.95). The side dishes are great fun, with good spareribs (£3.75) and guo tie (£4.50), which are pan-cooked dumplings filled with either vegetables or pork. Spring onion pancakes (£3) are a Beijing street food made from flat, griddled breads laced with spring onions and served with a dipping sauce.

✳ Try Dr Xu's cleansing tea (£1.85): "a light tea for strengthening the liver and kidneys".

La Poule au Pot

Very French £20–£55

221 Ebury St, SW1 ☎ 020 7730 7763

Station Sloane Square/Victoria **Open** Mon–Sat 12.30–2.30pm & 6.45–11pm, Sun 12.30–3.30pm & 6.45–10pm **Accepts** All major credit cards

You are in trouble at La Poule au Pot if you don't understand at least some French. It is unreservedly a bastion of France in England, and has been for more than three decades. What's more, several of the staff have worked here for most of that time, and the restaurant itself has hardly changed at all, with its huge dried-flower baskets and a comfortable rustic atmosphere. The wide windows brighten lunch and there are tables outside under parasols, but by night, candlelight ensures that La Poule is a favourite for romantic assignations. Many a Chelsea affair has started here, fuelled by the decidedly basic house wine.

A small dish of crudités in herb vinaigrette is set down as a bonne bouche. Different fresh breads come in huge chunks. The menu is deceptive, as there are usually more additional fresh daily specials than are listed. As a starter, the nine escargots (£8) deliver classic French authenticity with plenty of garlic and herbs. The soupe de poisson (£8.75) is not the commonly served thick soup, but a refined clear broth with chunks of sole and scallop, plus prawns and mussels. A main course of bifteck frites (£14.50) brings a perfectly cooked, French-cut steak with red-hot chips. The gigot aux flageolets (£14.50) is pink and tender, with beans that are well flavoured and not overcooked. There's calf's liver (£13.75), and carré d'agneau à l'ail (£17) – rack of lamb with garlic. The pudding menu features standards such as crème brûlée (£4.50) – huge, served in a rustic dish, and classically good. The wine list is unadventurous.

✳ Good prix-fixe lunch (£15.50 for two courses, £17.50 for three).

Roussillon

French £40–£100

16 St Barnabas St, SW1 ☎020 7730 5550

Station Sloane Square/Victoria **Open** Mon & Tues 6.30–10.45pm, Wed–Fri noon–2.30pm & 6.30–10.45pm, Sat 6.30–10.45pm

Accepts All major credit cards except Diners ⓦwww.roussillon.co.uk

Despite a dining room that has always looked rather stuffy, Roussillon has built up a decent reputation and gathered a shelf-full of awards. The mainspring is a young French chef called Alexis Gauthier, who is obsessed with the quality and freshness of his ingredients. To see the advantages of being season- and market-driven, try the set lunch, £30 for three courses and coffee. The main menu runs in at three courses for £45, so you will probably feel the urge to splash out on one or other of the nine-course showing-off menus – the vegetarian "Garden Menu" and the "Seasonal Menu" are both £60. Service is formal and slick.

The menu has various sections to it: the classics, the garden, the land, the sea and river – and changes with the seasons. Open with a terrine of duck foie gras with conference pear. Into "the garden": thin cream of broad beans and radish leaves, royale of chicken liver; or autumn vegetables and fruits cooked together in a pot with aged balsamic. Fish dishes may include roast Dublin Bay prawns, salad of purple artichoke and lemon pepper; or grilled halibut, steamed clams, young carrots, garlic leaves. "The land" brings pan-fried lightly battered sweetbreads, sautéed ceps and creamed flat parsley; or Gloucester Old Spot pork prepared in two ways – tenderly braised and pink-roasted, with pommes boulangère. This is gastronomic stuff. Onwards to cheese, fruit and chocolate. You have to warm to anyone so keen on chocolate puddings. There's white and black chocolate pyramide; chocolate praline finger; and a chocolate soufflé.

VICTORIA

✳ Vegetarians can dine particularly well here.

Further choices

The Goring Hotel
British

15 Beeston Place, Grosvenor Gardens, SW1
☎020 7396 9000

Splendid, old-school, pricey defender of traditional cooking and traditional values. Jackets and ties please!

Seafresh Fish Restaurant
Fish & Chips

80–81 Wilton Rd, SW1

Pukka fish and chip shop selling proper fish and chips. Always try and have your fish cooked to order.

Waterloo &
South Bank

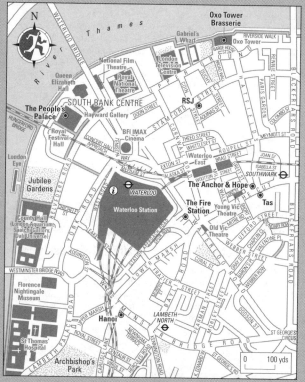

Anchor & Hope   British/Gastropub £25–£45

36 The Cut, SE1 ☎020 7928 9898

Station Southwark/Waterloo **Open** Mon 6–10.30pm, Tues–Sat noon–2.30pm & 6–10.30pm
Accepts Mastercard & Visa

Wherever you may be eating, there is one marker that signals really excellent food. You might spot it in the way the menu is written; in the presentation of the dishes; or in the way things taste…but the key quality is confidence. The kitchen at the Anchor & Hope have confidence aplenty. This gastropub opened late in 2003 and it has already won a shed load of awards – for once they are deserved. It's a rough looking dining area; there is no booking (which may mean queuing unless you are ready and waiting when the doors open); but the pricing is fair and the cooking is very confident indeed.

The menu changes twice a day, but the starters may include: smoked sprats with horseradish (£4.80); or crab on toast (£6.80) – how understated is that? Leeks gribiche (£5); a warm snail and pig's head salad (£6.40); or Spanish ham and green tomatoes on toast (£7.80). Among the mains are the economically named tripe and chips (£10.80); roast pigeon and semolina gnocchi (£11.80); scallops

escarole and morels (£16); and slow-cooked Middle White pork with choucroute (£14). Then there are a few dishes that are for sharing such as a slow-cooked stuffed duck (for three or four, £48). The cooking is inspired and owes a good deal to the time one of the chef proprietors spent at St John (see p.108). The wine list is ungraspingly priced and service, which can get ruffled, is in tune with the surroundings. Puds are pukka – chocolate pot (£4.80); pear and almond tart (£5); or a lemon and almond cake with blood oranges (£4.80). The Anchor & Hope is strongly recommended.

✳ Lancashire hotpot – for six (£72).

The Fire Station   Modern British £18–£35

150 Waterloo Rd, SE1 ♿ ☎020 7620 2226
Station Waterloo **Open** Mon–Fri noon–2.45pm & 5.30–11pm, Sat noon–10.45pm, Sun noon–9.30pm–3pm **Accepts** All major credit cards

When you arrive at The Fire Station it's hard to imagine that the food will be of much

distinction. This is a big barn of a place with pumping music, and to get to the restaurant at the back you have to fight your way through noisy waves of colourful-drink-swillers. Decoration is scant, consisting mostly of red and cream paint, and blackboards painted with popping champagne corks. At first glance, it looks exactly like a theme hamburger bar. But if you look a little closer you'll see an open-plan kitchen preparing good-looking food, and a lot of happy diners. It's worth persevering.

The menu changes daily but there are some simple things that often feature, including starters such as pan-fried squid, coriander and lime (£6.50); smooth liver terrine (£5.75); or crab, salmon and potato cake (£6.50). Equally appealing are mains such as roast spiced pork belly with sticky rice, pak choi and soy sauce (£10.95); and tandoori-seared yellow-fin tuna loin (£12.50). Or how about parsley-crusted calf's liver (£12.50)? Or the Fire Station bouillabaisse (£15.50), a large casserole containing a rather unauthentic mix of prawns, calamari, crab, mussels and salmon? The cooking is sound enough, and the service is friendly. Thankfully, puddings are simple: four huge scoops of caramel ice cream with butterscotch sauce (£3.95). To wash it all down, there's a decent wine list with five reds and whites by the glass, as well as a 50cl carafe (£7.95 for the house white, £9.80 for Rioja).

✳ Set menu (up to 7pm): two courses £10.95 and three £13.50.

Hanoi

Vietnamese £15–£35

139 Westminster Bridge Rd, SE1 ☎ 020 7207 9747

Station Waterloo/Lambeth North **Open** Mon–Fri noon–3pm & 5.30–11.30pm, Sat & Sun 5.30–11.30pm **Accepts** All major credit cards

This is still the Long family's restaurant. Until 2004 it was called Little Saigon, but now it has been re-named Hanoi. It still sells good, homely Vietnamese food from a comprehensive menu. You will eat best by sticking to the pukka dishes, and should take this opportunity to get to grips with Vietnamese spring rolls – both the crispy deep-fried kind and the "crystal" variety. The latter are round discs of rice pastry like giant, translucent Communion wafers, which you soak in a bowl of hot water until pliable, and then roll around a filling of fresh salady things, interesting sauces, and slivers of meat grilled on a portable barbecue.

Run amok with the starters. Vietnamese imperial spring rolls (£3) are of the crispy fried variety, but they are served cut into chunks and with lettuce leaves to roll them up in. Topping the bill are crystal spring rolls (£3) – delicate pancakes, (in this case "pre-rolled") which are quite delicious. Also good is the strangely resilient Vietnamese fish cake (£3.60). Each of the starters seems to come with its own special dipping sauce, and the table is soon littered with an array of little saucers – look out for the extra-sweet white plum sauce and the extra-hot brown chilli oil. For mains, Hanoi grilled chicken with honey (£5.50); stir-fried monkfish with lemon grass and chillies (£7); special Saigon prawn curry (£6.80), and the house special, fried crispy noodles (£6), which comes with chicken and shrimps, can all be recommended.

✳ Hot and sour salmon soup (£3.50).

The People's Palace

Modern British £16–£45

Level Three, Royal Festival Hall, South Bank, SE1 ♿ ☎ 020 7928 9999
Station Waterloo **Open** Mon–Sat noon–2.30pm & 5–11pm, Sun noon–3pm & 5.30–8pm **Accepts** All major credit cards ⓦ www.peoplespalace.co.uk

The Festival Hall is a very large place and finding the People's Palace can prove tricky. Many diners seated in front of the splendid river view are either pre- or post-concert, and that makes timing crucial. The food is well presented and accurately cooked. There are occasional flashes of innovation but the menu is mainly composed of well balanced, satisfying dishes at reasonable prices. Add the sound service, a child-friendly policy (they're nice to kids, and provide highchairs and children's menus), and it all adds up to an attractive package.

The bargains at The People's Palace are its fixed-price menus. Daily lunch menus are £14 for two courses, £19 for three, while the pre-theatre menu is £17 for two courses, £23 for three. On the à la carte you'll find starters such as mussel soup with Gruyere crisp (£7.50); warm Stilton and red-onion tart with frisee and chives (£6.50); frogs legs, garlic mousse, parsley butter (£8); smoked eel, treacle-cured bacon, fried egg and horseradish (£9); and venison carpaccio with roast apple (£8.90). Mains may include roast salmon with butter beans (£14.50); coq au vin with parsnip mash (£14.50); lamb rump, pumpkin mash, tomato fondue, mint pesto (£16.75); lemon sole fillet with crevettes and clams (£18); or on a heavier note, braised ox cheek bourguignon (£18). Puddings

(£5.95) ring the sweet-tooth bell: fig and ginger pudding with cinnamon custard; or banana and pecan pudding with clotted cream and toffee sauce. Wines are available by the glass with recommendations beside each dish.

✳ Figure the Festival Hall concert programme into your plans.

RSJ

Modern European £19–£55

13a Coin St, SE1 ☏ 020 7928 4554

Station Waterloo **Open** Mon–Fri noon–2.30pm & 5.30–11pm, Sat 5.30–11pm
Accepts All major credit cards ⓦ www.rsj.uk.com

Rolled Steel Joist may seem a curious name for a restaurant, but it is appropriate – they can point out the RSJ holding up the first floor if you wish! What's more interesting about RSJ is that it's owned by a man with a passion for the wines of the Loire. Nigel Wilkinson has compiled his list mainly from wines produced in this region, and it features dozens of lesser-known Loire reds and whites – wines which clearly deserve a wider following. Notes about recent vintages both interest and educate, and each wine is well described.

The menu is based on classical dishes, but with a light touch and some innovative combinations as well. The starters might include purple sprouting broccoli and garlic leaf risotto (£5.25); smoked haddock soup with baby spinach and crème fraîche (£5.25); or terrine of free-range chicken and foie gras (£8.95). Moving on to the main courses, typical choices might include roast cod fillet with a casserole of spicy butter beans (£12.95); fillet of beef, black pepper and chive butter, braised potatoes (£16.95); and breast of guinea fowl, Jersey royal potatoes, spring greens, shallot and carrots (£12.95). The menu also features an above-average number of vegetarian options, such as fresh sage gnocchi with a blue cheese sauce, new season peas and broad beans (£10.95). The puddings can be serious stuff: white chocolate and passion fruit mousse (£5.50); or pear and pistachio tart with camomile ice cream (£5.25). At £17.95 for three courses the set meal represents jolly good value.

✳ Use the website to check out the RSJ Wine Company.

Tas

Turkish £9–£38

33 The Cut, SE1 ☎020 7928 1444
Station Waterloo **Open** Mon–Sat noon–11.30pm, Sun noon–10.30pm
Accepts All major credit cards except Diners Ⓦ www.tasrestaurant.com

Tas is a bright and bustling Turkish restaurant where eating is cheap. The various menus and set menus offer a baffling choice and there is often live music. No wonder the place is heaving with office parties and stag or hen nights. Expect colourful crockery and an overdose of noise and liveliness. Consider the set menus as a simple way through the maze. Sahan menu (£7.95 per person) includes starter and main; renk menu (£9.95) is a mixed mezze.

The menu rushes off in a great many directions at once. There are four soups, a dozen cold starters, a dozen hot starters, eight salads, a dozen vegetarian dishes, plus casseroles, fish, and grilled meats aplenty. Take a breath and then treat Tas like a simple Turkish eatery. Start with some meze. There's tarama salata (£2.95); calamari (£3.95); hummus (£3.35); cacik (£3.35), a simple cucumber and yogurt dip; hellim (£3.95), which is grilled cheese – in fact all the usual suspects. Then go on to some grilled meats: tavuk shish (£7.85) is chicken kebab; kofte (£7.85) is a minced lamb kebab. Or there are the casseroles. Hunkar begendi (£8.85) is aubergine topped with lamb;

and incik (£9.25) is lamb cooked on the bone. One element of the menu which makes Tas stand out from most Turkish eateries is the long list of fish and shellfish dishes. As

well as kalamari (£8.25), there is balik bugiulama (£9.95) which is steamed cod, and pirasali mercan (£14.45) which is pan-fried Dorade. Baklava (£3.45) is all very well but it is probably outsold by chocolate cake (£3.55).

✳ £18.50 buys you the "Aslan" menu – for the lion-sized appetite?

Wembley

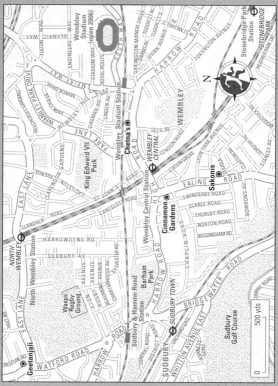

© Crown copyright

Chetna's

420 High Rd, Wembley ☎ 020 8900 1466

Station Wembley Central **Open** Tues & Wed 12.30–3pm & 6.30–10.30pm,
Thurs & Fri noon–3pm & 6.30–10.30pm, Sat & Sun 1–10.30pm
Accepts Mastercard & Visa ⓦ www.chetnasweetmart.co.uk

Chetna's is a remarkable Indian restaurant – busy enough to need a queuing system. You register your interest at the counter and are given a cloakroom ticket, and when your table is ready your number is called. The restaurant has smart wooden tables and chairs, ceiling fans and some seriously ornate brass chandeliers, but despite these trappings it is still awesomely cheap. The food is very good indeed and the menu is a bit of a surprise, opening with a section headed "seaside savouries" – presumably in homage to Chowpatty Beach.

Start with a truly amazing mouthful: Chetna's masala golgapa (£2.60). These are small, crisp golgapas filled with potatoes, onions, moong, chana, green chutney and sweet-and-sour chutney, and topped with sev. You load them into your mouth and, as you chew, different tastes and textures take over. It's an astonishing sensation. Order more portions than you think you'll need. Also try the kachori (£2.40): a crisp coat encases a well-spiced ball of green peas. Or there's alu tikki (£2.60) – spicy mash with chickpeas deep-fried. Or there's a dry potato curry (£2.80) – simple and good. The most visually striking dish must be the paper dosa (£4), a giant chewy cone of nutty-tasting pancake with a vegetable sambhar and coconut chutney for dipping. The award for most comprehensive dish must go to the Delhi Darbar thali (£7.80), which is served with one sweet, one farsan, three vegetables, chutney, vegetable biryani, dhal, raita, papadum and paratha. The minimum charge here of £3.50 is presumably to stop whole families sharing one.

✱ There's now a brisk takeaway trade in sweets at the counter.

Cinnamon Gardens

42–44 Ealing Rd, Wembley ☎ 020 8902 0660

Station Wembley Central **Open** Daily noon–midnight **Accepts** Cash or cheque only

Cinnamon Gardens is a bright and modern restaurant at the Wembley end of Ealing Road. The dining room is all minty green and apricot with a tiled floor and some ostentatiously modern chairs, which thankfully prove comfortable. The walls are also home to a virulent series of murals. This is a Sri Lankan restaurant, and things proceed at a Sri Lankan pace. Don't worry – simply relax and assess the relative merits of Lion lager and Lion stout; soon you will be in just the right mood.

Starters include most of the Sri Lankan favourites. There are mutton rolls (two for £1.75), crab claws (£2.75) and chicken 65 (£5.25). There is also a section on the menu devoted to "fried specials", any of which make a great starter when teamed with some bread – try fried lamb (£4.95) or fried squid (£5.25). Another section features devilled dishes, ranging all the way from a devilled potato (£3.95) to devilled king prawn (£6.95). There's a whole host of hoppers, or rice pancakes, including egg (£2.50 for two) and jaggery (£2.50 for two) – the latter rich with unrefined sugar. The Cinnamon special biryani (£5.95) is stunning: dark and richly flavoured, it comes with a bit of everything, including a lamb chop and a hard-boiled egg! It is also worth noting that the rotis (£1) are very good here, light and flaky, as are the sambols. The seeni sambol (£1.25) is a relatively mild, sweet onion jam, while the katta sambol (£1.75) is an incredibly wild chilli concoction. The service is friendly if a little dozy.

✳ Try the Portello (£1.50), a lurid-purple soft drink with an almost radioactive glow.

Geetanjali   Indian £12–£32

16 Court Parade, Watford Rd, ☎ 020 8904 5353
Station Wembley Central **Open** Daily noon–3pm & 6–11.30pm
Accepts All major credit cards

There are a good many Indian restaurants in Wembley, and it would be easy to write off Geetanjali as just one more of the same. On the face of it, sure, the menu is pretty straightforward, with a good many old, tired dishes lined up in their usual serried ranks – chicken tikka masala, rogan josh and so on and so forth. But Geetanjali has a secret weapon, a dish that brings customers from far and wide. Word on the street is that this place serves the best tandoori lamb chops in North London.

This chop lover's haven has a large, roomy dining room, and the service is attentive, if a little resigned when you pitch up and order a raft of beers and a few portions of chops – or, as the menu would have it, lamb chopp (£4.20). Of course, the chops are good. Very good. Thick-cut, exceedingly tender and very nicely spiced. Accompany them with a luccha paratha (£2.50), warm and flaky and presented in the shape of a flower with a knob of butter melting into its heart. The alternative is the intriguingly named bullet nan (£2.50), which promises to be hot and spicy, and delivers in good measure. Even if you're not a complete chopaholic, you can also do well here. Go for starters such as the good chicken tikka (£4.20) – made with chicken breast. Rashmi kebab (£3.90) is also good, made from minced chicken and spices. Main courses include mathi chicken (£6.90), which is chicken with fenugreek; and lamb badam pasanda (£6.90). And should this emphasis on meat leave you craving some of the green stuff, there's sag aloo (£4.20) or karahi corn masala (£4.50).

✳ Best tandoori chops in North London.

Sakonis

127–129 Ealing Rd, Alperton ☎ 020 8903 1058

Station Alperton **Open** Mon–Thurs & Sun 11am–11pm, Fri & Sat 11am–midnight
Accepts Mastercard & Visa

WEMBLEY

Sakonis is a topnotch vegetarian food factory. Crowded with Asian families, it is overseen by waiters and staff in baseball caps, and there's even a holding pen where you can check out the latest videos and sounds while waiting your turn. From a decor point of view, the dining area is somewhat clinical: a huge square yardage of white tiling, but the Indian vegetarian food here is terrific. It's old hat to many of the Asian customers who dive straight into the "Chinese" dishes. These tend to be old favourites such as chow mein (£5.95) and haka noodles (£4.25), cooked with the Indian spicing. Unless curiosity overwhelms you, stick to the splendid South Indian dishes.

Sakonis is renowned for its dosas. These are pancakes, so crisp that they are almost chewy, and delightfully nutty. They come with two small bowls of sauce and a filling of rich, fried potato spiced with curry leaves. Choose from plain dosa (£3.50), masala dosa (£4.50), and chutney dosa (£4.60) – which has spices and chilli swirled into the dosa batter. Try the farari cutlets (£3.50), not cutlets at all, in fact, but very nice, well flavoured dollops of sweet-potato mash, deep-fried so that they have a crisp exterior. Also worth trying are the bhel puri (£3.30), the pani puri (£2.50) and the sev puri (£3.30) – amazingly crisp little taste bombs. Pop them in whole and the flavour explodes in your mouth. Some say that the juices at Sakoni's are the best in London, and while that may be hyperbole they certainly are very good indeed. Try madaf (£2.50), made from fresh coconut.

 At the weekend there's a breakfast buffet between 8–11am.

Further choices

Maru's Bhajia House
Indian/Vegetarian

230 Ealing Rd, Alperton, Wembley
☎ 020 8903 6771

Astonishingly cheap bhajia house. Lumps of veggie stuff brought to life by adept deep frying. Tamarind sauce.

Palm Beach
Sri Lankan

17 Ealing Rd, Wembley
☎ 020 8900 8664

A reliable old-established resto. Dosas, vadas, plus some good curries. Rather scruffy, not expensive.

Westminster

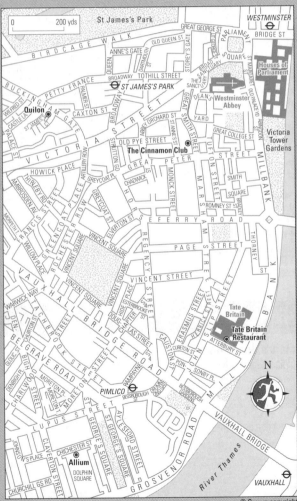

© Crown copyright

Allium

French £20–£100

Dolphin Square, Chichester St, SW1 ☎020 7798 6888

Station Pimlico **Open** Tues–Fri noon–3pm & 6–10.30pm, Sat 6–10.30pm, Sun noon–2.30pm **Accepts** All major credit cards Ⓦ www.allium.co.uk

Allium is a very sophisticated restaurant; it has a somewhat mannered style, but the cooking is first rate. The chef-proprietor is Anton Edelmann who spent several decades heading the Savoy kitchens during that establishment's glory years. At Allium he is following the same star – carefully sourced, top-quality ingredients cooked carefully: Buccleuch beef, foie gras, frogs' legs, everything fresh and every dish designed to bring out the intrinsic flavours. Sitting in the dining room is rather like being in the first class lounge on a transatlantic liner – there's a plush feel with plenty of dark blue and chrome.

The menu comes in three sections. There's a prix fixe – two courses £17.50, and three £22.50: poached skate; loin of pork with sautéed potatoes and wild mushrooms; hazelnut parfait – very competitive. Then there's the "daily special" (£11.90) which could be anything from a stuffed oxtail with celeriac purée to deep-fried lemon sole with warm

Allow twenty minutes for the raspberry soufflé.

Jersey potato salad. The à la carte is full on. Starters include seared scallops on caramelised sweetbreads, lemon and thyme reduction (£14); or a tortellini of ceps (£8.10). The menu changes gradually and continually but mains may include herb crusted loin of lamb on rosemary Provençal vegetables (£18.70), or roast suckling pig with black-pudding spatzle (£17) – the spatzle are absolutely marvellous. Puds are delicious (all £7.20): whole baked peach with ginger; or blueberry financier with lemon curd ice cream. The wine list offers good scope and you do not have to spend wildly.

WESTMINSTER

Cinnamon Club

Indian £25–£75

Old Westminster Library, Great Smith St, SW1 ♿ ☎020 7222 2555

Station St James's Park **Open** Mon–Fri 7.30–10.30am, noon–3pm & 6–11pm, Sat 6–11pm **Accepts** All major credit cards Ⓦ www.cinnamonclub.com

The Cinnamon Club occupies what was formerly Westminster Library. Libraries and restaurants can have a good deal in common – lofty ceilings, large doors, old wood floors, plenty of panelling – just the features for a cracking formal restaurant.

The Cinnamon Club is elegant, substantial and very pukka. Service is polished and attentive, the linen is snowy-white, the cutlery is heavy, the ashtrays stealably elegant, the toilets opulent, and there are huge flower arrangements. The cooking is accomplished, and each dish offers a finely judged combination of flavours, every one distinct. There's an informed wine list. And yes, unlikely as it may sound, this is an Indian restaurant.

From the "Appetisers" section of the menu there's tandoori halibut in Rajasthani spices (£10); or sandalwood-flavoured chicken breast (£7.50); or Bengali style grilled half lobster (£14.50). Such dishes and prices set the tone. Mains are also well conceived: spice-crusted tandoori monkfish with tomato and lemon sauce (£20); or Goan style wild boar chop with "vindaloo" sauce (£22); or smoked saddle of lamb with morels and corn curry (£20) – not something you'd find on the High Street. There's also a hot, Hyderabadi biryani made with goat (£15.50). Go for the basket of breads (£6) as a side dish, a selection of unusual parathas, naans and rotis. Desserts are elegant: try the warm apple lassi with champagne granita (£6), or the spiced banana tarte Tatin (£6.50), which comes with a deep-purple berry sorbet.

✱ Power breakfast? Full English (£16) or Bombay scrambled eggs on layered bread (£11).

Quilon

Indian £20–£70

41 Buckingham Gate, SW1 & ☎020 7821 1889
Station St James's Park **Open** Mon–Fri noon–2.30pm & 6–11pm Sat 6–11pm
Accepts All major credit cards ⓦwww.thequilonrestaurant.com

Quilon is about as swish as Indian restaurants get – as you'd expect when you learn that it is owned by the Taj Group, which also runs a dozen of India's most up market hotels. Quilon has the appearance of a sophisticated restaurant, you get the service you'd expect in a sophisticated restaurant, and you get the quality of cooking you'd expect from a sophisticated restaurant. And, unsurprisingly, you get the size of bill you'd expect from a sophisticated restaurant. The menu, built around "Coastal Food", showcases the splendid cuisine of Kerala – lots of fish, seafood, fresh peppercorns and coconut.

Start with the Coorg chicken (£6) – chunky chicken with rich spicing and a hint of Coorg vinegar. Or pepper shrimps (£6.50) – prawns fried in batter with plenty of chilli and a touch of aniseed. Moving on to the mains, seafood tempters include prawns Byadgi (£18.50) – enormous prawns grilled with the specially imported and pleasantly hot Byadgi chillies. Or try Mapla lamb curry (£16), mild and rich; or the guinea fowl salan (£14), cooked with coconut milk and yoghurt. These are all fairly spicy choices, but there is also gentler fare, with plenty of chicken options and several duck dishes.

All the main courses come with a vegetable of the day. Standouts include masala-stuffed aubergine (£7.50) – whole baby aubergines stuffed with coconut and poppy seeds; and a spinach poriyal (£7.50), made with freshly grated coconut, mustard leaves and split Bengal gram. Or how about mango curry (£7.50) cooked with yogurt, coconut and green chillies?

✳ Good value set lunches – £12.95 for two courses, £15.95 for three.

Tate Britain Restaurant

Modern British £15–£35

Tate Britain, Millbank, SW1 ♿ ☎020 7887 8825
Station Pimlico **Open** Mon–Sat noon–3pm, Sun noon–4pm
Accepts All major credit cards Ⓦ www.tate.org.uk

In these days of a "sandwich at the desk" office culture, you have to think long and hard before recommending a restaurant that is only open for lunch. For the foodie, the Tate Britain Restaurant is worth a visit; for the winey, it is an essential pilgrimage. This restaurant's love affair with wine began in the 1970s, when the food was dodgy and it seemed as if the only customers were wine merchants smug at the impossibly low prices. Today there are fewer florid gents enjoying a three-bottle lunch, but the atmosphere is soothing and the wine list not only fascinates, but offers outstanding value as well.

The menu changes on a regular basis and offers admirably seasonal dishes. Although there is no indication on the menu, there are dishes to suit the oenophiles, and dishes for civilian diners. Thus wine folk might choose simple starters such as dressed Cornish crab mayonnaise (£6.95), while the others can opt for eggs Benedict with smoked haddock (£7.50). Mains touch most of the bases: seared skate wings with capers, parsley and crisp potatoes (£16.75); roast squab pigeon with butternut squash and cranberry jus (£18.50). The food is fresh and unpretentious. There are enough tempting puddings to team with dessert wines. The wine list is wonderful, and constantly changing as bins run out. Don't be intimidated by the vast book – take your time, the wine waiters are knowledgeable. Bottles are served at the right temperature and decanted without fuss when necessary. Two tips – look at the half bottles, and ask advice.

✳ An oenophile's set lunch: two courses at £17.50, three at £20.50.

Wimbledon & Southfields

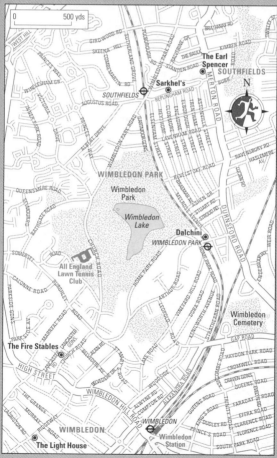

© Crown copyright

Dalchini

Indian/Chinese £12–£35

147 Arthur Rd, Wimbledon Park, SW19 & ☎ 020 8947 5966
Station Wimbledon Park **Open** Mon–Thurs & Sun noon–2.30pm & 6–10.30pm, Fri–Sat noon–2.30pm & 6–11pm **Accepts** Mastercard & Visa ⓦ www.dalchini.co.uk

Dalchini serves the kind of Chinese food that has emigrated to Bombay. This is Chinese with a pronounced Indian accent – lots of spice and a good deal of chilli. The restaurant is run by Udit Sarkhel's (see p.378) wife Veronica, who is Hakka Chinese and comes from a long line of Chinese restaurateurs based in Bombay. In 2003 the Sarkhels convinced the planning authorities to allow them to convert the ground-floor shop and deli into a restaurant dining room, and Dalchini was able to move up out of the basement into more agreeable surroundings.

A good strategy is to toy with a few starters and then turn to the specials list for the classic Indo-Chinese dishes. Start with the chicken lollipops (£4.25); or the sliced fish with burnt ginger (£4.25) – Tilapia that has been given an Indo-Chinese twist. Or perhaps the red pumpkin fritters (£3.95) appeal? Whether you are keen on Indian or Chinese food, the Dalchini main courses are great fun. There is chilli chicken (£6.50), a big seller in Bombay, sweet and chilli-hot; or "American chicken chop suey" (£7.25) – the story goes that chop suey was a dish first devised by Chinese coolies working on the American railroads. Or crispy lamb with celery and carrots (£6.75) – an interesting variation on "crispy shredded beef". Or the house signature dish, which is ginger chicken (£6.50). As an accompaniment to all this, vegetable Hakka noodles (£3.95) fit the bill. For pudding, how about honey noodles with ice cream (£4.25)? These are egg noodles as you've never seen them before!

✳ There's an "express" lunch – £5.

The Earl Spencer

Gastropub £10–£40

260 Merton Rd, SW18 ☎ 020 8870 9244
Station Southfields **Open** Mon–Sat 12.30–2.30pm & 7–10pm, Sun noon–3pm & 7–9.30pm
Accepts Mastercard & Visa ⓦ www.theearlspencer.co.uk

The Earl Spencer is a cracking gastropub. It is sibling to the long-established Havelock in Brook Green (see p.303), and the lessons learned over the years in W14 have been put to good advantage here in Southfields. The room is plain, large and bare. The bar serves decent beer. Portions are large, prices are very reasonable. Service is friendly, and the wine list offers sound value. The menu is an ever-changing one: things run out, dishes are seasonal. The standard of cooking is always very high.

"Mulligatawny soup, coriander and raita" (£4) is a real blast from the past, but a welcome one for all oldies who remember the hot sweet taste of the Heinz tinned version. The most pricey starter turns out to be stunning value: for £6.50 you get a plate of sound Caesar salad with two large, perfectly cooked scallops, each wrapped in crisp bacon. There's no pretentious presentation, no towering mounds of rocket, no artfully balanced scallops. You get good, fresh, well-cooked food. There's a game terrine served with toast and spiced crab apples (£6); or deep-fried squid, ox tongue, black- bean sauce (£6). If anything the main courses are even more satisfying: slow roasted shoulder of lamb, sweet potato Dauphinoise, purple sprouting broccoli (£12.50); a pork, peanut and coconut curry is served with sticky rice and pak choi (£9.50); or for vegetarians a gratin of Munster, new potato and melted onions (£7.50). Puds range from the straightforward sticky toffee pudding (£4) to the downright self-indulgent – deep-fried ice cream with dulce de leche (£4). This is how gastropub food should be.

✳ The Earl Spencer was London Evening Standard Pub of the Year 2003.

The Fire Stables

Modern British/Gastropub £12–£40

27–29 Church Rd, SW19 ♿ ☎020 8946 3197

Station Wimbledon **Open** Mon–Fri noon–3pm & 6.30–10.30pm, Sat noon–4pm (brunch) & 6–10.30pm, Sun 11am–4.30pm & 6–10pm **Accepts** All major credit cards

By gastropub standards The Fire Stables (which opened as long ago as 2001) is now something of a veteran. And it is a veteran that has won its share of awards. Even in busy Wimbledon the bar does good trade, and the spacious restaurant also prospers. The chairs are comfortable and the tables big enough, the high ceiling and large windows give a spacious feel, the floor is made of painted floorboards – in short everything is "gastropub-normal".

The menu changes daily and the food is well presented and reasonably priced. Starters range from fennel and potato soup (£4.75) to a foie gras and chicken liver parfait w̲ red onion marmalade (£5.75). You may have spotted the typographical idiosyncrasy, which wears pretty thin pretty quickly. They don't write "with" at the Fire Stables, what they put is "w̲". So you get duck spring rolls w̲ teriyaki dressing (£6.50) – this could get irritating by the time you get to farmhouse cheeses w Bath Olivers (£6). Other starters may include smoked chicken and mango salad (£6.25), or tomato, mozzarella and red-onion tart (£6). Among the main courses may be pumpkin risotto (£10.25); slow-roast belly pork w mash (£13.50); stuffed leg of rabbit wrapped in prosciutto w new potatoes (£14); spaghettini w smoked salmon and chervil cream (£11.50); and sea bass w roast fennel and potato salad (£16). Puds (all £5) are desirable if predictable numbers: bread-and-butter pudding; sticky toffee pudding w vanilla ice cream; pear and almond tart w crème fraîche; and baked cheesecake w raspberry coulis.

✳ Saturday means brunch, Sunday means a roast dinner.

Light House   Modern European £20–£50

75–77 The Ridgeway, SW19 & ☎020 8944 6338

Station Wimbledon **Open** Mon–Sat noon–2.30pm & 6.30–10.30pm, Sun 12.30–3pm
Accepts All major credit cards except Diners

Light House is a strange restaurant to find marooned in leafy suburbia – you would think that its modern, very eclectic menu and clean style would be more at home in a city centre than in a smart, quiet, respectable neighbourhood. Nevertheless it continues to do well. First impressions always count, and a light, bright interior – cream walls and blond wood – plus genuinely friendly staff make both arriving and eating at Light House a pleasure.

At first glance, the menu is set out conventionally enough in the Italian style: antipasti, primi, secondi, contorni and dolci. But that's as far as the Italian formality goes – the influences on the kitchen here are truly global. Starters may range from black bean marinated mozzarella with pickled carrots (£6.50); to celeriac soup with rocket and almond purée (£5). It would be very easy to get this sort of cooking wrong, but in fact Light House makes a fair job of succeeding. Among the "primi", dishes like tempura soft-shell crab with soba noodle salad (£8) jostle with combinations like broccoli and Taleggio ravioli with asparagus and rocket (£7.50). Mains range from sea bass with wild garlic leaves, salsa verde and olive oil mash (£15.50); to red roast duck with sweet potato, bok choy and smoked chilli jam. Puddings have a retro note but can still delight – fudge and vanilla semi freddo with chocolate sauce (£5,20) or lemon tart with crème fraîche (£5.20) The wine list features twenty each of whites and reds, and crosses as many frontiers as possible.

✳ "Set lunch" (Mon–Sat) is a steal at £14 for two courses, £16.50 for three.

Sarkhel's

Indian £15–£40

199 Replingham Rd, SW18 & ☎020 8870 1483

Station Southfields **Open** Mon–Thurs noon–2.30pm & 6–10.30pm,
Sat noon–2.30pm & 6–11pm, Sun noon–2.30pm & 6–10.30pm

Accepts All major credit cards except Diners ⓦ www.sarkhels.com

Sarkhel's is a large, elegant restaurant, serving well spiced food with a number of adventurous dishes scattered through the menu – the hot, fresh Chettinad dishes are particularly fine. Moreover, it's a pleasant, friendly, family-run place offering good cooking at prices, which, though not cheap, certainly represent good value (particularly the bargain lunch thali at £9.95 or the Express at £5 – but neither available on Sunday). Booking is recommended.

Start by asking Udit or his wife if there are any "specials" on. These are dishes which change according to what is available at the markets. You might be

offered a starter of Tareli macchi (£4.50), fish cooked in a spicy batter – a famous Bombay Parsee dish; or murg ke chaap sixer (£4.50), andhra style fiery hot chicken "lollipops". The seekh kebab (£4.25) is as good as you'll find anywhere. For main course dishes, check the specials again – it might be something wonderful such as a kolmi nu Patia (£8.95), a spicy Parsee prawn dish. On the main menu, try the galina cafreal (£7.50), a rich Goan chicken dish; or perhaps the jardaloo ma gosht (£7.50), a sweet-and-sour lamb dish made with apricots. All are delicious, without even a hint of surface oil slick. Be sure to add some vegetable dishes – perhaps the baigan patiala (£5.95), which is a dish of cubed aubergine and cashew nuts stewed with a touch of ginger and chilli. The menu also has frequent regional festivals – ask if you're puzzled by strange dishes, as you'll get good advice and fabulous food.

✳ Look out for frequent regional festivals.

Further choices

Calcutta Notebook
Indian

201 Replingham Rd, SW18
☎020 8874 6603

Part of, and next door to, Sarkhel's (see review above). Named after the Bengali recipes of Udit Sarkhel's mother which he jotted down in a notebook.

Thai Tho
Thai

20 Wimbledon High St, SW19
☎020 8946 1542

Tardis-like Thai restaurant (bigger inside than it looks from the outside), workman-like Thai dishes. Friendly service.

Index and small print

SMALL PRINT

A Rough Guide to Rough Guides

The Rough Guide to London Restaurants is published by Rough Guides. The first *Rough Guide to Greece*, published in 1982, was a student scheme that became a publishing phenomenon. The immediate success of the book – with numerous reprints and a Thomas Cook prize shortlisting – spawned a series that rapidly covered dozens of destinations. Rough Guides had a ready market among low-budget backpackers, but soon also acquired a much broader and older readership that relished Rough Guides' wit and inquisitiveness as much as their enthusiastic, critical approach. This philosophy was also succesfully applied to Rough Guides' reference titles, the first of which, *The Rough Guide to World Music*, was published in 1994. It was followed by a host of other lively music books, ranging from Opera to Hip-Hop plus nearly everything in between. Other reference series include computing titles, like the best-selling *Rough Guide to the Internet* ; popular culture guides, ranging from Superheroes to Shakespeare; compact histories of countries including England, India and the USA; and detailed guides to the Weather, the Universe, and Unexplained Phenomena. Rough Guides now publish:

- Travel guides to more than 200 worldwide destinations
- Dictionary phrasebooks to 22 major languages
- Maps printed on rip-proof and waterproof Polyart™ paper
- Reference books on many wide-ranging topics from Classical Music to James Bond
- World Music CDs in association with World Music Network

Visit **www.roughguides.com** to see our latest publications.

Publishing information

This 7th edition published Oct 2004 by
Rough Guides Ltd, 80 Strand, London WC2R 0RL.
345 Hudson St, 4th Floor, New York, NY 10014, USA.

Distributed by the Penguin Group
Penguin Books Ltd, 80 Strand, London WC2R 0RL
Penguin Group (USA), 375 Hudson Street, NY 10014, USA
Penguin Group (Australia), 487 Maroondah Highway, PO Box 257, Ringwood, Victoria 3134, Australia
Penguin Group (Canada), 10 Alcorn Avenue, Toronto, Ontario, Canada M4V 1E4
Penguin Group (NZ), 182–190 Wairau Road, Auckland 10, New Zealand
Typeset in Bembo and Helvetica to an original design by Henry Iles.
Printed and bound in Italy by Graphicom

424pp includes index
A catalogue record for this book is available from the British Library

ISBN 1-84353-341-3

The publishers and authors have done their best to ensure the accuracy and currency of all the information in **The Rough Guide to London Restaurants**, however, they can accept no responsibility for any loss, injury, or inconvenience sustained by any diner as a result of information or advice contained in the guide.

1 3 5 7 9 8 6 4 2

Help us update

We've gone to a lot of effort to ensure that the seventh edition of **The Rough guide to London Restaurants** is accurate and up-to-date. However, things change – restaurants open and others close, opening hours are notoriously fickle, restaurants raise prices or lower standards. If you feel we've got it wrong or left something out, we'd like to know, and if you can remember the address, the price, the opening times, the phone number, so much the better.

We'll credit all contributions, and send a copy of the next edition (or any DIRECTIONS guide or Rough Guide if you prefer) for the best letters. Everyone who writes to us and isn't already a subscriber will receive a copy of our full-colour thrice-yearly newsletter. Please mark letters: "**The Rough Guide to London restaurants**" and send to: Rough Guides, 80 Strand, London WC2R 0RL, or Rough Guides, 4th Floor, 345 Hudson St, New York, NY 10014. Or send an email to **mail@roughguides.com**

Have your questions answered and tell others about your dining experience at **www.roughguides.atinfopop.com**

Rough Guide Credits

Series editor: Mark Ellingham
Managing editor: Peter Buckley
Text editor: Michelle Bhatia
Layout: Michelle Bhatia, Peter Buckley
Cartography: Ed Wright

Picture research: Michelle Bhatia, Celia Gibson
Proofreader: Jan Leary
Production: Julia Bovis
Design: Henry Iles

Acknowledgements

Michelle and Peter would like to thank Jan Leary for proofing, Ed Wright for all his hard work on the maps, Celia Gibson for her help with picture research, Andrew Clare for his eleventh hour input and all the restaurants and agencies for their co-operation.

SMALL PRINT

Photo credits

p.1 Dim sum sign © Michelle Bhatia
p.6 Le Cercle © Le Cercle
p.6 Rasoi Vineet Bhatia sign © Rasoi Vineet Bhatia
p.7 Inn the Park © Inn the Park
p.7 The Wolseley © The Wolseley
p.7 Yauatcha © Yauatcha
p.8 The Square © The Square
p.8 Racine © Network London
p.9 South © South
p.9 The Capital © The Capital
p.9 Gordon Ramsay (restaurant) © Sauce Communications
p.9 Chez Bruce © Chez Bruce
p.10 The Rocket © The Rocket
p.10 The Barnsbury © The Barnsbury
p.11 The Anglesea Arms © The Anglesea Arms
p.11 The White Swan © The White Swan
p.11 The Eagle © The Eagle
p.11 The Anchor and Hope © The Anchor and Hope
p.12 The Painted Heron © The Painted Heron
p.12 Chutney Mary © Chutney Mary
p.13 Cinnamon Club © Cinnamon Club
p.13 Indian statuette © Rasoi Vineet Bhatia
p.13 Sarkhel's © Sarkhel's
p.13 Madhu's © Madhu's
p.14 Jaffna House © Peter Buckley
p.14 Masala Zone © Michelle Bhatia
p.15 Centrale © Michelle Bhatia
p.15 Chowki © Michelle Bhatia
p.16 Yi Ban © Yi Ban
p.16 Fung Shing © Michelle Bhatia
p.17 ECapital window © Michelle Bhatia
p.17 Dim sum © Yauatcha
p.18 Fergus Henderson © St John
p.18 Vineet Bhatia © Vineet Bhatia
p.19 Richard Corrigan © Richard Corrigan
p.19 Phillip Howard © The Square
p.19 Gordan Ramsay © Sauce Communications
p.19 Giorgio Locatelli © Locanda Locatelli
p.20 Morgan M © Morgan M
p.21 The Gate © The Gate
p.21 Roussillon © Peter Buckley
p.21 Kastoori © Peter Buckley
p.21 Wild Cherry © Michelle Bhatia

p.22 Zefferano © Zefferano
p.22 Locanda Locatelli © Locanda Locatelli
p.23 Enoteca Turi © Enoteca Turi
p.23 Sardo © Sardo
p.23 Riva © Riva
p.23 Assaggi © Assaggi
p.24 Dim sum © Yauatcha
p.32 Redmond's © Redmond's
p.34 Sonny's © Sonny's
p.38 Fabbrica © Fabbrica
p.39 Ransome's Dock © Ransome's Dock
p.43 Champor Champor © Champor Champor
p.45 The Garrison © The Garrison
p.50 Arkansas Café sign © Arkansas Café
p.58 Olley's © Olley's
p.59 Satay © DK Images
p.62 Shrimp © DK Images
p.64 Wagamama © Wagamama
p.67 Chutney Mary © Chutney Mary
p.68 Dish at Darbar © Darbar
p.69 Eight over Eight © Eight over Eight
p.78 Gerrard Street © Michelle Bhatia
p.82 Dim sum © Michelle Bhatia
p.82 Pak choi © Michelle Bhatia
p.89 Café Spice Namaste © Café Spice Namaste
p.92 Prism © Prism
p.94 Rosemary Lane © Rosemary Lane
p.98 The Freemasons © The Freemasons
p.106 The Eagle © The Eagle
p.102 Tabaq © Peter Buckley
p.110 Souvlaki & Bar © Peter Buckley
p.112 The White Swan © The White Swan
p.114 Belgo © Belgo
p.116 Hamburger Union © Charles Campion
p.117 Incognico © Incognico
p.121 At the Punjab © Peter Buckley
p.125 Mosaica © Mosaica
p.132 Yi-Ban © Yi-Ban
p. 136 Herbs
p.144 Collander © Peter Buckley
p.146 Al San Vincenzo © Peter Buckley
p.152 Eagle Bar Diner © Eagle Bar Diner
p.154 Fino © Fino
p.155 Sake © DK Images

382

"Coming to a screen near you"

The Rough Guide to London Restaurants
Full text download

The Rough Guide to London Restaurants is now available online as a free full-text download for you to use at home with your PC or Mac, or on the move with PC or Mac laptops and PDAs, including Palm Pilots and Pocket PCs. The book is available via a password-protected page on the Rough Guides website and can be downloaded in either Adobe PDF format, complete with maps, weblinks and illustrations, or formatted for Pocket PC and Palm. Adobe PDFs are readable on any Windows or Mac-OS computer.

For more details and to find out how to download **The Rough Guide to London Restaurants** visit:

www.roughguides.com/londonrestaurants

Index of restaurants by cuisine

Categories below are pretty self-explanatory, though note that "Indian" includes Bangladeshi, Indian and Pakistani restaurants. Also note that "further choice" restaurants are listed in italics. Where this "further choice" is the branch of a chain (see Wagamama for example) the neighbourhood is listed in italics.

INDEX

Burmese

Caribbean

Chinese

INDEX

INDEX

INDEX

INDEX

INDEX

Index of restaurants by name

A–Z note: The Eagle appears under E not T, La Trompette, and Al Duca under D. But Café Pacifico is a C and Alistair Little an A. Also note that "further choice" restaurants are listed in italics.

INDEX

INDEX

INDEX

INDEX

INDEX

...MUSIC & REFERENCE

ADVERTS

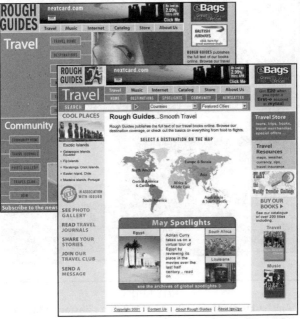

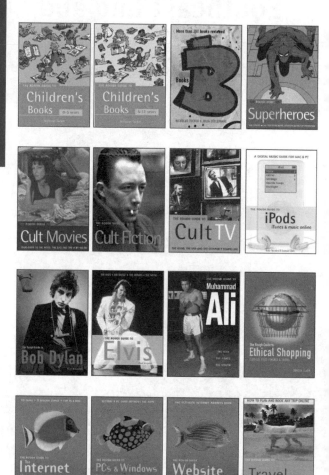

ROUGH GUIDES
MUSIC SERIES

ADVERTS